Educating Special Children

Educating Special Children is an indispensable companion for anyone requiring an overview of provision that has proved effective for children with learning disorders and disabilities.

Dr Michael Farrell guides the reader through what can be labrythine complexities of special education, providing educators with a road map to the most effective methods of provision currently being used. By concentrating on individual disabilities and disorders and not relying on the education system of any one country, Dr Farrell explores issues surrounding:

- Communication disorders and autism and Asperger's syndrome
- Developmental co-ordination disorders
- Reading, writing and mathematics disorders
- Disorders of conduct, anxiety and depression
- Attention deficit hyperactivity disorder
- Mild, moderate to severe, and profound cognitive impairment
- Sensory impairments
- Orthopaedic and motor disabilities, health impairments and traumatic brain injury

In addition, this authoritative text provides advice and support that is relevant to educating pupils in a range of settings. The importance of multi-professional working is explored and analysed.

Based on many years of experience, and drawing on expertise from all corners of the globe, this is *the* definite guide to special education today.

Michael Farrell is a special education consultant working with schools, local authorities/school boards, voluntary organisations, universities and others in Britain and abroad. He has published extensively in the area.

WITHDRAWN

D0549739

Educating Special Children

An introduction to provision for
pupils with disabilities and disorders

Michael Farrell

 Routledge
Taylor & Francis Group

NEW YORK AND LONDON

UNIVERSITY OF CHICHESTER

First published 2008 by Routledge
2 Park Square, Milton Park, Abingdon, Oxon, OX14 4RN

Simultaneously published in the USA and Canada
by Taylor & Francis Inc
270 Madison Avenue, New York, NY 10016

Routledge is an imprint of the Taylor & Francis Group, an informa business

© 2008 Michael Farrell

Reprinted 2009

Typeset in Garamond Three by Keyword Group Ltd
Printed and bound in Great Britain by TJ International Ltd, Padstow,
Cornwall

All rights reserved. No part of this book may be reprinted or
reproduced or utilised in any form or by any electronic, mechanical, or
other means, now known or hereafter invented, including photocopying
and recording, or in any information storage or retrieval system, without
permission in writing from the publishers.

Every effort has been made to ensure that the advice and information in
this book is true and accurate at the time of going to press. However,
neither the publisher nor the authors can accept any legal responsibility
or liability for any errors or omissions that may be made. In the case of
drug administration, any medical procedure or the use of technical
equipment mentioned within this book, you are strongly advised to
consult the manufacturer's guidelines.

British Library Cataloguing in Publication Data
A catalogue record for this book is available from the British Library

Library of Congress Cataloging-in-Publication Data
Farrell, Michael, 1948-
    Educating special children : an introduction to provision for pupils with
    disabilities and disorders / Michael Farrell.
        p. cm.
    Includes bibliographical references and index.
    ISBN 978-0-415-46312-6 (hardback : alk. paper) —
    ISBN 978-0-415-46315-7 (pbk. : alk. paper) 1. Special education—
    Great Britain. 2. Children with disabilities—Education—Great Britain.
    3. Behavior disorders in children—Great Britain. I. Title.
    LC3986.G7F3683 2008
    371.90941—dc22   2007045210

ISBN 10: 0-415-46312-2 (hbk)
ISBN 10: 0-415-46315-7 (pbk)
ISBN 10: 0-203-92763-X (ebk)

ISBN 13: 978-0-415-46312-6 (hbk)
ISBN 13: 978-0-415-46315-7 (pbk)
ISBN 13: 978-0-203-92763-2 (ebk)

371.
9
FAR

Contents

Preface

Educating Special Children: An introduction to provision for pupils with disabilities and disorders appears at an exciting time for those involved in special education. A body of knowledge and an understanding and an appreciation of the range of necessary skills for special education are being accumulated and refined. The twin elements of evidence-based practice and professional judgement/knowledge are indicating with increasing clarity effective provision for different types of disorder and disability.

There is further work to do in ensuring that the categories of disorder/disability used (for example 'reading disorder', 'traumatic brain injury' or 'profound cognitive impairment') enable further research and professional knowledge to be as focused and informative as practicable. Possibly some of the present contours of classifications may be modified in the light of future developments in, for example, neuropsychology. But it is likely that some form of categorisations of disorder and disability will continue to be useful in helping to guide research and to build evidence-based and professionally informed provision. This is in part because different types of disorder/disability suggest different kinds of special educational provision.

Educating Special Children aims to help readers consider what might constitute effective provision. By 'special children' is meant children with a disorder/disability. The term 'educating' in the present context refers to educational and related provision for learners with a disability/disorder enabling optimum educational progress and personal and social development. This encompasses curricula and assessment, pedagogy, resources, therapy, and school and classroom organisation – hence the broad term 'provision' in the book's sub-title.

In surveying the nature of the disorder/disability and related provision, the book does not emphasise any one national context and it is hoped the volume will be read in many countries and areas where English is the main language or is very widely spoken. The contribution of colleagues as critical readers has been invaluable, allowing the book to be informed by views from around the world:

- Australia
- Europe (Germany, Spain, Malta, Eire, United Kingdom)

- Asia (India)
- The Middle East (Israel)
- North America (Canada, The United States of America)

Among the book's readers might be the following:

- Teachers of special children in ordinary and special schools and other settings
- Newly qualified teachers following courses of continuing professional development
- School governors, managers and administrators
- Professionals whose work covers a wide range of disorders/disabilities
- Students following initial teacher training courses
- Undergraduate and postgraduate students of education
- Those who train teachers and other professionals working with special children
- Lecturers and researchers in universities whose work relates to special education
- Local and national politicians
- Anyone recognising the importance of working in a holistic manner, for example, integrating aspects of education and therapy.

I hope the text will be helpful to readers seeking a guide through the labyrinthine complexities of special education and aiming to establish suitable provision.

Michael Farrell
Consultant in Special Education in private practice
Epsom, United Kingdom
dr.m.j.farrell@btopenworld.com
www.drmjfarrell.co.uk

Acknowledgements

I am most grateful to the following colleagues who kindly commented on earlier versions of the various chapters of the book.

Chapter 2   Profound mental retardation/profound learning difficulties
   Dr. Michael Arthur-Kelly, University of Newcastle, Australia.
Chapter 3   Moderate to severe mental retardation/severe learning difficulties
  Dr Audrey Fenech Adami, Malta.
Chapter 4   Mild mental retardation/moderate learning difficulties
   Dr John Borkowski, University of Notre Dame's Centre for Children and Families, Indiana, United States of America.
Chapter 5   Hearing impairment
   Mr Paul Simpson, British Association of Teachers of the Deaf, United Kingdom.
   Ms Maria Wisnet, Head teacher, Johannes-Vatter-Schule, Friedberg, Germany.
Chapter 6   Visual impairment
   Mr Rory Cobb, Royal National Institute for the Blind, United Kingdom.
Chapter 7   Deafblindness
   Mr Akhil S. Paul, Director, Sense International, India.
Chapter 8   Orthopaedic impairment
   Ms Sandra Everitt, McGill University, Quebec, Canada.
Chapter 9   Health impairment
   Dr Elizabeth McCaughey Paediatrician, United Kingdom.
Chapter 10   Traumatic brain injury
   Ms Vivienne Streeter, British Institute for Brain Injured Children, United Kingdom.
Chapter 11   Disruptive behaviour disorders
   Dr Karen Proner, child psychotherapist, New York, United States of America.
Chapter 12   Anxiety disorders and depressive disorders
   Professor Alan Carr, University College Dublin, Republic of Ireland.

Chapter 13   Attention deficit hyperactivity disorder
Professor Lyndal Bullock, University of North Texas, Denton, United
States of America.
Chapter 14   Communication disorders: Speech
Professor Jannet Wright, DeMontfort University, Leicester, United
Kingdom.
Chapter 15   Communication disorders: Grammar and comprehension
Dr Susan Moon-Meyer, Kutztown University, PA, United States
of America.
Chapter 16   Communication disorders: Meaning and use
Dr Pam Smith, Bloomsburg University, PA, United States of America.
Chapter 17   Autism
Dr Laurie Sperry, University of Colorado, Denver, United States
of America.
Chapter 18   Developmental co-ordination disorder
Dr Naomi Weintraub, Hebrew University, Israel.
Chapter 19   Reading disorder/dyslexia
Dr Fernando Cuetos, University of Oviedo, Spain.
Chapter 20   Disorder of written expression
Dr Alan Beaton, Swansea University, Wales, United Kingdom.
Chapter 21   Mathematics disorder
Professor Russell Gersten, Professor Emeritus, University of Oregon,
United States of America.

While the comments of these colleagues certainly strengthened the book, any
shortcomings are of course entirely my own responsibility.

I would also like to thank Alison Foyle and all the team at Routledge for
their continued support and encouragement.

Ruth Hunt (www.flickr.com/photos/kitti) took the photograph of the
author and his bulldog Harry.

About the author

Michael Farrell was educated in the United Kingdom. After training as a teacher at Bishop Grosseteste College, Lincoln, and obtaining an honours degree from Nottingham University, he gained a Masters Degree in Education and Psychology from the Institute of Education, London University. Subsequently, he carried out research for a Master of Philosophy degree at the Institute of Psychiatry, Maudsley Hospital, London and for a Doctor of Philosophy degree under the auspices of the Medical Research Council Cognitive Unit and London University.

Professionally, Michael Farrell worked as a head teacher, a lecturer at London University and as a local authority inspector. He managed a national psychometric project for City University, London and directed a national

project developing course structures and training materials for initial teacher training for the United Kingdom Government Department of Education.

His present work as a special education consultant includes policy development and training with local authorities, work with voluntary organisations and universities, support to schools in the private and maintained sectors, and advice to government ministries.

Among his books, which are translated into European and Asian languages, are:

Standards and Special Educational Needs (Continuum, 2001)

The Special Education Handbook (3rd edition) (David Fulton, 2002)

Understanding Special Educational Needs: A Guide for Student Teachers (Routledge, 2003)

Special Educational Needs: A Resource for Practitioners (Sage, 2004)

Inclusion at the Crossroads: Concepts and Values in Special Education (David Fulton, 2004)

Key Issues in Special Education: Raising Pupils' Achievement and Attainment (Routledge, 2005)

The Effective Teacher's Guide to Dyslexia and Other Specific Learning Difficulties (Routledge, 2005)

The Effective Teacher's Guide to Moderate, Severe and Profound Learning Difficulties (Routledge, 2005)

The Effective Teacher's Guide to Autism and Communication Difficulties (Routledge, 2005)

The Effective Teacher's Guide to Sensory Impairment and Physical Disabilities (Routledge, 2005)

The Effective Teacher's Guide to Behavioural, Emotional and Social Difficulties (Routledge, 2005)

Celebrating the Special School (David Fulton, 2006)

The Special School's Handbook: Key Issues for All (Routledge/Nasen, 2007).

Chapter 1

Classification and provision

How children are identified as having a disability/disorder and the provision made for them are central to special education. This chapter describes the classification systems for disability/disorder in two countries; outlines the types of disability/disorder considered in the present book and examines criticisms and justifications of the usefulness of classification. Turning to provision, the chapter explains elements of curriculum and assessment; pedagogy; resources, therapy and organisation in relation to learners with disabilities and disorders. Relationships between classification and provision are then explored leading to a consideration of evidence-based practice and other matters.

Classifications of disability/disorders in two countries

Fletcher *et al.* (2003) argue that classifications imply deciding upon a set of defining qualities or attributes and, from a larger group, differentiating coherent (and more homogeneous) smaller groups according to the extent to which they relate to the defined qualities. Identification involves individuals being allocated to subgroups constituting the classification and represents the operationalising of the definitions that arise from the classification. Assessment is seen as the process of applying the operational definitions to children to decide membership in one or several partitions. The validity and reliability of these partitions are critical. Among qualities of the partitioning making up a *valid* classification is that it can be differentiated according to attributes that are not used to establish the subgroups. Good classifications are *reliable* in the sense that they are not dependent on the method of classification and 'replicate in other samples'. Furthermore, good classifications have sufficient coverage allowing suitable identification and help communication and prediction (ibid.: 34–35 paraphrased).

One of the benefits of suitable classification is that it can have useful practical implications. For example, identifying learning disability or attention deficit hyperactivity disorder (or learning difficulty and attention deficit hyperactivity disorder occurring together) has implications for provision (academic remediation, behaviour modification and medication) and prognosis (Fletcher *et al.*, 1999).

On such bases, classification systems have developed in many countries. For example, in the United States of America, pupils considered to need special education covered by federal law have both a defined disability and are considered to need special education because the disability has an adverse educational impact. Categories of disability under federal law as amended in 1997 (20 United States Code 1402, 1997) have been set out and are reflected in subsequent 'designated disability codes' as follows:

1　Mentally Retarded;
2　Hard-of-hearing;
3　Deaf;
4　Speech and Language Impaired;
5　Visually Handicapped;
6　Emotionally Disturbed;
7　Orthopaedically Impaired;
8　Other Health Impaired;
9　Specific Learning Disability;
10　Multi-handicapped;
11　Child in Need of Assessment;
12　Deaf/Blind;
13　Traumatic Brain Injury;
14　Autism.

In England, a similar classification (Department for Education and Skills, 2005, passim) comprises:

- Specific learning difficulties (e.g. dyslexia, dyscalculia, dyspraxia);
- Learning difficulty (moderate, severe, profound);
- Behavioural, emotional and social difficulty;
- Speech, language and communication needs;
- Autistic spectrum disorder;
- Visual impairment;
- Hearing impairment;
- Multi-sensory impairment;
- Physical disability.

In the American system, mental retardation is broadly equivalent to the English classification of moderate, severe and profound learning difficulties (see also Farrell, 2001: 1–5).

It will be apparent that several types of disability/disorder concern broad areas of development relating to all children whether or not they have a disorder/disability. For the categories in the United States of America, areas of development and related disabilities/disorders are as follows:

- Cognitive development – Mentally retarded
- Emotional and social development – Emotionally disturbed
- Communication development – Speech and language impaired
- Physical and motor development/health – Orthopaedically impaired/ other health impaired.

Regarding autism, the syndrome has an impact on several interacting areas of development: social, communicative and flexibility of thinking and is sometimes grouped with communication difficulties under a wider notion of 'communication and interaction'. The category of 'traumatic brain injury' refers to the potential cause of a range of possible disabilities/disorders having effects on communication, cognition, motor and emotional development.

In the case of sensory impairment, the classification has to do with typical functioning and impairment; so that only when typical ranges of vision or hearing are absent or deteriorate does it becomes usual to speak of disability/disorder as follows:

- Sight – Visual impairment/blindness
- Hearing – Hearing impairment/deafness

Concerning 'specific learning disability' it is thought a major factor is atypical brain processing involved in understanding spoken and written language showing itself in poorer than typical ability to listen, speak, read, write, spell and do mathematics.

In developmental co-ordination disorder the planning and execution of co-ordinated movement is affected.

It will be seen that the various disabilities/disorders relate to conceptions of typical development, syndromes or injury affecting several areas of development, the functioning of sensory faculties and the supposed effects of brain processing.

Classifications used in the present book

The aim of the present book is to illustrate provision for different types of disability/disorder, enabling readers to reflect on interactions and relationships between different types of disability/disorder to the benefit of the children concerned. This includes bearing in mind that some aspects of the approaches described in relation to disability/disorder may be transferable to children without a disability/disorder and that it is also necessary to respond to emerging individual issues as one comes to know a particular child.

The contents of the present volume reflect aspects of classifications such as those used in the United States of America and England. The classification within specific learning disabilities of 'reading disorder', 'disorder of written expression' and 'mathematics disorder' is used. Mild and moderate cognitive impairment (mental retardation) are considered together while severe cognitive impairment and profound cognitive impairment are examined separately. 'Emotional disturbance' (United States of America) or 'behavioural, emotional and social difficulties' (England) are considered in terms of 'disruptive behaviour disorders' (including conduct disorder), 'anxiety disorders' and 'depressive disorders'. The book also examines 'attention deficit hyperactivity disorder' which in the United States of America is seen as a health impairment and in England as an emotional, behavioural and social difficulty (Department for Education and Skills, 2001b). These examples follow classifications used in the *Diagnostic and Statistical Manual of Mental Disorders Fourth Edition Text Revision (DSM-IV-TR)* (American Psychiatric Association, 2000).

Speech and language impairments/communication disorders are considered in relation to speech; grammar; comprehension; semantics and pragmatics drawing on aspects of *DSM-IV-TR* (American Psychiatric Association, 2000) and speech and language pathology distinctions related to therapy and teaching approaches. The categories of 'orthopaedic impairment and motor disorder', 'developmental co-ordination disorder', 'health impairment' and 'traumatic brain injury' are considered separately. The present book's categorisations therefore makes it possible to draw on research and professional opinion concerning therapy and related educational initiatives that use these distinctions.

The reader will notice that the term 'Multi-handicapped' used in the United States of America is not included. 'Multi-handicapped' has some overlap with what in the United Kingdom might be categorised as 'profound and multiple learning difficulties' (PMLD). PMLD is a common alternative to 'profound learning difficulties' indicating that other impairments are often associated with profound cognitive impairment.

The classifications used in the present book are set out in Figure 1.1 the list corresponding to the order in which the chapters are presented. The figure gives equivalents of disorders and disabilities:

- as they are delineated in the present text;
- how they might be categorised in the United Kingdom;
- how they might be categorised in the United States of America.

Text: Profound cognitive impairment
UK: Learning difficulty (profound)
USA: Mentally Retarded (profound)

Text: Moderate to severe cognitive impairment
UK: Learning difficulty (severe)
USA: Mentally Retarded (moderate to severe)

Text: Mild cognitive impairment
UK: Learning difficulty (moderate)
USA: Mentally Retarded (mild)

Text: Hearing impairment
UK: Hearing impairment
USA: Hard-of-hearing/Deaf

Text: Visual impairment
UK: Visual impairment
USA: Visually Handicapped

Text: Deafblindness
UK: Multi-sensory impairment
USA: Deaf/Blind

Text: Orthopaedic impairment and motor disorder
UK: Physical disability
USA: Orthopaedically Impaired

Text: Health impairment
UK: Physical disability
USA: Other Health Impaired

Text: Traumatic brain injury
UK: No specific category
USA: Traumatic brain injury

Text: Disruptive behaviour disorders (including conduct disorder)
UK: Behavioural, emotional and social difficulty
USA: Emotionally Disturbed

Text: Anxiety disorders and depressive disorders
UK: Behavioural, emotional and social difficulty
USA: Emotionally Disturbed

Text: Attention deficit hyperactivity disorder
UK: Behavioural, emotional and social difficulty
USA: Other Health Impaired

Text: Communication disorders (speech)
UK: Speech, language and communication needs
USA: Speech and Language Impaired

Text: Communication disorders (grammar, comprehension)
UK: Speech, language and communication needs
USA: Speech and Language Impaired

Continued

```
Text:   Communication disorders (semantics, pragmatics)
UK:     Speech, language and communication needs
USA:    Speech and Language Impaired

Text:   Autism
UK:     Autistic spectrum disorder/autism
USA:    Autism

Text:   Developmental co-ordination disorder
UK:     Specific learning difficulties (dyspraxia)
USA:    Specific Learning Disability (developmental co-ordination disorder)

Text:   Reading disorder
UK:     Specific learning difficulties (dyslexia)
USA:    Specific Learning Disability (reading disorder)

Text:   Disorder of written expression
UK:     Specific learning difficulties (often as an aspect of dyslexia)
USA:    Specific Learning Disability (disorder of written expression)

Text:   Mathematics disorder.
UK:     Specific learning difficulties (dyscalculia)
USA:    Specific Learning Disability (mathematics disorder)
```

Figure 1.1 Broadly comparative terms.

Criticisms and justifications of classification

Social and individual perspectives and classification

The use of classification was sometimes negatively considered to imply adherence to an individual 'medical' model of disability/disorder and alternative social models were sometimes suggested. For example, a social model might take a social constructionist view of disability emphasising the way society includes or excludes disabled people. Because disability was considered a product of social arrangements it was thought it could be reduced and even eliminated. Impairment was seen as the biological component and disability the social response of oppression and disempowerment. If it was society that was responsible for disability, then it was thought, changing society so that disabling 'barriers' are removed would reduce disability. From this standpoint, criticism was made of the perceived inadequacies of the medical model (e.g. Campbell and Oliver, 1996).

In the medical model, people were regarded as disabled 'as a result of their physiological or cognitive impairments' (Drake, 1996: 148). The emphasis was on deficits and personal and functional limitations that were the responsibility of the person concerned, these functional limitations being seen as the cause of any disadvantage the person experiences that could be rectified only by treatment or cure (Barnes and Mercer, 1996). Notions of individual loss and inability were seen as linked to the idea of dependence on society and such a dependency model was considered to affect the identity of many disabled people (Campbell and Oliver, 1996). The *International Classification of Functioning, Disability and Health* (World Health Organisation, 2001: 20), presented the medical model as viewing disability 'as a problem of the person, directly caused by disease, trauma or other health condition, which requires medical care provided in the form of individual treatment by professionals'.

To the extent that a medical model was considered to influence special education including classifications of disorder and disability, the supposed negative impact of a medical model was not always easy to sustain. For example, the medical approach does not have to focus only on impairment but can be more holistic, taking into account what a child can do as well as what he cannot. (See also Farrell, 2004a: 67–77 and 2004b: 19–20). Furthermore, limitations of the social model with its intractable debates about paradigm, system and theory became increasingly apparent. One writer comments, 'Above all, it hardly matters whether the social model is a system, model, paradigm, idea, definition or even tool. What matters is that the social model is wrong' (Shakespeare, 2006: 53). A view that seems more likely than the medical – social dichotomy to attract growing assent is that disability is more accurately regarded as 'a complex interaction of biological, psychological, cultural and socio-political factors ...' (ibid.: 38). In practice too, the supposed dichotomy between the medical and social perspectives rarely arises and an interactive view is taken which seeks to use insights from individual and social perspectives and elsewhere. Within such an interactive view, classification can have an important place so long as it is not seen as an end in itself but as a means of potentially drawing on research and professional experience developed in relation to particular disorders/disabilities.

The editors of *DSM-IV-TR* (American Psychiatric Association, 2000) outline the benefits of classification. *DSM-IV-TR* is a categorical classification that divides mental disorders into types 'based on criteria sets with defining features' (ibid.: xxxi). The care required when drawing on such an approach is recognised; for example, there is no assumption that each category is a 'completely discrete entity' with 'absolute' boundaries that divide it from other mental disorders or from no mental disorder (ibid.: xxxi). Professional judgement is also needed and, in recognition of the heterogeneity of clinical presentation, *DSM-IV* often includes 'polythetic criteria sets' in which the individual is diagnosed using only a subset of items from a fuller list. Dimensional models are rejected because they are considered to have been less useful in clinical practice and in stimulating research, and because numerical dimensional systems are less familiar than the categorical names for mental disorders (ibid.: xxxii). While there has been disagreement on which disorders should be included and the optimal method of their organisation, it is argued, 'The need for a classification of mental disorders has been clear throughout the history of medicine' (ibid.: xxiv).

Negative or positive labelling?

The question of labelling, which is related to categorising, is sometimes presented as part of a deeper issue relating to the way language is viewed in relation to the self and the world. Ford (1999: 145–146), writing not about disability/disorder, but about theology draws pertinent distinctions. He uses a triangle to illustrate three features: 'world', 'language' and 'self' (as indicated in Figure 1.2). The line of the triangle joining 'language' and 'world' is designated 'truth'. The line connecting 'world' and 'self' is 'knowledge'. The line between 'language' and 'self' is 'meaning'. While there are views emphasising one of the elements of 'world', 'self' or 'language' (respectively, extreme objectivism, extreme subjectivism or extreme views of the self and world as constructs of language), more sustainable positions are ones trying to give an account of how two or all three might inter-relate.

Issues relating to disability and disorder can be seen in this context. Where views overemphasise the *knowledge* link between 'self' and 'world' there may be a tendency to accept labels (and classifications) as solely objective features simply waiting to be discovered. If views overplay the *meaning* relationship between language and the world, labels and classification and the disability/disorder they seek to describe appear mere constructs of language. A subtler picture of the influences of world, self and language suggests that neither of these extreme positions is useful.

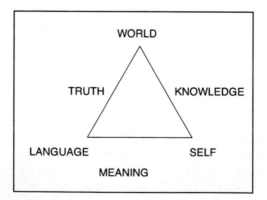

Figure 1.2 Inter-relationships of world, language and self (after Ford, 1999; 145–146).

Regarding labels, it is sometimes assumed that labelling for disabilities/ disorders is inevitably negative. Also, over time, certain terms that were perhaps neutral in their day become negatively perceived. It is hard to believe that those who developed terms such as 'moron', imbecile' and 'idiot' in previous centuries did so from a malign desire to offend the children and adults they were seeking to identify. Yet these and similar terms have become disparaging. More recently, in England, the expression 'educationally sub-normal' was used indicating a child was assessed to be below the statistical norm of educational functioning. But the term gradually came to be perceived as negative and was replaced by references to profound, severe or moderate 'learning difficulties'. In the United States of America similarly, some commentators are suggesting the expression 'mental retardation' might be replaced by 'cognitive impairment'.

It is useful to ask how and why the terms, if originally neutral, have come to be perceived as negative. One can question whether this is an aspect of the language itself or a feature of the negative attitudes of others to those with a disability or disorder. If the latter is the case, then changing terms is largely irrelevant and will have little impact given that the new terms will in time become as negative as the old. There is a view emphasising the role of language in shaping 'world' and 'self' that suggests that by changing the language we use, we change the way these are perceived. Those who hold this sort of view take great care with language as the shaper and arbiter of perception. Others who doubt this perspective may regard proposed changes to terminology as misguided political correctness, missing the point of tackling more relevant and – to them – 'real' issues.

Many would accept that it is appropriate to listen to the views of those who express a dislike of some of the terms used with regard to disability and disorder. Also, anyone using a label with its potentially positive or negative connotations needs to be aware of avoiding stereotyping and overgeneralising from a label, while at the same time using labels as an indicator of saying specific things about learner groups.

But set against the notion that labelling can be negative is the view that labelling as a part of identification can be helpful. It is a positive emancipatory process not a negative oppressive one in this perspective. Parents may express relief when a label has been given to a disorder/disability, which they viewed with confusion. The label offers a route to understanding and the support of others in a similar situation.

Two examples relating to special schools in England illustrate the potential for positive labelling. One child's parents write, 'Our son was sent to Brooklands School with no language/no diagnosis/severe learning difficulties and very little understanding of the world he lived in and within one year of being within this amazing school with its fantastic staff he is now a delightful, happy, confident, bright child with a diagnosis of autistic spectrum disorder' (Farrell, 2006a: 36). A student attending another school, states,

'I think it's a very good school. I think it should be all over the country and all over the world for pupils with behaviour difficulty problems ... when I'm here with a bunch of boys that's got emotional disabilities, I feel more comfortable and more confident' (ibid.: 41).

The challenge of delineating disorders/disabilities

If categories and labels can be potentially positive, the shape of the categories themselves is sometimes difficult to agree and justify. Classifications of disability/disorder may be considered too imprecise and the category boundaries too blurred. These questions in relation to particular disorders/disabilities such as attention deficit hyperactivity disorder and developmental co-ordination disorder are considered in individual chapters later. This section examines the extent to which groups of disorders/disabilities might be meaningfully considered as a wider category or unitary syndrome.

Learning disability (LD), under the United States of America *Individuals with Disabilities Act* (IDEA), is 'a disorder in one or more basic psychological processes involved in understanding or in using language, spoken or written, that may manifest itself in an imperfect ability to listen, think, speak, read, write, spell, or to do mathematical calculations ...' (34 C. F. R. section 300.7 (b) (10)). Despite appropriate learning experiences being provided, the child does not achieve 'commensurate with his or her age and ability levels in one or more of the areas listed ...' and there is a 'severe discrepancy' between achievement and intellectual ability in one or more of the specified areas (oral expression, listening comprehension, written expression, basic reading skill, reading comprehension, mathematics calculation, or mathematics reasoning) (34 C. F. R. section 300.541 (a)). The definition also excludes factors that might be expected to contribute to lower achievement (visual, hearing, or motor disabilities, mental retardation, emotional disturbance and environmental, cultural, or economic disadvantage) (Lyon *et al.*, 2001). More briefly, LD has been described as 'a heterogeneous set of disorders that include difficulty (not predicted from measures of general cognitive aptitude) in a variety of cognitive and social domains' (Cutting and Denckla, 2003: 125).

However, it has been argued that classification research has provided little evidence that IQ discrepancy marks out a specific type of LD differing from other types of underachievement (Fletcher *et al.*, 2002). The classification validity of most of the exclusion criteria have also been questioned as there is little evidence that children with 'expected' forms of achievement differ from children with 'unexpected' underachievement beyond the identification criteria (Lyon *et al.*, 2001). Also, as knowledge accumulates about possible genetic influences on LD, a point may be reached where LD can no longer be conceptualised as 'unexpected'. In 2004, the reauthorisation of IDEA (House Bill 1350) among its provisions, removed the requirement that schools show that students identified as having a learning disability have a discrepancy between ability and achievement.

To take another example briefly, there is debate about the extent to which developmental co-ordination disorder, specific developmental disorder of motor function (ICD-10, World Health Organisation, 1992) and developmental dyslexia can be considered a unitary syndrome with regard to symptoms, aetiology, treatment response and outcome (Cantell *et al.*, 2001).

Issues of category boundaries also arise in relation to the co-occurrence of various disorders/disabilities. For example, approximately half of clinic-referred children with attention deficit hyperactivity disorder also have oppositional defiant disorder or conduct disorder (American Psychiatric Association, 2000: 88). This may reflect conceptual overlap or possible underlying factors that predispose a child to several disorders and may ultimately suggest another category. To take other examples, disorder of written expression and mathematics disorder are often associated with reading disorder and it is relatively unusual for either to be present in the absence of reading disorder (American Psychiatric Association, 2000: 52). Language deficits and perceptual motor deficits may accompany disorder of written expression (ibid.: 55).

Important in response to such debates are the principles of classification outlined earlier (Fletcher *et al.* 2003: 34–35). The validity and reliability of categories can be tested leading to clearer and more robust categories. For classification to be useful, it is important that terminology is made as clear as possible. But equally important is the relationship between constructs and forms of assessment, and between assessment and interventions (e.g. Larkin and Cermac, 2002: 90). It is also possible that future research, for example, in genetics, brain imaging and neuroscience, may lead to a reshaping of some of the categories presently used.

Despite the challenges of delineating such disorders, it can be argued that much that is useful to teachers and others can be identified in research and professional practice referring to categories to provide for children with such disorders. This includes useful practical implications for provision and prognosis (Fletcher *et al.*, 1999).

Elements of provision

Curriculum

Doll (1996: 15) defines the curriculum as 'the formal and informal content and process by which learners gain knowledge and understanding, develop skills, and alter attitudes, appreciations and values under the auspices of that school'. While Doll sees curriculum with regard to both 'content and process', the present book sees it relating more to the 'what' of education. It is the content of what is taught and learned including the aims and objectives of teaching and learning, and the design and structure of what is taught in relation to areas of learning and programmes within those areas. The curriculum may be envisaged and organised by subjects (mathematics, science) or areas (communication, personal education). Related to this, aspects are sometimes considered as permeating the whole curriculum and might include literacy, numeracy, computer skills and problem-solving skills. In the United States of America, these may be termed 'basic skills' and in England 'curriculum strands' or 'key skills' but the intention is similar.

Curriculum can be considered with regard to differences in level, balance and content. In examining the curriculum for pupils with disabilities/disorders, one can consider the *level* of the curriculum in broad terms in relation to what is expected for children attaining typically for their age. For pupils with mild, moderate to severe, and profound cognitive impairment, the levels of the curriculum subjects and areas taken overall will be several years below what is age typical. For pupils with profound cognitive impairment, the curriculum may build on sensory and perceptual development typical of a child below the age of one year.

Also, the level of particular subjects or areas of the curriculum, may be lower, reflecting the difficulty the child has had and the slower progress he has made in certain areas. Examples are the lower progress made in reading by a child with reading disorder reflected in the content of the reading aspects of the curriculum being lower than is age typical (while still being stimulating and age relevant in relation to interests).

With regard to the *balance* of the curriculum, elements within its overall structure may differ from what is typical. These elements (subjects or areas) may be emphasised so that, for example, 'personal education' or 'communication' or 'reading' is highlighted both in relation to the time devoted to it and the extent to which it is embedded within other areas of the curriculum. Similarly, within particular curriculum subjects and areas there may be a distinctive difference in the balance of the programme. For example, in a physical education programme for pupils with developmental co-ordination disorder, there may be a particular emphasis on carefully graded steps to improving co-ordination and developing confidence in movement.

Areas of learning and programmes might have a different *content* for pupils with different disabilities/disorders and pupils without such difficulties/disorders. For example, a pupil with communication disorders might require to be taught alternative ways of communicating. A pupil with a health or orthopaedic impairment for whom aspects of the usual content of programmes for independence were inapplicable might be taught some self-care skills involving different ways of carrying out tasks, for example using different dressing procedures with modified clothing and aids. Although it can be argued that the principle of such programmes is the same as for other children (the child is still learning how to communicate), the specific content (*what* is taught) is different.

Assessment in relation to the curriculum concerns educational and related assessments, for example, small steps assessment used to recognise progress in phonics and other aspects of reading for a pupil with reading disorder or to recognise progress in basic social skills for a pupil with autism.

In summary, the curriculum may differ according to:

- the levels of all subjects or some being lower than age typical;
- the balance of subjects and areas being atypical; and/or the balance of components of subjects being atypical;
- the content of certain areas of the curriculum being different from those for most children and
- assessment being different usually in that it involves very small steps to indicate progress in areas of difficulty.

Pedagogy

In the present book, 'pedagogy' refers to the methodology (the 'how') of teaching. It is what the teacher plans and does, in the classroom and elsewhere, to promote and encourage pupils' learning. Of pedagogy, it may be said that 'the essence of what goes on in the classroom is the way in which the content of education, whether it is the knowledge, skills or attitudes, is learned by the pupil and taught or facilitated by the teacher'. Teaching methods include active learning, individualised learning, group work, discussion, audiovisual approaches, whole class teaching and other approaches (Farrell *et al.*, 1995: 4).

Pedagogy includes the sensory modality or modalities the teacher emphasises in presenting information (or encourages the pupil to use in communicating or responding). For example, a pupil with moderate to severe cognitive impairment may find it easier to understand and remember information presented visually than aurally. A child who is blind may write in Braille communicating in a medium requiring interpretation by touch rather than sight. Pedagogy may involve approaches distinctive to a particular disability/disorder such as 'Structured Teaching' (Schopler, 1997) used with children with autism.

It may emphasise an approach used also with children who do not have a disorder/disability, for example having a slower pace in lessons for pupils with mild cognitive impairment. Related to this, teaching that appears qualitatively different for pupils with disorders/disabilities is sometimes considered a variation on a continuum of teaching strategies characterised by 'more intensive and explicit teaching' representing the 'greater degree of adaptations' to common teaching approaches used with all children (e.g. Lewis and Norwich, 2005: 5–6). For example, in providing examples to learn concepts, such as 'big' and 'small', a more intensive version might provide many different examples while emphasising what is distinctive about them while the low intensity version might provide few. Although this view questions presenting such approaches dichotomously, it recognises that teaching 'geared to pupils with learning difficulties might be inappropriate for average or high attaining pupils' (ibid.: 6).

In brief, pedagogy for special children may be depicted as:

- emphasising particular sensory modalities or using alternative sensory modalities;
- using approaches different to those used with most children and
- using approaches similar to those for all children but with a particular emphasis or intensity.

Resources

The book uses the term 'resources' rather broadly. It is taken to include relatively fixed aspects of school building design, for example, those that aid access for pupils with orthopaedic impairment. Classroom design includes available space, lighting, acoustics and potential distractions and facilitators to learning. Furniture is included, such as adjustable tables and other surfaces and adapted seating to help good posture and give physical support.

Also described are learning resources, which may be categorised as sensory/physical aids and cognitive aids. Among physical/sensory aids is equipment adapted for various purposes such as alternative keyboards and tracker balls; low vision aids for pupils with visual impairment; hearing aids for pupils with hearing impairment; postural or mobility aids (e.g. wheelchair, walking aids, postural supports) for pupils with an orthopaedic impairment and computer technology enabling links to be made between the child's behaviour and what happens in the environment.

The heading also includes resources for augmentative communication (involving ways to supplement or augment partially intelligible speech) and alternative communication (means of communicating other than speech or writing) (Bigge *et al.*, 1999: 130). Cognitive aids include: computer software encouraging responses; symbols used for communication and computer programmes that break down tasks into very small steps. There may be an overlap between the two types of learning resources, for example aids to communication may involve sensory and cognitive help.

Therapy

In the present context 'therapy' refers to provision intended to help promote skills and abilities or well-being. For children and young people with disabilities/disorders, these may include elements that are predominantly: physical (e.g. aspects of occupational therapy and physiotherapy); psychological (e.g. psychotherapy and the various arts therapies); communicative (e.g. speech and language therapy) and medical (e.g. drugs).

The allocation of time for therapy can be seen as part of the whole school curriculum broadly defined. The areas of development on which therapy focuses (personal development, physical, speech) and its relationship with more conventional curriculum areas such as personal education, physical education and speaking and listening are part of curriculum planning, perhaps involving teacher and therapist working together. Therapy and aspects of care are intended to lead to changes in behaviour; attitudes and self-valuing that are similar to some of the aspirations of education and are in this broad sense educational. For example, aspects of cognitive behavioural therapy aim to help the child rethink and reinterpret his perceptions of the actions of others. In the care aspects of a day school and in residential schools, staff aim to be good examples (from which pupils can learn) of how to care for others.

Also, it is widely accepted that educators need to understand the aims of therapists and carers and support each other's work in order to be most effective. This is part of the trend to encourage multi-disciplinary working and is evident in close working in some settings to achieve shared assessments of pupils' functioning. Furthermore, aspects of special education are informed by what works therapeutically. Teaching pupils with speech and language disorders is informed by what works in speech and language therapy. Teaching pupils with conduct disorder takes account of findings in psychotherapies. For example, there may be implications for the curriculum, teaching and other aspects of provision from psychotherapeutic evidence that social skills training and anger management coping skills training can help reduce mild conduct problems in pre-adolescents.

Organisation

Organisation may be seen in terms of school and of classroom organisation. School organisation may involve flexible arrival and departure times for lessons for some pupils with orthopaedic impairment. The level of supervision necessary for recess times will take account of the need to encourage socialisation and independence. Organisational aspects relating to safety are also considered. Flexible arrangements for pupil absences can include home tuition and emailed work to support home study.

Classroom organisation may be different from that for most children. For pupils with profound cognitive impairment, classroom organisation may draw on room management approaches. Regarding a pupil with hearing impairment, the classroom may be organised to optimise seeing and listening to other speakers.

There may sometimes be an overlap between aspects of provision considered as 'resources' and those regarded as 'organisation'. For example, where physical resources are rearranged to facilitate access for a child with an orthopaedic impairment, this may be seen as part of classroom organisation as well as the use of resources.

Classification, provision and evidence-based practice

Having examined issues relating to classification and looked at the range of provision to be considered in the book, it remains to explain the relationship between the two informing the approach to the present volume and the link to evidence-based practice.

This inter-relationship operates within the context on an interactive view of disability/disorder. The book does not take the view that disability/disorder is solely within the child so that criticisms that might apply to a caricature of a medical model do not arise. Nor does it take the equally extreme view that disability/disorder is socially constructed (or even created) and if only teachers and others would try hard enough to remove supposed institutional 'barriers' disability would diminish. The book takes the position that disability/disorder is most helpfully and accurately understood as involving an interaction between individual, social and other influences in varying degrees for different types of disability/disorder.

Lewis and Norwich (2005) focusing on two positions relating to difference, question the usefulness of some groupings in relation to 'pedagogic *principles*' (italics added) (ibid.: 216). In their *general difference* position, group specific needs of pupils with disability/disorder are foregrounded although needs common to all learners and needs unique to individual learners remain important. The *unique difference* position (conversant with strong support of inclusion) emphasises unique differences, de-emphasises common pedagogic needs and eschews group specific needs. From this standpoint, while learners are in one sense all the same, they are all also uniquely different, so pedagogic strategies are considered relevant for all pupils irrespective of social background, ethnicity, gender and disability. Differences between individuals are accommodated in terms of personal uniqueness and their dependence on social context. Common pedagogic needs are approached through principles general and flexible enough to enable individual variations to be possible within a common framework (ibid.: 3–4).

Lewis and Norwich's contributors to their edited volume consider whether differences between learners, by special needs group, can be identified and systematically linked with learners' needs for differential teaching. Contributors recognised a general differences position (acknowledging group specific differences) for: autistic spectrum disorder, attention deficit hyperactivity disorder, deafness, visual impairment and profound and multiple learning difficulties. A more individual differences position (rejecting group specific differences) typified: deafblindness; severe learning difficulty; speech, language and communication needs; dyslexia; social, emotional and behavioural difficulties; and moderate learning difficulties (Lewis and Norwich, 2005: 215–216). ('Down's syndrome' and 'low attainment', not distinctively identified in American or English special education classification, were also considered). From this mixed picture, Lewis and Norwich (2005: 220) conclude, 'the traditional special needs categories ... have limited usefulness in the context of planning, or monitoring, teaching and learning in most areas'.

Perhaps, this conclusion is a little premature given that a general difference position was supported among the book's contributors for five of the 11 disabilities/disorders often considered in classifications. The present book will maintain that what Lewis and Norwich call a 'group difference position' can be maintained for other types of disorder too and not just with regard to pedagogy but also to wider provision. In doing this it is sometimes necessary to further differentiate classifications within amorphous headings. For example, within the broad range of 'social, emotional and behavioural difficulties' patterns of effective provision can be identified in terms of 'disruptive behaviour disorders', 'anxiety disorders and depressive disorders', and 'attention deficit hyperactivity disorder'.

However, the distinction made by Norwich and Lewis (2005: 3–4) is helpful here. It will be recalled that in the *general difference* position, group specific needs of pupils with disability/disorder are foregrounded, although needs common to all learners and needs unique to individual learners are important. It is this position that is taken in the present text and it is argued that there are group specific factors and relevant provision associated with them. But the book does *not* deny that provision for special children sometimes includes approaches that may be common to all children. It is assumed that from their generic training, teachers and others will know such general approaches. Neither is it claimed that provision for special children excludes approaches tailored to individual children. Teachers will learn from the individual child, parents and others what these individual factors are and how they might best respond using professional flexibility and creativeness. What the present book focuses on, however, is the range of provision that appears effective with regard to types of disability/disorder.

This position maintains that for children with an identified disorder there are approaches that may well be common to all children, approaches that are particularly effective with the children with the disorder and approaches for particular children with the disorder that may be individual to them. The book focuses on the second of these – those approaches appearing particularly effective with children with that particular disorder.

Although the book sets out a range of provision regarding each disorder/disability, it is *not* claimed that some elements of the range of approaches that work particularly well with children with a certain disorder have no application whatever to children who do not have the disorder. For example, visual structure may be effective for children with autism, but may also have application for children who do not have autism. However, this does not imply that all approaches that are effective for a pupil with autism will be suitable for all children. Similarly, if it is accepted that for children with

mild cognitive impairment effective provision includes: a curriculum significantly below the level followed by typically developing children of the same
age; slower lesson pace than usual and emphasis on concrete learning beyond
what is age typical, it does not follow that this provision is suitable for all
children who do not have mild cognitive impairment.

The framework of general difference, group difference and unique difference positions Norwich and Lewis (2005: 3–4) may have parallels with current
interests. The general difference may overlap with work being developed that
is suitable for children with a disability/disorder and children who do not
have such a disability/disorder, an aspect of so-called inclusive pedagogy. The
group difference position relates to the approaches presented in the present
book although the remit of the present text is wider than principles of pedagogy. The unique differences position may have similarities to the current
fashion for 'personalised learning'.

The growing influence of evidence-based practice relates to the interaction
of classification and provision discussed above. In the United States of
America, an enactment of the *No Child Left Behind Act 2002* is that all students, including those with disabilities, will demonstrate annual yearly
progress and perform at a proficient level on state academic assessment tests.
Identifying scientific methods and evidence-based practices has much to offer
to meet such aspirations. But it not a miracle solution. There are major
challenges in identifying, implementing and evaluating practices that are
scientifically valid and effective. Also, families and professionals have to
decide on the suitability of an intervention or approach for a particular child,
looking at various options.

Simpson (2005), considering evidence-based practice and autism, makes
observations having relevance to disability/disorder more generally. Ideally,
evidence will involve peer review and the validation of products and materials through research designs using random samples and control and experimental groups (ibid.: 141–142 paraphrased). However, other methods may
be appropriate in different circumstances because of 'limited student samples,
heterogeneous clinical education programmes, and the need for flexibility
in matching research designs to specific questions and issues ...' (ibid.: 142).
Alternatives might include single subject design validation or correlational
methods.

Basic questions for parents and professionals to ask relate to the efficacy and
anticipated outcomes in connection with a particular practice and whether
the anticipated outcomes are in line with student needs; the potential risks
(including risks to family life and cohesion of long-term very intensive interventions); and the most effective means of evaluation (ibid.: 143 paraphrased). Overall, evidence-based practice can inform the way forward, but
other dimensions are also relevant including professional judgement and the
views of the child and family.

Subsequent chapters

Subsequent chapters consider the disabilities/disorders mentioned earlier. For each of these, the relevant chapter considers definition; prevalence; causal factors; identification and assessment and any other relevant matters; then examines provision in terms of curriculum and assessment, pedagogy, resources, therapy and organisation. The conclusion chapter refers to each aspect of provision with regard to the various types of disorder/disability.

Thinking points

Readers may wish to consider:

- the degree to which, in an interactive approach, individual, and social considerations might inform understanding of different disabilities/disorders;
- the strengths and limitations of categories with reference to particular disorders/disabilities;
- the issues relating to the positive and negative potential of labelling and
- the extent to which the elements of provision suggested (e.g. curriculum, pedagogy) adequately describe and cover what is provided for learners with disability/disorder.

Key texts

American Psychiatric Association (2000) *Diagnostic and Statistical Manual of Mental Disorders,* Fourth Edition Text Revision, Washington, DC, APA.
This increasingly widely used reference seeks to define and provide identification criteria for many of the categories of disability/disorder covered in the present text.

Carr, A. (2006) (2nd edition) *The Handbook of Child and Adolescent Clinical Psychology: A Contextual Approach.* London, Routledge.
This book, written mainly for post-graduate psychology students and those undergoing professional training in clinical psychology, provides an account of a wide range of problems in childhood and adolescence. Chapter 3, 'Classification, epidemiology and treatment effectiveness', includes a discussion of issues of reliability, validity, coverage and co-occurrence of conditions and related matters.

Coch, D., Dawson, G. and Fischer, K. W. (2007) *Human Behaviour, Learning, and the Developing Brain: Atypical Development.* New York, Guilford Press.
This book outlines work on biological aspects of 'neurodevelopmental' disorders including autism, attention deficit hyperactivity disorder, conduct disorder, dyslexia, dyspraxia and dyscalculia and educational interventions.

Shakespeare, T. (2006) *Disability Rights and Wrongs*. London, Routledge.
This is an example from the area of 'disability studies' of the recognition of the weakness of an exclusively social view of disability and that a position recognising individual differences as well as social and other factors is more supportable.

Chapter 2

Profound cognitive impairment

Introduction

The chapter concerns children and young people that in the United States of America are defined as having 'profound mental retardation', and in England, in recognition of the frequent accompanying disabilities and disorders, as having 'profound and multiple learning difficulties'. Equivalent terms to 'mental retardation' include 'mental handicap' (Hong Kong and other parts of Asia), 'intellectual disability' (Australia and New Zealand) and 'cognitive impairment' (an alternative usage in the United States of America).

The chapter considers definitions; prevalence; causal factors; identification and assessment and provision. Regarding provision, it looks at: curriculum and assessment; pedagogy; resources; therapy and organisation, and examines challenging behaviour, which occurs with some children having profound cognitive impairment.

Definitions

'Profound mental retardation' is defined in the *Diagnostic and Statistical Manual of Mental Disorders, Fourth Edition Text Revision* (*DSM-IV-TR*) (American Psychiatric Association, 2000: 42) according to limitations in both intellectual functioning and in adaptive behaviour. It is associated with an intelligence quotient (IQ) range of below 20 or 25 although IQ levels are interpreted with care, not being the sole criterion. Most children with profound mental retardation have an 'identified neurological condition' that accounts for the retardation (ibid.: 44). In early childhood, impairments of sensory neural function are evident. Referring to possible development, including that in adulthood, and the sort of provision to encourage it, *DSM-IV-TR* states, 'Optimal development may occur in a highly structured environment with constant aid and supervision and an individualised relationship with a caregiver. Motor development and self-care and communication skills may improve if appropriate training is provided. Some can perform simple tasks in closely supervised and sheltered settings' (ibid.: 44). The diagnostic criteria for mental retardation also include 'co-current deficits or impairments in present adaptive functioning ... in at least two of the following areas: communication, self-care, home living, social/interpersonal skills, use of community resources, self-direction, functional academic skills, work, leisure, health and safety' (ibid.: 49).

In 2002, the American Association on Intellectual and Developmental Disabilities (AAIDD) agreed a supports-based definition in which cognitive impairment was regarded not so much as a relatively static disability as a condition able to be enhanced by the provision of supports. However, it is difficult to see how any support thought to be required could be allocated fairly unless there was some previous judgement of 'need' ultimately referring to characteristics of the person considered to require the support. Nevertheless, the notion of support provision could supplement existing definitions of cognitive impairment and might also point the way to possible pedagogic approaches.

> In England, a definition of profound and multiple learning difficulties in government guidance states that in addition to 'severe and complex learning needs' pupils have 'other significant difficulties, such as physical disabilities or a sensory impairment. Pupils require a high level of adult support, both for their learning needs and for their personal care. They are likely to need sensory stimulation and a curriculum broken down into very small steps. Some pupils communicate by gesture, eye pointing or symbols, others by very simple language ...' (DfES, 2005: 7).

The guidance adds that, throughout their school careers, the attainments of these students is likely to remain in a range typified by the lowest levels of widely used 'performance scales' ('P-scales'). The relevant levels (P1-4) begin with generic aspects of development such as that pupils 'encounter' and 'show emerging awareness' of activities and experiences and extend to emerging understanding relatable to areas such as mathematics and communication, for example that they are aware of cause and effect in familiar mathematical activities (Qualifications and Curriculum Authority, 2001a, 2001b, 2001c and later amendments).

Given that children with profound cognitive impairment have associated disabilities, the reader may wish, when consulting the chapters in this volume on 'Visual impairment', 'Hearing impairment', 'Deafblindness' 'Orthopaedic impairment' and 'Health impairment' to reflect on the extent to which approaches described there can be adapted taking into account the child's profound cognitive impairment.

Prevalence

Studies suggest agreement on the prevalence of profound cognitive impairment with Western Australia (Wellesley *et al.*, 1992) and several European countries (e.g. France) (Rumeau-Rouquette *et al.*, 1998) finding prevalence rates between 0.6 per cent and 0.8 per cent. In the United States of America, it is estimated that, of the population with mental retardation (mild, moderate, severe, profound), the group having profound mental retardation constitute about 1 to 2 per cent, (American Psychiatric Association, 2000: 43).

Although prevalence rates do not vary as widely as some other conditions, such as developmental co-ordination disorder or reading disorder, and although it is widely accepted that profound cognitive impairment is in comparison easier to define and identify, some small variation is nevertheless evident.

Part of the reason for the variation taking the *DSM-IV-TR* (American Psychiatric Association, 2000: 49) definition as an example may be the difficulty in being precise about the level of the 'co-current deficits or impairments in present adaptive functioning' as required by criteria. Another reason may be the variety of areas that can be considered relevant in the *DSM-IV-TR* criteria being 'communication, self-care, home living, social/interpersonal skills, use of community resources, self-direction, functional academic skills, work, leisure, health and safety' (ibid.: 49). Because the criteria specifies that 'at least two' of these areas should show deficits or impairments, the definition and assessment can include a child with two such impaired areas or all of them.

Also, definitions vary from country to country, as the example from England compared with that of *DSM-IV-TR* indicates. The definition in England tends to include sensory and physical disabilities that often accompany profound cognitive impairment as part of the definition, while *DSM-IV-TR* appears to view such disabilities as less fundamental to the definition, although it does recognise that the greater the mental retardation, especially if it is severe or profound, the greater the likelihood of other conditions, including 'neurological (e.g. seizures), neuromuscular, visual, auditory, cardiovascular' (ibid.: 46).

Causal and related factors

Almost all children with profound cognitive impairment have organic brain damage. During their childhood period, 'considerable impairments' in sensory motor functioning are evident (American Psychiatric Association, 2000: 44). Many rare syndromes each account for a small percentage of instances of profound cognitive impairment.

As already indicated, *DSM-IV-TR* observes that the greater the cognitive impairment, and especially if it is severe or profound, the greater the likelihood of other conditions (ibid.: 46). It is widely agreed that the vast majority of people with profound cognitive impairment are also multiply disabled (e.g. Arvio and Sillanpaa, 2003). Many causes of cognitive impairment may lead to different degrees of impairment, so the reader is also referred to the section on causal factors in Chapter 3, 'Moderate to severe cognitive impairment'.

Conditions that do not of themselves lead to profound cognitive impairment may be associated with such impairment. For example, cerebral palsy (a physical impairment affecting movement and linked with damage to the developing brain) is associated with 20 per cent to 30 per cent of instances of profound mental retardation (Evans and Ware, 1987; Wellesley *et al.*, 1992).

Identification and assessment

The identification of profound cognitive impairment includes the identification of profoundly impaired cognitive functioning and of other significant difficulties, such as physical disabilities, sensory impairment or a severe medical condition. Just as definitions and related application of criteria may vary, so identification and assessment is not clear-cut and the validity of assessments and how they can be improved is a matter of debate.

Educational assessments determine areas of relative strengths and weaknesses using intelligence tests (with particular attention to analysing performance on subscales) developmental scales (judiciously) and other assessments. In the use of such assessments, teachers and others will be concerned that the assessments are, among other things:

- valid (measuring what they are designed to measure);
- useful (serving a clear purpose that benefits the child) and
- purposeful (for example, indicating instructional approaches).

In using assessments of adaptive functioning, testers also look for a profile of strengths and weaknesses. For example, the *Vineland Adaptive Behaviour Scales* (Vineland II) (2nd edition) (Sparrow *et al.*, 2006) designed as a measure of personal and social skills required for everyday living from birth to adulthood, is used to support the identification and assessment of children with cognitive impairment. Information emerging from the scales which cover the domains of communication, daily living skills, socialisation and motor skills, are also used to inform educational and treatment planning and to track progress.

If assessment is informed by such developments as the 2002, American Association on Intellectual and Developmental Disabilities (AAIDD) supports-based definition described earlier, the provision of supports may be part of the assessment process. A more dynamic process of assessment might result that could also point the way to long-term pedagogic and support strategies.

Provision

Curriculum

Because of the very early developmental level of children and young people with profound cognitive impairment, the curriculum is informed by knowledge of typical early infant development. One working assumption is that the child may be developing in a similar way to a child without cognitive impairment but at a slower speed. However, it is not assumed that in all instances a pupil with cognitive impairment will develop in the same way as a typically developing infant and provision takes account of idiosyncratic development and the effect of other disabilities.

Planning ensures a rich variety of curriculum experiences and draws on what appear to be the pupils' developmental learning 'needs'. Crucial additional curriculum requirements such as therapy and special programmes (for example for communication) are integrated into provision.

Priorities such as those expressed in an Individualised Education Programme/Individual Education Plan are likely to involve the acquisition of basic and fundamental skills that do not necessarily fit into school curriculum subject categorisations. Given the impairments in adaptive functioning associated with mental retardation (American Psychiatric Association, 2000: 49), the curriculum will also ensure that practical, functional activities are planned in areas including: 'communication, self-care, home living, social/ interpersonal skills, use of community resources, self-direction, functional academic skills, work, leisure, health and safety'.

Assessment

It has been suggested (Ouvry and Saunders, 2001) that an assessment system suitable for pupils with profound cognitive impairment should (among other things) be able to:

- record experiences as well as responses or achievements and processes additionally to outcomes;
- be completed by a range of staff;
- record achievement in subject-specific understanding and individual priorities;
- relate directly to each pupil's Individual Education Plan;
- accommodate a wide variety of pupil responses to a situation;
- record responses in whole class, small group, and individual sessions (ibid.: 253, paraphrased).

As already indicated, the progress of pupils with profound cognitive impairment might be idiosyncratic and not necessarily conform to assumptions of hierarchical child development underpinning assessments of vertical progression. Therefore, assessment will include recognition of the breadth of a pupil's experiences, such as the opportunities they have had to develop a skill or knowledge in different ways, and the technological or adult support necessary to achieve a particular outcome. It will include the assessment of understanding and skills across different situations, at different times and with different people.

Many countries use curriculum-related assessments; standardised assessments of various aspects of attainment and development and portfolios of achievement. For example, in England, curriculum-related assessments, so-called 'P' scales (performance scales) recognise progress below level 1 of the National Curriculum. National Curriculum level 1 is usually entered by a typically developing child at about the age of 5 to 6 years (Qualifications and Curriculum Authority, 2001a, 2001b, 2001c and later amendments). More detailed commercially available assessments are also used.

Related to curriculum-based assessments is task analysis, allowing detailed assessments to be made of a task or activity and enabling educators to identify aspects requiring further instruction (e.g. Bigge *et al.*, 2001: 121–148). Although task analysis emerged from behavioural perspectives, the flexibility of the method has led to its being used by teachers and others influenced by other approaches including cognitive ones. Task analysis may be applied in various ways, for example, to a task seen as a prerequisite to other ones (picking up an item before using it) or to tasks logically linked as part of a procedure (such as dressing).

Broadly, task analysis typically involves:

- deciding the aims and objectives for teaching and learning;
- determining and specifying the desired learning outcome;
- specifying in detail the tasks and elements of tasks the pupil will be carrying out;
- prioritising and sequencing the tasks;
- agreeing suitable ways of teaching and learning likely to lead to the desired learning outcomes;
- deciding the support needed and the optimum learning environment;
- setting up ways of assessing the pupil's progress and achievement and evaluating the whole process.

Recording the results of assessments enables a starting point to be determined for a proposed intervention and allows progress to be monitored. From a baseline assessment, a target is set, the aim being to reach the target through a particular pedagogic approach, or extra time being allocated and so on. After a specified time a further assessment is made to indicate progress from the baseline and also to give an indication of the success or otherwise of the approach/extra time.

Also important is contemporaneously recording notable developments such as something the pupil has not been observed to do before or some skill the pupil appears to have transferred to a new situation. For example, a child may have used a manual sign in the classroom to request a 'drink' when the environment supports this as when daily routine preparations are being made for snack time. After a while, he may be observed making the sign in a different context such as the play areas or at a different time such as when he first arrives at school. This would be recorded, but even more importantly the teacher and others would respond to the sign!

Pedagogy

Communication

It will be remembered that the diagnostic criteria in *DSM-IV-TR* (p. 49) for mental retardation refer to 'co-current deficits or impairments in present adaptive functioning' in at least two areas, which include communication and social/interpersonal skills. The importance of supporting the communication of students with profound cognitive impairment can hardly be overemphasised.

Care needs to be taken interpreting apparent signs and constantly checking the adult's response seems suitable in the student's terms. For example, behaviour having the potential to be communicative may be physiological such as 'freezing' or being apparently startled. But temporary rigidity of the body or a limb may indicate dislike or fear or may be related to physical and motor impairment. Smiling or grimacing may respectively indicate pleasure or displeasure at something happening in the surroundings or may be related to an inner state. Facial expressions may not invariably indicate what they commonly convey.

Other aspects of non-verbal behaviour to which the teacher and others may seek to respond include: posture; withdrawal or approach responses; arm waving or other gestures; pushing someone or something away; reaching for something and many other movements that may be indications of feeling, preference or some other communication. Turning towards a sound or showing apparent attention through fixing one's gaze or following a person or object with one's gaze are other potentially communicative indications. But some behaviour may be ritualistic or obsessive and not relate to the present environment either internal or external in the usual way. Sounds may indicate feelings or preferences or other matters. These may include apparently contented sounds such as babbling or excited noises; or they may be seemingly unhappy sounds such as shrieking or crying. Again, the adult will be alert to their possible intended meaning and their own response.

Some early behaviours and responses may be spontaneous, but where an adult in turn responds to them, they can come to have communicative significance, such consequences being part of the development of communication for all children (e.g. Pease, 2000: 41–42). These patterns of response might take a long time to become routine and secure, sensitivity on the part of the adult communicative partner to what the pupil does and how he reacts being essential. Pupil behaviours/responses can lead to the teacher/adult responding in a way that lays the basis for the gesture or sound or glance to be invested with communicative intent. Sensitivity is also necessary if and when the pupil begins to point or gesture to ensure attempts to communicate are not missed.

'Intensive Interaction' for example is an approach using one-to-one sessions and seeking to 'help the person learn fundamentals of communication – eye contacts, facial expressions, turn taking' (Nind and Hewett, 2001:17). Intensive Interaction can involve encouraging interaction as it were for its own sake or can enable interaction with other children and help the pupil gain access to the curriculum through improving communication and interpersonal behaviour. It involves 'regular, frequent interactions between the practitioner ... and the individual with learning disabilities, in which there is no task or outcome focus, but in which the primary concern is the quality of the interaction itself' (Hewett and Nind, 1998: 2). (The term 'learning disabilities' in the context just quoted appears to refer to cognitive impairment.) Data were collected for a group of five children with 'profound and multiple learning difficulties' over a year during teacher-led group time (not directly aimed at developing communication) and in intensive interaction. It was found children demonstrated more consistent and advanced behaviour in the latter (Watson and Fisher, 1997). Single child reports also suggest that daily Intensive Interaction sessions can develop communication, increase participation in positive social interactions and sometimes lead to reduced stereotyped behaviour (e.g. Nind and Kellett, 2002).

Some students with profound cognitive impairment may respond to and use symbolic communication. Objects of reference may be used if it is apparent that the object can be invested with meaning for the student. Care will need to be taken that the item that appears to be an object of reference (for example a plate indicating meal time) is indeed acting in a symbolic capacity and is not simply a conditioned stimulus in a classical conditioning sense, only associated with the reward of food. The student may learn to use and understand visual symbols, for example conveying various activities or places. Or symbols may be used to indicate preferences, choices and feelings (e.g. a smiling face or angry face).

Where a pupil can communicate by simple language, it is important that this too is encouraged and that adults and other pupils are ready to respond. The spoken language used by adults to a pupil does not have to be overloud, stilted and telegraphic, but neither should the pupil be swamped with streams of talk. Key words can be naturally stressed and repeated and accompanied by the item to which the speaker is referring. Manual sign language is used to communicate and to supplement verbal communication.

Also, where a child has profound cognitive impairment and is also deaf, manual signing and lip reading take on particular significance. If the child is blind, aural-oral communication and opportunities to develop close familiarity with surroundings come to the fore. Should the child with profound cognitive impairment also be deafblind, then training in the significance and importance of touch is central and hand-over-hand work (e.g. Hodges, 2000: 179) may be used for communication.

Where such symbolic communication is learned, it opens up the opportunity to communicate about items or people that may not be present or about proposed activities. (See Chapter 3 on severe to moderate to severe cognitive impairment for further discussion.) The later sections on resources, organisation, and challenging behaviour also provide further information on communication.

Task analytic instruction

Task analysis has already been mentioned in relation to assessment (e.g. Bigge *et al.*, 2001: 121–148). The reader will have recognised that as well as being a form of assessment, there are implications for intervention. This section considers how the approach can inform teaching and learning, outlining an example of teaching a child to drink from a covered cup holding it in both hands.

The desired learning outcome is that the child, when thirsty and when a covered cup containing drink is placed on a tray in front of him will pick up the cup and drink from it. The elements of the task are to look at the cup, to place both hands round it, to raise it to the mouth and tilt it so the contents can be drunk. The sequence of subtasks might be taught in the order just explained. Alternatively, they might be taught using so-called backward chaining where the child is helped or prompted for all but the final part of the sequence and encouraged to finish that, progressively being encouraged to complete earlier parts of the sequence without support.

A suitable way of teaching this might be through using physical prompts for each part of the sequence and gradually fading these out, or by using time delay. The support needed might be one adult the child knows well, and a quiet environment without distractions. The pupil's progress might be recorded in terms of the parts of the sequence. Where there is more rapid progress on certain occasions, the possible reasons might be noted so that they feed into the evaluation of what worked best and why.

Multi-sensory approaches and daily living experiences

Three ways of using a multi-sensory approach have been suggested: to stimulate the senses; to be part of meaningful activities; and to help access to subject based activities (Ouvry and Saunders, 2001: 254).

First, stimulating the senses is a way of encouraging responsiveness in a child who may be less inclined or (because of accompanying physical or motor difficulties) less able than other children to explore the environment without considerable support and encouragement. Sensory stimulation is a way of introducing different experiences to the pupil and encouraging his interest and response. Senses are stimulated to develop perceptual skills to gain information from the environment. To the extent that this approach uses specialised equipment with no inherent meaning in situations lacking meaningful context, it might provide a starting point for the functional use of sense but has 'limitations as a long term teaching technique' (ibid.: 245).

A sensory stimulation room may be used where devices that respond to touch or sound by producing sounds or visual effects, may encourage responses from the pupil. There may be a soft room perhaps with a ball pool, a projector, bubble tubes, fibre optic lighting and a transmitter of sound effects or music. As well as stimulating the senses and encouraging responses, the rooms can also create an environment with soothing sounds and soft lighting to help a child relax if he is frustrated or distressed. Schools may wish to ensure they make the assumed educational and therapeutic effects of sensory rooms explicit in their policy development and planning, and rigorously evaluate their supposed educational gains (including a critical look at the likely meaningfulness of the experiences for the pupil) and the supposed personal impact.

The second way is to incorporate sensory experiences into activities having their own 'structure and meaning' but that have been devised to give opportunities for sensory work. The sensory experiences are based on what are judged to be the priorities for the child (for example attending to and visually tracking an object), but will incorporate this in an activity such as drama (handling then watching a glove puppet as part of a story).

The third way of using a multi-sensory approach is to enable participation in subject-related activities. Subjects such as mathematics, science and history have skills and understanding associated with them, some aspects of which may be accessible to pupils with profound cognitive impairment. For example, in science topic on plant growth, the student may be encouraged to touch, smell, observe and perhaps taste a fruit at early and later stages of growth, perhaps reinforced by grouping paired examples of fruits that are 'small' and 'big'. A difficulty is that the topic may or may not have meaning and if the topic is outside the pupil's understanding, the sensory experiences may seem to the pupil fragmented and meaningless or may not convey what is intended.

The challenge for the teacher is to identify in teaching contexts opportunities to encourage sensory experiences for the pupil that aid further development. This might be progress from tolerating to attending, from attending to participating, or from participating to understanding. The intention is that the pupil should be able to grasp meaning in the sensory experience itself as well as developing an awareness of the meaning that the sensory experience has in relation to the context of the activity. The aim is that as the pupil attends to these, he begins to develop increasing familiarity with them leading to potential further learning.

There is increasing consensus that the level of access afforded by multi-sensory approaches should not be regarded as sufficient in itself because they do not necessarily have meaning for the pupil (Ouvry and Saunders, 2001: 245). Sensory experiences, it is suggested, should be extended to give opportunities for conceptual learning and to help the pupil understand better his surroundings, daily activities and everyday experiences (Carpenter, 1994). For example, preparing food (and eating it!), washing, taking part in a game or leisure activity, visiting a park or market, exploring a nature trail, making music, shaping pottery and a host of other activities can be stimulating to the senses and also have the potential to be meaningful.

Community-based vocational instruction

The *DSM-IV-TR* (American Psychiatric Association, 2000: 44) suggests with regard to people with profound mental retardation that some 'can perform simple tasks in closely supervised and sheltered settings'. Baroff (1999: 59) maintains that an adult who is 'profoundly retarded' may 'be unable to perform any useful work, although with training in an activity center may achieve a work-activity level of productivity'. For older students, as part of transition from school to post-school settings, vocational instruction, including community-based vocational instruction, can have an important role. Community-based instruction can have a positive impact on the development of adaptive behaviour of students. A study with 34 high school students with 'moderate to profound mental retardation' found that students made statistically significant gains in three of the four domains of the *Scales of Independent Behaviour* (McDonnell *et al.*, 1993). The co-ordination of all parties involved, including potential employers, school, rehabilitation counsellor, those making transport arrangements, volunteers and those involved in other support services, help maximise the potential benefits of this provision. Planning for community-based vocational instruction takes account of local circumstances and job opportunities.

Training schedules are devised to help students develop the necessary skills for employability and employment. Task analyses may be made of the main tasks that the student will be expected to carry out, for example, cleaning procedures or packing skills. Such training helps students develop choices about what they would like to do, for example indicated by expressions of pleasure or dislike when carrying out tasks. It also gives employers the opportunity to see what a student with profound cognitive impairment, perhaps with co-worker support, is able to do. Education supports suitable for students aged 18 to 21 have been outlined (Wehmeyer *et al.*, 2002) and include that they are provided in an age appropriate setting that allows social contact and encourages inclusion in the community and that the services are 'outcomes orientated'.

Resources

Activities may be enhanced and structured using the visual and auditory capabilities of digital videodiscs (DVD) or interactive compact disks.

Also, technology is employed to aid communication and social interaction. Initially, these approaches may enable the child to become aware that his actions can affect others.

Making choices, as well as being an aspect of communication, contributes to greater autonomy. Choice making may be taught using adult prompting and/or the use of a switch-activated reinforcer. Prompting may be used to teach switch activation or/and discrimination between different choices (Ware, 2005: 73). Case studies have indicated the usefulness of multiple micro switches for enhancing different responses in children with profound disabilities. The wider range of response opportunities and the more differentiated input from the environment lead to higher levels of responding (Lancioni *et al.*, 2002).

For any activity in school or an outside trip, a digital camera or video camera can be used to record events and very soon after the activity is completed images can be transferred to computer and projected. The teacher and others will need to observe the students' responses to see if there is any indication that what is being shown conveys to the student anything about the activity recently carried out as such images are a form of symbolic communication that the student may not recognise or understand.

For students able to use symbolic communication, computer technology allows the flexible use of many symbols, although the teacher may need to ensure the pupil links object, activity or person and the symbol (see also Chapter 14, 'Communication disorders: Speech' in the present volume). Dedicated communication devices may be used involving electronic communication systems speaking programmed messages when the pupil activates locations marked by symbols. Computer aided communication may involve a voice production device with a computer-based bank of words and sentences that can be produced by pressing the keyboard keys.

Therapy

Physical and motor disability may be associated with conditions such as spina bifida, which may accompany profound cognitive impairment. These disabilities will require the support and advice of a physiotherapist, occupational therapist and others to develop and oversee specific programmes encouraging suitable posture and optimum movement. Because movement and exploring the environment contribute so much to learning, where these are impaired, it is vital to make the most of what mobility there is for pupils with profound cognitive impairment.

Medical conditions have their own implications both for care and in their effect on education and these are assessed for each child. If a child with profound cognitive impairment has cystic fibrosis (a life-threatening condition in which thick mucus is produced on the lungs and pancreas resulting in cysts) this requires regular physiotherapy to clear the lungs. School staff may need to administer medication for seizures to a child with profound cognitive impairment who also has epilepsy.

Organisation

Underpinning much of the organisation of the learning environment for pupils with profound cognitive impairment is an acute awareness of and an ongoing assessment of the pupil's behaviour state. The importance of creating an environment responsive to pupils' signs of attention and other behaviour is highlighted when one reflects on the fact that much of the time the student may be asleep or drowsy. Guess and colleagues (1990) found that in a group they observed, students were awake and alert only about half their time in school. Such findings underscore the importance of teachers and others making continuing assessments of the behaviour state of each pupil to optimise opportunities for learning in the times when the pupil is more alert and responsive.

A range of approaches is brought together under the term, 'responsive environment' (Ware, 2003), which is considered important in the development of social, intellectual and communicative development. This is essentially the creation of an environment in which pupils with cognitive impairment 'get responses to their actions, get the opportunity to give responses to the actions of others, and have the opportunity to take the lead in interaction' (ibid.: 1).

Greater awareness of a pupil's behaviour state is an aspect likely to improve the effectiveness of approaches such as 'room management' which is used with groups of pupils and in which the adults are assigned to one of three roles: individual helper, group activity manager or mover (e.g. Lacey, 1991). The individual helper tends to be involved with one pupil at a time on intensive work, varying the time between several minutes to longer periods, depending on the pupil, the task and other factors. The group activity manager makes sure that the other pupils are occupied, perhaps experiencing a game or some other activity that is not focused intensively on skill building. The mover ensures the smooth running of the group, dealing with visitors, preparing materials or tidying away. The adult roles may be rotated about every hour.

Although this approach increases the levels of adult attention for each pupil, it does not necessarily ensure that pupils are more engaged in the tasks (Evans and Ware, 1987), suggesting that the level of pupil's engagement be monitored. The mover might do this if there are few interruptions, preparation is done jointly before the sessions begin, and there is not too much mess to tidy up. Factors that increase the pupil's engagement can then be noted and the approach gradually modified to ensure pupils are optimally engaged. These modifications will take account of the pupil, the task and the time of day, the aim being to get the best from room management while ensuring better pupil engagement.

It is important to create an environment that is sensitive to movements and sounds made by the pupil so that these environmental responses will in their turn bring about a response in the child. Pupils should be enabled, through their actions, to control aspects of their surroundings. Related to this is encouraging, perhaps initially with much support, choice and decision making, such as choice of food and drink, or leisure activity, whether to go out or stay in the classroom, and with whom to sit.

More specifically in creating an environment conducive to communication and development, establishing contingency awareness (the child being aware of the link between his behaviour and its consequences) is very important. Using switch operated reinforcers, the child may be prompted to use the switch so that he will experience his action and its consequences repeatedly and link the two. Indications that a link is being made are the child operating the switch more frequently (to receive the reinforcer) and his showing apparent pleasure in the activity.

School routines such as morning greetings, mealtimes and snack times and personal care procedures are used to extend pupils' understanding and skills by building on what is familiar to them. These can be linked to resources to further develop understanding. The resources themselves can come to acquire meaning by being associated with familiar activities. For example, a particular cup regularly used for mealtimes at school may come to be associated with these times.

Routines can also invest several items with meaning in the sense that one item might indicate to the pupil that another may follow and this notion of sequence can contribute to the activity being imbued with greater meaning. The pupil might be shown a cooking utensil to indicate that a food preparation session is imminent. The pupil then sees the bread and a toaster and begins to link the two items to toast being made. Each item, the cooking utensil, the bread and the toaster gains meaning and the activity begins to make sense as one associated with preparing food.

For students who may be able to understand symbolic communication, routines may be used to aid communication. For example, the cup regularly used can signal that a snack or mealtime is imminent (using the cup as an 'object of reference' for mealtimes). This gives the pupil an indication that there is about to be a change and what the change entails. Objects of reference can be developed in a similar way for regular classroom activities such as using a computer (a CD); food preparation (a cooking utensil); or swimming/hydrotherapy (a piece of swimming costume).

Challenging behaviour

The nature of challenging behaviour

By no means all pupils with profound cognitive impairment exhibit challenging behaviour (CB) and neither is behaviour that challenges staff, pupils and others exclusive to pupils with profound cognitive impairment. But there are particular challenges to parents and professionals managing such behaviours where a child also has profound cognitive impairment, where the child has difficulties communicating wants, and where other difficulties may make it hard for the child to comprehend that some behaviours are harmful, or in other ways undesirable.

There is not always agreement on what constitutes CB because of varying standards of what is considered acceptable relating to social class, culture, different chronological and developmental ages of children and different settings. Sometimes there is disagreement that CB is evident either because of different interpretations of particular behaviour or conflicting views about its severity. In the present context, CB is taken to be behaviour that is socially unacceptable and significantly blocks learning. Because of its intensity, duration or frequency, the safety of the person exhibiting the behaviour or that of others is at risk. Such behaviour is likely to limit access to community facilities or prohibit it altogether in the short term. CB includes aggression, self-injury, stereotyped behaviour and problematic sexual behaviour (Olley, J. G. in Baroff, 1999: 370–395). Examples are:

- self injury or injury to others;
- damage to surroundings;
- severe lack of compliance;
- repeated absconding;
- stereotyped behaviour (speech or movement)
- faecal smearing;
- pica (habitually eating substances other than food such as paper or dirt);
- inappropriate sexual behaviour (e.g. public masturbation or exposing the genitals to others);
- persistent screaming;
- repeated vomiting and
- extreme hyperactivity.

Causal and sustaining factors

In some cases CB is linked to particular conditions such as Lesch-Nyhan syndrome, which is associated with self-injurious behaviour and often violence to others, spitting and vomiting (see Goldstein and Reynolds, 1999 for a fuller description). Other factors that can contribute to CB are the side effects of drugs, pain, stress, anxiety and depression. Further reasons include being unable to convey basic needs; the effects of phobias; limited language and understanding; intolerance of perceived over stimulation; low boredom threshold; discomfort from physical impairment or incontinence and insecurity because of sensory impairment.

CB may have a communicative function for the child, suggesting the importance of individual communication programmes devised in conjunction with a speech and language pathologist/therapist. CB may be used to communicate a request for social activities (e.g. attention or interaction); a request for items such as food or a toy; a protest or refusal to comply with a request or a wish to escape from a situation. It may indicate dissatisfaction; a comment or declaration such as a greeting or compliance with a request; or boredom, pain or tiredness. Analysing the possible communicative function of CB can lead to effective interventions, which may relate to consequences or antecedents as both may support the CB.

Assessment of challenging behaviour

One approach is functional behavioural assessment. See, for example, the American Institute for Research (AIR) Center for Effective Collaboration and Practice (CECP) functional behavioural assessment (www.air.org/cecp and Crone and Horner, 2003). This is a problem-solving process for tackling pupils' problem behaviour, seeking to identify the purpose of the behaviour, and finding ways to intervene to address it. Factors are considered which influence the behaviour: social, affective, cognitive and environmental and behavioural interventions are informed by the apparent reasons for the behaviour so that its purpose and function for the child can be better understood.

Provision for challenging behaviour

Schools try to create optimal learning environments for children with CB and to work out intervention programmes taking into account medical care and developmental level. Specific programmes are individually planned, systematically implemented and rigorously assessed, then modified or changed if ineffective.

Interventions may relate to functional analysis, although their long-term effectiveness may be impaired if the elimination of unwanted behaviour is not supported by naturally occurring events reinforcing the new behaviour. One way of ensuring that natural contingencies are applied is to teach new functional behaviours. These must result in reinforcing consequences similar to those available following the unwanted behaviour, and the new behaviour must be reinforced by the same consequences that reinforced the unwanted behaviour.

Successful intervention depends on expanding the limited response repertories of individuals with cognitive impairment rather than just trying to eliminate the inappropriate behaviour. Some interventions are designed to teach new communicative behaviours to replace unwanted behaviour (teaching a child desiring food to use a non-verbal sign rather than be disruptive). Others are developed to teach alternative functionally related behaviour to replace unwanted behaviour (e.g. the child being taught to listen to peaceful music on a headset to suppress an overstimulating environment instead of shrieking).

Yet, other interventions involve changing the events that lead up to the inappropriate behaviour. Where unwanted behaviour suggests a wish to escape from a demanding activity, simplifying the tasks and using errorless learning might reduce it. Children with CB may need from time to time, additional staff or equipment, or a modified timetable. See also the chapter by Olley, in Baroff (1999: 359–395).

Thinking points

Readers may wish to consider with reference to a particular school:

- the extent to which the curriculum and assessment fit closely together to ensure progress and development for the child;
- how communication and the responsiveness of the environment is optimised;
- how the schools organisation, including pupil grouping and management, enhances provision;
- how effectively arrangements for medical procedures and care are integrated into the school day.

Key texts

Aird, R. (2001) *The Education and Care of Children with Severe, Profound and Multiple Learning Difficulties*. London, David Fulton Publishers.
Discusses both severe learning difficulties (moderate to severe cognitive impairment) and profound learning difficulties (profound cognitive impairment). The book covers a broad range of issues including ensuring the curriculum is sufficiently responsive to the learning and other 'needs' of the pupils as well as requirements for a broad curriculum.

Baroff, G. S. with Olley, J. G. (1999) (3rd edition) *Mental Retardation: Nature, Causes and Management*. Philadelphia, PA, Brunner/Mazel.
Considers the nature of mental retardation and its impact on affected individuals, their parents and siblings. The book examines the effects of cognitive disorder on personality, the causes of mental retardation and the services and supports available.

Crone, D. A. and Horner, R. H. (2003) *Building Positive Behaviour Support Systems in Schools: Functional Behavioural Assessment*. New York, Guilford Press.

Includes case examples of developing and using functional behavioural assessments within school systems. Appendices provide supportive charts and proformas.

Dykens, E. M., Hodapp, R. M. and Finucane, B. M. (2000) *Genetics and Mental Retardation Syndromes: A New Look at Behaviour and Interventions.* Baltimore, MD, Paul H. Brookes.
Identifies characteristics of various syndromes and related interventions.

Chapter 3

Moderate and severe cognitive impairment

Introduction

This chapter concerns children who in the United States of America would be considered to experience 'moderate to severe cognitive impairment' and who in England would be said to have 'severe learning difficulties'. To take another example, in Canada, Australia and Malta, the term 'moderate to severe intellectual disability' is used. Terminology as reflected in the names of organisations is changing in some countries; for example the former American Association of Mental Retardation is now the American Association of Cognitive and Developmental Disabilities (www.aaidd.org).

This chapter mainly uses the alternative term 'moderate to severe cognitive impairment', and also, where it is used in research or assessment, the expression 'moderate to severe mental retardation'. Where comments or research applies specifically to only *moderate* cognitive impairment or only to *severe* cognitive impairment, this is made clear.

The chapter explains definitions of moderate and severe cognitive impairment, prevalence, causal factors and identification and assessment. Regarding provision, it looks at: curriculum including cross-curricular links, and assessment; pedagogy (visual inputs, communication, developing autonomy and independence, and community-based vocational instruction); resources; therapy and organisation.

Definitions

One understanding of moderate and severe cognitive impairment is to consider its relation to mild cognitive impairment (where there is contention about definition, assessment and provision) and profound cognitive impairment (where definition, assessment and provision is more widely agreed). Clearly judgements of moderate to severe cognitive impairment relate to these. Definition, assessment and provision are more clearly understood than is the case for mild cognitive impairment, but not as clearly as for profound cognitive impairment. There is debate about the most suitable provision for children who appear to function in the area between mild cognitive impairment on the one hand and profound cognitive impairment on the other, making ongoing monitoring of progress and development essential.

The *Diagnostic and Statistical Manual of Mental Disorders Fourth Edition Text Revision (DSM-IV-TR)* (American Psychiatric Association, 2000: 42) relates 'moderate retardation' to intelligence quotient (IQ) levels of 35/40 to 50/55. 'Severe retardation' is associated with IQ levels of 20/25 to 35/40. Consequently, the range for moderate to severe cognitive impairment is of IQ levels from 20/25 to 50/55. These ranges are treated with care as IQ is not the sole criterion. The diagnostic criteria for mental retardation in general also includes 'co-current deficits or impairments in present adaptive functioning ... in at least two of the following areas: communication, self-care, home living, social/interpersonal skills, use of community resources, self-direction, functional academic skills, work, leisure, health and safety' (ibid.: 49).

Most people with *moderate* mental retardation acquire communication skills in early childhood. With some supervision they 'can attend to their personal care' (ibid.: 43). While benefiting from training in social and occupational skills, they are 'unlikely to progress beyond second-grade level in academic subjects' (ibid.: 43). Individuals with *severe* mental retardation tend to acquire little or no communicative speech in early childhood but during the school age period may learn to talk and can learn 'elementary self care skills'. They profit to a limited degree from teaching in 'pre-academic subjects' such as 'simple counting' and can master skills such as sight-reading of some survival words (ibid.: 43).

In England, 'severe learning difficulties' by convention broadly corresponds in IQ terms to the American 'moderate mental retardation' and 'severe mental retardation', that is an IQ range of 20/25–50/55 (Kushlick and Blunden, 1974). Guidance published by the government Department for Education and Skills (DfES, 2005: 3–4) (www.dfes.gov.uk/sen) states that pupils with severe learning difficulties have 'significant intellectual cognitive impairments'. It continues: 'This has a major effect on their ability to participate in the school curriculum without support. They may also have difficulties with mobility and co-ordination, communication and perception and the acquisition of self-help skills. Pupils with severe learning difficulties will need support in all areas of the curriculum. Some pupils may use sign and symbols but most will be able to hold simple conversations. Their attainments will be within the upper P scale range for much of their school careers (that is below level 1 of the National Curriculum)' (ibid.: 3–4). The description indicates that pupils with severe learning difficulties will for most of their schooling be working below a level (that is level 1 of the National Curriculum) usually entered by a typically developing child at about the age of 5 to 6 years.

Lower IQ levels are associated with greater possibility of the child having a medical background condition. Around 40 per cent of individuals with an IQ level of 70 have such a condition, but when individuals have an IQ below 50, then 80 per cent have a medical background condition (Gillberg and Soderstrom, 2003).

Prevalence

Given the flexibly applied nature of definitions, prevalence is not easy to establish. Organisation for Economic Co-operation and Development (2000) figures only serve to confirm this, varying from Italy with 0.88 per cent of the school population considered as having severe learning difficulties to the Netherlands with 0.44 per cent.

In the United States of America it is estimated that of the population with mental retardation (mild, moderate, severe, profound) that the group having moderate mental retardation constitute around 10 per cent, and the group having severe mental retardation make up approximately 3 per cent to 4 per cent (with mild mental retardation accounting for around 85 per cent and profound mental retardation for about 1 per cent to 2 per cent) (American Psychiatric Association, 2000: 43).

Causal factors

Classifications of mental retardation used in research tend to adopt severity criteria, such as the IQ range discussed earlier, or aetiology as touched on below (Hodapp and Dykens, 1994).

The *DSM-IV-TR* (American Psychiatric Association, 2000) considers pre-disposing factors for mental retardation in terms of various elements. These include:

- heredity (e.g. Tay-Sachs disease, tuberous sclerosis, translocation Down's syndrome, fragile X syndrome);
- early alterations of embryonic development (e.g. chromosomal changes such as Down's syndrome due to trisomy; or prenatal changes owing to toxins, such as maternal alcohol consumption or to infection);
- pregnancy and perinatal problems (e.g. foetal malnutrition, prematurity, hypoxia, infections including viral infections, and trauma);
- general medical conditions acquired in infancy or childhood (e.g. infections, trauma, or poisoning, for example lead poisoning) (ibid.: 45–46, paraphrased).

Estimates have been made of the percentages of cognitive impairment attributable to different broad causal factors:

- about 15 per cent was attributed to events occurring at conception which include abnormalities of chromosomes as in Down's syndrome (10 per cent) or genes as in phenylketonuria (5 per cent);

- about 47 per cent was attributed to events after conception, which include prenatal (32 per cent), perinatal (11 per cent), and post-natal (4 per cent);
- about 12 per cent was attributed to non-biological causes such as deprivation;
- about 26–30 per cent causal factors are unknown (Crocker, 1992).

For further information on causal factors covering chromosomal and genetic, and non-genetic biological factors (pre-natal, perinatal, and post-natal), see Baroff (1999: 95–201).

Identification and assessment

Cognitive impairment is diagnosed by looking at two areas: intellectual functioning and adaptive behaviour/adaptive functioning (e.g. Algozzine and Ysseldyke, 2006: 17). Criteria such as those described in relation to the *Diagnostic and Statistical Manual of Mental Disorders Fourth Edition Text Revision* (DSM-IV-TR) (American Psychiatric Association, 2000: 42) inform the identification and assessment of moderate to severe cognitive impairment. It will be remembered that the diagnostic criteria for mental retardation include 'co-current deficits or impairments in present adaptive functioning' in at least two of 'communication, self-care, home living, social/interpersonal skills, use of community resources, self-direction, functional academic skills, work, leisure, health and safety' (ibid.: 49).

Commercial assessments include intelligence tests, where there is particularly careful analysis of performance on sub-tests. For example, the *Wechsler Intelligence Scale for Children – Fourth Edition (WISC-IV)*, (Wechsler, 2003) standardised in various countries for children aged 6 to 16 years has sub-tests for verbal comprehension, perceptual reasoning, working memory and processing speed. Commercial assessments of adaptive functioning are also used which set out a profile of strengths and weaknesses, for example relating to personal and social skills and may be referred to as adaptive behaviour scales. Similarly, assessments relating to educational provision include determining areas of relative strength and weakness. Assessments of adaptive behaviour may involve evaluations by parents, teachers and others familiar with the student's response to the demands of home, school, community and work.

Adaptive behaviours may be considered in three areas: daily living skills such as getting dressed; communication skills; and social skills, such as positive interactions with others (e.g. Algozzine and Ysseldyke, 2006: 17). The American Association of Mental Deficiency suggested the skill areas: communication, community living, employment, functional academics, health and safety, home living, leisure, self-care and advocacy, and social skills (for a summary see ibid.: 21–23). Expectations of the level and range of adaptive behaviours vary according to the child's age, for example vocational and social responsibilities take on particular meaning in later adolescence.

Provision

Given the comments made earlier in relation to provision for pupils who appear to function in the borders between mild cognitive impairment on the one hand and profound cognitive impairment on the other, ongoing assessment is important to ensure that the pupil is progressing well. In such instances, approaches described in the chapters concerning mild cognitive impairment and profound cognitive impairment may be considered if professional judgement and other considerations suggest it.

Curriculum

Working at earlier age levels and building on familiar, practical experiences

Although, as indicated in the relevant chapter in this volume, the curriculum for pupils with profound cognitive impairment is informed by very early infant development, that for children with moderate to severe cognitive impairment builds on this foundation and moves more securely into areas of the curriculum and activities with a more recognisable subject basis. The term 'functional academic content' (e.g. Wehmeyer *et al.*, 2002: 190–203) may be used to convey the need for practicality and relevance. Given the levels of attainment associated with moderate to severe mental retardation, it is important that the curriculum provided is broad and relevant but also that there is flexibility for children to work on areas of the curriculum at levels typical of much younger pupils. At the same time, every effort is made to ensure the activities are chronologically age appropriate. Small steps in the development of knowledge and skills in the curriculum will be reflected in schemes of work.

When building up, adapting and refining schemes of work, curriculum developers seek to use familiar activities before progressing to the less familiar. Among particularly important elements are communication, literacy, numeracy and personal and social development, each of which draws on the familiar and the practical.

Communication will focus on direct, relevant activities. Literacy may involve functional reading and functional writing. The former can include the use of common signs such as 'toilet' 'washroom', as well as for example business names known to the student, restaurant menus and newspaper extracts. Practical and relevant activities may include reading a street map of the local area, finding required sections labelled by names in the library or categorising a CD music collection. Functional writing can include daily writing activities such as keeping a diary, making a list of items to be bought from a shop, or noting down tasks to be accomplished during the day, taking down a telephone message, writing a note or letter, sending an email, or preparing part of a news letter (see also Algozzine and Ysseldyke, 2006: 38–41).

Numeracy and functional mathematics may involve day-to-day tasks such as budgeting and using money, laying a table, sharing several items, telling the time, writing and following a weekly schedule, reading transport timetables, reading energy meters, and measuring areas for practical activities such as gardening (ibid.: 38–42).

Personal and social education may include: developing a sense of self, self-awareness, self-esteem and self-knowledge. Another way of considering the content of personal independence programmes is in terms of self-care, home management and community skills. Self-care skills include washing and bathing, hair care, oral hygiene, feminine hygiene, toileting, dressing, eating and drinking and knowing one's belongings and keeping them safe. Sex and relationships education is likely to include the specific teaching of some aspects that typically developing pupils of the same age might learn incidentally such as what 'private' means. Home management skills might involve selecting a menu, cooking and house cleaning.

Community skills encompass: using local transport, knowing and responding to social sight vocabulary, shopping, choosing and pursuing hobbies, using community facilities and making choices and decisions. Understanding the roles of people who live in the local community might begin with those who work in the school (teachers, therapists, secretary, maintenance workers) and those who visit it (parents, people from other schools), those at home (parents, siblings) and those who visit home (relatives, newspaper delivery, postal worker). Opportunities and activities planned into the curriculum might include: opportunities to show visitors round, coping with changes in anticipated routine such as going out for lunch when expecting to eat in school and taking turns in a recess activity or game.

Leisure skills can be taught, encouraged and supported. These include the rules of sports and games such as turn taking, working in a team and the specific rules of activities. Also, the student may be helped to be more aware of opportunities for different activities at school, at home and in the community. Other skills might include being able to arrange to get to a leisure venue on time, and knowing when to leave a leisure venue to get home.

Cross-curricular links

Cross-curricular links between subjects/areas of the curriculum reinforce subject understanding and skills. Skills and understanding associated with mathematics can be tracked into the schemes of work for other subjects/areas, for example in science, physical education, history, geography, technology and modern foreign languages. The use of practical, relevant activities helps ensure the application of mathematical skills, but the contribution of other subjects is important in giving further opportunities to apply and develop these.

Teachers will recognise when a mathematical skill such as telling the time and measuring duration is involved in what they are proposing to teach and this will be highlighted in planning. For example, in physical education the student may be asked to take a turn at timing a partner carrying out a fitness circuit. The teacher will not assume that, even if the mathematical aspect has already been taught, it will be remembered or successfully transferred to the new context. The teacher will appreciate that the practical demands of the new task might make it harder for the pupil to apply any knowledge they may have. Such links aim to help the pupil generalise skills and transfer knowledge to different situations at first in a guided and structured way to help reinforce and develop understanding.

Assessment

Small steps in assessment, perhaps with intermediate targets, will be necessary to ensure that a pupil's progress is recognised. Related to cross-curricular planning is the assessment of understanding and skills across different situations, at different times and with different people. Regarding communication, this may involve teachers and others engaging with the pupil in a way and at a level the pupil can understand and to which he can respond. This provides opportunities to recognise and record the pupil's progress using communication strategies:

- in different areas of the curriculum (music, mathematics);
- with different people (various adults, other pupils, visitors, people in the community in visits to shops, cafes and on walks) or
- in different circumstances (with one person, with several people, with familiar people and with strangers).

In mathematics, a skill in counting to five can be applied and assessed when buying items in a shop, laying a table, or setting out chairs for others. Particularly where skills are just developing, evidence of such applications represent progress in beginning to generalise knowledge gained and the skills acquired.

Many countries use curriculum related assessments and/or standardised assessment of various aspects of attainment and development. For example, in England, curriculum related assessments are available to recognise progress below level 1 of the National Curriculum, the so-called 'P' scales (performance scales) (Qualifications and Curriculum Authority, 2001a, 2001b, 2001c) and commercially available packages may be used for more detailed assessments.

Portfolios of achievements, developed gradually over time with the fullest involvement of the pupil, are also used to give a wideranging celebratory indication of achievements in school and elsewhere, including evidence of leisure pursuits. Related to assessments is the setting of individual learning targets, for example as reflected in Individual Education Programmes/Plans. The participation of pupils in this process is important and may involve the teacher discussing with the pupil the targets and what might be the best ways of achieving them.

Pedagogy

Visual inputs

A sometimes overlooked – if perhaps obvious – advantage of presenting material visually to a child is that normally the visual impression remains constantly available, for example in the case of a symbol (although more fleetingly with regard to manual signing). By contrast, auditory information tends to be briefly accessible to the child unless it is deliberately repeated, for example when a request is made several times.

Regarding literacy, sight recognition approaches tend to be preferred to phonological ones especially where the pupil has:

- poor phonological awareness (that is, difficulties with an awareness that relates speech sounds to changes in meaning);
- problems with auditory memory and
- hearing impairment.

Sight recognition methods may include the use of graphical symbols as described later in the section on 'communication'.

In mathematics, where a pupil has poor auditory memory, he will tend to find difficulty using oral methods of teaching numeracy including mental arithmetic. Visual approaches are likely to be preferred especially where real-life contexts are used promoting problem solving. Reviewing strategies for teaching mathematics, Butler and colleagues (2001) found that for students with moderate mental retardation, predominant approaches involved structured direct instruction.

Where pupils with moderate to severe cognitive impairment do not have visual impairments, provision may capitalise on visual input. The chapter has already alluded to the importance of visual input where a child has problems with phonological processing, auditory memory, or hearing and linked this with the use of sight recognition approaches to literacy and visual methods of teaching numeracy. The use of visual symbols and whole word approaches for teaching and learning literacy also capitalises on visual input.

It has been suggested with reference to children with Down's syndrome that where a pupil has difficulty with short-term auditory memory, an icon or pictogram can help make a connection enabling the child to link letter sounds to letter names. Also, teaching reading (perhaps indicated through the responses of signing, vocalisation or verbal approximations) may help reinforce and encourage language skills (Alton, 2001). Where there are particular difficulties making phoneme-grapheme correspondences (that is linking sounds and written marks), whole word approaches use the possibly stronger visual skills of pupils by linking the sight of the whole word with the spoken response.

Visual discrimination can be guided by using strategies to improve success in visual discrimination tasks. Training begins with an item (say a blue item) and eight identical distracters (say red items). The task is to match the key item with one provided (in this case an identical blue item). The number of distracters is gradually reduced so the pupil has a choice of only two items from which to choose the correct match (MacKay *et al.*, 2002). It will be seen that this strategy can be adapted to teaching in many areas of the curriculum. For example, the provided item might be a coin of a particular value, say a high value coin such as an American dollar or an English pound and the key item would be an identical coin. The distracter items would be other coins of smaller values, perhaps all American cents or all English pence. The gradual removal of the distracters leaving only two coins from which to discriminate will help the student recognise and discriminate higher value coins when using money. It will be important that the use of such skills-based approaches is supplemented by opportunities to put the learning (i.e. discrimination) to practical use, in the example given perhaps selecting and using the higher value coin in a shop purchase once it can be reliably identified.

Where manual signing is taught and used, the visual aspects of this are important. Furthermore, signing programmes enable the adult to correct and refine communication because it is visual and three dimensional; and such signing systems can also encourage verbal communication.

Communication

General approaches and specific strategies

Difficulties in speech and language have already been mentioned and include limitations in the expressive communication skills of children with severe cognitive impairment (Mar and Sall, 1999). In general, it is important that the school setting encourages the child to communicate. Daily structure might include a brief arrival greeting session, snack times and recess activities where communication with other pupils is encouraged, group activities, paired activities and so on. Additionally, ongoing opportunities are taken to encourage and respond to pupils' communication and to use situations in which communication is necessary and valued.

Among specific strategies is the behaviour chain interruption strategy, which is used in already established contexts and routines. In this approach, a stream of well-established behaviour is interrupted so that the pupil is required to adopt new types of communication (Carter and Grunsell, 2001). For example, the pupil may be preparing a snack, perhaps making toast. Previously the teacher has always laid out the bread on a plate for the pupil to put into an automatic toaster and this has become a well-established procedure. A behaviour interruption strategy might involve starting snack time with the bread in a container so the pupil has to request (perhaps subsequently initially being guided towards) the bread. The motivation for communication is the momentum of the routine task and the expectation that it will be completed. Also in the present example the tangible reward of the food is likely to act as a further incentive.

Professional judgement and skill is required so that the behaviour interruption strategy acts as an incentive to the child's communication, not as a frustration and a trigger for inappropriate behaviour. This suggests that: the strategy is not overused, the required communication is within the child's capacity, the approach is used to trigger not to teach the communication, and the child is rewarded (for example by praise) for communicating.

Augmentative and alternative communication

Augmentative and alternative communication uses single or combined approaches, according to a pupil's skills and preferences, to enable communication. The skills necessary for developing competence in communication have been described as:

- linguistic skills such as learning what pictures and symbols mean and combining symbols to make sentences;
- learning the technical skills required to operate the communication system, such as the layout of symbols;
- developing the knowledge and skills in social rules of interaction;
- developing skills to communicate effectively beyond the limits of competence in augmentative and alternative communication (Light, 1989).

Approaches in augmentative and alternative communication include the use of signing, photographs and speech synthesisers. Other examples, discussed below, are objects of reference and symbols.

An *object of reference* is used to indicate an event or activity that may not be happening in the present, perhaps to remember something that has happened or something that it is planned will happen later. It is also used when the pupil wishes to indicate a choice or decision. The object of reference is not the actual object or event but is symbolic of the object or event. Objects of reference can be used to indicate a proposed activity, signal a proposed change of activity, help the pupil anticipate a task, or enable him to make a choice/decide an activity.

Visual *symbols* capitalise on visual input and are often used in connection with computer technology. Symbols are used to support emerging literacy (King-de Baun, 1990). They can be employed in a way that relates to language sequencing skills as pupils select and place the symbols in order, and for reading and writing.

An approach used to supplement alternative and augmentative communication is talking mats (www.speechmag.com/archives) developed by the members of the Alternative and Augmentative Communication Unit at the University of Stirling, Scotland. A textured mat such as a household mat is used on which various card symbols can be attached. Three sets of symbols covering 'issues', 'emotions', and 'influences' are used which the pupil can indicate in various ways including if he has a physical impairment, eye pointing. The innovative and flexible use of these symbols enables quite extensive communication. For example, a smiling face and a frowning face can be attached to different halves of the mat and beneath them can be sorted things and experiences the student likes and dislikes. Or a task can be represented such as using a computer and the student can indicate what they find helpful and unhelpful in learning computing by indicating symbols that are grouped according to this criteria.

Developing autonomy and independence

Developing autonomy and independence builds on aspects of provision such as having security and routine. Choice is the other side of the coin to routine, the former offering the security of predictability and regularity, the latter giving the opportunity for variety and exploration. Routines might include morning greetings, snack times, end of day farewells, personal care routines and more complicated ones such as preparing for a school trip. Encouraging choice and decision-making contributes to developing autonomy and independence and each lesson or activity plan can be examined to seek opportunities for offering choices. This might include choice of drink and food, leisure activity, musical instrument, or whether to examine a fruit or vegetable in a science lesson. At first, there might be only two options but this can be later extended. Initially, adult support may be necessary to enable the pupil to begin to make choices.

More complex decision-making can also be encouraged. The teacher might ask one pupil which of the other pupils should be asked to carry out a task – for example taking a message – then ask why that particular pupil was chosen. When required to complete three activities, the pupil can be asked to decide in which order he will carry them out and why (personal preference, makes it easier, favourite task first or last).

One way for the teacher to optimise choice and decision-making is to develop a matrix listing daily activities down the side (greeting session, numeracy, literacy, leisure activities, visit to post office) and setting opportunities for choice across the top ('chooses between one or more activities'; 'chooses between two or more items' and 'chooses a work partner'). The intersections indicate that opportunities are offered in the ways indicated.

In numeracy, the pupil might choose between two activities leading to the same learning outcome, perhaps 'counting to five' either to plant seeds in five pots or to count cups to prepare drinks for five pupils. In leisure activities, he might choose from several hobbies. On trips outside the school the pupil will choose items of clothing to wear. The same matrix can be used from time to time to record the range of choices offered and to record the progress the pupil is making in exercising choice. Parents may use a similar approach at home.

Children with cognitive impairment tend to have difficulties using strategies for remembering and monitoring their performance (Henry and Maclean, 2002). Examining several studies, Copeland and Hughes (2000) considered the effects of encouraging and guiding pupils' goal/target setting on performance. Visual cues were often used to remind pupils of their targets or to give a clear indication of progress. Giving pupils information on the accuracy of their performance was an important factor in the success of the approaches.

Practical applications will also be used: laying the lunch table using tablemats with outlines for setting out cutlery (matching), planting bulbs in the garden and spacing them well (measuring); reading a bus or subway timetable (grid data). Related to these, opportunities for problem solving can be built into curriculum schemes. For example 'How will we know when to go and catch the subway train?' and 'How will we know how many bulbs to plant?' 'How can we make sure we have enough table settings?'

The progression in such approach is likely to range from offering in a structured situation limited choice from two items or activities and later to extending this to wider choice; to enabling pupils to use problem-solving to develop autonomy. Throughout, communication is encouraged and developed so that the child can make his wishes known.

Community-based vocational instruction

The *DSM-IV-TR* (American Psychiatric Association, 2000: 43) suggests that most people with *moderate* mental retardation tend to be able to benefit from training in social and occupational skills. Individuals with *severe* mental retardation tend to profit to a limited degree from teaching in 'pre-academic subjects' like 'simple counting' and can learn skills such as basic social sight-reading.

Chapter 2, on 'Profound cognitive impairment', mentioned the importance of vocational instruction, including community-based vocational instruction. Similar arguments apply to pupils with moderate to severe cognitive impairment. In fact, it will be remembered that the McDonnell *et al.*, (1993) study relating to vocational instruction mentioned in the earlier chapter and indicating significant student gains concerned high school students with 'moderate to profound mental retardation'. The school can help the student develop work skills such as following directions, punctuality, staying on task and completing assignments by directly teaching these and providing settings where they are put into practice and encouraged (Algozzine and Ysseldyke, 2006: 49–50).

Resources

Regarding access technology, three kinds of access have been identified (Day, 1995): physical, supportive and cognitive. Physical access concerns using technology to eliminate or limit the physical barriers to learning. Examples are a communication aid speech synthesiser with a bank of words and the flexibility to create new words, or a device such as a 'BIGmac' allowing brief phrases to be programmed into it enabling a pupil to participate and respond. Physical aids to using a computer such as a roller ball can allow a pupil to demonstrate and develop an understanding of mathematical concepts such as matching and sorting objects, perhaps, in three-dimensional graphics, manipulating shapes which the pupil may not be able to handle physically.

Supportive access involves technology aiding a pupil in carrying out a task that is difficult for him, such as using a word processor to help with presentation where handwriting skills are poor; or speech output devices such as speech synthesisers and speech recognition software to enable writing.

To allow *cognitive access*, technology is used to present the curriculum in ways that make it more accessible. Three ways have been suggested (Detheridge and Stevens, 2001: 164): 'simplifying the writing process' (e.g. using an on screen grid of words, or symbols, and phrases that pupils can transfer to their own text to assist the writing process); 'allowing pupils to explore ideas and try things out before committing themselves to the final outcome' (e.g. using word processors that allow redrafting and editing before deciding to print the final version) and 'presenting information in small quantities that can be easily assimilated' (e.g. using talking book or CD-ROMs presenting manageable pieces of information, often enhanced with pictures, video clips, animation, spoken commentary or music).

Therapy

As necessary, therapy will be provided for areas of development such as physical development, where the involvement of the physical therapist and/or the occupational therapist may be required. Speech and language therapy may be necessary to help phonological difficulties and other aspects of language development. For teachers, it is important that liaison with therapists is close including when teachers and therapists assess pupils, plan interventions and implement them together. Curriculum time needs to be allowed for this to be done successfully. There is debate about the levels of language difficulty and other factors that might influence a decision about whether a child should work at least some of the time individually with a speech and language pathologist and whether a consultancy or other approach is used. In a consultancy approach, the speech and language pathologist would work closely with teachers and others in making assessments and interventions. An alternative is to have trained assistants to deliver parts of the agreed speech and language intervention.

Organisation

The classroom is organised so that the best use is made of pupils' senses of sight and hearing. For example, furniture arrangements can complement good classroom acoustics to help ensure pupils can hear as clearly as possible and minimise distracting noises. Given the importance of visual input, it is particularly important that the classroom is arranged so that pupils can notice and respond to visual cues and this may need to be reassessed throughout a typical day as furniture is moved and different grouping are adopted for different activities.

Thinking points

Readers may wish to consider, with regard to a particular school:

- the extent to which the curriculum and assessment provide an appropriate range of relevant learning opportunities on which progress is suitably determined;
- the degree to which pupil grouping is suitable to ensure progress;
- the extent to which the range of pedagogic approaches is effective and reflects the requirements of pupils.

Key texts

Algozzine, B. and Ysseldyke, E. (2006) *Teaching Students with Mental Retardation: A Practical Guide for Teachers*. Thousand Oaks, CA, Corwin Press.
A practically orientated book underpinned by professional knowledge and related research findings. Chapters cover definitions, prevalence, causes, diagnosis, associated characteristics, teaching, trends and issues. Chapter 6 concerns, 'What Teachers Should Know About Teaching Students with Severe Disabilities'.

Carr, A. (2006) (2nd edition) *The Handbook of Child and Adolescent Clinical Psychology: A Contextual Approach*. London, Routledge.
Written mainly for post-graduate psychology students and those undergoing professional training in clinical psychology, the book includes a chapter,

'Intellectual, learning and communication disabilities', which has a section on intellectual disability covering characteristics, epidemiology, clinical features, aetiology, assessment and differential diagnosis and interventions.

Drew, C. J. and Hardman, M. L. (2006) (9th edition) *Intellectual Disabilities Across the Lifespan*. Upper Saddle River, NJ, Prentice-Hall.
Examines the impact of intellectual disability on education, social and psychological issues from conception to old age.

Luckasson, R., Borthwick-Duffy, S., Buntinx, W., Coulter, D., Craig, E., Reeve, A., Schalock, R., Snell, M., Spitalnik, D., Spreat, S. and Tasse, M. (2002) (10th edition) *Mental Retardation: Definition, Classification, and Systems of Supports*. Washington DC, American Association of Mental Retardation.
Concerns understanding mental retardation, diagnosis and planning for a supports needs profile. It seeks to integrate the *DSM-IV TR* perspectives and considers other definitions.

Chapter 4

Mild cognitive impairment

Introduction

This chapter concerns children and young people that in the United States of America are defined as having 'mild mental retardation' although other terms such as 'mild cognitive impairment' and 'mild intellectual disability' are used interchangeably. In England the broadly equivalent term is 'moderate learning difficulties'. This chapter mainly uses the term 'mild cognitive impairment'. Other terms such as 'mild mental retardation' are employed where they are specifically used in research and assessment.

The chapter first outlines some issues that are debated relating to definition of, assessment of and provision for mild cognitive impairment. The chapter then considers definitions; prevalence; causal factors and identification and assessment. Under provision, it looks at: curriculum and assessment; pedagogy (communication; literacy and numeracy; behavioural, emotional and social development; slower but stimulating pace; concrete learning and ensuring relevance and generalisation); resources; therapy and organisation.

Some areas of debate

There is debate about the usefulness of the concept of mild cognitive impairment. This reflects in part the understandable disinclination to place the same confidence in demarcating mild disorders or disabilities as more severe ones. Consequently, there is more agreement about what constitutes profound or severe to moderate cognitive impairment than mild cognitive impairment.

Also, the more severe the cognitive impairment, the more likely it is that neurological and physical correlates can be identified. In the case of mild cognitive impairment, there is a correlation with poorer social backgrounds, which is taken by some commentators to indicate that it is fundamentally a socially constructed disability. Related to this, as discussed in the section on possible causal factors below, there is debate about the extent to which mild cognitive impairment is predominantly associated with 'within child' factors or environmental ones.

Despite these reservations, it may still be maintained that efforts to identify mild cognitive impairment, especially where it is associated with behavioural difficulties and speech and language difficulties, can enable provision to be made that can help the child progress educationally, personally and socially.

Definitions

'Mild mental retardation' is associated in the *Diagnostic and Statistical Manual of Mental Disorders Fourth Edition Text Revision* (DSM-IV-TR) (American Psychiatric Association, 2000: 42) with an intelligence quotient (IQ) range of 50/55 to 70. As with other levels of mental retardation, IQ levels are interpreted with care, as they are not the sole criterion. The diagnostic criteria for mental retardation also include 'co-current deficits or impairments in present adaptive functioning ... in at least two of the following areas: communication, self-care, home living, social/interpersonal skills, use of community resources, self-direction, functional academic skills, work, leisure, health and safety' (ibid.: 49). Children with mild mental retardation tend to 'develop social and communication skills during the pre-school years (ages 0 to 5 years)' (American Psychiatric Association, 2000: 43) and have minimal impairment in sensori-motor areas. By the late teens, they can acquire academic skills up to about sixth grade level.

It has been argued with regard to mild mental retardation (Greenspan, 2006) that there are limitations in an IQ based definition (e.g. because it does not capture the full range of ways of being 'unintelligent') and difficulties with functional based definitions (because they confound mental retardation with other forms of disability). An alternative has been proposed to ground a definition in its 'natural taxon' (that is a taxonomic group such as a class/classification) as determined from the behaviours of people widely considered to have mental retardation, key features being considered to be various forms of vulnerability.

Related to this, in 2002, the American Association on Intellectual and Developmental Disabilities (AAIDD) agreed a supports-based definition, viewing mental retardation as a condition that can be enhanced by the provision of supports rather than as a more static disability. One problem with such definitions is that it is difficult to envisage the support supposedly required being allocated fairly unless it is based on some judgement of 'need' that ultimately refers to characteristics of the person who is deemed to require the support. However, the notion of support provision could inform and clarify existing definitions of cognitive impairment and might also point the way to possible pedagogic approaches.

In England, a definition of moderate learning difficulties in government guidance states that these pupils 'will have attainments significantly below expected levels in most areas of the curriculum, despite appropriate interventions. Their needs will *not* be able to be met by normal differentiation and the flexibilities of the National Curriculum' (DfES, 2003: 3, italics added). They 'have much greater difficulty than peers in acquiring basic literacy and numeracy skills and in understanding concepts. They may also have associated speech and language delay, low self-esteem, low levels of concentration and underdeveloped social skills' (ibid.: 3). Attainments are low 'despite appropriate interventions' presumably because of the child's 'difficulty' in 'acquiring basic literacy and numeracy skills and in understanding concepts'. The guidance implies the child's home or family circumstances are not one of the factors that constitute special education need, stating, 'Under-attainment may be an indicator of SEN but poor performance may be due to *other factors* such as problems in the child's home or family circumstances or poor school attendance' (ibid.: 2, italics added).

Studies in England have indicated that pupils with 'moderate learning difficulties' tend to have other disorders/disabilities too. Pupils with moderate learning difficulties attending special schools were reported by head teachers to have associated difficulties (Male, 1996). The sample comprised 54 special schools in England for pupils with moderate learning difficulties in 1993. Some 87 per cent of head teachers reported that up to half of their pupils had language and communication difficulties while 80 per cent of head teachers reported that up to half of their pupils had emotional and behavioural difficulties. A more recent study in the south west area of England of pupils with 'mild to moderate general learning difficulties' also suggested a high percentage of pupils with other difficulties including language and communication difficulty (Norwich and Kelly, 2004: 13–14). Such claims need to be assessed in the context of the degree of clarity with which the 'additional' difficulties are assessed and possible financial incentives to find additional difficulties. But where there are such additional difficulties, provision can be modified.

Prevalence

Prevalence for mild cognitive impairment is difficult to establish because of lack of agreement on definitions across countries and within different areas of the same country. It is estimated that of the population with 'mental retardation' that the group having 'mild mental retardation' constitute around 85 per cent (with 'moderate mental retardation' accounting for about 10 per cent, 'severe mental retardation' for approximately 3 per cent to 4 per cent and profound for roughly 1 per cent to 2 per cent) (American Psychiatric Association, 2000: 43).

Where no biological causation, or indeed, any other cause can be identified (which is usually the case when the cognitive impairment is milder), more individuals from lower social classes are represented. Different assessments tend to provide different information with regard to different ethnic groups. For example, the Kaufman Assessment Battery for Children (KABC-II) (Kaufman and Kaufman, 2004) tends to find smaller discrepancies in the scores of African American and Caucasian children that did an earlier version of the *Wechsler Intelligence Scale for Children (WISC-III)* (Wechsler, 1991). Care is taken to help ensure that the prevalence for children of different ethnic or cultural backgrounds is reliably and validly determined (American Psychiatric Association, 2000: 43). For example, intelligence test procedures includes the use of:

- tests in which the individual's relevant characteristics are represented in the standardisation sample of the test and
- an examiner familiar with the ethnic and cultural background of the child.

Causal factors

There is debate about the degree to which mild cognitive impairment is attributed to individual or environmental factors and the extent of their interaction. Individual factors are taken to include cognitive impairments as indicated by assessments of cognitive functioning such as intelligence tests and other assessments. Social factors include the possible influence of impoverished social and economic backgrounds that has affected cognitive development. It will be remembered that earlier, when considering definitions, reference was made to guidance seeming to indicate that the child's home or family circumstances are not a factor constituted to special education need, and that, 'Under-attainment may be an indicator of SEN but poor performance may be due to *other* factors such as problems in the child's home or family circumstances or poor school attendance' (DfES, 2003: 2, italics added).

This quotation illustrates the complicated nature of the possible role of family circumstances and the interaction of environmental and 'within child' factors. On the one hand, low attainment may not be the result of a disorder such as 'mild cognitive impairment' but may be related to home and family circumstances so that the expectation might be that if these circumstances change, the child would progress better and attain better, perhaps to the level of a typical child of his age. On the other hand, it may be considered that home and family circumstances have been such that they have influenced (perhaps with other factors) the child's cognitive development so that, even if family circumstances were to change, there would still be evidence of mild cognitive impairment. (See also Baroff, 1999: 202–237.)

Identification and assessment

The identification of pupils with mild cognitive impairment is a challenge for schools and local boards/authorities because of lack of agreement on definitions. These might include levels of attainment in English and mathematics and other curriculum areas that would be expected (perhaps using percentage cut-off points); or cognitive levels as indicated by standardised tests or less frequently measures of difficulty in understanding concepts.

Related to this is the debate surrounding the additional use of 'dynamic assessment'. This form of assessment seeks to measure the responsiveness of an individual to teaching and practice (Bransford *et al.*, 1986). As well as providing a baseline assessment, dynamic assessment offers further information on the degree and form of assistance the child requires in order to reach a higher level of performance and how he responds to such help.

Provision

Provision for pupils with mild cognitive impairment involves: the level at which the curriculum is provided; and a cluster of approaches outlined below that take account of such factors as slower pace of learning and difficulties with concepts. Identifying children also enables preferential funding to be allocated enabling the pupil to be taught in smaller groups than is typical to encourage better progress and development.

Curriculum and assessment

The curriculum content for pupils with mild cognitive impairment is beyond usual curriculum flexibilities given that the level of attainment of pupils is significantly below that typical of pupils of the same chronological age. It involves content that is typical of younger children but presented in a way that takes account of the chronological age of pupils too. The level of the content of the curriculum is higher than that for pupils with moderate to severe mental retardation; and the curriculum tends to be securely subject based with lessons for literacy/English, numeracy/mathematics, science, history and so on. Communication, literacy, numeracy and personal and social development have particular emphasis through allocating more time than is usual in schools and by ensuring they are embedded in other subjects through cross-curricular planning.

Because of the difficulty of pupils with mild cognitive impairment in grasping concepts, the curriculum is carefully structured to ensure that knowledge and material is presented in a step-by-step way, as far as possible building conceptual understanding from basic practical experiences. Complex topics and procedures are broken down into simpler components that lead into more complex concepts at the level of curriculum schemes of work. For example, if the topic is the rain cycle, the components may be broken down into parts such as evaporation and condensation (both conveyed with practical examples and experiences) before the rain cycle was approached. At the same time the curriculum structure seeks to ensure that the separation of topics into component parts does not distort the whole and that what the pupil learns is not fragmented. The topics and schemes of work ensure that concepts are revisited in different contexts and related to everyday experience, and associated resourcing of the curriculum ensures that concrete experiences are given priority.

Assessment reflects the curriculum content and tends to be in subject terms, although with steps small enough to ensure that achievements are recognised and celebrated.

Pedagogy

Communication

In the development of language, repeated direct experience helps. So, when talking about fruit, having real fruits to see, smell, handle and taste is important. When discussing more challenging concepts, such as 'safety', real visual examples of 'safe' and 'unsafe' items and situations will aid the development of the concept. These are examples of the concrete approach to teaching and learning elaborated later.

To help develop speech (phonetics, phonology and prosody), approaches include raising phonological awareness by encouraging interest in and explicit teaching of new vocabulary. Error analysis and articulation exercises may be used to remediate speech sounds. To help with grammar (syntax and morphology), provision might include ensuring that the teacher's communication is direct, clear and understandable and that the pupil has extra time and opportunity for over learning as necessary. Planned opportunities for group discussion and the use of visual aids to support communication are other possibilities. To improve comprehension, helpful strategies include explicit teaching for and reminders of maintaining attention and listening behaviour. Other useful strategies are checking specific areas of understanding and encouraging pupil assertiveness to signal lack of comprehension.

Developing meaning (semantics) may be helped by improving a pupil's skills in and understanding of 'labelling' (through direct teaching and structured experience using objects and role play then pictures that represent objects and actions). 'Packaging' (the combination of conceptual and grammatical meaning in communication) can be improved through using exemplars and models and judicious reshaping of the pupil's utterances. 'Networking' concerns the way a lexeme (a lexical language unit of one or more words whose elements do not separately convey the meaning of the whole) gains meaning from its relationship with other words. Networking can be helped by direct teaching in a range of subjects and by the teacher using and explaining key polysemic words (words that have many meanings) in curriculum subjects.

The use of language (pragmatics) can be aided by developing conversational skills, such as introducing a topic, maintaining it and concluding it. This might involve role-play and being taught cues that are often used when a conversational partner wants to change or terminate the topic of conversation. The *Social Use of Language Programme* (Rinaldi, 2001) has been employed to promote the communication skills of young people with mild to moderate cognitive impairment and may be used to assess verbal and non-verbal communication skills and to implement an intervention programme.

Literacy and numeracy

Various approaches to literacy have been reported to be effective with pupils having mild mental retardation. 'Phonological Awareness Training' (Wilson and Frederickson, 1995) has been experimentally evaluated on a small group of pupils aged 9 to 11 years and which included 'some severe learning difficulties and some mild learning difficulties' (Brooks, 2002: 106, 37). The strategy uses a pupil's existing knowledge of letter sounds and words so that new words containing identically written endings present less of a difficulty in reading and spelling. Also effective was 'Reading Intervention' (Hatcher, 2000) which was evaluated with pupils having 'moderate learning difficulties', having IQ levels of 55 to 75 and uses a combination of phonological training and reading (Brooks, 2002: 38–39, 110). Pupils are helped to isolate phonemes within words to come to recognise that sounds can be common between words and that certain letters can represent specific sounds.

With regard to mathematics, it has been emphasised that the use of concrete and visual apparatus is helpful in teaching pupils with 'moderate learning difficulties' (e.g. Panter, 2001). This will include the use of concrete, visual apparatus such as real liquids to measure, real objects to classify, real money to use and real areas to measure. From such structured experience, the pupil gradually comes to be able to think concretely by visualising items. For example, he can visualise the height of order of three people when told their height relative to one another in pairs.

Concrete objects

It will be remembered that in England, a definition of moderate learning difficulties in government guidance considers these pupils will tend to 'have much greater difficulty than peers in acquiring basic literacy and numeracy skills and in understanding concepts' (DfES, 2003: 3). This difficulty with abstract concepts is reduced if the teacher and others use concrete objects and examples to illustrate points.

Mathematical concepts will be illustrated by concrete examples well beyond the chronological age when this might be necessary for pupils without mild cognitive impairment. Notions of time in history may be graphically indicated by time lines. The rain cycle might be demonstrated using steam and precipitation. While this is necessary with many pupils who do not have cognitive impairment, the regularity and intensity likely to be required for pupils with mild cognitive impairment is greater.

Behavioural, emotional and social development

Cornish and Ross (2003) explain a programme based on a multi-sensory cognitive-behavioural approach to social skills training that has been used in a special school for adolescents having 'moderate learning difficulties' to enable them to deal with social situations better so they might be transferred part time or full time to mainstream school. Sessions involve several activities and last about an hour and 40 minutes each, involving between six and ten students and two adults. Techniques used included rehearsal, modelling and reinforcement to teach students to use speech (internal and external) to influence their behaviour. Acceptable social behaviour and problem solving skills were taught. The techniques involved verbal instructions, although pictorial cues can also be used.

Self-regulation

Related to what has already been said about communication and behavioural, social and emotional development, is self-regulation. At the heart of self-regulatory approaches are the teacher's efforts to provide encouragement and structures to enable pupils to develop and evaluate their problem-solving strategies. Borkowski *et al* (2006) summarise the importance (in relation to students with cognitive impairment) of self-regulation, which in Borkowski *et al.*'s (2000) metacognitive model, plays a key role. Self-regulation is considered fundamental to most learning problems of individuals with cognitive impairment, who often do not use strategies efficiently, or who may not suitably generalise newly acquired strategies, perhaps because of immature forms of self-regulation.

Mental planning and monitoring is involved in everyday practical skills from preparing meals to social interaction. Goal orientation is an important aspect and a self-regulated student in a complex learning situation draws on strategies, sets realistic goals and monitors learning progress, adapting strategies to fit the current context and goals (e.g. Pintrich, 2000). But individuals with cognitive impairment often experience problems developing these skills. The context and choice of classroom tasks may help increase the self-regulatory functioning of pupils with cognitive impairment. In examining children's self-regulatory behaviour, Stright and Supplee (2002) compared small-group seat work to teacher-directed instruction, finding that small-group seat work facilitated children's active monitoring. Also, with regard to literacy teaching for young children, the type of task used by teachers for instruction appears to influence pupils' motivation (Turner, 1995). Open tasks requiring higher-order thinking tend to be more motivating than closed tasks involving memory skills. The pupil may be shown skills in self-monitoring by the teacher or parent or others and may practise these using role-play before being supported to use them in different situations and settings such as home and school.

Emotional regulation is strongly linked to the quality of social relationships, with more adept emotional regulators enjoying more successful social interactions. The same metacognitive skills needed for intellectual success appear crucial in managing one's emotional states. These include the abilities to recognise emotional states and to move from one emotional state to another to regain equilibrium. Some individuals with cognitive impairments may experience difficulty in forming and developing social relationships partly because of deficiencies in skills relating to emotional regulation (e.g. Borkowski *et al.*, 2006).

Language is important in guiding all domains of self-regulation, with inner verbalisation being influential in aiding self-reflection and inhibiting certain responses (e.g. Abbeduto and Hesketh, 1997). Children with specific language impairment tend to be rated much lower on teacher's reports of emotional regulation than more typically developing peers (Fujiki *et al.*, 2002). In this sense, language abilities and skills lay the groundwork for the emergence of mature forms of emotional and cognitive self-regulation.

Slower but stimulating pace

The pace of learning is a key feature of the education of pupils with mild cognitive impairment because the pupil is likely to have learned at a slower pace than others, leading to lower levels of attainment. In present learning the pupil may respond best to a slower pace of learning than typical pupils of the same age to ensure there is time to consolidate learning, over learn, and make sure that a learning point is fully understood.

However, there is a balance to be struck between a pace that ensures learning and one that keeps interest and enthusiasm. Teachers try to find a pace that ensures learning is secure but also that the lesson moves along sufficiently to maintain the pupil's interest. This can be fine-tuned by strategies of questioning such as a mixture of open and closed questions or by balancing difficult new material with more familiar material to be consolidated. Also, if the lesson is well structured and progresses from the practical to the more abstract and from the familiar to the less familiar, it is likely that an engaging pace will be sustainable because the lesson structure is providing a supportive framework for learning.

Ensuring relevance and generalisation

In seeking to make teaching and learning relevant, carefully planned and explicitly made connections that are linked to the pupil's own experience are considered helpful. For example, in making a moving toy, the teacher can ensure that the pupils: talk about their own toys or toys they had when younger; watch others play with moving toys and examine other moving toys and dismantle one to see how it works. Links with other subjects of the curriculum could include English (examining toys and learning the names of different toys and their parts); and mathematics (sorting and classifying toys and parts of toys, or measuring different toys or their parts).

When learning about electricity, practical experience of making circuits can be applied to making a working item such as a doorbell, making comparisons with battery-operated and mains-operated bells. Real household accounts for electricity can be studied and the electricity meter at home and at school can be read. Links can be made with mathematics (reading dials and numerals; geography (visiting a generating station or viewing pylons that carry electricity); and personal and social education (having practical experience of situations in which electricity is used safely).

In subjects such as history, real artefacts will be more pertinent than pictures. In geography real rocks and real ponds are more relevant than books about them. More generally, the teacher will seek to use real items and genuine situations: proper money in real shops, real weather observations, visiting a bank to deposit or withdraw money, writing real letters to post, reading daily newspapers and so on.

Pupils with mild cognitive impairment tend to have difficulties with generalising knowledge and skills (Meese, 2001). Emphasis on relevance can help the pupil generalise knowledge for the situation in which it was learned to new situations because the learning can be related to regularly occurring day-to-day experiences. As well as this, repeated opportunities can be built into the curriculum to develop and apply new skills and knowledge.

Resources

Resources used for pupils with mild cognitive impairment are not particularly distinctive from those used with all children, unless it is the extent to which physical examples are used that help the development of concepts.

Therapy

To the extent that pupils with mild cognitive impairment also have communication and language disorder, suitable provision will take this into account. A consideration of the approaches is discussed in Chapter 14 concerning: 'Communication disorders: Speech'; Chapter 15, 'Communication disorders: Grammar and comprehension'; and Chapter 16, 'Communication disorders: Meaning and use', may form a useful starting point. For all communication disorders, depending on their severity and complexity, the support of a speech and language pathologist/therapist may be necessary.

Where pupils with mild cognitive impairment have conduct or mood disorders, some of the approaches explained in Chapter 11 on 'Disruptive behaviour disorders' and Chapter 12 on 'Anxiety disorders and depressive disorders' may provide a useful starting point for deciding strategies. These include, for children aged 3 to 10 years with disruptive behaviour disorders, parent training, social skills training and anger management skills training, problem-solving skills, and classroom contingency management. For adolescents aged 10 to 17 years with disruptive behaviour disorders, provision includes family based interventions; combination packages of adolescent focused interventions and school-based interventions.

Turning to pupils' general anxiety disorder, cognitive-behavioural programmes have been used. For obsessive-compulsive disorder, medication, cognitive-behavioural therapy or the two in combination have been employed. Behavioural interventions and cognitive-behavioural therapy have been used with phobias. With regard to separation anxiety disorder, approaches drawing on group cognitive-behavioural therapy have been applied. For adolescents with mild depressive disorder, cognitive-behavioural therapy for adolescents (with the concurrent treatment of any maternal depression); Interpersonal Therapy Adapted for Adolescents and medication have had positive effects.

Organisation

The organisation of the classroom for pupils with mild cognitive impairment is not distinctive from that of classroom organisation for all children, except that education may emphasise small groups with a high adult pupil ratio that enables more attention to be given to each pupil.

Thinking points

Readers may wish to consider with reference to a particular school and local area:

- the extent to which there are suitable criteria for identifying pupils with mild cognitive impairment including any additional difficulties;
- the extent to which practical and relevant activities are used in the curriculum;
- how support for any communication and behavioural and emotional difficulties are ensured.

Key texts

Beirne-Smith, M., Ittenbach, R. F. and Patton, J. R. (2002) (6th edition) *Mental Retardation*. Upper Saddle River, NJ, Prentice-Hall.
This introductory textbook covers causes, assessment and pedagogy.

Norwich, B. and Kelly, N. (2004) *Moderate Learning Difficulties and the Future of Inclusion*. London, RoutledgeFalmer.
This looks at broad issues concerning 'moderate learning difficulties' considering justifications for and limitations of this category. It examines studies and perspectives relating to inclusion and moderate learning difficulty. The authors report on children's perspectives of their special provision, their perceptions of themselves and how others see them, and of labels associated with special educational needs. They consider social interaction, acceptance and bullying of pupils with moderate learning difficulties. The book concludes with a consideration of possible future strategies.

Switzky, H. N. and Greenspan, S. (2006) (eds) *What is Mental Retardation? Ideas for an Evolving Disability in the 21st Century*. Washington, DC, American Association on Intellectual and Developmental Disabilities.
This collection of essays includes discussion of the 2002 American Association on Intellectual and Developmental Disabilities (AAIDD) supports-based definition of mental retardation, viewing mental retardation as a condition that can be enhanced by the provision of supports rather than as a more static disability.

Wehmeyer, M. L. with Sands, D. J., Knowlton, H. E. and Kozleski, E. B. (2002) *Providing Access to the General Curriculum: Teaching Students with Mental Retardation*. Baltimore, MD, Paul H. Brookes.
Presents a functional model and a 'supports' view of cognitive impairment. The book explores topics such as a universal design for the curriculum, individualised learning and personalised planning.

Chapter 5

Hearing impairment

Introduction

This chapter explains definitions of hearing impairment and deafness; prevalence; causal factors; identification and assessment; implications of hearing impairment and issues relating to the education of deaf children. In examining provision, the chapter mainly focuses on pedagogy including general approaches; communication (oral/aural, sign bilingual and total communication approaches); literacy (in the sign bilingual and oral/aural approaches) and mathematics.

Definitions

In order to define hearing impairment and deafness, it is necessary to clarify two terms: 'frequency' and 'intensity/amplitude'.

Frequency concerns the rate at which sound waves vibrate and is usually expressed as cycles per second (c.p.s.), some countries, such as the United Kingdom, using the term Hertz (Hz). Sound frequency is perceived as pitch, with rapidly vibrating sound waves being perceived as high-pitched sounds and slower vibrating waves being perceived as low-pitched sounds. The human ear is normally responsive to sounds between 60 and 16,000 c.p.s. but it is most responsive to sounds between 500 and 4,000 c.p.s. Speech sounds occupy the most responsive band and particular speech sounds involve several frequencies. Vowels tend to occupy the lowest frequency range while fricatives, such as 's', 'f', 'th' and 'sh', tend to occupy the higher ones. Hearing loss rarely affects all frequencies equally, so hearing is usually distorted. With low frequency loss, the ability to hear vowels is impaired. Should there be higher frequency loss, the capacity to hear fricatives and sibilants is reduced and because consonants make speech intelligible, high frequency hearing loss is usually more serious.

Categorisations of hearing impairment relate to *intensity/amplitude*. The intensity of a sound is experienced as loudness and is measured in a decibel (dB) scale on which the quietest audible sound is given a value of 0 dB and the loudest sound has a value of 140 dB. Normal conversation is carried out at around 40 to 50 dB (Steinberg and Knightly, 1997). Hearing impairment can be measured on the dB scale in terms of dB loss. Categories of hearing impairment are recognised, although the cut-off points for the different bands vary from country to country (Westwood, 2003: 48). The following ranges give a broad indication.

- Slight loss: 15–25 dB
- Mild loss: 25–40 dB
- Moderate loss: 40–65 dB;
- Severe loss: 65–95 dB;
- Profound loss: above 95 dB (Westwood, 2003: 48).

Regarding severe loss and profound loss, a distinction, important for future communication, may be made between pre-lingual and post-lingual loss. A child who has experience of hearing and speech may already be speaking and may wish to continue, while a child with similar loss that occurred before speech developed would be likely to find communication using speech more difficult, although taking into account the age at which the child was diagnosed, and, very importantly, the date of fitting any hearing aid or cochlear implant.

Prevalence

It has been estimated that at a specified time almost 20 per cent of children in the range 2 to 5 years are affected by otitis media with effusion (one of the causes of conductive hearing loss), making it a very common disease, although the number of persistent cases is relatively few. Sensory-neural deafness occurs in about 1 in a 1,000 babies. (See the next section for explanations of these conditions.)

Causal factors

Deafness may be the result of an ear disease or injury, although profound deafness is usually congenital. A distinction is made between sensory-neural deafness and conductive deafness. In *sensory-neural* deafness, 'sounds' reaching the inner ear are not properly transmitted to the brain because of damage to the structures within the inner ear or to the acoustic nerve. Defects of the inner ear may be: congenital because of an inherited fault in a chromosome; owing to birth injury or owing to damage to the developing foetus (e.g. because of infection). The inner ear may also be damaged after birth because of severe jaundice or meningitis.

Conductive deafness occurs when sound is not properly propagated from the outer ear to the middle ear, usually because of damage to the tympanic membrane (eardrum) or to the bones of the inner ear. Common forms of impaired hearing in children are otitis media (middle ear infection) and otitis media with effusion, sometimes called glue ear, in which sticky fluid collects in the middle ear. Otitis media is the commonest cause of hearing loss in children under the age of 12 years (McCracken, 1998a: 155). Interventions comprise:

- the surgical insertion of tubes ('grommets') into the tympanic membrane to keep the middle ear ventilated;
- keeping the situation under review (watchful waiting) with regular hearing checks and the administration of antibiotics if acute infections occur; or
- the use of hearing aids with open ear moulds.

An estimate of the relative contribution of some of the different causes of hearing impairment is as follows (Moores, 2001)

- Otitis media – 3 per cent
- Maternal rubella – 5 per cent
- Meningitis – 9 per cent
- Heredity – 13 per cent
- Other causes at birth – 22 per cent

Identification and assessment

Hearing impairment may be identified through neonatal screening or by the parent, health visitor or equivalent, or later by the school through screening programmes. The 1982 American Joint Committee on Infant Hearing set out screening risk criteria for congenital or early onset deafness. In summary, (and with brief explanations of some of the terms) this is as follows:

- family history of hearing impairment;
- congenital perinatal infection;
- anatomic malformations involving the head or neck (e.g. cleft palate);
- birth weight below 1,500 grams;
- hyperbilirubinaemia (a raised blood level of bilirubin, a waste product formed from the destruction of red blood cells) at a level exceeding indications for exchange transfusion;
- bacterial meningitis (a life-threatening inflammation of the meninges, the membranes covering the brain and spinal chord), especially due to the bacterium Haemophilus influenzae and
- severe asphyxia (suffocation).

Habilitation strategies include hearing aid or cochlear implant fitting, counselling and guidance for parents and the involvement of a specialist teacher of the deaf.

Hearing tests determine whether hearing is impaired, the extent of the impairment and what part of the ear may be implicated. Audiometry, the measurement of the sense of hearing, often refers to hearing tests using a piece of equipment, an audiometer, to produce sounds of known intensity and pitch. The hearing in each ear is measured in relation to the range of normally audible sounds.

Types of test include pure tone audiometry, auditory evoked response and impedance audiometry.

Pure tone audiometry involves the use of an audiometer to produce and measure sounds of different frequency and intensity. The sounds are transmitted through an earphone into one ear while the other ear is prevented from hearing. First, the sound is reduced in intensity until it cannot be heard, then the intensity is gradually increased until the person signals they can detect it.

Auditory evoked response is the brain's response to sound stimulation provided by the audiometer, analysed using electrodes placed on the scalp. The technique is sometimes used if the child cannot indicate hearing thresholds, for example because of cognitive impairment.

Impedance audiometry is a test determining middle ear damage associated with conductive deafness. A probe fitted to the entrance of the outer ear canal emits a continuous sound while air is pumped into the probe. A microphone fitted to the probe detects the differing reflections of sounds from the eardrum as pressure changes in the ear canal, indicating the elasticity of the eardrum and the bones of the middle ear. This points to the type of disease causing the deafness.

Implications of hearing impairment

Among implications of hearing impairment are those relating to visuo-spatial skills, short-term memory (STM) and cerebral organisation.

Deaf children have demonstrated superior performance on a range of visuo-spatial tasks (e.g. Bellugi *et al.*, 1994). The extent to which this is attributable to sign language enhancing visuo-spatial skills or to deaf infants paying more attention to visual aspects of their surroundings is debated. Certainly, there are aspects of visuo-spatial processing at which deaf signers can excel, but rather than envisaging spatial cognition being uniformly better or worse in different populations, a clearer view might be recognising that different skills are implicated.

Studies testing STM, in terms of the order in which items are recalled, indicate that deaf participants recall fewer items than hearing participants (e.g. Campbell and Wright, 1990). Also, when STM is tested for order in the recall of sign stimuli, deaf participants recall fewer items than hearing signers using a verbal code (especially suited to recalling items in order) to remember signs (e.g. Logan *et al.*, 1996). If deaf children derive information from lip reading, which can form the basis of a speech-based code, such a code is probably qualitatively different from the speech-based code used by hearing people (Campbell and Wright, 1990). Variability in the level of speech-based code a deaf child will develop relates to factors such as the child's degree of hearing loss and speech intelligibility. While an alternative for deaf signers appears to be a STM code based on the properties of sign language, this may take up more memory capacity than speech representations, resulting in fewer items being recalled.

Turning to cerebral organisation, although brain hemispheres interact, hearing people process language predominantly in the left hemisphere, damage to which can lead to language difficulties. While not all deaf people use sign language, where it is used, it is visual and spatially conveyed, combining the functions of language and visuo-spatial information. A study of three deaf signers having left hemisphere damage showed they experienced sign language deficits in both expression and comprehension (Poizner and Tallal, 1987). The signer's ability to use gestures and motor skills was unimpaired so the impairment appears to be linguistic, suggesting similarities at the neurological level between the processing of sign language by deaf people and of spoken language by hearing people. But whereas spoken language can continue with left hemisphere support 'alone', sign language seems to require right hemisphere involvement. Deaf signers with right hemisphere damage had visuo-spatial deficits such as spatial disorientation just as hearing people would. But their production and comprehension of space used for mapping spatial relations with sign language was also impaired (although aspects of their sentence construction were intact).

Functional brain imaging techniques indicate that, for some aspects of visual processing, language background plays a part but not hearing status. For deaf and hearing people using sign language as their first language, structures in the 'visual' parts of the brain were more involved than they were for hearing non-signers. Some brain activity was particular to deaf people irrespective of their knowledge of sign language (e.g. Neville et al., 1997). The age verbal language is acquired and the age of onset of deafness appears to have different roles in any cerebral reorganisation occurring during development (Marcotte and Morere, 1990).

Further issues related to educating deaf children

This section touches on issues relating to the deaf child's family, cultural 'Deafness'; support in mainstream schools; the use of hearing aids and cochlear implants.

Regarding the family, a Northern Ireland survey indicated that 90 per cent of deaf children are born to non-deaf parents (Phoenix, 1988). Among issues with which the family deals are responding to the initial diagnosis and matters arising at times of transition, for example when a young person enters adolescence or when a child changes school. Factors influencing the family's choice of language to be used with the deaf child include whether the parents are deaf or hearing, and the degree of hearing loss experienced by the child. (The significance of degree of hearing loss has reduced where features such as early diagnosis and cochlear implants are well established.)

Some writers, to signal a view of 'cultural Deafness' use 'Deaf' with an initial capital. It has been suggested, 'The use of the term, "Deaf" is based on the premise that deaf children whose deafness means that they do not acquire spoken language through oral means are likely to develop to become culturally Deaf young people' (Ridgeway, 1998: 12). The expression 'culturally Deaf' refers to 'those Deaf people who share similar beliefs, values and norms and who identify with other deaf people' (ibid.: 12). Some writers appear to make the unjustified assumption that people viewed as 'Deaf' necessarily share the same beliefs and values.

Turning to the matter of support in mainstream schools, this relates to understandings of inclusion. Views on that aspect of inclusion concerning the numbers of children educated in mainstream schools, special units and special schools ranges from those preferring placement in neighbourhood schools, to separate education in preparation for later integration into society. Both these positions are sometimes expressed in terms of supposed 'rights' but are incompatible. There is a concern that anticipated social results are not achieved either personally and regarding peer interaction (Kirchner, 2004) or academically because work content level is lowered or is not relevant to current class work (Antia, 1998). Developments such as coenrolment in which a class has a substantial number of deaf and hearing students (e.g. 50/50) are one attempt to address these issues (Kirchner, 2004). Among considerations involved in providing support in mainstream schools are: the teaching style used by the mainstream teacher; the pupil's age; the physical environment of the school and the mode of communication in which support is provided.

Different issues arise according to whether support is provided in an oral/aural approach, a total communication approach or in the county's deaf sign language (these are explained in later sections). Within an oral/aural approach, issues include ensuring amplification aids (hearing aids and classroom amplifications) are in best working order and are used optimally; and that in-class support is effective. Note taking may be done by a teaching assistant using a laptop computer connected with one used by the pupil with the teaching assistant close enough to explain any new vocabulary. Within a total communication approach, the teacher or assistant may from time to time provide sign support, carefully co-ordinated so as not to clash with teacher explanations. Regarding support in the deaf sign language used in the country concerned, this may involve interpreting the lesson and/or providing pre-tutoring or post-tutoring. Pre-tutoring or post-tutoring also takes place in oral/aural settings as does other individual withdrawal work with a specialist teacher of the deaf or a teaching assistant.

After assessment by an audiologist determining the child's particular requirements, a hearing aid (either behind/in the ear types or radio frequency aids) may be prescribed. A radio frequency (FM) aid involving the teacher wearing a small microphone, which transmits to the child's hearing aid, allows the teacher's voice to be heard with minimum background noise from the environment (see also Pagliano, 2002).

A cochlear implant is a device that electrically stimulates the auditory nerve, producing the sensation of sound and comprises electrodes implanted on or in the cochlear and an external receiver fitted in the temporal bone (Turnbull *et al.*, 2002). While cochlear implants are usually recommended for children who are profoundly deaf and unable to benefit from other types of hearing aid, use of the procedure appears to be extending to children with less severe hearing loss too, which has been the subject of ethical debate (Stewart and Ritter, 2001).

Provision

Curriculum and assessment

Whatever the approach used, whether oral, sign bilingual and total communication methods predominate, the aim is to provide the fullest access to the curriculum unless there are additional difficulties. Curriculum content and related assessment is influenced by whether oral, sign bilingual and total communication methods predominate.

Pedagogy

Professional knowledge of teachers

In Europe there have been specialist teachers of the deaf since the 1700s, and their specialist knowledge and skills and their support of other teachers are highly valued. More generally, teachers who may not have specialist qualifications need be aware of how practice can be adapted to ensure the participation of deaf students. This includes providing visual support for learning such as class handouts, visual aids on what is being discussed and writing new vocabulary on the white/black board. Ensuring the deaf pupil can see and hear who is talking implies: the teacher facing the class and ensuring the deaf student is looking; having groupings where pupils can see what others are saying; repeating for the deaf pupil any comments made by another pupil in class discussion where the pupil may not have been visible and not giving instructions when classroom background noise is likely to be distracting. The daily checking of hearing aids and cochlear implants has to be guaranteed.

Communication in an oral/aural approach

An oral/aural approach (hereafter an 'oral' approach) aims to teach children who are deaf or have hearing impairment, and whose parents are hearing, to learn to speak intelligibly and to understand the spoken language (Steinberg and Knightly, 1997). (Although there are deaf parents, oral and signing, who wish their child to have an oral education.) One intention may be that, later, the person can choose whether to learn sign language. A cochlear implant may be made at an early age to promote the early use of residual hearing. For those who support an oral approach, increasingly earlier identification of deafness enhances the opportunity to use an oral approach early, although (for example for very young children), natural gesture is accepted as being important to communication.

While there have been variations in the approach, common features are discernible: residual hearing is used and enhanced (e.g. by hearing aids or cochlear implants); children unable to comprehend speech using hearing alone can gain information from lip reading and natural gesture (although as far as possible speaking and listening has precedence); cochlear implants may be used; communicating is emphasised and the rules of language are assumed to be learned over time through using language; every effort is made to provide favourable listening conditions; active listening skills are encouraged; and the child is encouraged to use contextual clues and knowledge of the world to aid communication and understanding.

Speech training and auditory training (Reddy *et al.*, 2000) may be provided by speech pathologists/therapists or language teachers using speech and articulation drawing on behavioural principles of rewarding and shaping and the social learning principles of imitation and modelling. This sort of formal speech and auditory training is becoming more rare with the advent of more powerful hearing aids, cochlear implants and earlier diagnosis. Also language development will be encouraged through using naturally occurring classroom activities aiming at better generalisation of vocabulary and patterns of language to daily life.

Communication and sign bilingualism

The sign languages used in different countries (American Sign Language, Auslan, British Sign Language) have many similarities but also distinctive features. Sign bilingualism uses both the sign language of the deaf community and the spoken and written languages of the hearing community. The aim is to enable the deaf child to become bilingual and participate fully in both the hearing and deaf society.

A sign-bilingual-approach involves the planned, systematic use of both the sign language of the country concerned and the spoken language, the balance varying according to perceived individual needs. An aim of sign bilingual education is that each child becomes sufficiently competent in the sign language and the spoken language for their needs as a child and as an adult. This is likely to require the planned use of sign language and spoken language both before school and throughout schooling.

Total communication

Total communication includes the full spectrum of language modes, child devised gestures, the language of signs, speech, speech reading, finger spelling, reading and writing, with the choice of methods being based on children's individual requirements.

To take the British context as an example, four broad options in total communication are: spoken English without signing; sign language (in this case British Sign Language/BSL); sign supported English and signed English. *Sign languages* have their own vocabulary, syntax and grammar, but no written form. In BSL, the subject is stated first and then the verbs, adverbs and adjectives. Most signs do not come directly from English words and cannot always be translated in a one-to-one fashion, although finger spelling is used for technical terms and proper names. Signs have meaning not just because of the manual shapes but also from the position of the hands in space, for example in relation to the body of the person signing. *Sign supported English* uses signs derived from BSL to support the use of natural English. Users may hold the view that to sign every aspect of spoken English could provide too much information for the child receiving the communication. *Signed English* is a representation with signs (mainly derived from BSL) of all aspects of spoken English. The vocabulary, plurals, tenses, gender and other features of natural English are all represented. An attempt is made to sign every aspect of what is spoken, thereby facilitating good English.

Literacy within an oral approach

There are often reported findings that the literacy levels of deaf children fall below that typically achieved by hearing peers, perhaps three or four years behind. In the United States of America, 18-year-old deaf students were found to be reading on average at 4th to 6th grade level, with only 3 per cent having comparable levels to the average for their hearing peers (Karchmer and Mitchell, 2003). Nevertheless, many deaf students are very accomplished readers. Encouraging levels of attainment have been reported in reading using an oral/aural approach with a quarter of the sample reading at or above chronological age on reaching school leaving age (Lewis, 1998). The approach emphasises creating and exchanging meaning, not decoding words in isolation. It accepts that the reader's previous experience, the context of the reading and the text, all interact to create meaning and draws on top-down and bottom-up, approaches as necessary.

Lewis (1998: 104, paraphrased) has suggested that three conditions need to be satisfied if reading is to progress well: a basic level of linguistic understanding must be established before formal reading programmes are introduced; the integrity of reading as a receptive process and as a reflective activity should be preserved and the language of ideas used to promote deaf children's earliest reading insights must be accessible to them.

Early reading material should be chosen to ensure the vocabulary relates to the child's linguistic competence and that meanings relate to the child's experience. Home-made books or the child's version of a story or event may be used. Helping the pupil with strategies for reading comprehension may be more effective than overemphasising decoding skills, vocabulary and grammar (Banks *et al.*, 1990).

In phonic work, unless sounds that are part of the deaf child's phonic system are used, phoneme-grapheme correspondence cannot be effectively taught. In later reading, discussing what has been read is beneficial. Pre-teaching can prepare the pupil for ideas that will come up in the text, allowing fuller participation. Directed Activities Related to Text (DARTs) helps the pupil's ability to access text through, for example, paired or small group work or discussion. DARTs is an activity-based approach enabling a pupil to read for meaning despite limited reading skills. Information is gained from the text through structured analysis and reconstruction tasks, encouraging the pupil to regard reading as a way of learning across the curriculum.

The written expression of deaf children is also reported to be problematic (Power, 1998) including difficulties with sentence structures, verb tenses and plurals and incorrect word order. In early writing, the teacher will consider attempts in their developmental context (that is in terms of what is developmentally appropriate) and in the context of the pupil's present linguistic functioning. Shared writing activities for various purposes are numerous and include: messages, shopping lists, jokes, postcards and birthday cards. From early stages, pupils are encouraged to read back what they have written and as appropriate self-correct their work.

Story retell programmes contribute to children remembering what they have read and to self-confidence in writing. The pupil is told a story or reads a story at his present level of verbal recall and understanding. The teacher then asks the pupil to retell the story (unprompted). This is video recorded (as are several subsequent attempts). Each time, the teacher transcribes the videotape verbatim with the pupil. This might be repeated twice a week for two or three weeks, over which time a steady improvement in the pupil's verbal retelling of what he has written is expected.

Literacy within a sign bilingual approach

A sign bilingual approach recognises that sign language is the preferred or main language for some children who are deaf. Where this is so, it is maintained that the sign language is used for teaching and learning, including the teaching and learning of spoken and written English. It distinguishes sign language, and sign systems such as sign-supported English, whose purpose is to encode and to be used in parallel with spoken English. The approach does not accept that sign systems supporting English (simultaneous communication/simcom) necessarily improve a child's English (e.g. Maxwell, 1992).

Because sign language has no orthography, bilingual deaf children have not had the opportunity to develop literacy skills in their primary language. It is important that a pupil's sign language skills are used in literacy teaching (by deaf and hearing adults) for 'presentation, discussion, analysis and explanation of tasks in a way that can bring reading and writing alive for deaf children' (Swanwick, 1998: 113). Metalinguistic understanding and awareness (being able to think and talk about language, its characteristics and structure) developed in sign language and used in constructing the second language (e.g. English) is also important.

Various activities support a sign bilingual approach. These include: Directed Activities Related to Text (DARTs) offering strategies to approach a text (Swanwick, 1993); dialogue journals (Baker, 1990) involving pupil and adult communicating with each other by writing a shared journal with the adult in responding modelling the correct written English so the pupil can learn from it; and video analysis (Partridge, 1996) to make a bilingual version of a reading scheme, offering opportunities to raise metalinguistic awareness and improve skills through being able to compare and contrast the two languages.

It is considered important that deaf and hearing adults teaching literacy in a sign bilingual approach understand the structure of both languages so they can make explicit comparisons between the languages and anticipate potential areas of difficulty. It is suggested that,

> Alongside ... support through discussion in sign language, deaf pupils also need plentiful exposure to the different conventions of writing English through wide and guided reading activities. This implies a reading programme which aims to focus the learner's attention on the structures and conventions of written English, in addition to developing their individual reading skills. Deaf children's early writing might then be further supported by the use of structured materials such as writing frames and models.
>
> (Swanwick, 2003: p. 135).

Mathematics

The teacher can introduce mathematical problems taking into account the order of written language and the order of the required mathematical operation. A study of mathematical problem solving ability involving 8 to 12-year-old profoundly deaf children of average or higher intelligence suggested that a problem was easier if the presentation of its segments reflected the order in which the mathematical calculation was carried out (Pau, 1995). This suggests working on problems such as 'Jane is ten years old. Tom is three years older than Jane. How old is Tom?' before going on to problems in the form of 'Jane is 10 years old. Tom is 13 years old. How much older is Tom than Jane?' once the language has been explained and understood.

It is important that sufficient emphasis is placed on teaching young children with hearing impairment to count in school, taking care to avoid confusions that might arise between counting and signing. Knowledge of the sequence of counting appears to be a significant predictor of performance on some numerical problems (Nunes and Moreno, 1997a). More emphasis on teaching young children with hearing impairment in school to count is therefore expected to improve their numerical knowledge. The two process of counting by pointing to objects one at a time, and signing can be separated to avoid confusion (Nunes and Moreno, 1997b).

The use of spatial ability is important. A review of 208 studies involving 171,517 deaf participants found the mean IQ from all studies was 97; the mean verbal IQ 86 and the mean non-verbal IQ 100. For deaf pupils with deaf parents, it was found that non-verbal IQ was 108, significantly higher than hearing people (Braden, 1994). Where a deaf pupil has this higher ability, spatial ability can be used as a strength in teaching and learning mathematics.

A promising project to teach deaf children the four arithmetic operations through spatial representation in problem solving and examples of teaching fractions and graphs is reported by Nunes (2005).

Children who are deaf and have multiple disabilities

It has been reported that 35 per cent of children who are severely or profoundly deaf have a visual impairment (Armitage *et al.*, 1995).

Video recording can help with recording and assessing observations of the fine details of pre-verbal behaviour relative to the pupil's behaviour and the communicative behaviour of the partner.

Provision for pupils who are deaf and have other disabilities involves taking into account the different difficulties and the way they may interact. If a pupil has behavioural difficulties, these may be compounded by hearing impairment if information or instructions are misunderstood, and further exacerbated if the hearing impairment is insufficiently recognised. Also, a consideration of the pupil's developmental level and an assessment of his communication skills are important. A suitable system of communication depends on factors such as the pupil's cognitive ability, vision and motor skills and may involve, as well as oral and sign language, alternative and augmentative communication systems.

A helpful chapter on 'Educating deaf students with multiple disabilities' is provided by Van Dijk (2004).

Resources

Hearing aids may be of various types. A hearing aid may be behind/in the ear type or a radio frequency (FM) aid (Pagliano, 2002). A cochlear implant comprises electrodes implanted on or in the cochlear and an external receiver fitted in the temporal bone (Turnbull *et al.*, 2002) and their fitting has been subject to ethical debate (Stewart and Ritter, 2001).

Therapy/care

No specific therapy/care other than the maintenance and optimum use of any hearing aids appears essential, unless the child has additional difficulties.

Organisation

Classrooms are organised to optimise listening to other speakers and seeing them clearly.

Thinking points

Readers may wish to consider with reference to a particular school:

- how communication is facilitated between those working with pupils with hearing impairment;
- how interventions are developed, evaluated and refined to ensure an evolving pedagogy and
- how it is ensured that the acoustic conditions in each teaching area are optimal.

Key texts

Moores, D. F. (2001) (5th edition) *Educating the Deaf: Psychology, Principles and Practices*. Boston, Houghton Mifflin.
Concerns definitions, identification, causes and treatments.

Power, D. and Leigh, G. (eds) (2004) *Educating Deaf Students: Global Perspectives*. Washington, DC, Gallaudet University Press.
Part 1 deals with 'Contemporary Issues for All Learners'; Part 2 covers 'The Early Years'; Part 3 'The School Years' and Part 4 'Contemporary Issues in Postsecondary Education'.

Stewart, D. A. and Kluwin, T. N. (2001) *Teaching Deaf and Hard of Hearing Students: Content, Strategies and Curriculum*. Boston, MA, Allyn & Bacon.
Covers various school subjects considering how they may be taught to students with hearing impairment.

Turkington, C. and Sussman, A. E. (2001) (2nd edition) *Encyclopaedia of Deafness and Hearing Disorders*. New York, Facts on File.
Information on deafness and hearing disorders including types of conditions and types of treatment.

Chapter 6

Visual impairment

Introduction

This chapter defines visual impairment, blindness and low vision and outlines some developmental implications of visual impairment. It looks at prevalence and causal factors. After considering identification and assessment of visual impairment the chapter examines provision including low vision devices and lighting, orientation and mobility, gaining rapid and efficient access to information, and reading using tactile methods. Finally, the chapter briefly considers visual impairment and multiple disability.

Definitions of visual impairment, blindness and low vision

In this chapter, the term 'visual impairment' is used to indicate a continuum of loss of sight, which includes blindness unless it is made clear that the expression is being used in a particular way. Where blindness is specifically referred to, it describes a level of sight loss of children who depend mainly on tactile methods of learning. The expression 'low vision' is used with reference to children whose learning and teaching involves predominantly methods relying on sight.

Examples of starting points for gathering further information on the Internet are the American Foundation for the Blind website which includes links to publications (www.afb.org) and 'VI Guide', a pointer to Internet resources for parents and teachers (www.viguide.com).

Some developmental implications of visual impairment

Visual impairment affects social and emotional development, language development, cognitive development and mobility and orientation. The combination of these effects on development influences the functioning and learning potential of a child with visual impairment.

In the early years, visual impairment impacts on a child's ability to interact with surroundings at a global level, especially if the child is born with no sight. The implications of this for enabling the child's development, well-being and education require sensitivity and reflection on the part of those who educate the child. Practical steps can also help. For example, a pre-school child who cannot see what other children are doing in a play setting can be invited to join in, and an adult can initially structure co-operation with the other children.

Before a child with visual impairment starts elementary/primary school, a specialist teacher or similar professional will usually provide the school with details of assessments of the child's vision and set out the educational implications. A specially assigned professional or a teacher will help the child find his way around the new school. The teacher and others will need to take care that the classroom environment is safe and welcoming and that such features as illumination, the use of tactile displays with Braille labelling and the print resources being used, all aid the pupil's learning.

During adolescence, there are implications relating to visual impairment and physical, cognitive, social and emotional development. A fully sighted young person can see the physical and sexual changes associated with adolescence and compare them to similar changes experienced by peers. However, an adolescent with visual impairment cannot see these changes and has to rely mainly on verbal descriptions. At the same time, touching taboos constrain the opportunity to explore the bodily changes in others. As children grow older, there is often an increasing awareness of differences.

Challenges also arise in transitions to adulthood, in higher education and in preparing for and pursuing a career, all of which require support and practical guidance.

Prevalence

Studies of childhood vision impairment from 1988 to 2000 have found prevalence rates ranging from 3.0 to 18.1 per 10,000 with the variation possibly being owing to methodological differences in case definition and the exact age range being considered, and the procedures for ascertaining cases (Mervis and Boyle, 2002).

In the United States of America a population-based study of childhood vision impairment, including moderate impairment levels (best corrected visual acuity in the better eye 20/70 or worse), found a prevalence rate of 10.7 per 10,000 of children aged 6 to 10 years old in metropolitan Atlanta, Georgia. Nearly two-thirds had coexisting disabilities (Mervis and Boyle, 2002).

In a report published in 2003, it was estimated that in England 20,870 children up to the age of 16 experienced visual impairment, suggesting a prevalence rate of 2.5 per 10,000 (Keil and Clunies-Ross, 2003: 13). Of these children, 30 per cent had additional 'complex needs' including severe learning difficulties/moderate to severe cognitive impairment or profound learning difficulties/profound cognitive impairment. The great majority of pupils with visual impairment who read and write use print, while about 4 per cent aged 5 to 16 years use Braille as the main medium for their learning (ibid.: 28).

Causes and types of visual impairment

Causes of visual impairment may involve factors that are genetic; that arise during foetal development or during the birth process or that occur in childhood. Various conditions and syndromes, some genetically determined, can be passed to the child by a parent or both parents who may be unaware they carry the condition. Genetic counselling enables parents carrying such conditions to plan for children with this information available to them. Factors affecting foetal development or affecting the baby during the process of birth can cause visual impairment. For example, maternal rubella can lead to a baby having visual impairment, or visual impairment may be the result of disease or injury. While the eyes may seem normal, visual messages to the brain are neither correctly interpreted nor acted upon. In childhood, the causes of visual impairment include viral infections, brain tumours and injury.

Among types of visual impairment are refractive errors (myopia or short sightedness, hypermetropia or long sightedness and astigmatism) and other types such as cataract, nystagmus and retinitis pigmentosa.

Refractive errors are often straightforward and corrected by spectacles or contact lenses worn for specified purposes. A child is considered to have visual impairment only if the best corrected vision is significantly outside the normal range for near and distance visual acuity (clarity or sharpness of vision).

In myopia, the eyeball is too long so that parallel light rays coming from a distance do not focus on the retina at the point where they should (the central point of the macula – the fovea). Instead, the light rays are focused between the lens and the macula so distance vision is blurred, requiring corrective concave spectacles or contact lenses.

Hypermetropia is a condition in which the eyeball is too short and light rays focus behind the retina so that vision is blurred or in extreme cases not effective. In straightforward instances, convex lens spectacles or contact lenses can correct hypermetropia so that light rays are focused on the fovea. But, when other conditions such as cataracts co-occur visual acuity is reduced even when prescribed spectacles are worn. Children with hypermetropia should avoid long periods spent on 'close' tasks such as reading because they cause discomfort. Low vision devices such as closed circuit television may be prescribed for some pupils.

In astigmatism, the main cause is that the eye lens (cornea) has irregularities in its curvature that lead to variable refractive power causing the image on the macula to be distorted. A cylindrical correction built into the lens of spectacles can correct this but where astigmatism is accompanied by myopia or hypermetropia, correcting vision can reduce visual acuity.

Turning to other types of visual impairment, retinopathy of prematurity and cortical visual impairment have already been mentioned. Further examples are cataract, nystagmus and retinitis pigmentosa.

A cataract is an opaqueness or cloudiness of the cornea preventing some light rays passing to the retina. The school must have advice from an ophthalmologist or an optometrist because a suitable response depends on factors such as the position of the cataract. For example, if the cataract affects the lens periphery, the child will need increased levels of illumination, while if the centre of the cornea is opaque, low lighting will aid vision.

Nystagmus is a repetitive, rhythmic involuntary movement of the eyes often accompanied by other visual impairments such as congenital cataracts. Children with nystagmus have considerable difficulty fixing the eyes on a specified point, although some can be helped to find an eye position in which involuntary movement is reduced. Line markers for reading and the use of reading materials with bold, well-contrasted print can help.

Retinitis pigmentosa is a group of progressive conditions affecting the retina, particularly the peripheral area that contains the cells (rods) sensitive to vision in dim light. This leads to night blindness and 'tunnel vision'. As the condition is usually progressive, for some children eventual loss of sight is expected so that provision for using Braille and mobility training should be part of the curriculum.

Cortical visual impairment (CVI) is not strictly an eye condition because it relates to the brain's interpretation of visual information. However, it is one of the commoner visual problems affecting children with additional or complex difficulties.

Identification and assessment

Most severe visual problems are identified within the first few months of a baby's life, perhaps by the maternity hospital, health visitor (or equivalent) or parents, although some difficulties may not be appreciated until the child starts school.

Assessment of vision

When a child is very young or is unable to co-operate verbally, methods of gaining information about vision include testing blinking reflex or measuring the electrical responses of the visual cortex. A full assessment of vision is expected to include the following (Mason *et al.*, 1997: 53):

1   a distance vision test;
2   a near vision test;
3   a field of vision test;
4   a test of colour perception;
5   a contrast sensitivity test and
6   an assessment of visual functioning.

For tests 1 through 3 above, each eye is usually tested independently then both eyes are tested together. Distance vision and near vision are usually tested with and without aids such as spectacles that the child might use.

Distance vision is commonly tested using the Snellen test chart, comprising letters, numbers or pictures arranged in rows of descending smallness. Assuming letters are being used, each row of letters is designed to be recognised at a certain distance by a person with normal vision, for example 60, 36, 24, 18, 12, 9, 6 or 5 metres. If a child stands 6 metres from the chart and is able to read all the letters down to the row typically read at 6 metres, the child's vision is said to be 6/6. Should he only be able to read to the row typically read at 18 metres, while standing 6 metres away, his visual acuity is 6/18. Should the child be unable to read the top line of the chart (typically readable at 60 metres) from 6 metres away, vision is less than 6/60 and the test is continued at a shorter distance. If the child can read the top line from 3 metres away, 3/60 is recorded and if from only a metre away, visual acuity is 1/60. In a classification of visual acuity, 6/6 to 6/18 represents 'normal vision', worse than 6/18 but better than or equal to 3/60 represents 'low vision' and worse than 3/60 represents 'blind'. Among alternatives to the Snellen test chart, which are being increasingly used, are LogMAR type tests allowing more finely graded assessments of visual acuity.

Near vision acuity, important for close work such as reading and writing, may be assessed by an 'N print' test involving print of different sizes. Each print size is given an N number so that the larger the N number the larger the print. N5 is the smallest print size. For the test, the print size is recorded along with the distance in centimetres from which it is read, for example N6 at 25 centimetres. Alternatives for young children include tests using pictures graded for size. A child with visual impairment may use very large print size. N print sizes roughly accord with font point sizes on a computer although this depends on the font used. For many educational tasks, near vision is more important than distance vision.

The field of vision is the area a person sees from all parts of the eye when looking directly ahead and any field of vision defect is mapped out on a circular chart representing the field of vision in each eye.

A well-known test of colour vision is the Ishihara test comprising plates of coloured dots among some of which are numbers or symbols. A person with normal colour vision can distinguish these while someone with a loss of colour vision will either not be able to distinguish them or will interpret them incorrectly.

Problems with contrast sensitivity are indicated by a poor response to medium and low frequencies in a contrast sensitivity test. A child with such difficulties will be unable to read easily unless illumination is good and print is very dark against a white background.

A key difference is between problems with central vision, making it difficult to see detail and difficulties with peripheral vision, which make it hard to get around.

Visual functioning concerns how well a child makes use of vision in day-to-day activities. Two children having the same visual acuity may differ in visual functioning; for example, one may be more willing to use the vision he has and benefit from better mobility and orientation skills than the other. A specially qualified teacher normally makes an assessment of visual functioning, which involves consulting the child and others who know him. The assessment investigates strengths and weaknesses in the way the child uses vision, taking into account cognitive and social development.

Educational assessments

The assessment of vision and educational assessment are related. With regard to intelligence tests, certain sub-tests are considered suitable for use with children who are blind or have low vision. Tactile versions of some sub-tests are also available. Reading tests have been standardised for use with blind children. Such tests, standardised in the country concerned, are available from commercial test suppliers.

Within all forms of assessment, the child is at the centre and it is the child's attitudes, aspirations, motivation, views and other individual and personal factors that inform provision that will be beneficial.

Provision

Curriculum

Indications of approaches to the curriculum will be evident in the section on pedagogy below. In general, concrete experience is important to help the pupil develop concepts, as are clear teacher explanations and opportunities for the pupil to engage in discussion. Approaches and aids in different subjects help access to the curriculum.

In mathematics, Braille notation is used in different countries while in music there is an international system of Braille notation. Regarding science, a light-sensitive device such as a light probe allows the pupil to conduct experiments on shadows, reflection and refraction. Equipment such as an electrical thermometer or balance may have a speech output or a large display on a computer screen. History can be enlivened by visits to places of historic interest and 'living' museums and the use of artefacts from earlier periods. In geography, visits to transport facilities and areas with different geographical features (lakes, beaches, rock formations) can be experienced. Adaptations can be made to physical education equipment, for example using a ball containing a bell so it can be heard. Artwork is available through paintings represented using a bas-relief technique with raised edges and an accompanying audiotape, while raised lines may be drawn using 'german film' (a plastic drawing film) and spur wheels used to produce raised lines of different heights and textures when drawn across Manila paper.

Extra-curricular activities including sports, leisure pursuits, clubs, social gatherings and fitness offer opportunities for a pupil to make contacts and friends in the local community that can continue into adult life. Those organising such activities who may not have knowledge of visual impairment will need to become conversant with the specific implications of the particular visual impairment, and of such matters as the importance of lighting and the need for good contrast on items such as gymnasium equipment (see also, Lieberman, 2002).

In examinations, depending on circumstances, a pupil with visual impairment may use Braille or large print, use a word processor, have a scribe and a reader, and be allowed extra time. Examination papers may be in Braille, large/modified print or on audiotape. Schools may be allowed to open papers early to check content and a specialist teacher may modify the papers by removing visual bias and complexity while testing the same skills.

In study of the percentage of children with and without visual impairment who could achieve independent living skills, it was found that only very few children with a visual impairment could walk independently to a friend's house (Lewis and Iselin, 2002). The areas of orientation and mobility form a distinctive aspect of the curriculum are associated with independent movement and travel. Orientation involves awareness of space and where one is within it ('Where am I?' 'Where do I want to go?' 'How do I get there?'). Mobility is the ability to move around safely. To travel safely, the child may use a sighted guide or a long cane and young adults may also use a guide dog or an electronic aid. Mobility specialists teach more complex skills such as travelling using a long cane in town.

School layout and other features can aid orientation and mobility. A tactile or large print plan of the school in the reception area can help the pupil build up a notion of the general layout of the school and particular routes to be followed. This would be supplemented by mobility training. Recessed radiators and surfaces reducing glare from floors improve safety. Specific adaptations are necessary for particular curriculum subjects such as in technology where machinery is used and where it must be well-defined by colour and lighting.

It is difficult to overstate the importance of orientation and mobility, given their contribution to improving physical fitness, raising self-esteem, providing opportunities to socialise, and increasing the ability to travel to and from a place of employment.

Pedagogy

Tactile representation and hands on experience

The term 'tactile' is sometimes reserved for a passive touch such as that of clothing on the body. The expressions 'tactual' and 'haptic' are then used to refer to a more active use of touch, such as that involved when exploring the qualities of an object or material and recognising qualities such as temperature, texture, shape and weight. Tactile representations include maps, diagrams, graphs, charts, pictures and mathematical constructions, and may be supplemented by labels and instructions in Braille. Tactile diagrams may use collage (string, sandpaper, wire) or 'swell' paper having raised black lines contrasting to a flat white background.

The use and processing of tactile representations and their educational applications is subtle. Tactile information is processed sequentially, the parts being used to make up a picture of the whole. When information is processed visually, the whole may be processed together and then the detail of the components. For such reasons, when the teacher introduces tactile diagrams, she will need to offer explanations and guidance and the pupil will need time to explore the diagram so that it becomes meaningful. For fully sighted pupils, the conventions of portraying three-dimensional items or scenes in two-dimensional photographs or illustrations have to be learned. For the child using tactile materials, conveying three-dimensional representations two-dimensionally in tactile form is even more difficult as conventions such as perspective need also to be transmitted.

Regarding hands-on experience, it is important to allow and encourage the pupil with visual impairment to handle materials, objects and artefacts. This can often be arranged through advance planning in museums, sites of historic interest, art galleries (sculptures, friezes), farms and so on. In mathematics, for example, hands-on experience is vital in handling money, weighing, measuring, exploring geometrical shapes and making fractional parts.

Listening and speaking

It has been estimated that 80 per cent of information received by people who are fully sighted comes through the visual mode (Best, 1992). Listening is also important to enable the person with visual impairment to move around safely and efficiently, for example by listening for sound signals at pedestrian road crossings. Listening to curriculum material through talking books, electronic reading devices and computer programmes using synthesised speech provides important information. A variable speed audio recorder can be used for higher level study to give faster listening speeds and 'compressed speech' devices ensure that the original pitch of the voice is maintained while speaking rate is accelerated. Digital audio, which is increasingly used, is more versatile.

A classroom with carpeted areas will reduce unwanted background sounds, allowing the pupil to attend more effectively to relevant sounds. The teacher should speak clearly, remembering that visual clues from her body language may not be available to the pupil with visual impairment. When speaking directly to the pupil, if the teacher uses the pupil's name first, he will know he is the one being addressed.

Turning to speaking skills, an important aspect for a pupil with visual impairment is learning skills such as looking at the person being addressed when the pupil himself is speaking. Turn-taking skills in conversation and in discussion groups are facilitated by visual clues about body language which may be unavailable to the pupil with visual impairment. Therefore, the interpretation of the other person's tone of voice, rhythm of speaking, pauses and other verbal features are important clues in timing conversational exchanges.

Reading using tactile methods

Tactile readers are a minority of children with visual impairment, as indicated earlier. Braille uses a 'cell' of six raised dots, combinations of which make up letters, punctuation and contracted words. For example, in British Braille, there are two grades: first, consisting of alphabet and punctuation signs, and second, comprising contractions of words such as 'RCV' for 'receive'. The early teaching of Braille reading and writing is usually based on contracted Braille from the beginning. An average reader of Braille reads two or three times slower than the average print reader, the respective rates being about 100 words per minute and 250 words per minute (Aldrich and Parkin, 1989). In part, this is because a Braille reader cannot scan ahead in the same way as a sighted reader of print, there being no peripheral touch equivalent to peripheral vision. The reading rate differs similarly between children reading Braille and print. Computer programs can translate print files into Braille files, which are then downloaded to Braille embossers. Moving from print reading to Braille for a pupil whose sight is worsening requires sensitivity as the pupil may resist Braille reading as an acknowledgement of deteriorating sight. Reading schemes are available to develop Braille skills for pupils transferring from print to Braille.

Moon is a tactile medium based on a simplified raised line adaptation of the Roman print alphabet that may be used for pupils with visual impairment and additional difficulties who are unable to learn Braille. Moon is slow to read and provides a basic access to literacy.

Writing in tactile codes and handwriting

Electronic Braille typewriters use a six-key format for input, each key corresponding to a dot in the Braille cell. Output may be through synthetic speech or a renewable tactile display on the machine. Text may be stored in the machine's memory to be transferred later to a standard printer or Braille embosser. Braille text downloaded to a conventional printer is translated by software into print. There is debate about whether or not older students should be taught to use dedicated Braille writing devices as the main medium for recording information, the alternative being to teach students who are educationally blind to touch type using the conventional QWERTY keyboard in elementary/primary school in order to develop word processing skills early. In high school/secondary school, students may use conventional computers with adaptive software and synthesised speech as their main way of writing and storing information.

Moon characters may be written by hand on special plastic material ('german film'). Moon fonts have also been developed for computers through which Moon text is typed onto the computer screen then downloaded through a conventional printer onto paper. The Moon is then copied onto 'swell' paper and raised by being passed through a stereo-copying machine.

Handwriting tends to be difficult for a pupil with low vision because he cannot easily see and self-correct work, which may be untidy. Word processing skills may be taught from an early age. For older students who are blind, handwriting should be sufficiently developed so that one can sign one's name. Typing skills are also a vital means of gaining access to the wider benefits of modern technology including the Internet.

Personal and social development and leisure

Self-help skills are most meaningfully taught in context so the pupil is motivated to exercise and develop the skill in order to achieve a particular goal (e.g. selecting clothing and dressing taught at home in the morning and at bedtime or at school for physical education lessons). Day-to-day items can be made more helpful to children with visual impairment if they are carefully chosen (e.g. a light-coloured plate makes dark foods like beef easier to see). Kitchen equipment such as a microwave cooker can have tactile controls, labels and instructions. Specialist equipment may be used such as liquid level indicators.

School lunchtime can provide a good opportunity for socialising and the teachers might tactfully ensure that the child with visual impairment is in a well-lit, less crowded environment close to friends. The student can be enabled to develop independence skills to arrive at the table independently with their lunch tray (Shapiro et al., 2003).

To encourage a pupil's increasing independence and autonomy in studying, a balance is sought between offering adult help where necessary and ensuring that a pupil's work is differentiated sufficiently so that task demands are not excessive. For example, extra time may be allowed for reading in Braille compared with reading in print for a fully sighted pupil.

In general, counselling can raise self-esteem by providing a situation in which the child can be listened to and given unconditional regard as well as offering the opportunity to talk through any problems and look at ways they might be resolved. Counselling can allow the child to express feelings, for example in relation to deteriorating sight. It may help the pupil come to recognise and accept when the time is approaching to begin learning Braille and mobility training because of deteriorating eyesight. See also, *Teaching Social Skills to Students with Visual Impairments: From Theory to Practice* (Sacks and Wolffe, 2005).

Visual impairment inhibits some physical activities that many sighted children take for granted. Children who are visually impaired tend to have lower levels of physical fitness than peers (e.g. Lieberman and McHugh, 2001) making opportunities for participation in leisure pursuits, for example sports, important. Among ways in which children with visual impairment (and children who are deafblind) can access sports are:

- using a guide wire system, a sighted guide or a caller for running;
- tandem, duo or stationery bicycles for cycling;
- the use of a 'bonker' (a pole with a tennis ball on the end used to tap the swimmer as he approaches the end of the pool for turning) for lap swimming;
- health club exercise training and
- yoga (Lieberman, 2002).

Resources

Resources to aid rapid and efficient access to information

Developing the ability and skills to gain efficient access to information is an important aspect of study skills and a way of gaining greater independence. For example, the pupil may use a tone indexing facility on audio recordings, or consult contents summary pages in a Braille book before reading a lengthier treatment of the subject. CD-ROMs offer quick access to information through synthesised speech or large character displays. There are various ways to help ensure the pupil has easy access to work he has produced. Boxes of computer disks can be suitably labelled and the pupil can have a series of labelled files for different topics/subjects in which work is kept on numbered pages. Using reference materials such as a Braille dictionary is time consuming and subject-orientated word lists with definitions may be more efficient for some purposes.

Low vision devices and lighting

The most suitable low vision devices for a child's requirements are determined through consultation with various people including: the child, parents, an optometrist, a specialist teacher of the visually impaired and a specialist in rehabilitation.

Ways of achieving magnification include: increasing the size of the image of the object; decreasing the working distance to the object and increasing the visual angle, for example by using a telescope or other multi-lens device. Devices include a hand magnifier; a stand magnifier; a flat bed magnifier (with a plane base in contact with the surface to be viewed and a hemispheric plano-convex top); a line magnifier; spectacle mounted devices; telescopic devices and closed circuit television (a television camera mounted on a movable table and connected to a video display monitor). A distinction may be made between near devices for viewing items such as printed materials through the use of magnifiers and microscopes; and distance devices for viewing such things as sporting events through the use of bioptic lenses. Filter lenses are used for medical conditions such as cataracts or cone dysfunctions where light impairs vision and reduces visual acuity. Where suitable for the student, large-print books may be used.

Important for pupils with visual impairment are ambient lighting around school and task lighting to maximise the use of the pupil's near vision while studying. The school should ensure that lighting is glare free and control artificial and natural lighting to ensure the level is suitable for particular areas of the classroom. The type of visual impairment influences suitable illumination, for example, pupils having photophobia require reduced lighting while other pupils will prefer higher levels of illumination. Blinds, louvre and tinted glass are used to control natural light and dimmer switches enable artificial ambient lighting to be adjusted.

Computer technology

Aspects of computer technology have been discussed in earlier sections. It allows a pupil to write an essay by speaking it into a computer and offers access through sight (e.g. using a magnified or large print), hearing (e.g. speech synthesis) and touch (e.g. converting conventional print text into Braille). Information from Internet sites is accessed by being downloaded onto a computer then read by a screen reader using speech synthesis, magnification or Braille. Optical character machines and scanners enable the pupil to read from printed text that is translated into synthesised speech. CD-ROMs having electronic or spoken versions of the same text are replacing talking books, while CD-ROM writers and recorders are now available. Specialist tape recorders (desk or compact) used by pupils with visual impairment include multi-track models with speed control, voice indexing facility and control switches with tactile markings. A tone indexing facility allows signals to be inserted onto a tape, which can be heard when the tape is rewound or fast forwarded. Some pocket memo recorders are voice activated and have a tone indexing facility. Digital software such as the Digital Accessible Information SYstem (DAISY) (www.daisy.org) and MP3 are increasingly used.

Therapy/care

There appear to be no aspects of therapy or care essential for provision for visual impairment as such beyond safety implications for mobility and orientation already mentioned. However, many children with visual impairment have additional difficulties requiring speech therapy, physiotherapy and other support.

Organisation

The organisation of schools and classrooms supports safe and easy access to all areas of learning. Classroom design and layout can help to reduce background noise. For pupils with low vision, preferential seating near the teacher's board can help.

Other aspects

Specialist teachers

A child with visual impairment may have access to the services of a specialist teacher. For example, in the United States of America, a child who meets the criteria for visual impairment in his state is eligible to receive the services of a certified teacher of students with visual impairments. Such a teacher may be responsible for carrying out initial assessments and advising on adaptations and modifications and individual education plans/programmes.

A specialist teacher for the visually impaired may work in a special school or nursery, in a unit or centre in a mainstream school, or as an advisory teacher visiting and working in special and mainstream settings. A specialist teacher working mainly in a special school may be well placed to provide services elsewhere if the service is well funded and the special school staffing is enhanced to allow such work as outreach, in reach (educating pupils from ordinary schools in the special school for part of the timetable), training and consultancy. Joint work with families and schools may also be offered. Advice, support and help may centre on: assessment; the physical environment; specialised teaching strategies; the sensory curriculum; modifications to classroom resources; movement and mobility skills; directly teaching and facilitating visits to other schools and centres.

Visual impairment and multiple disability

An essential aspect of multiple disabilities is the interaction of the disabilities and the combined impact on the child's development. Communication is a major challenge for children with complex needs if they have severe visual impairment. Orelove and Sobsey (1991) refer to individuals with moderate to severe or profound cognitive impairment/severe or profound learning difficulties and 'one or more significant motor or sensory impairments and/or special health care needs'. Hearing impairment, visual impairment, physical disability and motor difficulties may have been identified by staff in the maternity hospital or by the health home visitor or parents. Other disabilities/disorders such as moderate to severe cognitive impairment or communication disorders may be noticed only later. Commercially produced structured assessments are available for use with children having multiple disability and visual impairment suitable for the country concerned.

The curriculum for children with multiple disability and visual impairment includes a flexibly interpreted general curriculum, a developmental curriculum (which concerns areas of early development which may include motor development, communication, cognition and personal/social development) and additional curriculum provision such as physiotherapy, mobility education and motor development programmes. Appropriate provision is made for pupils who need to use communication methods other than speech, non-sighted methods of reading and aids or adapted equipment for writing or for practical activities.

Co-ordination is assisted by a cross-curricular approach involving a variety of professionals such as the teacher, mobility specialist, speech pathologist, physical therapist/physiotherapist, occupational therapist and social care worker. Individual education plans with jointly agreed targets and strategies to achieve them can help pull together the shared work of these professionals. Such multi-professional working requires time to enable face-to-face communication, joint planning sessions, and money to pay for the higher staffing levels necessary to create this non-contact time.

For some pupils with multiple disability and visual impairment, communication may not be primarily through spoken language or writing. Non-verbal skills may be used, including a manual signing system. Signing can be used to give visual/gestural support to aid a child's comprehension of spoken language. A switch with a voice input system may be used. Other means of communication may be objects of reference or tactile symbols. For pupils who are unable to understand and use formal communication systems such as speech and manual signing systems, their potential communication signals may be non-intentional or unconventional. A communication partner may be helpful to seek to relate such signals to meaning and more generally ensuring that stimulation that is structured and suitable is provided in an interactive context.

Thinking points

Readers may wish to consider:

- whether their local authority/school board offers a range of educational places for pupils with visual impairment including mainstream school, nursery, units and special schools;
- how effectively training, supervision and liaison with specialist teachers develops the skills of the non-specialist teacher working with children with visual impairment and enhances the child's education.

Key texts

Heller, M. A. and Ballesteros, S. (eds) (2006) *Touch and Blindness: Psychology and Neuroscience*. Hillsdale, NJ, Lawrence Erlbaum Associates.
Considering touch and blindness from a psychological and a neuroscience perspective, this book includes an examination of processing spatial information from touch and movement; and the role of the visual cortex in tactile processing.

Mason, H. and McCall, S. with Arter, C., McLinden, M. and Stone, J. (1997) (eds) *Visual Impairment: Access to Education for Children and Young People*. London, David Fulton Publishers.

Covers visual impairment and the curriculum, the role of the specialist teacher, and teacher education. Seven chapters concern children with multiple disabilities and visual impairment.

Sacks, S. Z. and Wolffe, K. E. (2005) (eds) *Teaching Social Skills to Students with Visual Impairments: From Theory to Practice*. New York, American Foundation for the Blind Press.
Part 1 concerns personal viewpoints; Part 2, theories of social developments; Part 3, elements of social success and Part 4, interventions and practice.

Koenig, A. J. and Holbrook, M. C. (eds) (2000) *Foundations of Education Volume 2: Instructional Strategies for Teaching Children and Youth with Visual Impairments*. New York, American Foundation for the Blind Press.
The title is self-explanatory.

Lewis, S. and Allman, C. B. (2000) *Seeing Eye to Eye: An Administrator's Guide to Students With Low Vision*. New York, American Foundation for the Blind.

Orr, A. L. and Rogers, P. A. (2002) *Solutions for Success: A Training Manual for Working with People who are Visually Impaired*. New York, American Federation for the Blind Press.
The title is self-explanatory.

Sardegna, J., Shelley, S., Shelley, A. and Steidl, S. M. (2002) (2nd edition) *The Encyclopaedia of Blindness and Vision Impairment*. New York, Facts on File.
An A to Z format guide to topics such as research, surgery, social issues and economic matters.

Chapter 7

Deafblindness

Introduction

This chapter defines deafblindness, considers its prevalence, outlines some of its causes and examines implications for a child who is deafblind or whether hearing impairment and/or visual impairment are congenital/early inset or are acquired. The chapter considers the identification and assessment of deafblindness. It explains various approaches to the education of children who are deafblind, focusing mainly on developing communication but also touching upon mobility and finding out information.

An example of further information on the Internet is Minnesota's online resource about combined vision loss and hearing loss which includes pages on well-know deafblind people in history, a parent and family resource guide and a frequently asked questions page with many further links (www.deafb lind-info.org).

Definitions

Deafblindness is also referred to as 'multi-sensory impairment'. Sometimes 'deafblind' is written as a single word, which may be taken to suggest the combined effect of being deaf and blind is greater than the sum of its parts. It may be written as two separate words 'deaf blind' or as hyphenated words 'deaf-blind'. The range of definitions that are found for deafblindness is associated with a range of possible interventions that may work for pupils who happen to fall into the remit of one definition but may not work for pupils covered under another definition. For example, many aspects of provision associated with deafblindness relate to children who are congenitally deafblind and without other disabilities.

A document by the United Kingdom Qualifications and Curriculum Authority states:

> Pupils who are deafblind have both visual and hearing impairments that are not fully corrected by spectacles or hearing aids. They may not be

completely deaf and blind. But the combination of these two disabilities on a pupil's ability to learn is greater than the sum of its parts.
(Qualifications and Curriculum Authority, 1999: 7).

A child who is deafblind may or may not have other difficulties or disabilities such as:

- profound cognitive impairment/profound learning difficulties;
- severe cognitive impairment/severe learning difficulties;
- mild to moderate cognitive impairment/moderate learning difficulties and
- physical or motor difficulties.

Some functional definitions emphasise the effects of deafblindness on communication, mobility and gaining information. One reason for this emphasis in functional assessment is that assessment of vision and hearing impairment generally does not lead to suggestions for interventions, which functional assessment is designed to do.

In the United States of America, the *Individuals with Disabilities Act 1997* uses the following definition,

'Deaf-blind' means concomitant visual and hearing impairments, the combination of which causes such severe communication and other developmental and educational problems that they cannot be accommodated in special education programmes solely for deaf or blind children.
(Section 330.7 (c) (2))

The New England Centre for Deafblind Services definition was adapted by a United Kingdom project on curriculum access for deafblind pupils (Porter *et al.*,1997, appendix 1) as follows:

1   Individuals who are both peripherally deaf or severely hearing impaired and peripherally blind or severely visually impaired according to definitions of 'legal' blindness and deafness; acuity to be measured or estimated in conjunction with a recognition of level of cognitive development supported by medical description of pathology.
2   Individuals who have sensory impairments of both vision and hearing, one of which is severe and the other moderate to severe.
3   Individuals who have sensory impairments of both vision and hearing, one of which is severe, and/or language disabilities, which result in the need for special services.
4   Individuals who have sensory impairment of both vision and hearing of a relatively mild to moderate degree and additional learning and/or language disabilities, which result in need for special services or who have been diagnosed as having impairments which are progressive in nature.

5   Individuals who are severely multiply handicapped due to generalised nervous system dysfunction, who also exhibit measurable impairments of both vision and hearing.

The effect of the loss of vision and hearing has led to the needs of children who are deafblind being those of 'multisensory deprivation' (McInnes and Treffry, 1982: 1). Indeed, the work of van Dijk, an influential European figure in developing pedagogy for deafblind children, drew on concepts of deprivation, attachment and socialisation to inform pedagogy (Nelson *et al.*, 2002).

Prevalence

It is estimated that the incidence of deafblindness among children is about 3 in every 10,000 (Sense, 2004: 7). In the United States of America it is estimated that about 0.01 per cent of the school population are deafblind. For example, in the school year 2000–1 about 1,500 pupils identified as deafblind received special education services (United States Department of Education, 2002)

Causal factors

Congenital or early onset deafblindness

Infections, genetic or chromosomal syndromes, or birth trauma may cause congenital or early onset deafblindness. Children who are deafblind as a result of such causes often have other impairments such as cognitive impairment/learning difficulties or physical disabilities. A parasite, bacteria or virus may transmit *infection*. The rubella virus used to be the main cause of deafblindness before the rubella vaccine came to be widely used. Cytomegalovirus (CMV) is a herpes virus that can cause damage to the nervous system of the foetus and can also lead to deafblindness. Among *genetic or chromosomal syndromes* that can result in deafblindness is CHARGE syndrome. Thought to have a genetic cause, it is a rare condition the name of which is formed of the initials of its common features. These are: Colomba (eye defects); Heart defects; choanal Atresia (nasal blockage); Retardation of growth and developmental delay; Genital abnormalities and Ear abnormalities, including deafness. Similarly, Goldenhaar syndrome, which appears to have a genetic cause, can lead to malformations of the ears and to eye abnormalities. *Problems at birth* or soon after that are associated with deafblindness relate to prematurity, low birth weight, anoxia (insufficient oxygen), or other trauma or to injury.

Acquired deafblindness

Acquired deafblindness in children may be the result of genetic syndromes whose effects may emerge later in a child's development, or of accidents or other trauma. Usher syndrome results from a gene defect, which is present from birth but whose effects appear as the child grows. Retinitis pigmentosa develops in late childhood or even in adulthood, causing difficulties in changing light conditions and a gradual reduction in peripheral vision. An accident may damage part of the brain involved in processing vision or hearing, which can lead to deafblindness.

Implications of congenital and acquired hearing and visual impairment

A child who is deafblind has inter-related difficulties in finding out information, communicating with others and in moving around the environment (Aitken *et al.*, 2000: 3–4). Common patterns may be discernible depending on whether hearing impairment, or visual impairment or both are congenital/early onset or have a later onset.

When a child experiences *congenital/early onset hearing and visual impairment*, it is important to establish and develop communication, perhaps using special signing and to develop mobility skills and access information.

For a child with *congenital/early onset hearing impairment and acquired visual impairment*, sight may become progressively more impaired, often in adolescence. Where the hearing impairment was profound, sign language may have been learned, which may need adapting because of impaired vision; and specialised interpreter services may also be necessary. Information and communications technology may help access to information, and mobility training will be helpful.

Where a child has *congenital/early onset visual impairment and acquired hearing impairment*, the child may have learnt Braille, mobility and other skills in his early education. Reading and writing in Braille may be developed (because speech and hearing were intact earlier) and can assist later learning of deafblind finger spelling, keyboard skills and mobility, and can allow for the later development of Braille skills.

If *visual and hearing impairment are both acquired*, the child or young adult's already developed skills in communication, mobility and accessing information will be affected. Support to cope with the emotional difficulties of losing sight and hearing in later childhood or adolescence will be needed by the young adult and his family.

Identification and assessment

Maternity hospital staff, parents or health home visitors may identify congenital deafblindness. Parents, teachers, specialist teachers, audiologists or ophthalmologists may observe later acquired deafblindness. Identifying deafblindness is informed by the definition of deafblindness adopted. It may be argued that the degree of visual impairment that on its own would indicate blindness and the extent of hearing impairment that alone would constitute deafness, could, taken together, indicate deafblindness. However, if the combined effect of having both hearing and visual impairment is considered greater than the sum of its parts, it can be maintained that lower levels of hearing impairment and visual impairment together constitute deafblindness. Where there is any residual vision or hearing it should be encouraged.

Specialists assess the degree of deafblindness: an audiologist (an audiological scientist trained to perform hearing assessments and fit and monitor hearing aids) and an ophthalmologist (a medical doctor specialising in the diagnosis and treatment of diseases of the eye). Also contributing to the assessment are the child, the parent, speech and language pathologist/therapist, physiotherapist, occupational therapist, school/educational psychologist and others. Where the child knows the person carrying out the assessment and therefore co-operates well, the assessment is more likely to be accurate and useful.

While it is essential that when a child is being assessed as deafblind, any other disorders and disabilities are identified and assessed, it is equally important they are not wrongly attributed. Because a child who is deafblind learns slowly and requires intensive support, it can be incorrectly assumed that he has cognitive impairment too. Similarly, motor impairment can be wrongly attributed because the child's movements may be hesitant. A functional assessment is likely to provide much useful information because it is contextual, the environment being structured to give opportunities to see skills in practical use.

As well as ophthalmological and audiological assessments, the sense of touch, taste, smell and proprioception are assessed. Assessing tactile development might include determining if the child can explore objects to make fine distinctions between them. An assessment of cognitive abilities may involve seeking information about the child's awareness, attention, memory, curiosity (including problem solving skills), recognition, imitation, classification, symbolic understanding and number concepts.

Observations relating to assessment involves forming a clear description of what the child did and an interpretation of its context and meaning. The teacher, parents and others may all make observations and the purpose of the observation should be clear, for example to establish what skills the child learns most easily. Commercial assessments are also used, an example being the *Callier Azusa Scale* (Stillman, 1978), a developmental guide designed for use with deafblind learners.

Assessing communication

Communication may be assessed in functional and linguistic terms. Assessing functional communication includes determining whether for example the child shows interest in, or participates in, any form of two-way interaction and 'whether the child associates any gestures, signs, pictures, objects or words with an activity or person' (Eyre, 2000: 133–134). Linguistic communication involves examining the forms of communication used, the functions that language fulfils for the child, and the level of language the child uses, and includes assessing whether and how the child can 'express wants and needs' and can 'refer back to previous events' (ibid.: 134).

Assessing physical skills

Physical skills may be assessed by a physiotherapist, whose report may include information on the child's potential for movement, harm that may occur to the child in connection with certain movements and medical aspects of managing their physical impairments. This sort of information is used to optimise the child's ability for movement and ensure the best access for learning.

Assessing social skills

An assessment of social skills might include examining the extent of the child's awareness of himself and others and the child's degree of independence or dependence on other people. Personal factors might be the child's likes and dislikes, what motivates him and how well developed are his self-help skills. A report on the child's medical history may contain information, such as whether the child has been in hospital for long periods. There may also be reports from any previous school the child has attended.

Provision

Where a pupil who is deafblind has some vision, certain strategies and resources mentioned in Chapter 6, 'Visual impairment', can be considered, such as low vision aids suitable lighting. If the deafblind pupil has some hearing, then some of the suggestions made in Chapter 5, 'Hearing impairment', can be considered, such as making every effort to provide a suitable listening environment.

The curriculum and cross-curricular skills

The overall curriculum for pupils who are deafblind will be broad and well designed and will include support such as the use as necessary of manual signing or Moon (a tactile medium based on a simplified raised line adaptation of the Roman print alphabet that may be used for pupils unable to learn Braille).

The curriculum may draw on developmental models, especially models of early communication. It will take full account of the importance of the environment, the communication partners and other 'systems' influences. Opportunities for free play and self-occupation between adult led tasks are considered important as is the opportunity for the pupil to engage in activities he appears to enjoy or in which he, at least, is willing to participate (Pease, 2000: 83–118).

Cross-curricular skills and understanding may be audited and recorded using a skills matrix (set out in columns and rows) presenting a plan of how key targets are integrated across curriculum areas (e.g. Hodges, 2000: 177). The left-hand column might list regular or daily activities such as 'morning greeting' or 'drink'. A key target such as 'choosing between two activities' might head the other columns, with elements listed below to show how the target is applied in different situations. In 'morning greeting' the choice might be between greeting by a 'sign' or a 'song', while in the drink sessions the choice might be between 'apple' or 'biscuit'. As targets and their elements are identified in the columns, the rows indicate how a particular activity contributes to the targets.

Communication

Pedagogy

General requirements

Factors impeding communication for deafblind pupils include 'direct effects of sensory impairment: effects of motor impairment; [and] effects of ill health and medication'. There are several things lacking which hinder communication: 'lack of opportunities to interact; lack of interactive strategies; lack of information; [and] lack of knowledge about the world'. Other factors are: 'poor self-image; impaired communication from other people; and "doing for" the child' (Aitken, 2000: 40).

The teacher uses her knowledge of the ways communication and interactions typically develop in children to inform setting suitable learning goals. The school also provides opportunities to interact naturally in the context of activities that have meaning for the deafblind pupil. At the same time, the teacher will take account of the specific ways in which the child who is deafblind develops, identifying and building on tiny responses and idiosyncratic behaviours, and perhaps using object cues to signal activities. The teacher should use every opportunity and avenue to enable the child to understand that he, the child, can make things happen.

Some approaches to encourage communication

Among approaches aimed at encouraging and developing communication are: cocreative communication, resonance work, coactive movement and signing, burst-pause activities, routines and 'scripts' and hand-over-hand work. An important theme of such approaches is the opportunity for the adult to encourage and develop the child's competence and sense of action or 'agency'.

Cocreative communication emphasises the importance of the relationship between the child and the communication partner, which has been aptly described as 'symmetrical' (Nafstad and Rodbrøe, 1999). It has been stated that one of the roles of partners is to recognise the deafblind pupil as an extraordinary version of oneself, leading to a more equal relationship.

Resonance work (van Dijk, 1989) tends to be an initial form of encouragement of communication that involves an adult reflecting back to the child, the child's movements or vocalisations, the idea being that this encourages the child's awareness of self. In other words, the adult resonates the child's actions and vocalisations, continuing when the child continues and stopping when the child stops.

In coactive movement (another aspect of van Dijk's work) the child tends to be more aware of the adult and of the idea of interchange than is the case with resonance work. The adult and the child are in close bodily contact: for example, the child may be sitting on the adult's lap. The movements (e.g. swaying from side to side a number of times, or bouncing on the adult's lap a number of times) are carried out in a sequence until the child is familiar with them. Once the child has grasped the pattern, the adult can evoke 'signal behaviour', for example by interrupting the sequence, observing the pupil's reaction, and responding immediately to reinforce the signal (e.g. Pease, 2000: 76). The closeness of the physical contact is gradually lessened and the pupil may hold the adult's hands for coactive movement.

Regarding burst-pause activity, the adult ensures that the child has time to respond and provides prompts for further activity. Initially, the adult leads the activity, then stops, allowing the pupil to pick up the activity. The adult then keeps the activity going until the next pause. For example, if the child is making a cooking mixture, the adult will first lead then stop to allow the child to continue. The adult will then encourage the activity until the next pause.

Routines might be built into mealtimes or a movement sequence. So long as they do not become over rigid, routines provide security and predictability, helping learning because they involve repetition. In giving a framework in which a child can come to recognise sequences, routines can encourage a pupil to signal as he anticipates the next part of a series of events. Where routines are intended to encourage early communication, it is helpful if they are predictable and frequent, and occur at the same place and time, perhaps each day.

In the early stages of developing routines, 'scripts' help ensure they are followed closely. Scripts involve recording and following an action sequence such as a mealtime routine in steps in which adult actions and child actions are specified. Choice can be built into these steps so they are not rigid and, as routines become more established, further options can be provided for pupils by varying the structure through changing what is anticipated.

In working hand-over-hand, the adult moves the child's hands slowly and with sensitivity to show him how to do something. The adult is careful to respond to any signs of discomfort or resistance from the child. If a child's main source of information is his hands, he may not like another person 'taking them over' and may resist. The adult can encourage hand-over-hand learning, but should not of course enforce it.

Using non-symbolic communication

Non-symbolic communication (e.g. reflexive responses, signals, place or object cues) is direct and does not rely on symbolic understanding. *Reflexive responses* are very basic responses to the external environment, or (as in the case of hunger) to the internal bodily environment. Examples are stilling, changes in body tone, and cooing or shouting. While the child has no control over these responses and they have not been taught, they can suggest what a child is aware of and his likes and dislikes. *Signals* are intentional responses to the environment that have a particular aim. They may include, depending on the child's mobility, picking up a desired object or pushing an object away, rolling to one side to get away from an activity, or pulling at a person's hand. While such actions may not always be intentionally communicative, where the teacher and others respond as if they were, the child may learn they have a certain effect. The child is encouraged to attract attention before making such a signal. *Place or object cues* are used in structured routines so that certain objects and places come to typify activities for the child. When this link is made, the child can, for example, use the object to indicate a desire for an activity.

Using symbolic communication

Symbolic communication involves something standing for a concept, such as an object, picture, a manual sign or the spoken word, allowing the child to refer to things other than in the here and now.

Object cues, where certain objects come to typify activities for the child, have already been mentioned as examples of non-symbolic communication. It was stated that, when a link is made between an object and an activity, the child might use the object to indicate, for example, a desire to participate in an activity. Understanding of an *object of reference* may develop from this. The object of reference may be used to indicate an event or activity when it may not be happening in the present, perhaps to remember something that has happened (a ribbon to remember a past gift) or something to happen later (a piece of swimming costume to indicate that the child will go swimming later that day) or importantly to indicate a choice. The object of reference is not the actual object; for example, it is not the real gift that was received, but is symbolic of the object or event. Calendar boxes, a development from the work of van Dijk (e.g. Pease, 2000: 77–79) use sequences of objects of reference to indicate the order of activities and events in the pupil's day, acting as a sort of tangible timetable. Tactile objects of reference can be used to: indicate a proposed activity, signal a proposed change of activity, help the pupil anticipate a task or help the pupil make a choice/decide an activity.

Tactile symbols may be used where a pupil understands objects of reference but has difficulties seeing or interpreting pictures and visual symbols.

Developing from an understanding of tactile objects of reference, some pupils may be able to use tactile symbols such as Moon script to recognise letters or words.

Parts of an object may be used so long as they convey what is intended. A length of leather rein can indicate horse riding. Symbols involving texture or shape can also be used as when different shapes represent different timetabled subjects or activities. Various textures can represent different times of day (morning, afternoon, night). Materials with raised outlines, perhaps using a Thermoform machine, can represent items or events, and can act as a link to literacy using Moon script.

Miniature objects may be used, such as a toy horse to represent the activity of horse riding. The adult will need to make sure that the pupil is making a link between the real horse and the activity and the miniature object, perhaps by encouraging the child to explore the miniature object while involved in horse riding and gradually introducing the miniature object to stand for the activity when it is scheduled later in the day.

For a child who is deafblind, using manual sign language may involve drawing with the finger the shapes of the letters of a word on another person's hand. Another form of signing involves the communication partner tapping a position on the other person's fingers and palm to correspond to different letters of the alphabet. For such signing to be effective, the school needs to take into account the pupil's cognitive, physical and visual skills. In finger spelling, words and sentences from speech are spelled out using a particular hand shape for each alphabetic letter. The deafblind manual alphabet is based on the visual alphabet with modifications to enable the sender to spell out onto the receiver's left hand. Finger spelling can also be used in its own right or to supplement manual sign language by spelling out names or features for which there may be no sign in the system. In co-active signing, the adult guides the child's hands through the shape and movement of the sign.

A communication book is a further aid. It is a collection of tactile symbols on the pages of a book that the child can turn to convey different messages. The symbols can be accompanied by written messages so the child can turn to a particular page and show it to others who do not understand the symbol system to convey the message. For example, in a shop, the book can be used to request items.

Communication during an activity and group work

Pease (2000: 52) describes communications during a cookery lesson with a student aged 16 years who is profoundly deaf and thought to be totally blind. Strategies included preceding the visit to the kitchen by the teacher putting objects of reference on a board and the teacher putting the student's hand on her walking frame to signal that it is time to go to the kitchen. The teacher puts the student's hand on the door handle to indicate, 'here is the kitchen' and places the student's hand on the chopping board to convey, 'here are the ingredients'. When the teacher taps the student's hand on the student's chest it indicates, 'you do this please'. When the teacher puts the student's hand on the teacher's chest, it indicates, 'I'll do this bit'. The student's signals include standing up ('I know where I'm going); sitting and co-operating ('I know what I'm doing') and shaking her head from side to side ('I'm not happy').

Group work requires careful structuring for the child who can neither see nor hear what other participants are saying or doing. The pupil will need to be taught behaviours such as turn taking; when it is time to listen and to speak and similar features of group work that other pupils will tend to pick up with less effort. For such reasons, the child who is deafblind may initially sit close to the teacher or another adult who can prompt the child as necessary and provide cues as to what is expected.

Mobility

Improving mobility begins with developing trust with a child and building the child's confidence and motivation to move. For deafblind children with additional difficulties, such as physical disability or disorders of movement and communication, clearly mobility is going to be more difficult and any aspect of the environment that can facilitate mobility needs to be considered. The provision of a tactile environment recognises that it is important for a pupil who is deafblind to be able to explore and build up a mental map of each space. Strips of carpet, textured surfaces and handrails can be used to mark out different spaces and levels. It is helpful if furniture is kept in the same positions, routes through a room or building are obstacle free, and tactile clues are added to objects such as specific lockers and doors. Tactile pictures can also be used as wall clues.

Finding out information and encouraging meaningful experiences

Being unable to access information that is readily available to people who have sight and vision makes it much more difficult for the deafblind child to build up knowledge of the world, which in turn affects communication. Perception, interpretation and learning are limited, and it is therefore often necessary to provide experiences in a more structured and planned way. The teacher will ensure that information is provided to encourage the deafblind pupil to exercise choice, for example by deciding on an item of clothing according to texture. Also important are, 'structured opportunities within which to interact with people, the physical environment, objects, places and activities (Aitken, 2000: 23). Part of this is building routines to encourage anticipation and help the pupil begin to make sense of a sequence of events.

It is important a pupil who is deafblind recognises an activity, works with other people and learns from experience. To accomplish this, the pupil has to be able to identify and recognise an object, the activity performed, the time when it is done or the person with whom it is done. Identifying and recognising a place in which activities often occur is part of this sort of orientation too. To help a pupil identify and recognise an object, the adults may all agree to identify the same distinctive features of the object. An adult coactively lifting a hairbrush with the child and feeling the bristles and then the handle before brushing the hair can help the child identify the item (Hodges, 2000: 195). Gradually, different hairbrushes may be introduced; identifying the same features so that the pupil's notion of a brush can be extended. A place such as a room can be identified by encouraging the pupil to move in the room and by indicating features that are distinctive to the room, such as a chopping board in a kitchen or a bed in the bedroom. Identifying others is helped if the person has a feature that is identified and recognised, for example a necklace that they always wear and that is held for the child to touch as an indication of who the person is.

Further familiarity with items, their use and the time when things are done can be combined in such occasions as mealtimes. The pupil may get knives, forks and spoons from a cutlery drawer, identify each and lay the table for lunch.

Resources

The emphasis is on exploring and understanding the environment and aspects within it, rather than on specialist resources. Where the child has residual vision or residual hearing, then some of the physical resources mentioned in the chapters on visual impairment and hearing impairments will be considered.

Therapy/care

Speech and language therapy and occupational therapy are among the therapies provided.

Organisation

Co-ordinating multi-professional contributions

Professionals involved with children who are deafblind and his parents may include:

- specialist teacher;
- other teachers;
- home health visitor;
- general practitioner/general medical doctor;
- ear, nose and throat specialist;
- ophthalmologist and
- orthoptist (a technician providing exercises aimed at restoring or developing the co-ordination of the eye system);

- a technician dealing with hearing aids;
- audiologist;
- speech and language pathologist/therapist;
- occupational therapist;
- social worker and
- school psychologist/educational psychologist.

When it is remembered that several of the particular personnel with whom the child and parent have had contact with over the years may move on, the number of people involved is daunting. One implication is that it is important for the school to draw together information and advice from these many sources and use them to make educational and other judgements about what will enable the child to learn and develop best.

With a secretariat in New Delhi, India, Deafblind International promotes services for deafblind people and their web site includes a link to a publication 'Guidelines on Best Practice for Service Provision to Deafblind People' (www.deafblindinternational.org/).

Thinking points

Readers may wish to consider:

- steps that may be taken to develop further understanding of provision for deafblind children, such as school visits to observe provision, discussion with specialist teachers for deafblind children and further reading.

Key texts

Sense (2004) *Reaching Out: A Toolkit for Deafblind Children's Services*. London, Sense.
This booklet indicates the importance of social care services to the well-being of children who are deafblind and their families and to their social needs outside school. It briefly explains the nature of deafblindness; the impact of deafblindness on communication, independence skills and sensory information; and how local services should identify and assess deafblind children. Explains the range of services that are appropriate and the importance of co-ordination.

Smith, M. and Levack, N. (1997) *Teaching Students with Visual and Multiple Impairments: A Resource Guide*. Texas, Texas School for the Blind and Visually Impaired (www.tsbvi.edu).
Includes assessment guidelines, strategies for developing Individual Education Plans, teaching and transition planning and information on adapting materials and environments.

Chapter 8

Orthopaedic impairment and motor disorders

Introduction

This chapter considers orthopaedic impairment and motor disorders. Orthopaedic impairment refers to disorders of bones and joints and associated muscles, tendons and ligaments and physical disability. Motor disorders may be associated with neuromotor impairment (involving the central nervous system and affecting the child's ability to use, feel, control and move certain parts of the body).

This chapter therefore considers several orthopaedic impairments (spinal curvature; limb deficiencies and talipes). Also considered is juvenile rheumatoid arthritis, a chronic inflammatory disease. The chapter looks at several conditions considered under the umbrella of neuromotor disorders (muscular dystrophy; cerebral palsy; and neural tube defects). Developmental co-ordination disorder, another neuromotor disorder, is considered in a separate chapter. With regard to each, this chapter defines the condition and considers its prevalence, causal factors and implications for provision. It then outlines some general points in relation to provision for students with orthopaedic impairment and motor disorders regarding curriculum and assessment; pedagogy; resources; therapy and care and organisation.

Orthopaedic impairment and motor disorders defined

The prefix 'ortho' means 'straight' or 'correct' and in the term 'orthopaedics' conveys the notion of a 'straight child', because this form of surgery was initially concerned with the correction of children's skeletal deformities. Orthopaedics, today, is a branch of medical science concerned with disorders of the bones and joints (and the muscles, tendons and ligaments associated with them). It can involve setting fractured bones, putting on casts or other orthotic devices, treating conditions of the joints (e.g. arthritis, dislocations, back problems); treating skeletal birth defects and replacing/repairing joints (e.g. the hip).

In the United States of America, under federal law (the Individuals with Disabilities Education Act or IDEA) an orthopaedic impairment is defined as a severe impairment adversely affecting the child's educational performance. The Code of Federal Regulations definition is:

> impairments caused by congenital anomaly (e.g. club foot, absence of some member, etc.), impairments caused by disease (e.g. poliomyelitis, bone tuberculosis, etc.) and impairments from other causes (e.g. cerebral palsy, amputations, and fractures or burns causing contractures)
>
> (34 CFR, section 300.7 [c] [8], 1999).

It will be seen that under this definition, the term 'orthopaedic' is not used strictly and embraces both orthopaedic conditions and also neuromotor impairment. However, both types of impairments can limit movement (the type of limitation is different) and broadly the provision of education, therapy and care has similarities. Also, a child with a neurological impairment causing him to be unable to move limbs can develop orthopaedic impairments. General causes of orthopaedic impairments may be congenital or acquired and involve deformity, disease, injury or surgery.

Spinal curvature

Definition

Three types of spinal curvature are identified: scoliosis, kyphosis and lordosis. In scoliosis, there is a lateral (sideways) curvature of the spine which ressembles an 's' shaped curve. As a result, one hip is higher than the other and one shoulder blade more prominent than the other. With kyphosis, there is a posterior curvature of the upper spine (stooped shoulders) leading to shortened stature and decreased lung capacity. Lordosis is a forward curvature of the lower spine when it is viewed from the side.

Causal factors

Three types of causal factors are identified: congenital (abnormal development of spine in the foetus), neuromuscular (localised muscle weakness or muscle weakness from a neuromotor disorder) and idiopathic (no known cause). The symptoms are somewhat predictable, given the nature of the condition: shortened stature, altered posture and decreased lung capacity.

Prevalence

The prevalence of spinal curvature is difficult to determine, as it is associated with other conditions in varying degrees.

Provision

A body brace or jacket may be used to correct the posture. Corrective surgery may fuse some of the spinal vertebrae and/or insert metal rods in the back to help the child maintain a more upright posture. Where pain killing medication is prescribed, the school might administer this.

Pupils may experience low self-esteem because of their physical difference, and aspects of personal and social education and pastoral support including counselling can help improve this. If the pupil requires frequent hospital treatment he may miss schoolwork, although there should be teaching in the hospital for pupils who are staying for longer periods. Pupils may experience pain and as a result become very tired, so the curriculum could require adapting.

Some pupils may not be able to take part in the usual school physical activities. They may not be able to participate fully in physical education lessons or an adapted course may be developed. Rough physical play could be too risky and a quiet place for break time leisure activities might be helpful. Seating may need to be adapted or specially moulded seating designed to provide for difficulties with posture. The pupil might require extra time to travel around school, so flexible start/finishing times for lessons could be adopted.

Limb deficiencies

Definition and causal factors

Limb deficiency refers to the absence or partial loss of a limb. The causes of congenital limb deficiencies are not always known but among identified causes are chromosome defects and constriction in the uterus during pregnancy. Acquired limb deficiency may be owing to accident or disease or may be part of surgery to prepare a limb for prosthesis.

Prevalence

Congenital limb deficiency occurs in about 1 in every 2,000 births, with acquired limb loss (amputations) occurring less frequently (Scott, 1989).

Provision

Pupils may be fitted with artificial limbs (prostheses). Depending on the particular limb deficiency, the pupil may use a wheelchair, crutches or a walking aid. Children are taught to use any prosthesis effectively from an early age. The teacher will work with the occupational or physical therapist finding ways to help the correct use of the prosthesis and encouraging independence as well as ensuring that the environment is supportive, for example, seating and desk surface height facilitate efficient and comfortable movement. Where a large skin area is lost (for example where the legs are absent) the child may find it difficult to regulate body temperature and become dehydrated so that it may be necessary to add or remove items of clothing (Mason and Wright, 1994).

The student should be encouraged to be as independent as possible, but children whose use of the prosthesis is recent and who have little experience of it may need help with the toilet, dressing and eating. Older pupils could benefit from strategies to support and develop self-esteem through pastoral support and counselling. This may be helpful if a pupil loses a limb through accident or medical necessity when it can be difficult to adjust emotionally both for the child and his family. Adapted seating might be necessary and the use of a lift or stair lift to gain access to upper parts of the school building.

A pupil may use the mouth or feet to write or a prosthesis. If a pupil's writing speed is affected by the loss of a limb, arrangements for examinations could allow extra time, taping of responses or the use of a scribe.

Talipes

Definition

The various kinds of talipes, sometimes called 'club foot', are conditions present at birth in which the foot or both feet are twisted out of position or shape. In the most common type, 'talipes equinovarus', the heel is turned inwards and the remainder of the foot bent downwards and inwards.

Prevalence

Talipes affects about 1 baby in every 900.

Causal factors

The exact cause of talipes is not known, although most cases are thought to involve pressure on the baby's feet from the mother's uterus late in the course of pregnancy which may be related to there being insufficient amniotic fluid surrounding the foetus (oligohydramnios). A genetic factor is suggested by the fact that relatives of affected individuals have a higher incidence of the condition. Talipes equinovarus is twice as common in boys as girls.

Provision

Physiotherapy involving the manipulation of the foot and ankle is used to treat talipes. A plaster cast, a metal splint or adhesive strapping may be used to hold the foot into a correct position. Where these methods are ineffective, surgery may be used to lengthen the tight ligaments and tendons after which the limb is immobilised in a plaster cast for several months. The child having a plaster cast will have a wheelchair with an extended leg support.

In school, provision will be made to enable the pupil requiring a wheel chair with a leg extension to have suitable access to the school's facilities including halls, other rooms, toilet facilities and his own classroom, which might be on the ground floor. Within the classroom, the arrangement of furniture will facilitate easy movement in and out of class and around it, and the height of tables and desks will allow access for the extended leg.

Curriculum adaptations will be required for physical education lessons where challenging activities will be provided that allow the pupil to participate safely. Where physiotherapy is required, while this is integrated into school provision, it does not have to be assumed that physiotherapy is the alternative activity when other pupils do physical education. Routines and activities under the oversight of a physiotherapist and occupational therapist may also be integrated into different periods in the school day.

Juvenile rheumatoid arthritis

Definition

Rheumatoid arthritis is a chronic systemic disease characterised by inflammatory changes occurring throughout the body's connective tissues. It is associated with pain of the joints, stiffness and swelling. The causes are unknown although it is thought there are several causal factors. Juvenile arthritis, also called Still's disease, fluctuates in its effects so that various joints may be affected and children may be better on some days than others.

Prevalence

Prevalence for juvenile rheumatoid arthritis is about 1 child in every 1,000.

Causal factors

The causes of juvenile arthritis are not securely known.

Provision

Anti-inflammatory drugs can ease the condition. Physiotherapy and occupational therapy help to improve the function of joints as well as easing pain. Occupational therapy advice may relate to daily living activities, school tasks and leisure activities and the protection of joints.

Provision in school is sensitive to the changing nature of the condition and responds accordingly. As with other conditions resulting in pain, the child may become very tired and motivation may be low. The fluctuating impact may mean that for some of the time the pupil can move around satisfactorily and be relatively free of pain, while at other times he could require a wheelchair, perhaps one that is powered, and might require regular breaks from written work.

Curriculum implications include provision to adapt to fine motor movements being affected for tasks such as handwriting and dressing. Programmes for movement, physiotherapy and occupational therapy are often integrated into the overall curriculum in a planned way so that other work is balanced and the arrangements are not *ad hoc*. In personal and social development, the restrictions in movements can have implications for personal hygiene and arrangements will be made for discrete support and help as necessary.

Classroom organisation may involve ensuring that the child is sitting in a suitable posture with a sloping writing surface and the chair and table at a suitable height.

As with many conditions, juvenile arthritis can lead to absences from school, and the school will make arrangement for home tuition to support the child's return to school. School friendships may also be disrupted by absences and the school can seek strategies to alleviate the effects of this, for example encouraging members of the child's class to write to the absent pupil.

Muscular dystrophy

Definition

Muscular dystrophies are types of genetic, progressive muscular disorders in which breakdown of muscle fibre leads to weak and wasted muscles. While some types affect both sexes, Duchenne muscular dystrophy, the most common form, affects boys exclusively. The life expectancy of individuals with muscular dystrophy is shortened, some dying in their late teens, although, because of developments in scoliosis treatments and pulmonary care, life expectancies are increasing. The main symptom is a gradual weakening of the muscles because they are damaged and not regenerated adequately, so that the muscle is replaced by fibrous tissue and fat. There may be times of remission, as well as periods of rapid deterioration.

Prevalence

Muscular dystrophy is rare, the commonest type, Duchenne muscular dystrophy, affecting around one in 3,300 boys (Emery, 1991).

Causal factors

Duchenne muscular dystrophy is inherited through a recessive, sex-linked gene so that only males can be affected and only females can pass on the condition. Other forms include: limb-girdle, facioscapulohumeral and Becker's, which affect children and adults and are the result of autosomal or sex-linked defects.

Provision

Because lack of physical activity tends to increase the progression of symptoms, students with Duchenne muscular dystrophy are encouraged and supported to be ambulatory as long as possible (Heller *et al.*, 1996). Pupils may require aids to mobility such as callipers and walking aids and, as the condition progresses, will need a manual or powered wheelchair. Some children have metal rods inserted surgically in the back to help maintain an upright posture. Children with muscular dystrophy require occupational therapy and physiotherapy.

As the condition progresses, the pupil may need increasing amounts of help with activities such as using the toilet, dressing and eating. Later, one-to-one support, perhaps from a teaching assistant, may be necessary throughout the day, both during and outside lesson times. Particular sensitivity is needed from others as the student reaches adolescence and may be becoming increasingly dependent, as peers are getting increasingly independent. If parents agree, counselling may be offered, perhaps by local support groups to help the pupil come to terms with shorter life expectancy.

Mobility is aided as required, arrangements being similar to those for individuals with spina bifida, including wheelchair access and flexible arrival and departure times for lessons. The pupil may need support in class to help him use equipment and resources (Kenward, 1997: 34).

Most children with muscular dystrophy have levels of intelligence typical of other children of the same age. But as the illness progresses, the pupil may be more frequently absent from school and progress in school subjects may therefore be slower. Generally, especially as the condition progresses, the pupil will tire easily and the whole curriculum may be reviewed to ensure activities and the way lessons are dispersed throughout the day and the week keep demands realistic. Homework is often waived or adapted, for example accepting taped oral responses rather than written ones (e.g. Bigge *et al.*, 2001: 55). Handwriting may be affected as the condition weakens the arms and hands. For practical activities, the teacher needs to ensure work is pitched within the range of which the pupil is physically capable. Computer technology may be used as an alternative way of recording work and adaptations such as keyboards with larger keys and keyboard guards and voice-activated computers can be beneficial.

If the pupil has rods surgically inserted in the back, he is vulnerable if knocked, so that contact sports cannot be played. In examinations a scribe may be used and extra time allowed and with careers guidance particular sensitivity is needed.

Cerebral palsy

Definition

Cerebral palsy has been defined as 'a disorder of movement and posture that is due to non-progressive abnormality of the immature brain' (Kurtz, 1992: 441).

It is a physical impairment affecting movement and has different forms: spacticity, athetosis and ataxia. Spacticity is characterised by disordered control of movement. Athetosis involves some loss of posture control and a tendency to make involuntary movements. Ataxia is typified by unsteady gait and problems with balance, and sometimes a child with ataxic cerebral palsy has irregular speech and tremorous hand movements. A child may experience a mixture of the above types with different effects. About 60 per cent of individuals with cerebral palsy also have some degree of cognitive impairment (Turnbull *et al.*, 2002). Epilepsy affects about 30 per cent of children with cerebral palsy (Capute and Accardo, 1996). Symptoms may include:

- quadriplegia (all four limbs are affected), hemiplegia (one side of the body is affected) or paraplegia (trunk and legs are affected); diplegia (the same parts on both sides of the body, either arms or legs are affected);
- loss of control of movement and increased reflex activity;
- limited range of movement;
- still and/or immobile legs;
- poor control of the head;
- difficulty with articulation and
- problems with visual perception.

Prevalence

Cerebral palsy is evident in around 2 cases in every 1,000 live births and the prevalence rate appears constant despite advances in pre-natal and antenatal care (Heller *et al.*, 1996).

Causal factors

Intrauterine causes of cerebral palsy include brain malformation, infection and lack of oxygen (anoxia). Among perinatal causes (during birth) are infection and poor oxygen supply. After birth, cerebral palsy may be caused by traumatic brain injury, an infection of the central nervous system, or situations limiting oxygen supply such as near drowning or suffocation.

Provision

The treatment of cerebral palsy may include the use of orthotics (e.g. braces or splints), medication (e.g. muscle relaxants) or surgery (e.g. to release contractures) (Pellegrino, 1997). Most children require a structured programme of occupational therapy and physical therapy. Pupils using a wheelchair may need to spend part of the day standing, using specialised equipment. Advice is sought from physical therapists and occupational therapists. There are also particular medical implications where the child also has epilepsy.

Some pupils may need help with many tasks such as dressing, using the toilet and eating, while others will require limited help with only some activities. Where feeding and swallowing assessment and programmes are necessary, these include correct positioning of the child, using suitable feeding utensils and choosing appropriate food or drink (e.g. Bigge *et al.*, 2001: 504–535).

Sensitivity is needed in adolescence. Most forms of cerebral palsy are not progressive and the student will not become more dependent, but as the activities of peers become more advanced, pupils may become or feel more 'different'. Regarding mobility, the pupil may need wheelchair access and flexibility of arrival and departure times for lessons. Also, the pupil may need to sit at a desk with ankles at right angles resting on the floor or on a foot block. Particular care is needed if the pupil is seated on the floor, as posture is important and chairs are more comfortable.

Teachers also need to be aware that the movements of pupils with cerebral palsy may be characterised by so-called primitive reflexes which are involuntary movements originating in the brain stem. These may require the teacher to help the pupil maintain positions conversant with learning and taking part in the lesson. Such support and help will be enhanced where the teacher is properly trained by and liaises with a physical therapist and where special seating requirements are assessed and provided by an occupational therapist.

Help or/and adapted equipment may be needed for practical tasks, depending on the degree of the pupil's disability. The use of information and communication technology can aid in recording work. Also, there are other alternative recording strategies such as using a tape recorder for some activities or using an interactive whiteboard. Switches may be used.

Children with severe forms of the disability may require augmented communication devices such as voice synthesisers, which the teacher and teaching assistant may use under the guidance of a speech and language pathologist/therapist. Where the pupil has speech and language difficulties that may not be as severe, this may involve the child working on a programme developed by the speech and language therapist and delivered by support staff. Special arrangements may be made for examinations, such as an amanuensis and/or extra time. For further information about cerebral palsy and guidance on provision see Best and Bigge (2001: 92–117).

Neural tube defects

Definitions

Congenital malformations of the spine, brain or vertebrae are collectively referred to as neural tube defects. The three major types are:

- encephalocele (in which the skull is malformed and part of the brain material finds its way through the malformation);

- anencephaly (in which the brain fails to develop beyond the brain stem and the baby rarely lives beyond infancy) and
- spina bifida, the most common type and the main focus of the remainder of this section.

Spina bifida is a condition in which one or more spinal vertebrae fail to close properly, exposing the nerves ('bifid' means 'divided in two'). It is further classified as spina bifida occulta, meningocele and myelomenigocele. In spina bifida occulta, the spinal cord does not protrude and there is only a small defect in the bony covering of the spinal cord leaving little or no external signs of the condition. With meningocele, the meninges (membranes around the brain and spinal cord) protrude through the malformed spinal opening. Myelomenigocele is the severest and commonest form of spina bifida in which the meninges and spinal cord protrude. Associated symptoms include: total/partial paralysis of the legs; paralysis of the bladder and bowel; difficulties with activities involving the arms and hands; poor fine motor skills; poor balance; problems with blood circulation and visual impairment. Many children with spina bifida have hydrocephalus, a condition in which the obstructed flow of cerebral spinal fluid leads to the enlargement of the brain ventricles. Hydrocephalus may be congenital or may develop later (Griebel *et al.*, 1991). It is frequently controlled by a 'shunt' (a fine tube inserted in the ventricles to drain cerebrospinal fluid away, usually to the chest or abdominal cavity).

Prevalence

Neural tube defects occur more frequently in females than in males (Liptak, 1997). In the United Kingdom, about 30 babies in every 100,000 born have spina bifida, although the numbers are declining with the wide use of screening and prevention programmes.

Causal factors

The causes of spina bifida remain unknown, although both genetic and environmental factors appear to be implicated and vitamin deficiency seems to be a major factor.

Provision

For myelomenigocele, surgical treatment begins soon after birth, removing the protruding sac and closing the open area along the spinal column. Often some days later, further surgery is undertaken to place in the brain a shunt which helps avoid brain damage caused by cerebrospinal fluid pushing brain matter against the inside of the skull. Orthopaedic treatment helps prevent deformities of the spine, hips and legs and may involve standing and prone positioning to help prevent muscle contractures.

Braces and splints are used to help correct or reduce deformities. Braces are often used to support the trunk and legs and aid walking. For children unable to walk a wheelchair may be needed. The physical therapist helps the child in walking correctly, in using mobility aids and other matters. The occupational therapist helps the child develop self-care and independence skills, which may include working with the family and others in connection with catheterisation of the bladder and programmes to achieve regular bowel movements, working to improve school-related skills such as visual-motor co-ordination and dexterity for writing and encouraging appropriate leisure activities. Procedures in connection with tube feeding, catheterisation and colostomy/ileostomy care are summarised by Bigge *et al.*, (2001: 547–551).

Some health implications require immediate referral to a doctor or hospital, for example, if the shunt is blocked, perhaps giving rise to symptoms of drowsiness, disorientation, memory problems, squint and headache.

The school can ensure facilities are available that enable the pupil to be as little constrained by the condition as is practicable, for example providing adapted toilet facilities and help with dressing and help for younger pupils to change their catheter. Aiding mobility might include wheelchair access to the school building and classrooms and sufficient room to manoeuvre comfortably around the classroom. Further practical suggestions include seating near the door so there is easier access to and from the classroom, and flexibility in times of arrival and departure from lessons to avoid times when the corridors are crowded with pupils (Kenward, 1997: 32).

Motor difficulties and spatial problems may lead to particular challenges with handwriting and number work, and, while encouraging as much independent work as possible, a teaching assistant/classroom aid may help with practical tasks or act as an amanuensis. Similarly, an amanuensis may be required when examinations are taken. The use of computer technology can provide an alternative means of presenting and recording work.

While some pupils with spina bifida attain at the same academic levels as children who do not have the condition, others, especially if they also have hydrocephalus, may have cognitive impairment. Absences from school can also lower the pupil's attainment. The student may have speech and language difficulties, including difficulties comprehending language that may require speech and language therapy, either directly or as a consultant working with and through other adults. If a visual impairment makes it difficult for the pupils to judge distance or direction, multi-sensory teaching can help by drawing on other senses.

Orthopaedic impairment and motor disorders – general points

Several examples of orthopaedic impairment were outlined in this chapter to illustrate the sorts of conditions involved. Spinal curvature can affect stature and lung capacity and although it can be caused by or may be associated with conditions (such as spina bifida) that have other implications the focus was on the effects of the physical disability of spinal curvature, what ever is cause. With spinal damage, the main focus was consequent paralysis. Limb loss or damage; talipes and juvenile rheumatoid arthritis were similarly considered in terms of physical limitations associated with them.

The occurrence of an orthopaedic impairment does not necessarily lead to the child requiring special educational provision. For example, it cannot be assumed that cognitive development is affected for although pupils with physical disabilities may also have neurological or sensory impairments or cognitive impairment, the intelligence levels of pupils with physical disability cover the full range (e.g. Stieler, 1998). The examples considered allow some broader generalisations to be made about providing for children with orthopaedic impairment educationally and otherwise.

Curriculum

The curriculum will be reviewed to ensure the best involvement and support of the pupil in activities including art, technology and science where special equipment may be necessary. Within safety requirements, many activities may still be available in physical education for pupils with an orthopaedic impairment and joining in activities will be the first option. Often, games and the rules of games can be adapted to ensure the participation of all pupils. Where this is not possible or inadvisable, alternative activities can be arranged that lead towards similar learning goals. The teacher may seek advice from the physical therapist and occupational therapist and may work with the physical therapist to develop programmes that will engage pupils with physical disabilities. Where special programmes are necessary to develop skills or encourage movement, these are planned into the pupil's school day to ensure that the pupil still encounters a balanced range of subjects.

Pedagogy

Pedagogy for pupils with orthopaedic impairment is not in itself distinctive from the pedagogy for children not having a disability/disorder. The issue is gaining access to the curriculum and to learning activities and in this, the use of specialist resources is important as the section below illustrates.

Resources

This section owes much to the comprehensive and illustrated account of resources and their use provided by Bigge et al., (2001). The choice of resources and their use for children with orthopaedic impairment play a large part in appropriate provision, and guidance from the physical therapist or the occupational therapist will often be necessary. Resources are used to ensure that children are correctly positioned, for example, using pads and cushions or specially constructed adapted seat inserts and by adopting alternative positioning throughout the day, for example using a sidelyer, wedge or tricycle with a built-up back or standing. For comfortable and correct seating, consideration is given to the position of the pelvis, and supports may be used for the trunk and shoulders, for example using vest type supports or H straps. An abductor or leg separator may be used which may be part of the seat or a separate item of equipment. Alternative seating may include a chair without legs, a chair with arms and a footrest and corner seats (ibid.: 199, 201–204).

In general, furniture will take account of pupil's stature and need for good posture and support. During the teaching of subjects such as science where pupils might sit on high stools, a stool with a back support and arms may be used. Tables can be used which adjust to different heights and with surfaces that can be angled. Adaptable tables are commercially produced for certain subjects such as art and technology (e.g. Hull Learning Services, 2004: 83–4).

Hoists and other devices may be needed to support safe moving of the student. Among assistive walking devices are a PVC pipe walker and crutches, either forearm or underarm. Manual or powered wheelchairs may be used or toys as mobility aids, such as a hand-propelled wheeler. In different countries, supported by legislation or guidance or both, there is a trend to ensure that pupils with orthopaedic impairments have better access to classrooms and other facilities. This may involve wheelchair access ramps and continuous areas of smooth floor surfaces to enable movement.

Separate rooms where personal care procedures can be carried out in privacy and adapted toilets and sufficient room in clutter free corridors to allow easy access are typical requirements. Toilets will be adapted to take account of various requirements of students with orthopaedic impairments, including medical needs such as changing a colostomy bag. Where a specially moulded toilet seat was needed, an occupational therapist would advise and help arrange this. In the classrooms and elsewhere, there will need to be sufficient room for a pupil requiring a wheelchair or a walking frame or sticks to aid mobility to move around easily and space to keep equipment such as walking frames to hand but where they will not trip other pupils.

Environmental modifications have been described (Bigge *et al.*, 2001: 213–218) in terms of location of materials and equipment (e.g. a wheelchair backpack or modular stacking trays for storing materials accessible from the pupil's desk); work surface modifications (e.g. a supine stander with a cut-out tray, a wheelchair with elbow supports, or angled work or viewing surfaces) and object modifications. Finnie (1997: 127–160) and others have further delineated object modifications with regard to: object stabilisation (e.g. clamping the bases of items to tables); boundaries (e.g. edges on a wheelchair tray or holders for items); grasping aids (e.g. magnets on a glove for picking up metal items or enlarging items by wrapping tape around them); manipulation aids (e.g. long-handled brushes and combs or large-handled cutlery). The pupil may have his own set of equipments for various subjects modified as necessary, for example, adapted scissors or guillotine scissors, pencil grips. In food preparation lessons, adapted equipment may include special controls on cookers, a kettle tilting device to ensure safer pouring of hot liquids, devices such as food choppers that can be used with one hand, and sinks and cooking surfaces of adjustable height.

Environmental control may involve the use of appliances such as communication devices, computers, or home lighting that may be operated in various ways including electrically, by infrared, radio control or ultra sound. Switches enable the individual to gain some control over the environment and are designed to be operated by different movements and pressures. They can be activated by pushing, pulling, tilting, puffing, eye blinking, voice and so on (Bigge *et al.*, 2001: 219–221).

Therapy and care

The support of services other than education is generally required for the student to function successfully and maintain better life quality (Snell and Brown, 2000). Medical practitioners, physical therapists, occupational therapists, prosthetists and others contribute to the child's well being. Their services may be provided outside the school or within school and often they work in close liaison with teachers, for example where occupational therapists, physical therapists and teachers work together to assess, plan and provide programmes for children in school.

Intimate care procedures might include routines for toileting and hygiene; urostomy and colostomy care; catheterisation and emergency administration of rectal medication. Health care professionals provide training for school staff in intimate care procedures before these are carried out. In different countries, government, local authority and school specific guidance is provided and updated on these matters.

Pastoral care will support the development of high self-esteem and counselling may be available to allow the pupil to talk through issues such as restrictions on activities, developing relationships and so on.

Organisation (including safety procedures)

The school can consider whether having flexible arrival and departure times for lessons would be helpful to enable some pupils with orthopaedic impairment to start their route to the next lesson when corridors were relatively free. If the pupil requires adult oversight of movement between lessons, and he leaves with other students, the adult can keep at a distance that does not inhibit the student's social contact with peers.

Outside classroom, the level of supervision necessary for recess times will be determined to balance safety with encouraging socialisation and independence. This balance may change from time to time, and even from day to day. Similarly, in class where adult support is needed this should be given only as required, encouraging the pupil to develop independence. Where trips and visits are planned, pre-visits can help check details of physical access, for example for wheelchairs or with reference to the height of facilities and displays. Flexible arrangements for pupil absences can include home tuition and emailed work to support home study.

Where there are particular hazards, a risk assessment or similar procedure is carried out which usually involves identifying a potential hazard and taking steps to minimise the risk with reference to all children, a particular group of children or a particular child. Moving and handling some pupils with physical disability has potential hazards and risk assessments may be carried out on these procedures, supported by training for the adults involved. Fire procedures take into account any particular issues arising with, for example, easy wheelchair egress from a fire exit. Safety procedures are followed where adults help students in wheelchairs with steps using devices such as a 'stair climber'. Procedures and responsibilities for administering medication will be clear and supported by staff training as necessary.

Thinking points

Readers may wish to consider with regard to children with orthopaedic impairment:

- the training and supervision that staff will require to effectively educate and support pupils with orthopaedic impairment and how it is ensured that this is up to date;
- the broad and common features of provision for many pupils with orthopaedic impairment, such as wheelchair access and flexible lesson starting and finishing times and
- provision for more specifics to particular conditions.

Key texts

Dewey, D. and Tupper, D. (eds) (2004) *Developmental Motor Disorders: A Neuropsychological Perspective*. New York, The Guilford Press.
A chapter that may be of particular interest is: 'Neurodevelopmental motor disorders: cerebral palsy and neuromuscular diseases', which concerns muscular dystrophy as well as cerebral palsy.

Bigge, J. L., Best, S. J. and Heller, K. W. (2001) (4th edition) *Teaching Individuals with Physical, Health or Multiple Disabilities*. Upper Saddle River, NJ, Merrill-Prentice-Hall.
This book includes a chapter on 'Physical disabilities', which has sections on muscular dystrophy and limb deficiencies. The chapter on 'Multiple disabilities' focuses on cerebral palsy as an example.

Chapter 9

Health impairments

Introduction

After considering the nature of health impairments in general, this chapter looks at the following specific examples:

- allergy
- asthma
- epilepsy
- congenital heart condition
- cystic fibrosis
- diabetes and
- haemophilia.

With regard to each, it defines the condition and considers its prevalence, causal factors and implications for provision. Finally, the chapter examines broader implications of health impairments in relation to curriculum and assessment; pedagogy; resources; therapy and care and organisation.

Health impairments in general

In the United States of America, a Code of Federal Regulations definition of 'other health impairments' (taken to exclude orthopaedic impairment), is:

> ... having limited strength, vitality or alertness, including a heightened alertness to environmental stimuli, that results in limited alertness with respect to the educational environment, that (i) Is due to chronic or acute health problems such as asthma, attention deficit or attention deficit hyperactivity disorder, diabetes, epilepsy, a heart condition, haemophilia, lead poisoning, leukaemia, nephritis, rheumatic fever and sickle cell anaemia: and (ii) Adversely affects a child's educational performance.
>
> (34 CFR, section 3000.7 [c] [9] [I] [ii], 1999)

It will be remembered that 'orthopaedic impairment' in the United States classification includes:

- certain neuromotor conditions where there are orthopaedic consequences and where provision associated with orthopaedic conditions is necessary (e.g. cerebral palsy and neural tube defects) and
- certain degenerative conditions such as muscular dystrophy.

Therefore, the 'other' health impairments defined above tend to exclude these. Also, attention deficit hyperactivity disorder is considered under 'other health conditions', while in England, it is considered in government frameworks (e.g. Department for Education and Skills, 2001b), a type of emotional, behavioural and social disorder. These points illustrate the arbitrary nature of dividing health impairments and orthopaedic impairments, but the classification is not random, and some justification can be made of it where conditions lead to similar approaches or where understanding is enhanced by grouping certain conditions.

Allergies

Definition

Allergies are a group of conditions caused by the immune system overreacting or responding inappropriately to a substance. In a susceptible person, allergy may occur through different forms of exposure: if the skin is exposed to a particular substance; or the respiratory system is exposed through inhalation to particles of pollen or dust; or the digestive system is exposed to certain foods.

Prevalence

About one person in eight appears to have an inherited predisposition to allergies.

Causal factors

The body's protective immune system recognises antigens (proteins not usually found in the body) on the surface of microorganisms and forms antibodies and sensitised white blood cells (lymphocytes). On a subsequent immune system encounter with the same antigens, the antibodies and sensitised lymphocytes interact with them and the microorganisms are destroyed. In allergies, the immune system reacts to harmless substances ('allergens') because it incorrectly identifies them as antigens. The hypersensitivity reactions associated with allergies can have four different mechanisms (Types I to IV), the most widely known allergies being brought about by Type I reactions.

Allergens that can cause Type I reactions include: pollen, particles of animal skin, house dust, house dust mites, certain drugs and the constituents of bee and wasp sting venom. Foods containing substances that may bring about an allergic reaction include nuts, milk, eggs and shellfish. These allergens induce the immune system to produce certain antibodies of a type called immunoglobulin E (IgE) which coat 'mast cells' present in the skin, stomach lining, lungs and upper respiratory airways. When the allergen is encountered again, it binds to the IgE antibodies causing granules in the mast cells to release chemicals, including histamine, responsible for the symptoms of the allergy. Histamine causes blood vessels to widen, muscles to spasm and fluids to leak into tissues. Symptoms may involve:

- skin (swelling, rash);
- upper airways (sneezing in hay fever, narrowing of airways in asthma, inflammation, mucus secretion);
- eyes (inflammation) and
- stomach and intestines (vomiting and diarrhoea).

Sometimes, several organs may be implicated. Conditions associated with Type I reactions include asthma, hay fever, many food allergies and anaphylactic shock. Anaphylactic shock is a rare, severe, generalised allergic reaction requiring urgent medical attention. It may occur as a result of an insect sting, local anaesthetic, or, less commonly, eating a particular food. Symptoms can include itching; swelling of the face, lips and tongue; skins flushing or blotches; nausea; increased heart rate; difficulty breathing and collapse.

Identification and assessment

Skin allergy may be diagnosed using tests to identify particular reactions to allergens. Tiny amounts of suspected substances are applied to the skin, the reaction and its severity indicating sensitivity to the allergen.

Provision

The most effective treatment is to avoid the relevant antigen. For example, if the allergy is to nuts, these will be avoided both directly and as ingredients in other foods. If the allergy is to pollen, contact is avoided, for example, by avoiding the school fields on high pollen days. Medication includes the use of antihistamine drugs, to relieve symptoms.

Regarding anaphylactic shock, staff are trained to administer medication in an emergency (Epipen-adrenaline). Protocols should be agreed for sending for an ambulance in an emergency. Information sharing must be secure and clear. An individual health care plan is likely to cover a definition of the allergy, precautions, food management, treatment and emergency procedures, staff training and parental consent/agreement.

Asthma

Definition

Asthma, one of the most common childhood conditions, is a physical condition causing the airways of the lungs to narrow, making breathing difficult. Sudden narrowing of the airways brings about an asthma attack. Symptoms may include breathlessness, wheezing and repeated coughing, tightening of the chest and difficulty breathing. It ranges in severity from a mild condition to one that can be life threatening (Heller *et al.*, 1996). It is diagnosed using a range of tests: chest X ray, blood tests, and tests of lung function (e.g. Avery and First, 1994).

Prevalence

Estimates of the prevalence of asthma vary considerably (Kraemer and Bierman, 1983). About 1 in 10 children experience asthma. For example, it is estimated that in the United Kingdom, around 150,000 children are affected.

Causal factors

Allergies, exercise, stress, cold weather, viral infections and fumes (e.g. paint or vehicle exhaust) may precipitate asthma.

Provision

Asthma is managed through prevention or relieving symptoms when they appear. Medication that helps prevent asthma includes Intal or low-dose steroids so long as these are taken regularly. Symptoms are relieved by medication such as Ventolin or Bricanyl. In extreme cases, a short course of steroid tablets may be prescribed.

At school, staff should be aware of the symptoms of asthma and of what to do if an attack occurs. If a pupil is known to develop symptoms as a result of exercise, he should use his inhaler before the activity. Should an attack occur, the pupil should rest before he restarts the activity and should be reassured and calmed down. If symptoms persist or worsen, medical attention should be summoned and in severe cases, an ambulance called.

Pupils with asthma can attain similarly to children without the condition, but where asthma is not managed well, this can lead to frequent absences from school and the pupil can fall behind in work. The school can develop the flexibility to enable the pupil to catch up, for example by rescheduling homework, providing summary notes of lessons and providing homework clubs.

Opportunities should be available for pupils with asthma to talk about any frustration they may feel because of the condition and this can be followed up with further support as necessary. The pupil should be encouraged to use medication independently and responsibly to avoid attacks.

Participation in sports and other physical education may be restricted, especially if outdoors in cold weather. Short periods of exercise are less likely to bring on an attack than long ones, with obvious implications for the management of physical education lessons.

Epilepsy

Definition

Epilepsy is a neurological condition typified by recurring seizures that can present in different ways including sudden episodes of uncontrolled electrical activity in the brain. These are associated with convulsions (violent movements of the limbs or the whole body caused by muscular contractions), muscle spasms, involuntary movements and changes in perception and consciousness. It is distinguished from fainting and pseudoseizures, which appear similar but are not accompanied by electro-encephalogram abnormalities. Also epilepsy is distinguished from convulsions that occur only in febrile illnesses, hypoglycaemic seizures associated with diabetes and hypoxic seizures that occur in asthma attacks.

The International League Against Epilepsy (ILAE) (www.ilae-epilepsy.org/), an association of physicians and other health professionals seeking to enable better care and well-being for those with epilepsy and related conditions, outline a diagnostic scheme in their Commission report (Engel, 2001). Seizures may be classified as: partial (affecting only one lobe or part of one side of the brain) and generalised (affecting the whole brain). Partial seizures are further classified as 'simple partial' or 'complex partial'. In simple partial seizures, the child remains conscious and may experience a tingling feeling in the arms or legs, disturbance of feeling, or disturbance of the sense of perception (for example the sense of smell may be affected). In complex partial seizures, consciousness is impaired but not completely lost. Behaviour may be confused and the child may be unresponsive. He may walk aimlessly or make staccato movements such as plucking at his clothes. Some of these behaviours may be misinterpreted as emotional/behavioural difficulties. Complex partial seizures can, in seconds, generalise to the whole brain, when they are described as 'complex partial with secondary generalisation'. Generalised seizures are further classified as:

- Tonic: The body goes stiff and the child falls, but does not have spasms.
- Clonic: This involves spasms with muscles alternately contracting and relaxing.

- Tonic-clonic: The body stiffens and falls and then there are convulsions. The child may cry out, there may be saliva round the mouth and the child may lose bladder and bowel control.
- Atonic: The child falls limply to the floor.
- Absence: An absence seizure may be mistaken for loss of concentration. The child may stare into space with his eyelids flickering. He may appear vacant and it may be difficult to gain his attention.
- Myoclonus: This is typified by brief jerking of a part of the body.
- Unclassified: This does not follow the typical pattern of other seizures.

Epilepsy is also classified according to an epilepsy syndrome where this can be done (about 60 per cent of cases). Among the implications of all this for education is that it can help the parent and teacher better understand the implications for learning, language and cognition that typify some of these classifications. Briefly the classification involves an anatomical aspect, such as whether the epilepsy is localised or generalised and aetiology (Johnson and Parkinson, 2002: 9).

Prevalence

Epilepsy occurs in about 1 in every 200 children and more frequently among those with cognitive impairment. For example, in the United Kingdom, a frequently quoted figure for epilepsy is that is affects 0.7 to 0.8 per cent of all school children aged 5 to 17 years (Appleton and Gibbs, 1998). However, about a third of all epilepsies beginning in childhood will apparently disappear by the start of adolescence (Johnson and Parkinson, 2002: 2).

Causal factors

Causal factors relating to epilepsy are complex. It can occur as a result of accident or head injury that may be followed by brain haemorrhage; brain infections such as meningitis or encephalitis or infections causing abscesses that grow in the brain. Lack of oxygen at birth can cause brain damage that may lead later to epilepsy. Genetic factors appear to be implicated for some types of epilepsy, for example in some instances, photosensitive epilepsy appears to have a genetic component (Johnson and Parkinson, 2002: 3–4, 19). Many cases are idiopathic, that is, having no known cause.

Provision

The teacher needs to know whether there are arrangements for medication to be taken during the day; whether any side effects of medication are expected; and any changes in medication and their implications for school activities. In school all incidences of seizures are recorded and there are seizure description forms to assist this. Epilepsy protocols/basic procedures are followed if a child has a seizure (e.g. Johnson and Parkinson, 2002: 12 and 16). Procedures for tonic-clonic seizures include not moving the child unless he is in danger and placing him in the safety-recovery position.

Very occasionally, there are emergencies requiring specific responses, such as, where a seizure does not look as though it is stopping after several minutes, or the child has several seizures within a few minutes, (status epilepticus). In such instances, an emergency protocol is followed which the administration of rectal Valium or buccal midazolam. This procedure is only followed by trained staff with parental consent and with guidelines and procedures agreed with the school head teacher and staff. Where a child has regular tonic-clonic fits, or myoclonic or drop attacks, he may wear a protective helmet.

It has been suggested that staff teaching a child with epilepsy should find out the type of seizures the child experiences; their frequency and whether they occur at certain times; potential triggers such as fatigue and how the seizure should be dealt with should it occur (ibid.: 7). Staff being able to deal with seizures and to carefully record their progress is important as it has implications for the management of medication and other matters.

Epilepsy can be associated with difficulties in taking in large chunks of information; retaining, processing, categorising, prioritising and assimilating information; and formulating and expressing an appropriate answer whether in writing or verbally (ibid.: 59–60, paraphrased). A structured framework and routine in which to locate information therefore helps the student with information processing. The teacher can:

- present information in short chunks;
- reinforce verbal information with written notes or bullet-pointed handouts;
- offer direct support when a pupil is felt to have difficulty in maintaining a focus of attention – particularly when working in group settings (ibid.: 60).

Pupils may feel frustrated and have low self-esteem because of the condition. The pastoral system may include opportunities for counselling and other provision to help. The potential embarrassment if a child with tonic-clonic seizures loses bladder and bowel control may be eased if the school plans ahead seeking to ensure privacy and keeping a second supply of the child's clothing. Risk assessments are undertaken for some activities such as practical subjects, laboratory-based work and aspects of physical education to determine the balance between seeking to offer the pupil with epilepsy the widest curriculum opportunities and ensuring he is safe.

Congenital heart condition

Definition

A congenital heart condition is a heart abnormality present at birth and affects heart chambers, heart valves or major blood vessels such as the aorta.

Among types of heart condition affecting children are aortic stenosis and coarctation of the aorta. In aortic stenosis, the aortic valve (lying between the aorta and the left ventricle) is too narrow, causing heart stress because of the extra work required to pump blood through a small area. With coarctation of the aorta, part of the aorta itself is too narrow, restricting blood to the lower parts of the body, and surgery is usually required for babies.

Prevalence

Congenital heart condition affects around 8 in every 1,000 babies.

Causal factors

Errors of development leading to defects occur early in the life of the embryo. Although in most instances the causes are unknown, one well-recognised causal factor is maternal rubella.

Identification and assessment

Ultrasound scanning of the foetus during pregnancy allows the heart to be examined enabling many cases of congenital heart disease to be diagnosed so the plans can be made for the timing of treatment. After birth, if clinical examination suggests any defect of the heart, further procedures are used to investigate. In aortic stenosis, symptoms are chest pain, dizziness and loss of consciousness. With coarctation of the aorta in older children symptoms may include: cramps, tiredness, high blood pressure in the arms and weak pulse in the legs. Main symptoms in children are breathlessness and reduced exercise tolerance and fatigue.

Provision

Medical intervention can include surgery to try to correct the abnormality or improve function. Where the school building has stairs, the school may ensure that the classroom and other facilities are on the lower floor, or minimise the necessity of stair climbing for the child with a heart condition. Also, a lift or stair climber may be used. Belongings may be kept in lockers in central and easily accessible areas to reduce the necessity of carrying equipment around school.

Some aspects of lessons where there may be some inhalation of fumes such as metal shop or science may have to be avoided. A mask may be used in some lessons where there is a risk of inhaling dust, for example wood technology. Where lessons require physical demands the child may need extra adult support. In physical education lessons, alternative but interesting and participatory activities may be provided. Organisational flexibility that may be required includes flexible timescales for the return of homework where fatigue has delayed its return. Supported work at home may be arranged or home tuition may be provided if the child is absent for long periods. Resources include the possible use of standing aids where lessons require long periods of standing.

Cystic fibrosis

Definition

'Cystic' refers to cysts, while 'fibrosis' is an overgrowth of scar tissue or connective tissue. Cystic fibrosis is a progressive, multi system, inherited disease present from birth, in which thick mucus is produced in the lungs and pancreas resulting in cysts. The mucus causes lung infections and stops enzymes, which digest food, flowing from the pancreas to the intestines. In very few instances, cystic fibrosis is associated with other conditions such as cirrhosis of the liver, sinusitis, hay fever, arthritis, diabetes or a heart condition. The sexual maturity of a boy with the condition may be delayed. Symptoms may be a persistent, non-infectious cough, wheezing, lack of weight gain and chest infections.

Prevalence

Cystic fibrosis occurs in about 1 in every 2,500 live births among white Americans and Europeans, although the incidence in African, Asian and Jewish populations is much lower.

Causal factors

Cystic fibrosis is an inherited condition present from birth. It is caused by a defect in a gene on chromosome 7 (Weinberger, 1993). It is recessive, and therefore must be doubly inherited with one gene from each parent. Individuals who inherit only one affected gene are carriers.

Provision

To alleviate digestive problems, a child may have a substance 'pancreatin' with meals to replace missing enzymes, helping food to be absorbed. Older students may take intravenous equipment with them to the school or ensure they have access to it. Sometimes, the child may need a nebuliser or may be prescribed a course of antibiotics to help clear an infection. Daily physiotherapy and breathing exercises are necessary to clear the child's lungs and while this is often done before and after school, it may be necessary also in school time. A suitably trained teaching assistant may carry this out. Where pupils need intravenous treatment, arrangements are made between the head teacher, parents and school staff prepared to supervise. In general, school staff will need to liaise with others such as the child's doctor and the physiotherapist to ensure treatment plans are fulfilled. Pupils with cystic fibrosis should be able to participate in all school activities, but time may have to be allocated to physio-therapy. Learning and progress can be affected where the pupil needs frequent hospital care, although education is provided in hospital for pupils who may be there for long periods. Also, the school can be flexible in providing work if the pupil is at home and by allowing the pupil time to catch up any missed work.

Younger pupils and pupils who need help may need supervision at meal-times to ensure they eat well and remember to take any medication and food supplement capsules. A pupil may need additional pastoral support to help him deal with the frustrations to which the condition can give rise. Some may have emotional and behavioural difficulties related to their capacity to cope with the condition. Sensitive behaviour management strategies may be used if there are behaviour difficulties. Teachers need to be aware that the pupil may be teased about persistent coughing, small stature and the need to take tablets with food. It is suggested that because of undigested fat leads to stools being frequent and foul smelling, teachers should be ready to allow frequent toilet visits and that where there is embarrassment, the pupil might use the restroom when others are not present or use a private restroom supplied with strong deodorisers.

Counselling can help teenagers recognise and deal with the stress associated with delayed sexual maturity or other matters. Special arrangements may be made for examinations.

Diabetes mellitus (type 1)

Definition

Diabetes mellitus is caused by the pancreas not producing (or producing insufficient amounts of) the hormone insulin. This hormone enables glucose to be absorbed into cells for their energy needs and the liver and fat cells for storage. If there is not enough insulin, the levels of glucose in the blood become too high, causing extreme thirst and the passing of excessive amounts of urine. Because the body is unable to store the glucose, this causes tiredness and hunger and can lead to weight loss.

The two types of diabetes mellitus are type 1 (the insulin dependent type) and type 2 (the non-insulin dependent type). Type 1 is the more severe and usually develops in childhood. The insulin producing cells in the pancreas are destroyed and the production of insulin stops almost completely so that regular injections of insulin are needed. Type 2 usually develops in older people and risk factors include being overweight.

Prevalence

In the United Kingdom, about 1.4 people in every 1,000 develop insulin dependent (type 1) diabetes by the age of 16 years. (Non-insulin dependent diabetes is much more common).

Causal factors

While diabetes mellitus tends to run in families, only a small percentage of those inheriting the genes responsible for the insulin dependent form eventually develop the disease, when it is thought to be the delayed result of an earlier viral infection. Obesity, particular illnesses, certain drugs and infections may precipitate latent diabetes.

Provision

Diabetes mellitus type 1 is treated in two ways. The individual injects himself with insulin between one and four times per day. Also a diet is followed which regulates the intake of carbohydrates and ensures their intake is spread out during the day, avoiding marked fluctuations in the levels of glucose in the blood. Too much glucose leads to symptoms of the untreated disease (thirst and polyuria), while too little can cause weakness, sweating, confusion and even seizures and unconsciousness. The blood and urine levels of glucose are regularly self-monitored using a do-it-yourself test kit.

Teachers need to be aware of the medical and dietary requirements of the child with diabetes and should receive training in noticing possible signs of glucose imbalance, taking appropriate action and summoning medical assistance as necessary. Alertness and vigilance of staff is very important. The child needs to be encouraged and supported in ensuring the proper monitoring and treatment of glucose levels. Dietary requirements should be strictly adhered to.

Haemophilia

Definition

Haemophilia is an inherited disorder involving recurrent bleeding usually into the joints, which may occur spontaneously or after injury.

Prevalence

Haemophilia almost exclusively affects males with around 1 male in 10,000 born with the condition.

Causal factors

Haemophilia is caused by a deficiency in a blood-clotting agent. These are numbered from I to XIII and the two main types of haemophilia involve factor VIII (haemophilia A) and factor IX (haemophilia B). The lack of this protein is owing to a defective gene with a sex-linked pattern of inheritance. While affected males pass on the defective gene to all of their daughters (who become carriers), they pass it to none of their sons. Some of the sons of carrier females may be affected and some of the daughters of carriers may also be carriers. While about a third of people with haemophilia have no family history of the condition, many have an uncle, brother or grandfather who are affected.

Identification and assessment

Haemophilia is diagnosed by blood clotting tests, which indicate that factor VIII is very low. Symptoms reflect the fact that most bleeding episodes are to the joints and muscles causing pain. If left untreated this can lead to deformities of the joints. Internal bleeding can lead to blood in the urine or bruising.

Provision

Medical treatment involves controlling episodes of bleeding by controlled infusions of blood clotting factor and regular infusions can be given as a preventive measure. Older children and adults can inject the factor themselves. Screening techniques for viruses and the heat treatment of the coagulation factor concentrate considerably reduced the risk of infection from contaminated blood and the introduction of genetically engineered coagulation factor concentrate eliminated this risk of viral infection.

As children can often recognise the 'sensation' of internal bleeding before symptoms occur, it is important they report this to adults promptly. Health care plans are drawn up with the involvement of parents, health professionals and the school to identify such essentials as what procedures to follow if a pupil reports a bleed and whom to contact in an emergency should parents prove unavailable. Training is given to school staff in first aid procedures.

Children with haemophilia avoid activities with a risk of injury such as contact sports. Swimming, walking, dancing and similar activities are encouraged. Support for movement may be necessary after a bleed where there is swelling or pain.

Health impairments – general points

Having considered examples of health impairments, it is possible to consider whether anything more general can be said about provision for them.

Curriculum

Health impairments can lead to functional impairments and disability. The school will be aware that serious and chronic illness or disability can place stress on the child and family and will support families wherever they can and work closely with others seeking to do the same. Also, collaboration between parent, school and others such as the school health team, especially the school nurse and school doctor, can help ensure that the child is not excluded unnecessarily from any part of the school curriculum and that appropriate protocols and training are in place.

Curriculum flexibility is necessary to ensure that a wide and suitable range of learning experiences is provided, for example the provision of supervised swimming or walking and related activities where there is a risk from pursuits such as contact sports (as for children with haemophilia). Participation in sports and other physical education may be restricted according to weather conditions, for example for pupils with asthma.

Curriculum opportunities may be modified following risk assessments for some activities such as practical subjects, laboratory-based work and aspects of physical education. For some pupils, for example with cystic fibrosis, time may have to be allocated to physiotherapy, although the breadth and balance of the curriculum should not be affected.

Pedagogy

The impact of a health impairment can vary from time to time because of variations in the condition, but also because of different demands of the curriculum or the child's peer group. Therefore, the child's educational provision needs to be responsive to changes in the child's physical and motor abilities and sensitive to the physical, psychological and any other effects of the condition. Particular requirements arise such as, for a child with epilepsy, having a structured framework and routine in which to locate information to help the student with information processing.

Resources

As well as medication and access to medication as necessary, other resources may be required, depending on the condition and its severity. For example, standing aids might be used for a child with congenital heart defect where lessons require long periods of standing. Architectural/organisational implications include that, where the school building has stairs, the school may ensure that the classroom and other facilities are on the lower floor or minimise the necessity of stair climbing or a lift may be used (e.g. for a child with a heart condition).

Therapy and care

Medical intervention can include surgery to try to correct the abnormality or improve function, for example in the case of a congenital heart condition.

In a survey conducted in the United States of America (Heller et al., 2000), teachers and paraprofessionals stated that they regularly carried out specialised health care procedures, such as clean intermittent catheterisation, but only half considered themselves very knowledgeable about the procedures, suggesting the need for more training, help in developing policies and technical assistance.

An important contribution is made by the individualised health care plan, developed under the guidance and leadership of a health care professional. It includes: a description of the condition, a short health history, basic health status and health care needs, treatments or medication and their side effects, transportation issues, equipment needs, emergency plans and particular precautions or restrictions on activities. Regarding the medical aspects of health impairments, school staff clearly need to be aware of these, properly trained where they have responsibilities relating to medical needs and have the knowledge and skills to support health care plans, first aid measures and recording procedures. To help ensure the plan is effective, its development is likely to involve the child, school staff, health personnel and parents (Clay, 2004). This includes working closely with health (nursing) and therapy staff. The pastoral system may include opportunities for counselling and other provision to help. The training and support of staff to carry out any necessary procedures or to be aware of the implications of particular symptoms and how to act is important, as for example in the case of haemophilia.

The pastoral system may include opportunities for counselling and other provision to help raise self-esteem, help teenagers recognise and deal with the stress associated with delayed sexual maturity, support pupils with life limiting conditions or other matters.

Organisation

School building design and use is important and care is taken in ensuring where necessary the child does not unduly exert himself because of carrying equipment round school. Risk assessments are made to avoid situations and activities that may affect the child adversely. Where necessary, flexible timescales for returning homework and possible home tuition are employed. Higher levels of supervision may be needed. Extra supervision may be necessary sometimes at specific times such as mealtimes or recess to ensure dietary or medication procedures are followed by pupils.

Thinking points

Readers may wish to consider with regard to children with physical disability, motor disability and medical conditions:

- the training and supervision that staff will require to effectively educate and support pupils and how it is ensured that this is up to date;
- the broad and common features of provision for many pupils with physical disabilities or motor difficulties such as wheelchair access and flexible lesson starting and finishing times and
- provision more specific to particular conditions, such as counselling relating to reduced life expectancy.

Key texts

Bigge, J. L., Best, S. J. and Heller, K. W. (2001) (4th edition) *Teaching Individuals with Physical, Health or Multiple Disabilities*. Upper Saddle River, NJ, Merrill-Prentice-Hall.

This book comprises three parts. The first deals with the impact and implications of physical, health or multiple disabilities. The second part concerns 'facilitating participation across environments' and includes a chapter on augmentative and alternative communication. The third part covers curriculum adaptations and instructional strategies.

Clay, D. L. (2004) *Helping Children with Chronic Health Conditions: A Practical Guide*. New York, The Guilford Press.

Discusses specific health conditions to encourage school participation and social functioning. For example, a chapter on 'Making accommodations: Developing 504 plans and individual education plans (IEPs)', gives planning guidance regarding diabetes, asthma, juvenile rheumatoid arthritis and cystic fibrosis.

Chapter 10

Traumatic brain injury

Introduction

This chapter considers traumatic brain injury (TBI), defining the condition and related matters and outlining some of the implications. The chapter gives estimates of the prevalence of TBI, and considers causal factors, identification and assessment, and provision: rehabilitation, curriculum and assessment; pedagogy; resources; therapy/care and organisation.

Definitions and related terminology

The term 'acquired brain injury' is sometimes used to refer to an injury to the brain occurring after birth and caused by an accident or as a result of disease or infections. It therefore excludes congenital brain injury (e.g. Walker and Wicks, 2005: 1–2). Within the context of acquired brain injury 'atraumatic' brain injury is caused by illness and infection while 'traumatic' brain injury (TBI) is the result of accidents or other injuries.

In the United States of America, Code of Federal Regulations define TBI as follows:

> ... an injury to the brain caused by an external force, resulting in total or partial functional disability or psychosocial impairment or both, that adversely affects the child's educational performance. The term applies to open or closed head injuries resulting in impairments in one or more areas, such as: cognition, language, memory, attention, reasoning, abstract thinking, judgement, problem solving, sensory, perceptual and motor abilities, psycho-social behaviour, physical functions, information processing, and speech. The term does not apply to brain injuries that are congenital or degenerative, or brain injuries induced by birth trauma.
>
> (34 CFR, section 300.7 [c] [12])

Injuries causing TBI may be closed head injuries or open head (penetrative) injuries (e.g. Heller *et al.*, 1996). With a closed head injury, which might, for example, be sustained in a road accident or a fall, there is no penetration of the dura (the membrane inside the skull covering the brain). In a penetrative head injury there is an opening or penetration from outside of the skull and dura, which might be caused by an object such as a sharp instrument or a bullet. Also, the injury may have been focal or diffuse. Focal damage affects a relatively small brain area and may be caused by a penetrative injury to a specific site of the brain or an injury at the point where an external object hits the skull. As well as focal damage, closed head injuries may give rise to diffuse brain injury affecting several areas as the brain is moved about inside the skull.

Injuries may be immediate or delayed. The main types of immediate injuries are contusions (bruising) and diffuse axonal injury. Contusions may lead to some cells being irreparably damaged and others partially injured so that they cease functioning for a few seconds to several weeks. Diffuse axonal injury damages axons (extensions of neurons/nerve cells) diffusely throughout the brain. Delayed injuries include: haemorrhages, herniation syndrome, and edema (Christensen, 2001: 10–12) as explained below.

Haemorrhages can occur within the brain; into the ventricles; or into spaces surrounding the brain (between the skull and dura; beneath the dura; or under the arachnoid layer of the meninges into the cerebrospinal fluid). Consequences of bleeding depend on the amount of blood, how quickly it accumulates and the location. Any 'extra' blood in the space already occupied by the brain, cerebrospinal fluid and blood within the blood vessels can lead to increased pressure. Where the haemorrhage occurs slowly, the brain may adapt by squeezing some fluid out of the brain or the cerebrospinal fluid space, or decreasing the amount of blood in the blood vessels. But if haemorrhage is rapid and extensive, leading to intracranial pressure, the circulation has to adjust to ensure there is enough blood flow to the brain to keep it nourished, for if it is insufficient, further injury can be caused by lack of oxygenation and blood flow.

Herniation syndrome may occur if there is a localised mass or area of swelling that pushes on the brain and deforms it. Such a swelling occurs when the brain tries to squeeze itself into another space within the intracranial space, creating high pressure on focal areas of the brain and its blood vessels, which can lead to further localised brain injury and stroke.

Edema (swelling) of the brain can occur after a head trauma, can lead to intracranial pressure, and may be localised or diffuse, causing similar complications to haemorrhage. For the most severe head injuries, an intracranial pressure monitor is temporarily surgically placed inside the head relaying information to a monitor allowing medical staff to make necessary interventions (Christensen, 2001: 10–12).

Generally, the younger the child at the time of injury, the poorer the outcome is, possibly because the neurological deficits resulting from TBI (e.g. memory, attention and organisational problems) are important in learning new knowledge and skills so that a later adolescent, who has already learned a great deal before injury, will tend to function better than a young child having learned much less.

Some implications of TBI

An indication of the aspects of cognition that may be affected, the possible problems with these following brain injury, and illustrations of how these can manifest themselves in the school setting, is provided by Savage and Wolcott (1995).

Neurological problems

Types of neurological problems that can result from TBI include:

- post concussion syndrome;
- headaches;
- seizures and
- motor impairments.

A concussion is a mild head injury with or without loss of consciousness and includes such symptoms as: difficulty remembering new things, labile emotions, poor concentration and fatigue. It is important that where a child has these symptoms as a result of concussion, parents, teachers and others do not mistake them as signs of laziness or unco-operativeness.

Headaches may be related to the trauma to the head, tension headaches, head and neck pain associated with whiplash injuries, and migraine headaches. Headache, if it is extremely severe, may be a sign that emergency treatment may be required. For less severe headaches that recur, the physician may prescribe medication (Christensen, 2001: 35–36).

After a TBI, seizures are not uncommon, but repeated post-traumatic seizures are rare and late seizures occurring after the first week of injury are more predictive of developing post-traumatic epilepsy. The risk of developing epilepsy after a severe TBI is about 11 per cent.

Most children with TBI do not have major motor problems. Types of problems that can occur include: weakness, poor co-ordination, lack of ability to control or plan movements, abnormal muscle tone (e.g. increased muscle tone – spasticity or rigidity), loss of postural skills and balance reactions and tremors. Children with such difficulties are assisted particularly by the physical therapist and, for Activities of Daily Living (ADLs) such as feeding and dressing, by the occupational therapist. Also, many children with moderate to severe TBI develop secondary (acquired) attention deficit hyperactivity disorder for which medication may be prescribed.

While injuries to the bones and muscles may occur at the same time as the child receives a TBI, these usually heal well. Occasionally, however, orthopaedic problems may arise such as complications of muscle tone problems (such as scoliosis or spinal curvature) requiring treatment. Nutritional issues may include swallowing difficulties and while these are being relearned, feeding may involve using a tube: a nasogastric tube (passing through the nose, down the throat and into the stomach) or a gastronomy tube. The latter is inserted surgically by passing the tube through an incision in the abdominal wall to the stomach, or down the throat.

Effects on attention and memory

Attention problems are common after TBI and different locations of brain injury have implications for the way attention might be affected. Injury to the brain stem (responsible for arousal) can result in coma. Injury to the temporal, parietal, and occipital lobes can lead to omissions and mistakes in processing and integrating incoming information. Damage to the frontal lobe may interfere with the ability to manage, allocate and direct attention effectively. Sensory impulses are filtered in the primary zone of the brain, largely automatically. Information is further selected in the secondary zones, for example according to whether it is familiar or novel. The sensory input unit, being large, is often damaged in TBI and the reduced regulation of attention can lead to the child being oversensitive to stimulation or apparently shutting down attention. Damage to the frontal lobes can affect the child's ability to direct attention to goal relevant information and shut out unwanted distractions. The child may have difficulties with sustained attention; selective attention (including shutting out distractions); alternating attention (moving focus from one task to another) and divided attention (attending to multiple tasks) (Brady, 2001: 153–154).

After TBI, while old memories may be in place, the use of memory for new learning may be impaired. Declarative memory (for facts and episodes of personal experience) is more likely to be affected than procedural memory (for conditioning, motor skills and other types of memory stored and retrieved without evident conscious effort). Declarative memory may be regarded in three stages: attending and sensory registering; short-term memory (STM) and long-term memory (LTM). The STM and LTM differ in terms of capacity, storage format, duration and cognitive processes involved. STM last only for seconds although it can be extended by rehearsal (repeating the information) and other strategies. Contents of STM are lost if there is a distraction before the information is transferred to permanent storage in LTM. Rehearsal and 'chunking' information increase the likelihood that information in STM will be encoded into LTM. Both the process of transfer from STM to LTM and retrieval from LTM can be disrupted by traumatic brain injury. After TBI, while STM may be within age typical limits, it may be very unstable, being lost with the slightest distraction. Also, the child may find it difficult to adopt strategies such as rehearsal and chunking unaided.

The limbic system (structures in the temporal lobes near the centre of the brain), essential to transferring information from STM to LTM, may be less efficient after TBI. The child's rate of learning may therefore be slower, requiring many repetitions of new material before new learning occurs. Memory retrieval is often impaired because memories may not be efficiently laid down or the child may not be as able to plan and carry out an organised search of information in LTM.

Effects on the visual system

With TBI, if the optic nerve is damaged it can cause decreased acuity or permanent loss of vision in a particular portion of the visual field. Also, muscles responsible for eye movements are controlled by several cranial nerves, and cranial nerve dysfunction often occurs after TBI generally owing to pressure such as swelling. This can lead to difficulties such as striabmus resulting in double vision. Such problems tend to subside as swelling reduces a few days or weeks after the injury.

While most visual information travels from the retina to the occipital lobe, some impulses instead end in a structure in the upper brainstem. This pathway appears to provide information about the presence and location of an object but without giving information about the identity of the item or its features. Damage to this system can lead to difficulties in moving gaze and in orientating to, tracking and localising objects in the environment.

Visual perceptual problems after TBI, that is, difficulties in interpreting the visual signal reaching the occipital cortex, relate to whether damage occurred in the primary, secondary or tertiary zone of the occipital cortex. Localised injury to the visual primary zone of the visual cortex, where electrical signals from the retina via the optic nerve terminate, is rare in TBI. As information continues to the secondary zone of the visual cortex, the sensations (e.g. of colour) received in the primary zone are made into images of whole objects and scenes resembling aspects of the external world. Cells in this zone combine the input of cells from the primary zone that were activated together when a person looked at a certain object and when the brain recognises a previously fired pattern, this constitutes a visual memory. If there is damage to the secondary areas, the individual perceives particular features, but does not combine them into recognisable wholes reliably. The more complex the visual surroundings (e.g. a busy classroom), the more confusing it is likely to be. As visual information passes to the tertiary zone of sensory input, it is linked to other types of sensory input (e.g. tactile, auditory). Injury to this area leads to difficulties in complex processes of thinking and understanding. TBI often leads to defects in one or more aspects of tertiary zone functioning.

As visual pathways continue beyond the secondary occipital cortex into the tertiary association cortex, they form two streams. One leads into the temporal lobe and combines visual and auditory/verbal representations of information (the 'what' stream) enabling one to label and describe what is seen using words. The other leads into the parietal lobe and combines visual, touch and positional information allowing individuals to understand spatial relationships and move guided by vision (the 'where' stream). Should areas concerned with visual and auditory/verbal integration be disrupted, this interferes with many naming activities including reading.

If damage to the tertiary zone (especially the right side) is extensive, 'unilateral neglect' can occur involving inattention to/failure to respond to anything presented to the child's left side. The child is unaware, he is not attending to part of the environment and may bump into things on his left. More obvious signs tend to get better over time, but some may remain. The child may have difficulties interpreting visual information, so he may find moving around school difficult. Putting on clothes and constructing things will be challenging. Visual spatial words such as 'behind' and 'in front' will be difficult, as will interpreting pictures and charts and telling the time using an analogue clock. The child may have problems with understanding conceptual space (e.g. time and numerical reasoning) and there may be difficulties with visual motor integration (e.g. using fine motor skills to copy work from a blackboard) or writing (Brady, 2001: 162).

Executive functions

After TBI, executive functions, the cognitive processes necessary for organised and directed behaviour, are often impaired.

In the frontal lobes are centres for selecting, sequencing and initiating responses. The primary division of the frontal cortex comprises a 'motor strip' and impulses arising there lead to particular actions which in lower species are comparatively automatic and set in action by particular sensory stimuli. The secondary and tertiary frontal regions enable humans to respond much more flexibly. The frontal lobes allow automatic responses to be inhibited and alternative goals brought into play so that, when frontal lobes are damaged, inhibition may be less effective. Also, working memory interacts with impulse control to enable behaviour to be organised.

Through 'feedback loops' with the sensory input unit, the frontal lobes direct one's attention to aspects of surroundings that are relevant to future goals and to filter out distractions. A child with problems in executive function has difficulty in filtering out irrelevant features of his environment.

With the help of working memory, we can consider the many aspects of a situation and draw out common features, allowing us to develop rules, generalisations and concepts. A child with TBI may find it difficult to develop such generalisations and rules, finding it hard to transfer knowledge from one situation to another. This can lead to thinking in concrete literal terms and having difficulty with such language forms as humour and sarcasm. Frustration tolerance may be decreased and the child may have difficulty evaluating his own behaviour and its effect on others. Mental flexibility may be affected making it harder for the child to complete work independently (Brady, 2001: 165–169).

Effects on communication

Taking communication to be the giving and receiving of information, speech and language are its major components. Generally, the more widespread and diffuse the damage to the brain, the greater the likely effect on speech and language. Speech involves co-ordinating structures involved in respiration, phonation and articulation and TBI may affect any of these. A child with TBI may experience dysarthric (slow and laboured) speech or dysfluent speech (stammering/stuttering) in the early phases of recovery and these symptoms may subside or persist later. Other speech problems that may occur are difficulties with respiration affecting voice quality; difficulties with speech and sound production (e.g. dysarthria) or vocal problems with resonance and voice quality.

Taking language to be a set of symbols used to communicate (including written forms, speaking and gesture), the child with TBI may experience problems with receptive or expressive language or both that may be mild or severe, temporary or permanent. Language problems are much more common than speech problems for children with TBI. Language abilities are linked to cognitive functions and particularly executive functions of the brain such as attention, memory, conceptual organisation, processing speed and analysis/synthesis of environmental cues and conversation (e.g. interpreting facial expression to gather that the person addressed does not understand). When executive functions are disrupted by TBI, language difficulties may include difficulties in: learning new vocabulary, word finding, following complex directions, understanding figurative language and solving problems. The child may also have difficulties with conversation, which may, for example, be tangential or irrelevant (Schoenbrodt, 2001: 192–195).

Effects on behaviour

Many head injuries result in damage to the frontal lobes, which are involved in the oversight of brain functions such as decision-making and emotional expression and perform the brain's executive functions such as performing abstract thinking and regulating emotional expression. Some children with TBI may exhibit disruptive behaviour or may develop poor self-esteem, depression, anxiety or temper outbursts. There may be long-term difficulties with impulsivity, judgement and awareness of safety.

Different levels of emergence from coma have been identified reflected in the *Rancho Los Amigos Cognitive Scale* (Savage and Wolcott, 1995). At a certain level (IV) the child's behaviour tends to be confused, repetitive, bizarre and emotionally labile. Here parents and professionals manage the behaviour by keeping conversation simple and direct, giving calm praise for compliance and so on. Later stages are also associated with typical behaviours.

Among ways of understanding the effect on behaviour of frontal lobe damage is in terms of two global behaviour patterns. The first is associated with a tendency for the child to be easily aroused typified by such behaviours as hyperactivity, aggression and impulsivity; the second with a tendency for the child to be less easily stimulated characterised by behaviours such as social withdrawal, depression and shyness. The nature of the injury influences whether one pattern of behaviour, or the other, or a mixture of both is evident and behaviour patterns also differ from time to time and in different settings.

Another conceptualisation is considering frontal lobe functions and behaviours that might occur if these are damaged. These include deficits in attention, which may lead to behaviour such as distractibility, over concern with irrelevant details or confusion over choices. If the child's sense of coherence and predictability in his behaviour is affected, this might lead, for example, to lack of foresight and difficulty setting goals. Should emotional and interpersonal behaviour be affected this can be evident in behaviours like mood swings, poor self-control and opposition. If executive functions are involved, behaviour might include poor insight into one's behaviour, rigidity in thinking and acting, and inability to monitor oneself (e.g. Tucker, 2001: 219–210).

These may lead to behaviour, which includes impairment in safety awareness; impulse control; social skills and anger management. There may be memory problems and disorganisation, apathy and overdependence.

Prevalence

In the United States of America, by the age of 16 years, 4 per cent of boys and 2.5 per cent of girls sustain a TBI (mild to severe). There is a peak of incidence in the late teen years (and in the elderly). Most TBI are mild, but severe TBI is nevertheless the most common acquired disability in childhood (Kraus *et al.*, 1990). In the United Kingdom, there are around a million patients who present to hospitals each year with head injuries almost half of whom are under the age of 16 years (Royal College of Surgeons of England, 1999).

Causal factors

Among the most frequent causes of TBI are a traffic accident, fall, or sport injury (DiScala *et al.*, 1997) with other accidental causes including near drowning or an object falling on the head. The injury may be the result of an intentional act, such as attempted suicide, child physical abuse or other violent crime.

Identification and assessment

Determining the type and location of the child's injury is assisted by computerised tomography (CT) scans and by magnetic resonance imaging (MRI) scans which are non-invasive techniques showing cross-sections of the brain. Assessments of the child's functioning are also important in providing information about the brain injury.

The severity of the brain injury is usually classified as mild, moderate or severe, using three methods:

- the *Glasgow Coma Scale* (Teasedale and Jennet, 1974);
- observing the length of coma and
- observing the length of post-traumatic amnesia.

These help predict the depth and duration of neurologic dysfunction, providing an indication of how long and to what degree function is and will be normal.

The *Glasgow Coma Scale* (Teasedale and Jennet, 1974), used in intensive care settings to detect progress or deterioration, comprises subscales for eye opening, verbal and motor responses.

Whether the child is in a coma and if so for how long informs judgements about the severity of the brain injury, although there is debate about whether the end of coma is best signalled by spontaneous eye opening or by the child being able to follow simple commands. Mild TBI is associated with no loss or only momentary loss of consciousness, or with coma of less than one hour; moderate TBI with a coma of 1 to 24 hours and severe TBI with coma of 24 hours or more duration.

The length of post-traumatic amnesia (PTA) is a predictor of the severity of TBI, giving an indication of how memory and cognition are likely to be affected in the longer term. A PTA of less than one hour is associated with mild TBI; 1 to 24 hours with moderate TBI; 1 to 7 days with severe TBI and 7 days with very severe TBI. If PTA shows a higher degree of severity than other indicators, it takes precedence.

The level of severity of TBI gives an indication of the relative risk of certain problems. Very broadly, children and adolescents with mild TBI do well without long-term complications. Children with moderate TBI are at high risk of temporary (or permanent) cognitive and behavioural problems. Those children with severe TBI are at very high risk of permanent cognitive and behavioural problems and also of motor problems. Evaluations of functioning and difficulties are made by the rehabilitation team (see below). The *Rancho Los Amigos Cognitive Scales* (Savage and Wolcott, 1995) are used to help recognise and respond to early stages of recovery from TBI.

Provision

It is important that those seeking to help children with TBI including health, social service and education professionals and parents work closely together to clarify where the child is in terms of current presentation of symptoms and where future difficulties may arise. Ideally, this will encourage preventive measures to be put into place before difficulties arise or become entrenched.

Rehabilitation

'Rehabilitation' involves restoring to someone abilities they once had but lost owing to illness or injury. ('Habilitation' involves helping someone acquire abilities they did not previously have). Rehabilitation aims to optimise health and functional abilities, beginning in the intensive care unit and continuing as long as necessary. It involves relearning to do things the child can no longer do; and compensating for inabilities by using abilities (for example employing visual aids to compensate for memory difficulties).

The recommendations of the rehabilitation team might lead to modifications in the environment (e.g. at home) and the use of adaptive equipment and assistive devices (e.g. wheelchair, visual aids to memory). Rehabilitation might take place locally on an outpatient basis involving home, hospital and community facilities; or may involve the child staying in an inpatient rehabilitation hospital some distance from home before later using less intensive facilities locally.

The initial team may be large and include: physician, nurse, nutritionist or dietician, psychologist, speech and language therapist/pathologist, teacher, occupational therapist, physical therapist/physiotherapist, swallowing therapist (who may be a speech pathologist or occupational therapist), social worker and recreational therapist. As progress is made the team tends to become smaller, for example, a physician, teacher, psychologist and social worker.

Curriculum and assessment

Many children after TBI retain the memory of what they previously thoroughly learned. For example, if they attained at an age typical level in mathematics before the accident, they may well be able to perform at the same level once they are able to return to school. However, the TBI may affect the rate at which the child can learn new information, slowing subsequent progress. Therefore, the curriculum may need to be modified by breaking down content into smaller steps while ensuring it is not fragmentary. Reflecting this, smaller steps for assessment may be necessary to show progress.

If a child has had a TBI, it is very important to avoid a second injury, as the effects may be cumulative. Careful consideration is therefore given to physical activities where non-contact sports are encouraged and safe rules are followed.

Pedagogy

Blosser and DePompei (1994), referring to acquired brain injury, have pointed out that, 'Rehabilitation and education professionals agree that good teaching strategies designed especially for students with ABI are necessary and essential'. Research evidence also supports the view that children with TBI may require some educational approaches that are different from those commonly used (e.g. Ylvisaker, 1998). On the other hand, some of the approaches used are good practice for all classrooms at certain times and will not always entail additional adjustments.

Attention can be helped by developing a stable routine for the child and by giving any instructions in clear, straightforward language. The teacher can also give cues to the information being presented and can limit or break down the amount of information.

To aid memory, information may be broken down into smaller units and presented repeatedly enabling extra rehearsal. New information is more likely to be remembered if presented in a meaningful context, rather than as disparate items.

Also, new information can be linked explicitly to previously known or recently learned information as when previous learning is briefly recapped before new information is presented. Visual cues such as timelines and charts can help information recall. Giving an overview of what the lesson is about before it takes place can help as can other aids to prior organisation of information. The teacher may give instruction in memory aiding techniques such as rehearsal and chunking. Tangible aids are also useful such as notes, lists, timetable checks and assignment books. Cueing and prompting can help, for example, when posing questions a reminder might be given about the context or a cue about the activity being discussed. Such aids to memory as rehearsal, repetition and practice are best developed when the family and school work closely together given the importance of the home as a key learning environment for children.

Helping the child with visual functioning difficulties is likely to draw on assessments and advice of the ophthalmologist and occupational therapist. The child's positioning, for example at a desk, and the positioning of work surfaces, require care. The classroom environment is more comprehensible if it is not cluttered and if things are put back in a familiar place. In preparing food, utensils can be arranged so that they are easier to find and identify. In changing for physical education, clothing can be set out to be easier to find and put on. Where the child experiences visual perception problems, it can help if the materials such as texts used for teaching are simplified, for example using larger, darker print or ensuring pages are uncluttered. The amount of written work required might be reduced and extra time allowed to complete it. Computer technology can also be used, for example to enlarge print or to reduce writing demands through using writing frames. Where a child experiences unilateral neglect, he can be reminded to scan by turning his head fully. A left margin signal such as a dark line can be provided for printed material.

Turning to executive functions, impulse control can be helped by teaching the child 'self talk'; breaking complex tasks and instructions into smaller steps; encouraging the use of notes and lists. The adult can demonstrate thinking processes to the child by saying aloud how she is working out a problem or dealing with an issue, and then encouraging the child to do the same. Self-monitoring can be encouraged by getting the child to anticipate how he will deal with a task, then after the activity is completed, comparing the results with the predictions and learning from them. For younger children, social interactions might be more structured than usual to give the opportunity to develop and recognise some of the necessary social skills. Prompting the appropriate behaviour as necessary can be helpful.

The teacher and others contribute to helping the child communicate by working closely with the speech and language pathologist/therapist as necessary and by supporting communication themselves. Communications from the teacher need to be clear and understandable to the child, and instructions and information may need to be repeated. Clear signals of a change of conversation topic can help the child. Other systems of communication may be used temporarily, for example signing and symbols.

Among approaches to managing and behaviour and reducing problems are: behaviour management strategies, psychotherapy (individual and family) and environmental modifications and supports. Behaviour management strategies include defining the required behaviour (e.g. tidying away items when requested) and establishing a baseline (e.g. how many times a day/ a session the required behaviour occurs). The required behaviour might be not doing something (e.g. reducing or eliminating the number of times a child touches others to distract them in a lesson). Establishing the context of the target behaviour can include noting the antecedents, the behaviour and its consequences (ABC). Altering the events that appear to precipitate them may reduce unwanted behaviour. Contingency management involves arranging rewards and punishments to encourage appropriate behaviours and discourage unwanted behaviours. It is helpful if expectations are explicit and requests are made clearly and if the routine is secure and safe. The child can work on rules of behaviour where he is having difficulty, for example not calling out in class and not disturbing others so that he is clear what the rules are and when he has and has not complied. Suitable behaviours to replace unwanted behaviours can be taught; for example, if a child makes inappropriate comments when meeting others, he can be taught; a series of more suitable comments, practising them in role play. Anger management techniques may also be taught. Environmental prompts might be reminder signs posted at home or at school. Having smaller class groups, regular breaks, shorter activity periods and fewer distractions, and adapting these as and when the child improves, might help poor attention. Where a child is depressed or anxious or has other emotional difficulties, it is important to provide opportunities for him to express feelings with a trusted person such as a school counsellor or mental health professional.

Resources

Resources may include adaptive equipment to help function, such as a wheelchair (which may be used temporarily or for some activities and not others) and environmental modifications. Technology may be used for example to help manual dexterity. Depending on the exact nature and consequences of the TBI, some of the resources described in Chapter 8 on 'Orthopaedic impairment' may be useful.

Therapy/care

The speech and language therapist/pathologist has an important role in assessing the child with TBI drawing on standardised assessments of the child, interviews with parents and teacher, observing the child, making a curriculum based language assessment and sampling narrative (story) language. The SLP/ SLT may work directly with him or in a consultancy role through others such as the parents and teacher who have regular contact with the child. Some SLP/SLT specialise in working with children having TBI. For children with motor speech disorders, intervention may include: oral motor therapy (e.g. exercises to strengthen the tongue, lips and jaw); phonation exercises (i.e. breath control exercises) and articulation therapy (helping the child produce correct sounds). For children with language disorders, work may be undertaken on the child's vocabulary (e.g. through work on categories and on visualisation); pragmatic skills (language use) and organisational skills to facilitate language learning (e.g. categorisation, association and sequencing).

Support for the child and the family may be provided by a mental health professional: psychologist, family therapist, clinical social worker, or psychiatrist, ideally with particular experience of working with children with TBI. This may be necessary if the child is exhibiting behaviours harmful to him or others or if the family are overwhelmed.

Organisation

The level of supervision for a child with TBI is an important consideration, ensuring it assists safety but does not damage social contact with peers. To encourage attention, the classroom layout (and physical aspects) should minimise distractions and the child may be taught, at least for a time, in small groups.

Thinking points

Readers may wish to consider:

* how the general points made about TBI can be applied and interpreted for a particular child with TBI and
* how the specialist knowledge and skills of other professionals can be optimised in relation to the child's education.

Key texts

Schoenbrodt, L. (ed.) (2001) *Children with Traumatic Brain Injury: A Parent's Guide*. Bethesda, MD, Woodbine House.
This book, written primarily for parents, is also useful for teachers and others, providing a rich source of information on rehabilitation, education and family adjustment.

Walker, S. and Wicks, B. (2005) *Educating Children with Acquired Brain Injury*. London, David Fulton Publishers.
A clear, well-structured account for teachers, other professionals and parents that largely assumes a United Kingdom context.

Chapter 11

Disruptive behaviour disorders

Introduction

This chapter considers some of the most challenging disorders within the remit of special education: disruptive behaviour disorders. Drawing on the classifications in the *Diagnostic and Statistical Manual of Mental Disorders* Fourth Edition Text Revision *DSM-IV-TR* (American Psychiatric Association, 2000), it considers oppositional defiant disorder briefly and then conduct disorder more fully, commenting on the criteria for conduct disorder and related issues.

In examining interventions for disruptive behaviour disorders and implications for education, the chapter distinguishes approaches relevant for children (3 to 10 years) and those for adolescents (10 to 17 years). Illustrative interventions are chosen that could be used in schools, could be used to complement school provision or which suggest schools could learn from the effectiveness of these interventions in reviewing their own provision. The question of medication is then considered.

Finally, an attempt is made to summarise the aspects of provision in relation to curriculum and assessment; pedagogy; resources; therapy and care and organisation.

It is important to emphasise first the difficulty of educating and helping children and young people with disruptive behaviour disorders. For teachers and others such work can at times feel deskilling, impossibly stressful and unrewarding. To have to endure on top of that long hours, poor support, distant management and poor teamwork would make the work barely possible. The importance of support for those working with pupils with disruptive behaviour disorders is therefore probably self-evident and can include regular training, counselling, opportunities for discussing and seeking to resolve issues as a staff team, and a supportive and responsive management personnel and structure. Where these are in place, many who work with children and young people with disruptive behaviour disorders, whether in schools or secure settings, can find the work very rewarding.

In considering the points raised in this, chapter readers may wish to reflect on a particular pupil, how the teacher and others approach the disruptive behaviour, how and when the school senior staff and head teacher are involved, when and how other support such as that of the school psychologist is brought to bear and how parents are involved. Also, the reader may reflect on the strategies that are available to a specific school and how particular ones are chosen, monitored and evaluated in the setting.

Definitions, prevalence and possible causal factors

Disruptive behaviour disorders and schools

The main classifications of disruptive behaviour disorders in *DSM-IV-TR* (American Psychiatric Association, 2000) are oppositional defiant disorder and conduct disorder. For teachers, it is important to be as clear as possible about the nature of disruptive behaviour disorders, although this is made difficult by several factors.

There is debate about the criteria that are appropriate for these disorders and variability in the level of severity when applying any criteria. In schools, it is sometimes difficult to disentangle what appear to be disruptive disorders on the one hand, and poor teaching and poor pupil management on the other. Teachers who are working hard to encourage positive behaviour in pupils may not be receptive to suggestions that the source of their most disruptive pupil's behaviour might be their own poorly adapted teaching skills. Yet, such avenues will need to be explored before a confident assessment can be undertaken.

Tension exists between the extremes of assuming the difficulties lie very predominantly with the child and assuming that if the teacher only tries hard enough to remove supposed barriers to learning, any apparent problems will recede. It may be helpful therefore if a trusted colleague outside the usual school setting, and with access to the child's family, is involved in assessments of a child who is considered to manifest disruptive behaviour disorders.

Oppositional defiant disorder

As classified under the *DSM-IV-TR* (American Psychiatric Association, 2000) the essential feature of oppositional defiant disorder (ODD) is a repeated pattern (lasting at least for 6 months) of behaviour towards people in authority that is 'negativistic, defiant, disobedient, and hostile' (ibid.: 100). This behaviour leads to significant impairment in 'social, academic or occupational functioning' (ibid.: 100). Attention deficit hyperactivity disorder is common in children with oppositional defiant disorder

The prevalence of ODD varies from 2 per cent to 16 per cent, depending on the nature of the population sample and the methods of assessment. This may be an indication of the point raised earlier about the difficulty of determining whether apparent oppositional defiant disorder is predominantly (and rather loosely speaking) a 'within child' disorder or, in part, a consequence of poor teaching and inadequate behaviour management.

The disorder is usually evident before the age of 8 years and usually not later than early adolescence (ibid.: 101). In a significant proportion of cases, ODD is a developmental antecedent of conduct disorder. All the features of ODD are usually present in conduct disorder so ODD is not diagnosed if the criteria for conduct disorder are met.

Conduct disorder

Definitions and features

Conduct disorder can include a range of behaviours such as aggression, destroying property, stealing, housebreaking, truanting and other infringements of other people's rights and violations of social rules. It is commonly associated with other disorders including attention deficit hyperactivity disorder and substance abuse disorders.

The main aspect of conduct disorder as classified under the *DSM-IV-TR* (American Psychiatric Association, 2000) involves the violation of the rights of others or the transgression of 'major age-appropriate social norms' (ibid.: 98 criterion A). The behaviour forms a repetitive and persistent pattern. Fifteen behaviours are specified under four groupings:

- aggression towards people or animals (seven behaviours);
- damage to property (two behaviours);
- deceitfulness or theft (three behaviours) and
- 'serious' rule transgression (three behaviours).

Three or more of these 15 characteristic behaviours must have been present during the previous 12 months with at least one being evident in the previous 6 months.

Criterion B (American Psychiatric Association, 2000: 99) specifies that the behavioural disturbance causes 'significant impairment' in functioning: social, occupational or academic. A further criteria C applies to those aged 18 years and over and specifies that the criterion for another disorder, antisocial personality disorder, would have been excluded if a diagnosis of conduct disorder was determined (ibid.: 99).

A coding system allows the age of onset to be specified as either childhood onset, adolescent onset, or unspecified onset (where the age when the first signs appeared is unknown). In childhood onset, although the three or more behaviours will have been identified to give the diagnosis, at least one will have started before the age of 10 years. For adolescent onset, no criterion would have been identified before the age of 10. One reason for specifying age of onset is that this has different implications.

With childhood onset, the individual is usually male, frequently manifests physical aggression towards others, has 'disturbed peer relationships', and usually has symptoms meeting the full criteria for conduct disorder before puberty. Many children also have attention deficit hyperactivity disorder. They are more likely to have persistent conduct disorder and to develop adult antisocial personality disorder than those with adolescent onset.

By comparison, those with adolescent onset are less likely to show aggressive behaviours, or to have persistent conduct disorder, or develop adult personality disorder and are more likely to have normal peer relationships. The male-to-female ratio is lower than for childhood onset (ibid.: 95).

DSM-IV-TR (American Psychiatric Association, 2000) also outlines features and disorders associated with conduct disorder, which include lack of empathy; outbursts of temper and recklessness. The behaviours may lead to school suspension or exclusion from school and may preclude attending an ordinary school or living with parents or foster parents. Intelligence may be lower than average, especially verbal intelligence. Academic achievement, particularly reading and verbal skills, is frequently below age and intelligence level expectations (ibid.: 96).

The behaviours that are intended to indicate conduct disorder cover a range of levels of seriousness, although none are trivial. For instance, in *DSM-IV-TR* (American Psychiatric Association, 2000), within the broader scope of aggression to people and animals, criterion A3 refers to the use of a weapon such as a knife or a gun; and criterion A6 concerns stealing while confronting a victim and includes as an example armed robbery. By contrast, criterion A11 (under deceitfulness or theft) concerns often lying 'to avoid obligations' or for other reasons; and criterion 15 (within violation of rules) refers to being often truant from school, commencing before age 13 years.

This makes it important that the specific criteria that have been used for identification are known to those concerned: teachers, social workers, therapists and others. This is recognised in the specification of the severity of conduct disorder. 'Mild' implies a minimum number of criteria have been met to reach a diagnosis and that 'only' minor harm has been caused to others; while 'severe' indicates many conduct problems above the number required for diagnosis or that the conduct has caused 'considerable' harm to others.

Particularly where conduct disorder involves deceitfulness and lying, it is unsurprising that the child himself may not divulge his behaviour or that others, including parents, teachers and peers, may not always know about it. However, the persistence of conduct disorder usually implies that it is apparent in different settings: home, school, in the community, at youth clubs and elsewhere. Gender difference include a tendency for boys' conduct disorder to be associated with fighting, stealing, school discipline problems and vandalism; while in girls it may implicate truancy, lying, substance abuse, running away and prostitution (ibid.: 97).

Prevalence

Prevalence of conduct disorder varies considerably depending on the nature of the population sampled and on the methods used to ascertain it. In the general population reported rates range from 1 per cent to 10 per cent. Prevalence rates are higher among males than females (ibid.: 97). The points concerning the difficulty of ascertaining prevalence that were raised when ODD was examined may also apply to judgements of the prevalence of conduct disorder. The co-occurrence of conduct disorder and attention deficit hyperactivity disorder and anxiety and depression is high, especially in clinic populations.

Causal factors

There is debate about the possible causal factors relevant to conduct disorder. The role of genetically transmitted constitutional features is suggested by certain observations. For example, a much larger proportion of boys than girls experience conduct disorder and heritabilty coefficients are often between 0.4 and 0.7 (Simonoff, 2001). Another theory draws on evidence that children with conduct disorder tend to have lower arousal levels than others, leading them to be fearless, stimulus seeking and less responsive to reward (e.g. for socially accepted behaviour) and punishment (e.g. for unacceptable behaviour). Several studies indicate that low arousal as indicated by various physiological measures are typical of young people with conduct disorders (Raine, 2002). Atypically low arousal levels are thought to be inherited, a view in part supported by twin studies (Kazdin, 1995). The low arousal theory suggests that interventions such as very structured learning environments to help children internalise social rules may be justifiable.

Children with conduct disorders tend to have social skills deficits more generally (e.g. Spivak and Shure, 1982), lacking skills to understand or implement alternative solutions to problematic social situations. Group based social skills programmes developed to train young people tend to address skills such as:

- correcting hostile attributional bias;
- accurately judging difficult social situations;
- generating a variety of solutions to these problematic social situations;
- anticipating the effect of these solutions in the shorter and longer term;
- carrying out the best solution and
- learning from feedback (Carr, 2006: 379).

Among social learning theories of conduct disorder, modelling theory (Bandura and Walters, 1959) suggests that aggression is learned through imitation and modelling, sometimes of the aggressive behaviour of parents, the fathers of aggressive boys typically being aggressive themselves. Derived interventions involve helping parents to model appropriate behaviour for their children, or providing alternatives in foster care or residential settings.

Systems theories, which consider the role of family and society in relation to conduct disorder, include structural family systems theory. This focuses on certain characteristics that appear typical of families of children with conduct disorder such as disorganisation, unclear rules and roles and confused communication. Family therapy relating to such theories seeks to improve the coherence of the family through its members meeting together in subgroups to fulfil certain goals, for example improving communication styles and clarifying hierarchies. Systems approaches also link home and school systems (e.g. Dowling and Osborne, 1994). Recent summaries of aspects of systems approaches are available (e.g. Farrell, 2006b: 17–27).

Identification and assessment of disruptive behaviour disorders

Assessments of disruptive behaviour disorders include assessments of a child's behaviour in an interactional context. This may involve a clinician carrying out structured interviews with teachers and parents or behavioural rating scales being completed by teachers and parents. Direct observation of the child in different settings is also important. Another aspect of assessment is that involving child characteristics such as temperament, social skills and academic achievement.

Provision for disruptive behaviour disorders

The difficulties of identifying disruptive behaviour disorders have already been suggested in the widely varying estimates of prevalence. In addition, where research into treatments has been carried out, it has not always used criteria for conduct disorder or oppositional defiant disorder. The outcomes of some research are therefore suggestive of what works rather than clearly indicative.

Children (3 to 10 years old)

Approaches that have been demonstrated to be effective with some children with disruptive behaviour disorders include:

- parent training;
- social skills training and anger management coping skills training;
- problem solving skills and
- classroom contingency management.

Parent training

One rationale for parent training is that problems such as children's disorders of conduct are considered to relate to inappropriate patterns of family interaction, and that altering these patterns is likely to lead to positive changes in the child's behaviour. Typically, parent training is based on behavioural management principles drawn from social learning theory and may include role-play, behavioural rehearsal and homework exercises. One programme, the 'Incredible years training series' (e.g. Webster-Stratton and Reid, 2003: 224–240) consists of three training curricula for: parents, children aged 2 to 8 years and teachers. It seeks to improve parents' competence, for example, by encouraging them to work together, increasing positive parenting and reducing negative parenting.

An example successfully used in a range of contexts is the 'Oregon Social Learning Center Program' (Patterson and Forgatch, 1995), which addresses aggression and non-compliance in children aged 3 through 12 years. It normally begins by setting out how social learning principles apply to family life. Parents learn to identify and track various of their child's behaviours, usually focusing on two or three that concern them, such as non-compliance, and monitoring these for daily one hour periods over a week. Next the programme introduces a positive reinforcement system using points underpinned by reinforcers such as treats and social reinforcement including praise. Parents are taught to use time out for non-compliance and aggressive behaviour, and mild punishments (chores) and response cost (loss of privileges) are also used. Problem solving and negotiation strategies are taught to help with family crises and marital difficulties (Patterson and Chamberlain, 1988).

'Parent-child interaction therapy' (PCIT) (e.g. Eyberg et al., 1995), developed at the University of Florida, is intended to teach the parent how to develop a warm and responsive relationship with their child and to teach the child how to behave suitably. First, parents develop non-directive play skills intended to improve the quality of child-parent relationship. Next, within the play interaction, the parent learns to direct the child's play with direct instructions seeking to establish consistent consequences (praise for compliance and time out for non-compliance). Parents take turns to interact with the child behind a one-way mirror in the clinic, while the therapist coaches them using an ear microphone, and the interactions are later extended to the home setting. In an early study (Eyberg et al., 1995), children's behaviour in the treatment group fell from the clinical range to the normal range while a waiting list control group experienced no change. Classroom behaviour also improved. Subsequent studies have tended to confirm the success of the approach including the generalising of appropriate behaviour to the classroom (Funderburk et al., 1998).

Several factors tend to make parent training more effective (for a summary see Roth and Fonagy, 2005: 393). Among these factors are:

- the children are younger;
- the disturbance of conduct is less severe;

- there is less family socio-economic disadvantage;
- parents are together.

Conversely, factors have been identified which tend to be associated with failure to benefit from the programmes and attempts have been made to respond to these, for example partner support training where there is discord in the parents' marriage. Parent training may benefit the child's education because it can contribute to improved behaviour in the classroom.

Social skills training and anger management training

One perspective is that conduct disturbance relates to deficits in information processing and that a child with conduct disturbance tends to have distorted appraisals of social events. It is suggested that he will therefore benefit from treatments that seek to modify these distortions and that lead to better ability to regulate his emotional responses.

One approach to anger management training for aggressive children used a '... contextual social cognitive' model of prevention (Lochman et al., 2003: 264). Potential mediators to adolescent antisocial behaviour were recognised to be child level factors such as lack of social competence and parent level contextual factors such as poor child discipline. Within this model, an 'Anger Coping Program', included sessions such as 'using self instruction', 'perspective taking', 'choices and consequences' and 'steps for problem solving' (ibid.: 267).

A school-based strategy, 'Coping Power' (Lochman and Wells, 1996), involved primary school children with conduct problems. Thirty-three structured sessions were administered in the children's school days. Children review examples of social interactions discussing social cues and motives and there are problem-solving components to the programme. Particular skills are practised to manage anger arousal as well as anger control strategies such as self-talk.

Evidence from such interventions indicates that social skills training and anger management coping skills training can help reduce *mild* conduct problems in pre-adolescents (Quinn et al., 1999 provide a review).

Problem-solving skills training

Problem-solving skills training (PSST) developed from the work of Spivak and Sure (e.g. 1978) aims to influence interpersonal cognition. Aggressive children are considered to be more likely than non-aggressive children to attribute hostile intentions to others and anticipate rejection. Children with conduct problems are limited in creating different solutions to interpersonal problems and are poor at working out the motivations of others. Accordingly, PSST aims to help develop necessary interpersonal and cognitive problem-solving skills. Typically, this teaches children to recognise and alter how they think about and respond to social situations, for example using modelling and role-play. In about 20 clinic-based individual sessions the therapist examines the ways in which the child usually responds to interpersonal situations and encourages a structured approach to solving these problems. Structured tasks related to real-life situations are used. Social behaviours are encouraged by modelling and direct reinforcement.

A cognitive behavioural approach was used for children aged 2 to 13 years with conduct disorder which involve child problem-solving skills training (e.g. using 'stop and think' self statements) and parent management training (e.g. using positive reinforcement) (Kazdin, 2003: 241–262). The intervention focuses on '... facets within the individual (e.g. cognitive and behavioural repertoires and predispositions to respond to potentially problematic situations), as well as external and internal interactional events (e.g. antecedents and consequences from others) to promote pro-social behaviour' (ibid.: 258).

Evidence indicates that problem-solving skills training can be effective, particularly in combination with parent training. Smaller effects of the treatment relate to the severity of the child's dysfunction and higher perceived 'barriers' (e.g. Kazdin and Wasser, 2000).

Classroom contingency management

In one study (Barkley et al., 2000) many behavioural interventions, the effect of parent training and the combined treatments were compared (and compared with the results of a control group). Of 158 children screened for disruptive behaviour, 57 per cent met clinical criteria for ODD, 12 per cent for CD and over 50 per cent for attention deficit hyperactivity disorder (ADHD). Among the classroom interventions were a token system, over correction, response cost, time out, group cognitive-behavioural self-control training, group anger control training, group social skills training and support for home-based reinforcement. The parent training programme was based on the Oregon model. Although benefits in terms of outcome measures such as showing less aggression (CBCL-Teacher Report Form) were found for the multiple behavioural interventions, no effects were discernible for parent training. The latter finding may relate to the parents not having sought out the parent training for themselves and therefore perhaps not being as motivated and committed to it as they might otherwise have been.

Unfortunately, such approaches have not been shown to generalise to other settings such as the child's home or to continue beyond the end of the programme.

Adolescents (10 to 17 years)

By the time young people with conduct disorder have reached the age of adolescence, many behaviours relating to CD involve law breaking. Approaches that have been effective with adolescents include those drawing several interventions together in a multiple-level package. These include:

- family based interventions (Functional Family Therapy and Multi-systemic Therapy);
- Teaching Family Model in group homes; and fostering;
- combination packages of adolescent focused interventions;
- school-based interventions.

Family based interventions: Functional Family Therapy and Multi-systemic Therapy

One of the justifications for family based interventions for adolescent conduct disorders are that links are found between family difficulties and adolescent behaviour problems.

Functional Family Therapy (FFT) put forward by (e.g. Alexander and Parsons 1982) and developed further in later versions (Alexander et al., 1988) takes the view that an adolescent's difficult behaviour is serving a function (e.g. regulating distance between family members). Consequently, intervention seeks to tackle not just the adolescent's behavioural problems and cognitive dysfunction but also family interactions and aims to change patterns of interaction and communication so as to encourage adaptive family functioning.

Multi-systemic Therapy (MST) is considered one of the most promising interventions for serious young offenders. A home-based intervention provided by a single therapist, MST draws on a variety of techniques, such as family therapy, parent training, behavioural approaches and cognitive approaches, depending on circumstances. With delinquent adolescents, it has reduced recidivism, improved family pathology and improved individual pathology (e.g. Borduin, 1999). Multi-systemic Therapy (and parent training) has been reviewed indicating that for young delinquents, these interventions tend to reduce the time spent in institutions and the frequency of arrests (e.g. Wolfenden et al., 2003).

The Teaching Family Model in group homes; and fostering

Many group homes for aggressive and delinquent adolescents in the United States of America use Teaching Family Model (TFM) principles. Each home is run by a married couple with at least one year's training in TFM (Kirigin, 1996). Treatment includes academic tutoring, a reinforcement system for monitoring school behaviour, a multi-level points system, social skills training and self-government procedures. Although there is evidence of the benefits of the approach while the adolescents are on the programme, the effects tended to be lost when participants left the programme, indicating broader difficulties of generalising improvement made with behavioural programmes.

Treatment foster care (TFC) for serious juvenile offenders is rooted in the Oregon Social Learning Center model (Patterson and Forgatch, 1995). Community families are trained to provide alternatives to group homes and have been relatively effective in reducing the rate of recidivism (e.g. Chamberlain and Moore, 1998). The programme also uses individual therapy and case management.

Combination packages of adolescent focused interventions

Although it is difficult to endorse a positive impact of individual skills programmes such as social and problem-solving skills training, anger management and training in moral reasoning, there are indications that combinations may be more effective in addressing the multiple cases of conduct disorders.

One package, 'Equipping Youth to Help One Another' (EQUIP), brings together anger management, social skills training, moral reasoning training and problem-solving skills training in a group setting (Gibbs et al., 1996). Promising results have been demonstrated with a small sample of incarcerated male offenders aged 15 to 18 years where a year after release, the EQUIP group recidivism rate was 15 per cent compared with 41 per cent for the control group.

School-based interventions

An evaluation of a programme aimed at tackling gang involvement, Gang Resistance Education Training (GREAT), showed significant effects (Esbensen and Osgood, 1999). Law enforcement officers taught a nine-week curriculum to middle school students that included exercises and interactive approaches intended to underline the consequences of gang violence. Activities taught goal setting, conflict resolution and standing up to peer pressure. Participating students had lower-levels of self-reported delinquency and gang membership than a comparison group.

It is probably too simplistic, given the multiple causes of conduct disorders, to expect direct links between school related variables and delinquency. Yet the school is an important setting for programmes for conduct disorder and delinquency and there may be potential for drawing on school-based mental health resources to modify the school environment to change characteristics associated with delinquency (Fonagy et al., 2005: 171).

Medication

It is argued that medication cannot be justified as the 'first line of treatment' for conduct problems (Fonagy et al., 2005: 192). For educators, among the main issues are being aware of the intended effects and the potential side effects where medication is prescribed, including possible impact on learning and other aspects of behaviour. Also, the stronger and better evaluated are other strategies for dealing with disorders of conduct, the less likely the need to consider medication.

Psychostimulants are effective in reducing antisocial behaviour in adolescents who have both attention deficit hyperactivity disorder and attention deficit disorder/conduct disorder. Their effect is independent of the impact of the medication on the attention deficit and the hyperactivity symptoms. Combinations of psychosocial treatments and stimulant treatments appear to be more broadly effective and have a more lasting impact than either on their own. Various drugs are used, including methylphenidate (Ritalin) in the treatment of antisocial behaviour. There are suggestive indications that clonidine reduces aggressive and destructive behaviour.

Anticonvulsants have been used in the treatment of impulsive behaviour but strong side effects have been reported. While traditional neuroleptics seem to reduce aggressiveness, there are side effects including sedation and an interference with learning. Atypical antipsychotic drugs appear to reduce aggressiveness but weight gain is reported.

Summaries of evidence of the effectiveness of these drugs are available (see Fonagy *et al.*, 2005: 182–192).

Curriculum and assessment; pedagogy; resources; therapy and care; organisation

This final section seeks to summarise provision in terms of curriculum and assessment; pedagogy; resources; therapy and care; organisation.

Curriculum and assessment

The curriculum for pupils with disruptive behaviour disorders may well be at the same academic level as for pupils without a disorder/disability, although, if behaviour has led to long absences from school, the academic content level may be lower (although every effort will be made to keep the interest level age appropriate). As far as the balance of subjects is concerned, there is likely to be an emphasis on aspects of the curriculum encouraging and supporting appropriate behaviour such as social and personal development. In other subjects, the importance of social and personal development may be stressed, for example in physical education the importance of rules and why they are followed will be explained (coupled with strategies to help pupils comply).

Also subjects allowing communication such as drama, debates and arts subjects may be highlighted as well as subjects that may have a cathartic effect such as physical education and drama. Distinctive aspects of the curriculum might include programmes of anger management (for children) and gang resistance education training (for adolescents).

The curriculum may be designed to include extensive opportunities for training in social skills and related skills. Aspects of educational provision can be variously informed by the interventions. For example in lessons devoted to or involving personal and social development, sessions may involve the discussion and practice of social skills; approaches to dealing with anger and problem-solving skills related to social and personal situations. This can either be part of or supplement the more focused provision to develop these skills and attitudes.

In residential special schools, where residential staff and teachers work together to provide a 24-hour curriculum, the skills taught can be more consistent. Residential staff working with therapists can adopt positive parenting skills indicated to be effective.

Assessment may use small steps when applied to personal and social development to enable progress to be seen and acknowledged.

Pedagogy

For adolescents, teaching and learning approaches associated with such programmes as gang resistance education training may be used. For children, pedagogy might include: anger management coping skills training; social skills training and problems-solving skills training. Classroom contingency management may be used with children and where it is, for example, for children with conduct disorder, it can allow academic learning to take place where otherwise it would be disrupted.

In day-to-day contact with pupils, teachers, aware of the importance of the range of skills that are helpful to pupils (social skills, anger management, problem-solving skills) can support and encourage them. Pupils can be helped to develop the skills in daily settings, encouraged when they demonstrate the skills and supported when they cannot do so.

Resources

No distinctive resources appear essential for pupils with disruptive behaviour disorders.

Therapy/care

Psychotherapy will be part of provision, for example programmes such as anger management training may be delivered by therapists with specialist training. Medication may be prescribed.

Organisation

Multi-level/multi-agency approaches with adolescents necessitates the school working closely with others, including workers in the youth justice system, mental health professionals, social workers, health professionals and others. The school requires systems that support such multi-agency working including time being allocated for meetings, telephone contacts and other forms of liaison.

The school setting may include provision for the strategies mentioned. School staff may include, for example, therapists and others providing the relevant services, including supporting parents either in the school or at home. Teachers themselves may be trained in the skills and knowledge necessary to provide or support such services. School flexibility can allow multi-modal treatments such as day or residential, short term or longer term.

Teachers and others in the school not providing these services directly need to be aware of them and be able to work closely with colleagues that do provide the interventions. As part of parent training approaches an important feature is teachers and parents working as closely together as can be managed.

Where several pupils with conduct disorder are taught together and perhaps live together in residential accommodation, staff need to be fully aware of the potential of this contact increasing delinquency. Links with parents or foster parents or residential workers in group homes can support and encourage parent training for children with conduct disorder, and family support for adolescents with conduct disorder.

Other aspects of provision

Among other aspects of provision are: with regard to children, parent training; and concerning adolescents, family based interventions, and teaching family model in group homes/fostering. For both children and adolescents, multi-agency working is important.

Thinking points

Readers may wish to consider:

- how secure the identification and assessment of disruptive behaviour disorders is in the children and young people with whom they work;
- how the school might improve the process by which a teacher considers that a child may have disruptive behaviour disorders, within school assessment and the support provided to the school, for example from school psychologists;
- how the provision indicated by research and professional judgement can be best delivered in a particular school depending on such factors as available staff and their training and
- how the school can best support and complement intervention taking place elsewhere than the school, for example in the family home or in a clinic.

Key texts

Bloomquist, M. and Schnell, M. (2005) *Helping Children with Aggression and Conduct Problems*. New York, Guilford Press.
This describes interventions found effective with children aged 3 to 12 years with aggression and conduct problems. These include social competence training, parent and family skills building, and school-based approaches. Risk factors and protective factors are also described.

Fonagy, P., Target, M., Cottrell, D., Phillips, J. and Kurtz, Z. (2005) *What Works for Whom? A Critical Review of Treatments for Children and Adolescents*. New York, Guilford Press.
As part of the trend for evidence-based treatment, the book presents research evidence of what works. The most substantial chapter of the book, 'Disturbances of conduct' reviews a wide range of interventions mainly from a therapeutic point of view but also including school-based interventions. Chapter 1, 'Introduction and review of outcome methodology', and Chapter 2, 'Epidemiology', are helpful contextual reading.

Larson, J. and Lochman, J. (2005) *Helping School Children Cope with Anger: A Cognitive-Behavioural Intervention*. New York, Guilford Press.
This book presents guidance on the 'Anger Coping Program' for 8 to 12-year-old children.

Nelson, W. M., Finch, A. J. and Hart, K. J. (eds) (2006) *Conduct Disorders: A Practitioner's Guide to Comparative Treatment*. New York, Springer.
This book provides a broad picture of a range of approaches and models that may be used with varying degrees of success with conduct disorder. The practitioners in this case are therapists, but the book covers much that is relevant for teachers and others. Chapters cover description, prevalence and aetiology; psychoanalytical approaches to treatment; family therapy; cognitive-developmental psychotherapy; behavioural treatment; cognitive-behavioural psychotherapy; multi-systemic therapy; continuum of residential treatment care and comparative treatments.

Tremblay, R. (ed.) (2005) *Developmental Origins of Agreession*. New York, Guilford Press.
This book examines the interactions between biological factors, social and environmental effects, and sex differences in adaptive and maladaptive aggression.

Chapter 12

Anxiety disorders and depressive disorders

Introduction

For teachers and others, while conditions such as conduct disorder are all too evident, anxiety disorders and depressive disorders may not always be as readily recognised, yet their negative impact on school and home life can be profound. This chapter focuses on anxiety disorders: generalised anxiety disorder, obsessive-compulsive disorder, phobias, separation anxiety disorder, and selective mutism; and on depressive disorders: major depressive disorder and dysthymic disorder. The final section seeks to summarise provision in relation to curriculum and assessment; pedagogy; resources; therapy/care and organisation and other matters.

Anxiety disorders

In the *Diagnostic and Statistical Manual of Mental Disorders Text Revision* (*DSM-IV-TR*) (American Psychiatric Association, 2000) most anxiety disorders are adult syndromes the criteria for which can also be applied to children and include:

- generalised anxiety disorder;
- obsessive-compulsive disorder;
- specific phobia and
- social phobia.

The *DSM-IV-TR* (American Psychiatric Association, 2000) also includes, as disorders first diagnosed in infancy, childhood or adolescence:

- separation anxiety disorder; and
- selective mutism.

Overall for one or more of the various types of diagnosable anxiety disorders prevalence is estimated to be around 8–12 per cent of children and adolescents aged 4 to 20 years (e.g. Bernstein and Borchardt, 1991). About a third of children with one anxiety disorder also meet the criteria for at least one other anxiety disorder (Strauss and Last, 1993) and around a third also experience major depression (Bernstein and Borchardt, 1991).

Generalised anxiety disorder

Definition

Generalised anxiety disorder involves excessive anxiety and worry on most days for at least 6 months concerning several activities or events (American Psychiatric Association, 2000: 472 and criteria A). The worry is hard to control and includes, in children, an additional symptom such as difficulty in concentrating, restlessness or fatigue (ibid.: 472).

Prevalence

In a community sample, the prevalence for generalised anxiety disorder was around 3 per cent (American Psychiatric Association, 2000: 474). Reviews of epidemiological studies indicate that concerning children and young people of 4 to 20 years age of onset, 8–12 per cent of children in the age range experience one or more diagnosable anxiety disorders (e.g. Bernstein and Borschardt, 1991). Anxiety disorders are the most common type of psychiatric disorder in children.

Causal factors

Generalised anxiety disorder is a chronic and fluctuating condition but tends to worsen in times of stress.

Identification and assessment

Generalised anxiety disorder is identified and assessed according to criteria such as those outlined and by distinguishing it from superficially similar states such as non-pathological anxiety (the former interferes significantly with functioning for example). Commercial assessments also contribute.

Provision

Some cognitive-behavioural therapy (CBT) packages have been effective in treating generalised anxiety disorder and other anxiety disorders in children (e.g. Toren et al., 2000). A 'child focused treatment' of anxiety is described (Kendall et al., 2003: 81–100). This cognitive-behavioural programme was used to treat 'disturbingly anxious' 8 to 13 year olds. It involves child-therapist relationships and 'education into the physiological signs of anxiety, the normality of anxiety and behavioural skills to address the management of anxiety' (ibid.: 97). An initial educational (preparation) phase was followed by an exposure (practice) phase.

Individual CBT was compared with individual plus family cognitive behavioural work (Barrett *et al.*, 1996). Some 76 children aged 7 to 14 years with anxiety disorder were allocated to one of the three conditions (CBT only; CBT plus family management; waiting list control). CBT plus family intervention was found to be the superior condition, confirming earlier research by others that treatment was rendered more effective by adding family management.

A study at the University of Pisa (Muratori *et al.*, 2002) evaluated the effectiveness of a programme for 58 children with relatively mild anxiety disorder or dysthymic disorder (which involves chronically depressed mood). Treatments comprised 11 sessions of focal psychodynamic psychotherapy, which started with five sessions involving the whole family in which the therapist explored the dynamic formulation of the child's conflicts in terms of family relationships. Five sessions with the child only followed this with the therapist aiming to help the child make connections between his feelings and unconscious conflicts about the relationship with his parents. In the final session for the whole family, the therapist set out again the dynamic formulation of the child's conflicts rooted in family relationships. The control group was referred for community treatment. The family work, not considered family therapy, was intended to help the therapists in treating the child to focus on relationship issues. While only 60 per cent of children were in the clinical range of the Child Behaviour Checklist (Achenbach and Edelbrock, 1983), this was reduced to 34 per cent in the treatment group at follow-up testing while the controls increased to 65 per cent.

Obsessive-compulsive disorder

Definition

Obsessive-compulsive disorder (OCD) involves recurring obsessions and compulsions that take up more than an hour a day or bring about significant impairment or distress (American Psychiatric Association, 2000: 456). Obsessions are persistent ideas, thoughts, desires or images that cause significant distress or worry such as the need to have items in a certain order, thoughts about being contaminated through touching others and impulses to harm others. Compulsions are repetitive behaviours (e.g. hand washing or touching walls) or mental acts (e.g. counting to one's self) aimed at reducing anxiety or distress. Children may not always recognise that these actions and thoughts are unreasonable.

Prevalence

Community studies of children and adolescents have estimated a lifetime prevalence of 1 per cent to 2.3 per cent and 1 year prevalence of 0.7 per cent (American Psychiatric Association, 2000: 460).

Causal factors

Obsessive-compulsive disorder concordance rate is higher for identical than for non-identical twins, suggesting a hereditary element. A cause that is eliminated in the definition is substance abuse or medication. For a small number of children, obsessive-compulsive disorder may be associated with a group A betahemolytic streptococcal infection (e.g. scarlet fever).

Identification and assessment

The identification and assessment of obsessive-compulsive disorder is linked to criteria already outlined in the section on definition.

Provision

Although medication is used with several anxiety disorders, it appears to be most effective for OCD. The tricyclic antidepressant Clomipramine has been demonstrated to lead to significantly better improvement than a placebo (e.g. DeVeaugh-Geiss et al., 1992) but cardiac monitoring is necessary because of the small risk of sudden death from cardiac arrest (review by Geller et al., 1999). More positively, in research involving children and young people aged 8 to 17 years, scores on several measures relating to OCD were significantly lower for those given the selective serotonin reuptake inhibitor (SSRI) fluvoxamine than those given a placebo. SSRIs also tend to produce less serious side effects than tricyclics (Riddle et al., 2001).

Cognitive behavioural therapy, involving exposure and response prevention, is also used. For example, a small-scale open study with 14 children and adolescents meeting the criteria for OCD led to 12 of the patients having at least a 50 per cent reduction in the severity of symptoms, gains that were maintained after a 9-month follow up (Franklin et al., 1998). It has been recommended that the treatment of choice for childhood OCD is a combination of SSRI medication and cognitive behavioural therapy (March, 1999).

Phobias: specific and social

Definition

DSM-IV-TR (American Psychiatric Association, 2000) includes criteria for specific phobia (e.g. claustrophobia); social phobia and agoraphobia (with or without panic disorders). A *specific phobia* is a persistent unreasonable fear of certain situations, activities or objects leading to their avoidance and can bring about distress and disruption of social relationships. Whereas adults tend to recognise the fear as irrational, children may not.

Social phobia involves a marked, persistent and unreasonable fear of social situations or performance situations where the person may be embarrassed (American Psychiatric Association, 2000: 450). Exposure to such a situation triggers immediate anxiety. School refusal may be related to school phobia and/or to separation anxiety where the child fears separating from home.

Prevalence

Estimates of lifetime prevalence range from 3 per cent to 13 per cent (American Psychiatric Association, 2000: 453). For specific phobias, in community samples (not just children) estimates of prevalence range from 4 per cent to 8.8 per cent (ibid.: 447).

Causal factors

The fear of a stimulus (e.g. spiders) is usually present for some time before becoming distressing enough and restricting enough to be considered a specific phobia. Social phobia, which often emerges in the mid teens, is sometime preceded by a childhood history of shyness or inhibition.

Identification and assessment

Specific and social phobias are identified and assessed using criteria such as those outlined in the section on definitions.

Provision

Behavioural interventions have long been used effectively for many phobic children (Ollendick and King, 1998 for a review). Behavioural treatments of circumscribed phobias may involve desensitisation either through images of what is feared or actual experience of it (*in vivo* treatment). Childhood phobias have been effectively treated through modelling based on social learning theory (Bandura, 1977) and particularly effective is participant modelling involving *in vivo* exposure and the modelling of exposure by others (e.g. Blanchard, 1970). Contingency management drawing on operant conditioning has been shown to be effective with phobias in young children (e.g. Menzies and Clarke, 1993). School refusal has been effectively treated by so called 'flooding' in which the child is rapidly returned to school, although there are concerns about the humaneness of such an approach (e.g. Fonagy *et al.*, 2005: 87). One study, mainly of school refusers of secondary school age, indicated that behavioural treatment led to significantly better rates of maintenance in school than inpatient treatment and home tutoring (Blagg and Yule, 1984).

Cognitive behavioural therapy, including gradual exposure techniques, can be effective in treating circumscribed phobias such as school refusal especially in younger children (e.g. King *et al.*, 2001). One randomly controlled trial involved 34 children aged 5 to 15 years with school phobia. Those assigned to CBT showed significantly greater improvement during treatment compared with a waiting list control. The CBT involved six individual therapy sessions over a period of 4 weeks and a gradual return to school (King *et al.*, 1998).

Separation anxiety disorder

Definition

In *the Diagnostic and Statistical Manual of Mental Disorders Text Revision* (*DSM-IV-TR*) (American Psychiatric Association, 2000: 121) separation anxiety disorder is excessive anxiety to do with separation from the home or from someone to whom the child or adolescent is attached (criterion A). Under other criteria it must last for at least 4 weeks and begin before the age of 18 years. School refusal may be an indication of separation anxiety.

Prevalence

Estimates of prevalence of separation anxiety disorder average about 4 per cent in children and adolescents but prevalence decreases from childhood to adolescence (American Psychiatric Association, 2000: 123).

Causal factors

Separation anxiety may develop after a very stressful life event such as the death of a family member or pet, a change of school or a change of home.

Identification and assessment

Separation anxiety disorder is identified and assessed using criteria such as those outlined in the section on definitions.

Provision

Approaches drawing on group cognitive-behavioural therapy may be helpful with children and adolescents with separation anxiety disorder. An open trial of parent–child group cognitive behavioural therapy for children with anxiety disorders was conducted. Almost all had separation anxiety disorder and half had overanxious disorder of childhood (now subsumed under generalised anxiety disorder) and/or phobias. Some 24 children and their parents took part in 10 sessions using CBT approaches. Seventy per cent of these no longer met the diagnostic criteria by the end of treatment and 3 years later this applied to 91 per cent (Toren *et al.*, 2000).

Selective mutism (elective mutism)

Definition

In *the Diagnostic and Statistical Manual of Mental Disorders Text Revision* (*DSM-IV-TR*) (American Psychiatric Association, 2000: 125–127) defines selective mutism as a 'persistent failure to speak in specific social situations ... where speaking is expected, despite speaking in other situations'. The situations in which the child might not speak yet where speaking is expected to include school, or when with playmates and the situations in which the child does speak are typically at home. The criteria include that the disturbance interferes with educational achievement, occupational achievement or with social communication. It must last for at least a month and the first month of school should not be counted, as many children are reluctant to speak perhaps because of shyness. If the child does not speak solely because of lack of knowledge of (or lack of 'comfort' with) the spoken language required in the social situation, this is not considered selective mutism. Also, the condition is not diagnosed if the disturbance is better explained by other reasons: embarrassment because of communication difficulties such as stuttering, or if it occurs only during a pervasive developmental disorder, or a psychotic disorder (ibid.: 125–126).

Selective mutism may be associated with other features. There may be excessive shyness, fear of embarrassment, social isolation and withdrawal, clinging, compulsive behaviour, temper tantrums, or controlling or oppositional behaviour (particularly at home). Social and school functioning may be severely impaired. While the child usually has normal language skills, elective mutism may be associated with communication disorder (e.g. phonological disorder) or a general medical condition causing abnormalities of articulation. Hospitalisation, extreme psychosocial stressors or mental retardation may be associated with selective mutism. In clinical settings, children with selective mutism are almost invariably additionally diagnosed as having an anxiety disorder, for example social phobia (American Psychiatric Association, 2000: 126).

Prevalence

It is estimated the prevalence of selective mutism is less than 1 per cent of individuals seen in mental health settings (American Psychiatric Association, 2000: 126). It is slightly more common in females than males.

Causal factors

Selective mutism usually occurs before the age of 5 years, although it may not come to the attention of clinicians until the child starts school. It may persist for a few months or for several years. In some instances, particularly where the child has severe social phobia, anxiety symptoms may become chronic (American Psychiatric Association, 2000: 126).

Identification and assessment

The criteria outlined in the definition of selective mutism inform the identification and assessment. Also, children with elective mutism may communicate by gesture, nodding or shaking the head or pulling and pushing. In some instances, the child may communicate in utterances that are short, monosyllabic or monotone or may use an altered voice (American Psychiatric Association, 2000: 126).

Provision

Elective mutism is responsive to family based behavioural treatment (e.g. Carr, 2006). This typically involves the child and a family member with whom the child will speak having planned conversations in a setting where the child usually remains mute, for example the school classroom. In this example, the planned conversation would take place in the classroom when it is empty. Gradually in incremental steps people in whose presence the child does not usually speak in the setting concerned join the child and the family member. In our example this would be other school pupils, the teacher, the classroom aide and so on.

As the child becomes increasingly able to continue conversation with the family member in the presence of these others, the teacher and pupils gradually take part in the conversation. Eventually, the child and family member move further apart so that in the final stages, the child is conversing with others in the classroom with the family member positioned close to the classroom door. Finally the child asks the family member to leave and collect them at the end of the school day (ibid.: 521). (See also Sage and Sluckin, 2004.)

Depressive disorders

Definitions and other matters

Among depressive disorders in the *Diagnostic and Statistical Manual of Mental Disorders Text Revision* (*DSM-IV-TR*) (American Psychiatric Association, 2000) are major depressive disorder and dysthymic disorder. In major depressive disorder, there are one or more major depressive episodes (ibid.: 369). The depressed mood must be present for most of the day almost every day for at least two weeks. Severity is noted as mild, moderate or severe (with or without psychotic features).

Dysthymic disorder in comparison with major depressive disorder is characterised by less severe symptoms that are present more days than not over at least a 2-year period (American Psychiatric Association, 2000: 376). With children and adolescents, the mood may be irritable rather than depressed and the required minimum duration is a year (ibid.: 377). In children dysthymic disorder may be associated with other conditions including attention deficit hyperactivity disorder, anxiety disorders and conduct disorder. It occurs equally in both sexes and often leads to impaired school performance and social interaction (ibid.: 378). While depressed, two or more of other features have to be present to meet the criteria and these include: poor appetite or overeating, low energy or fatigue, low self-esteem and poor concentration or difficulty making decisions (ibid.: 380).

In children, depression is comparatively rare tending to be expressed through anxiety, frustration or somatic complaints (e.g. Birmaher *et al.*, 1996) while adolescents tend to show more biological complaints and thoughts of suicide or actual suicidal behaviour. For children and adolescents diagnosed as having major depression, 40 to 70 per cent have a second psychiatric disorder and 20 per cent or more have three or more disorders (Birmaher *et al.*, 1996). Although there is a high rate of recovery from episodes of depression, there is also a high relapse rate of 50 per cent within 2 years (e.g. Fonagy, 2005: 103).

Prevalence

Epidemiological studies of children and adolescents aged 4 to 20 years of age indicate a point prevalence rate of around 2 per cent for children and 2 to 5 per cent for adolescents for both depression and dysthymia (e.g. Lewinsohn and Clarke, 1999). Until adolescence, depressive disorders are equally distributed among boys and girls until after the age of 14 years when girls predominate over boys by a ratio of 2 to 1.

Causal factors

Major depressive disorder is up to three times as common among the first-degree biological relatives of people with the disorder than it is among the population generally (American Psychiatric Association, 2000: 373) suggesting a hereditary element. Dysthymic disorder is more common among first-degree biological relatives of people with major depressive disorder than among the population generally (ibid.: 379).

Identification and assessment

Major depressive disorder and dysthymic disorder are identified and assessed using criteria such as those outlined in the section on definitions.

Provision

While neither social skills training nor individual child psychotherapy has been demonstrated to be effective treatment for depression (Fonagy *et al.*, 2005: 101–104), cognitive behaviour therapy for adolescents (with the concurrent treatment of any maternal depression), Interpersonal Therapy Adapted for Adolescents, and serotonin reuptake inhibitors (SSRIs) look promising. The evidence points to the effectiveness of such interventions for adolescents with mild depression but the picture is less clear for adolescents with severe depression and for children with depression.

Cognitive behavioural therapy appears effective for treating adolescents with mild or moderate depression whether treatment is provided individually or in a group. Where there was no response to treatment of the usual duration, providing a longer course of CBT or booster sessions reduced relapse and improved recovery (e.g. Clarke *et al.*, 1999).

A series of studies comparing CBT, systemic-behavioural family therapy and non-directive support for 107 adolescents indicated that CBT showed the greatest improvement particularly for those adolescents also experiencing anxiety. Where the mother was clinically depressed, the treatment outcome for the adolescent was worse and CBT was no better than the other conditions. This leads to the suggestion that any such maternal depression should be concurrently treated (Brent *et al.*, 1998). At a 2-year follow-up, the superiority of CBT had not been maintained.

The 'Primary and secondary control enhancement training for youth depression' programme, used for treating depressed children and young people aged 8 to 15 years, draws on the cognitive-behavioural tradition (Weisz *et al.*, 2003: 165–183). It takes a two-process model of control and coping: primary and secondary control. 'Primary control' involves attempts to cope by making objective conditions (e.g. the activities in which one participates and one's acceptance by other people) conform to one's wishes. 'Secondary control' refers to efforts to cope by adjusting oneself to fit the objective conditions (e.g. adjusting one's beliefs, expectations and interpretations of events). The programme involves treatment sessions and assignments that are taken home.

Also, Interpersonal Psychotherapy Adapted for Adolescents (IPT-A) appears a promising treatment for adolescent depression (e.g. Mufson *et al.*, 1999). Interpersonal psychotherapy is a brief treatment for adults with depression that concentrates on certain interpersonal problems that may underlie the depression. This has been modified and manualised for the treatment of adolescents as IPT-A. A randomised controlled trial included 48 referred adolescents with major depressive disorder and 32 of them completed the programme. The control group was a clinical monitoring waiting list. As evaluated by rating scale scores, 75 per cent of the IPT-A group recovered compared with 46 per cent of the control group (Mufson *et al.*, 1999).

Regarding medication, the most promising appear to be selective serotonin reuptake inhibitors (SSRIs), which also appear to have fewer side effects than alternative medication. A randomised double blind placebo controlled trial of fluoxetine was conducted with 96 outpatient children and adolescents aged 7 to 17 years experiencing depression. This indicated fluoxetine is to be significantly more effective than a placebo (Emslie *et al.*, 1997).

Curriculum, pedagogy, resources, therapy and organisation for anxiety/depressive disorders

Curriculum

Aspects of the curriculum that encourage open communication are considered valuable including personal and social education sessions. Discussions, art, drama, dance, play and other sessions may all afford opportunities for the child to communicate concerns. Regular and ongoing opportunities for the child to communicate any worries are important with staff trained to listen and respond helpfully. This may include more formal systems such as counselling as well as an ethos in which pupil participation, consultation and communication is paramount.

Structures that may support this include group work the potential benefits of which include opportunities to share problems and experiences and build up mutual support. The role of the facilitator is central and the facilitating role may need to be explained to pupils and agreed with them. Parental consent is sought and the informed consent of the pupil established (see also Geldard and Geldard, 2001). An example of group work in schools is that used as part of the Coping in Schools programme which included reintegration groups developed in special schools although these were not solely for pupils with anxiety and depression but for a broader group of pupils with 'behavioural and social difficulties' (McSherry, 2001: 34–44). Circle time is a further approach involving peer group work focusing on sharing perceptions and seeking to deal with any problems as a group (Kelly, 1999). Where it is judged appropriate, peer counselling may be used in which trained and supervised students carry out 'interpersonal helping tasks' (Hornby *et al.*, 2003: 71).

Developing 'emotional literacy' includes that it aims to develop the language of feelings, encourages reflection on feelings, taking an interest in the feelings of others and engaging in dialogue about thoughts and feelings (e.g. Antidote, 2003: 33–56).

Perhaps such issues can be best summarised in aiming for a 'listening school' but the practicalities of how this is made a reality cannot be overlooked. There are implications for extra staffing, and training in counselling type skills and general supervision skills.

Pedagogy

In educating children with anxiety disorders, and depressive disorders, the teacher and the school will want to be aware of any psychotherapy the child may be receiving and be supportive of it. For example, in educating children with phobia, the nature of the phobia is relevant. Where usual school provision is likely to bring the child into contact with an item or situation that the pupil fears, teachers will need to work with therapeutic staff to determine the approach to be taken so opportunities for close professional liaison are necessary.

A training co-ordinator in a school may wish to consider the basic knowledge and skills a member of staff is likely to need to provide well for pupils with anxiety disorders and depressive disorders. A rolling programme of training involving other professionals as necessary can then be devised and monitored, supplemented by an initial training and induction programme for new staff. Supervision and support is important in less structured times such as breaks and lunchtimes and the staff mainly responsible for these periods may require special awareness training. Where teachers or other staff in the school are specially trained, they may deliver or contribute to aspects of the psychotherapeutic interventions. In some schools the treatment may take place on the school campus. Where it proves difficult to find therapists trained in the interventions mentioned, the role of teachers is likely to be one of support.

Resources

There appear to be no distinctive physical resources that are essential for pupils with anxiety disorders or depressive disorders.

Therapy

As indicated in the section on pedagogy, the provision of therapy is an important contribution with teachers and therapists liaising well. Cognitive behavioural therapy is used for separation anxiety; obsessive-compulsive disorder and (with family work) for anxiety disorders. For phobia, behavioural methods, social learning (modelling) and cognitive behavioural therapy are employed. For mild depression in adolescents therapy may comprise: cognitive behavioural therapy with treatment of any concurrent maternal depression; Interpersonal Therapy Adapted for Adolescents; or selective serotonin reuptake inhibitors. Medication such as selective serotonin reuptake inhibitors may be administered for obsessive-compulsive disorder. Staff need to be aware of any medication taken by children, its likely effects and its possible side effects, necessitating liaison between education and health service personnel.

Organisation

It is considered important that the organisation of the school encourages a calm and reassuring ethos, with teachers aiming to be supportive without being overprotective and routines being predictable and well understood by the child (without encouraging further rigidity in behaviour for pupils with obsessive-compulsive disorder). An organisational structure in which pupils as well as staff are encouraged to be supportive is helpful.

Many schools have transition arrangements for any child or young person starting school, coming from another school or area or returning to school after a long absence. This might involve initial visits with parents, a system to ensure that the new pupil has other pupils to help them settle in, procedures to help ensure that the pupil knows what is expected, where to go at different times of the day and so on.

Clearly where a child experiences school phobia, the staff will seek to ensure school is as welcoming and supportive as possible while still remembering that the phobia is by definition not based on reason. The phobia may relate to a particular child or group of children, a particular teacher or certain subjects and establishing these will inform the response of the school. It may be possible to develop special transition arrangement perhaps involving the pupil first attending a unit on the school campus then gradually reintegrating into the rest of the school. Separation anxiety may lead to the child being extremely reluctant to attend school and the school might arrange to provide shorter sessions for part of the day and part of the week to gradually bring the child to return to school. Support for parents also suffering anxiety can help.

Other aspects

Where family management is provided relating to child anxiety disorders or where the mother of a depressed adolescent is herself depressed, the school will want to do all it can in support. Where schools have facilities for therapy on site this can encourage parents to seek support themselves. Parents, where they feel harassed by persistent requests from a child with obsessive-compulsive disorder, may require particular understanding and practical support from the school and others.

Thinking points

Readers may wish to consider with reference to a particular school:

- how coherent is whole school provision given the range of anxiety disorders and the fact that they often occur together and given the range of depressive disorders;

- training implications for staff if they are to work with children with severe anxiety disorders and depressive disorders;
- practical ways in which parents can be supported.

Key texts

For anxiety

Chorpita, B. F. (2005) *Modular Cognitive-Behavioural Therapy for Childhood Anxiety Disorders*. New York, Guilford Press.
This book describes approaches for treating anxiety using exposure based techniques.

Rachman, S. (2004, 2nd edition) *Anxiety*. London and New York, Taylor & Francis.
A comprehensive introduction to current research and practice, the book covers: the nature of anxiety; influences on anxiety; theories of anxiety; the conditioning theory of fear and specific phobias; panic and anxiety; agoraphobia; obsessions and compulsions; social anxiety and general anxiety disorder.

De Silva, P., Rachman, S. and Rachman, J. (1998) *Obsessive-Compulsive Disorder: The Facts*. Oxford, Oxford University Press.
This covers definitions of obsessive-compulsive disorder; its relationship to other disorders; the effect on family, work and social life; prevalence; theories and explanations; assessment and evaluation and practical advice.

For depression

Goodyer, I. M. (ed.) (2001, 2nd edition) *The Depressed Child and Adolescent*. Cambridge, Cambridge University Press.
Mainly intended for psychiatrists, psychologists and other mental health professionals, this book discusses causes of depression, clinical characteristics and frequency. The importance of life events is considered and the difficulties around the onset and continuation of depression. The effectiveness of psychological interventions and of medication is covered. Chapters include: 'Suicidal behaviour in adolescents', 'Pharmacology of depressive states in childhood and adolescence' and 'The psychotherapeutic management of major depressive and dysthymic disorders in childhood and adolescence'.

Chapter 13

Attention deficit hyperactivity disorder

Introduction

This chapter outlines some of the debates currently relating to attention deficit hyperactivity disorder (ADHD). It presents a definition of ADHD and considers its prevalence then looks at identification and assessment of the condition. The chapter outlines some of the other disorders with which ADHD co-occurs and causal factors. Turning to provision, it explains some of the main approaches including behaviour management training, parent training, medication and educational approaches.

Examples of further information on the Internet that may act as starting points for further searches are the United States of America Attention deficit Hyperactivity Disorder Association (www.add.org) and the United Kingdom Attention Deficit Hyperactivity Disorder website (www.btinternet.com/~black.ice/addnet/).

Some debates concerning ADHD

Debates about ADHD reflect the broader issues mentioned in the introduction to this book concerning social, individual and interactionist understandings of disability/disorder and the balance of the influence of language, subjective and objective views. Other issues are also raised.

Shifting responsibility

There is a concern in some quarters that acceptance of ADHD as a 'condition' may displace parental responsibility for a child's unacceptable behaviour. It has been suggested that 'To millions of families, the label [of ADHD] provides a legitimate justification to "outsource" some responsibilities related to raising children' (Cohen, 2006: 12). Similarly, the label may provide an 'alibi' for schools to explain why they cannot make some children fit into their institution (ibid.: 13).

To the extent that this is a legitimate concern, schools, parents and others could work together more successfully than is often the case to try to ensure that other possible explanations of behaviour associated with aspects of ADHD are considered before an identification of the behaviour as ADHD is made. This might include examining the quality of teaching and ethos of the school, the family context and peer relationships as possible contributory factors.

Family location within society and socialisation

Another perspective in some ways contrasts to the view that the ADHD label may be used to displace responsibility mentioned above. This is the view that parents may feel pressured to accept the label of ADHD and perhaps accept medication for their child because of pressures from a judgemental society. In examining the possible 'social construction' of ADHD Davis (2006: 47) explores the view that top-down views of socialisation influence the public services of health, education and social care, and coerce mothers into co-operating with professionals, for example in defining their child's appropriate behaviour at different age stages.

It is suggested a 'moral discourse' exists that holds parents, especially mothers, responsible for the decline in moral standards and the child's lack of achievement. Irresponsible parents, especially single and teenage mothers, and breakdown in community ties are seen as part of the explanation of child educational failure. In relation to ADHD this 'discourse' is thought to, 'pressurise parents into using drugs to control their children's behaviour' (Davis, 2006; 49). Davis concludes that, 'the increase in the diagnosis of ADHD may be an indicator of a wider social problem that relates to a family's location within society' (ibid.: 49). Similarly it is suggested that society's need for, 'good children, normal young people and future productive citizens' underpins the emergence of ADHD (Davis, 2006: 52). Therefore 'medical model solutions' such as prescribing drugs fail to treat the 'root social causes' of ADHD (ibid.: 52).

It appears that Davis is maintaining that the root social causes of ADHD relate to wanting good children and future productive citizens. It is not clear whether Davis is suggesting that society should instead settle for bad children and unproductive future citizens so society is less demanding of others, especially supposedly oppressed groups. Also, a parent may have to wait a long time with a child whose behaviour is very challenging while the supposed root causes of society are put right.

Cultural influences and pressures

It has been argued that the apparent increase in ADHD may relate to cultural influences, such as the overstimulation of the mass media, the limited opportunities for active play and higher expectations of children from an earlier age (Armstrong, 2006: 41). Within this context, it appears important that understandings of ADHD take such influences into account and that ADHD is understood as behaviour over and above what might be expected given such possible influences and that it inhibits learning and interferes with daily life activities.

Parents may see the use of stimulants for ADHD as ways of helping to ensure the child does well in school. It has been suggested that to the degree medication may be being used as 'short-term school performance enhancers for children' this should be subject to open discussion rather than being masked behind what some perceive as an 'ostensibly medical condition' (Cohen, 2006: 19). Parental motives appear central here. If medication is seen as a performance enhancer in the absence of any difficulty or disorder there is reason to question its use. But if ADHD impairs a child's ability to concentrate and be less active when situations generally require it, this is likely to hinder learning. Should medication control some of this and allow learning to take place then learning is likely to be enhanced. In the latter case it is not necessarily correct that the medication is being used simply to enhance performance although that is its beneficial effect as it allows learning to take place.

The speed at which modern life is lived in developed countries it has been maintained may be affecting the consciousness of children. It has been argued that, 'As rapid-fire culture gives rise to rapid-fire consciousness – and, for children, an inability to manage their own behaviour – sensory addictions develop, motivating us to engage in more stimulus seeking behaviours' (DeGrandepre, 1998: 32). What is not clear in this explanation is why the purported sensory addiction appears to affect some children more than others and whether the classification ADHD identifies those children whose supposed sensory addiction goes beyond the levels at which usual adaptation is manageable.

Overzealous medicalisation

The identification of ADHD has been seen as 'medicalising' deviant and even ordinary behaviour. For example, some of the behavioural signs in the *Diagnostic and Statistical Manual of Mental Disorders, Fourth Edition Text Revision (DSM-IV-TR)* (American Psychiatric Association, 2000) are if taken singly merely aspects of normal childhood behaviour. It is the 'frequency and combination of signs' (Cohen, 2006: 16) that is taken to be dysfunctional. Related to this is that no discernible physical abnormality has been securely established for ADHD and that the symptoms can be seen as little more than a list of behaviours that annoy teachers (and parents). It is suggested that the diagnosis of ADHD 'cannot have any validity as a label for a genuine biological dysfunction' (ibid.: 21). Another difficulty is that identification can be criticised as only identifying the symptoms in medical terms but not the possible causes of the behaviours because the symptoms are synonymous with the condition.

This position has the problem that, while it is strictly correct so far as identifiable biological dysfunctions are concerned, the classifications of conditions do not always have clear physiological correlates yet may be useful constructs enabling support or more effective education to be provided to the person considered to experience the condition. Autism is an example of a condition thought to have a physiological basis but this has yet to be securely identified.

Incompatibility between child and environment

ADHD has also been seen in terms of a mismatch between a normal child and a normal environment. The child may have a normal temperament and no neurological impairment but have within normal variations 'low adaptability and low persistence/attention span' (Carey, 2002: 23). As Carey states, 'The dysfunction appears to be in the interaction between child and environment, both of which may be normal but incompatible with each other' (ibid.: 23).

The difficulty with this argument is that the lower than usual level of ability to adapt, persist and pay attention is not specified. The suggestion is that it is within usual or normal limits, yet this is not what is generally intended by the term ADHD. The behaviour associated with definitions of ADHD are beyond what is considered usual and disrupts learning and other aspects of functioning as a result.

Preferred diagnosis when ADHDs co-occurs with other conditions

ADHD may be a preferred diagnosis when it co-occurs with other conditions (co-occurrence is also discussed in the later section of this chapter on 'Prevalence and co-occurrence with other disorders'). For example, about a third of individuals with ADHD develop significant antisocial behaviour problems in adolescence with the problems persisting into adulthood leading to criminal behaviour for most of this subgroup (e.g. Carr, 2006: 423). Also, it has been estimated that 30–50 per cent of children with ADHD also have conduct or oppositional disorders (Biederman *et al.*, 1991). If some of the characteristics of these problems or conditions are unacceptable or uncomfortable for parents and others, the question arises if whether an assessment of ADHD is more acceptable than some other potential diagnoses where the diagnosis is unclear and characteristics are similar.

Possible further developments

While it is useful to be aware of possible distorting factors that may influence the definition, assessment and provision for ADHD, some of these arguments are not without their weaknesses, as has been suggested above. Also it is necessary to consider within the limits of current understanding the extent to which definitions, assessment and provision are helping children and young people. For example, it is not easy to completely explain away the evidence of the positive impact of medication in combination with other provision (see later in the chapter) in terms of the purported capitalist exploitation by drug companies, the malign effect of medical 'discourses' and abusive power relationships.

On the other hand, this does not imply that the understanding of what is presently considered to represent ADHD, its definition, assessment and provision cannot be refined and improved. Furthermore, some of the points raised by critics of the ADHD label require careful consideration and reflection. Among these is perhaps the concern that the label may lead to shifting of responsibility for parents and schools. Another is the possibility that cultural influences, such as mass media, limited opportunities for active play and higher expectations of younger children, may be contributing to a general increase in behaviour that is less compatible with the usual requirements of education and an overidentification of apparent ADHD.

Taking such points into consideration, there may be grounds for considering critically whether ADHD is overdiagnosed which suggest more careful assessment and a greater awareness of factors that may encourage such a phenomena. It is the view of this chapter that some children do experience very severe difficulties that cannot be explained away sociologically or by postmodern discourses. These can be identified by the category of ADHD with potentially helpful implications for provision for the child. At the same time it is possible – even likely – that the supposed condition is overdiagnosed. The challenge is to refine and be more robust about identification after seriously considering alternative explanations and approaches for elements of the behaviour associated with ADHD.

Definitions

There are several disorders relating to difficulties concerning over activity, impulsivity and problems sustaining attention. Among terms that have been used for these are: attention deficit disorder, hyperkinetic disorder, minimal brain dysfunction, hyperkinesis, minimal brain damage and disorder of attention motor control and perception (DAMP). Currently the most widely used term is attention deficit hyperactivity disorder.

Attention deficit hyperactivity disorder is a term that has emerged from attempts to describe inattentive, overactive and impulsive behaviour. The *Diagnostic and Statistical Manual of Mental Disorders, Fourth Edition Text Revision* (*DSM-IV-TR*) (American Psychiatric Association, 2000: 85–93) provides a definition of ADHD, which is preferred in the United States of America and Australia, setting out criteria relating to inattention, hyperactivity and impulsivity. The nine criteria for *inattention* include 'often fails to give close attention to details or makes careless mistakes in school work, work or other activities' and 'often has difficulty sustaining attention in tasks or play activities'. There are six criteria for *hyperactivity* such as 'is often on the go' or often acts as though 'driven by a motor'. The three criteria for *impulsivity* include 'often has difficulty waiting a turn' (ibid.: 92).

The diagnostic criteria state that six or more of the nine criteria for inattention *or* six or more of the nine criteria for hyperactivity-impulsivity should have persisted for at least six months to an extent that is 'maladaptive and inconsistent with developmental level'. Four further criteria must be met including that 'some impairment from the symptoms is present in two or more settings ...' such as at school and home and that 'Some hyperactive-impulsive or inattentive symptoms were present before age 7 years' (ibid.: 92).

It will be recognised that a child can meet the criteria if he manifests different combinations of inattention, hyperactivity and impulsiveness. He may show six or more of the nine criteria for inattention; or all six criteria for hyperactivity; or all three criteria for impulsivity and three or more for hyperactivity. These will influence whether the difficulty is seen as predominantly inattention, or hyperactivity or impulsivity with hyperactivity. There is debate about whether it is useful to combine these potentially disparate profiles under the wider criterion of ADHD or whether it would be more productive to consider 'hyperactivity-impulsiveness' and 'inattention' as to a greater degree as separate manifestations that may and often do overlap.

Perceptions of hyperactive-disruptive behaviour vary in different cultures. This is illustrated by a study in which health professionals from Japan, China, Indonesia and the United States of America were required to rate video clips of 8-year-old boys using standardised rating scales. Chinese and Indonesian professionals gave significantly higher ratings for hyperactive and disruptive behaviours than did the professionals from the other countries (Mann *et al.*, 1992).

Prevalence and co-occurrence with other disorders

In the United States of America, a Center for Disease Control and Prevention publication states that nearly 7 per cent of children aged 6 to 11 years were reported to have a diagnosis of ADHD (Pastor and Reuben, 2002: 3). Prevalence rates in other countries vary. For example, in Italy it is estimated the prevalence among children aged 6 to 15 years is 1 to 2 per cent (Bonati, 2006: 131). The variation may relate to which diagnostic criteria are used, how strictly they are applied and the location of cut-off points. A higher ratio of boys to girls is reported for ADHD in relation to children considered to have predominantly hyperactive behaviour, predominantly impulsive behaviours or those with both, although some of this may be owing to referral bias. The peak age for referral is between 7 and 9 years old.

About a third of individuals with ADHD develop significant antisocial behaviour problems in adolescence (including conduct disorder and substance abuse) and for most of this subgroup, the problems continue into adulthood, leading to criminal behaviour (e.g. Carr, 2006: 423).

Similarly, it has been estimated that 30–50 per cent of children with ADHD also have conduct or oppositional disorders; 15–75 per cent have mood disorder, and 25 per cent anxiety disorder (Biederman *et al.*, 1991).

One of the reasons why such co-occurrence is important is that some interventions appear to have different implications for children with different co-occurring disorders. For example, while psychostimulant drugs such as methylphenidate (Ritalin) are effective with regard to inattention, impulsivity and hyperactivity in the classroom, the co-occurrence of anxiety or depression with ADHD requires care as such medication may aggravate these emotional problems.

Causal factors

Possible causal factors are genetic, physiological, psychological and environmental. ADHD is more common in the biological relatives of children having ADHD than in the biological relatives of children who do not. Twin studies show a greater incidence of ADHD among identical twins than non-identical twins. Studies comparing the incidence of ADHD among children whose parents are biologically related with that of the children of parents where the child was adopted indicate a greater probability of ADHD appearing in parents and children when they are biologically related (Tannock, 1998). All this suggests biological factors may predispose children to ADHD.

Another suggestion is that ADHD may be related to dysfunction in the brain's neurotransmission system, which is responsible for making connections between different parts of the brain. In individuals with ADHD, brain-imaging research has indicated abnormalities in the frontal lobes where systems responsible for regulating attention are centred. Giedd and colleagues (2001: 44) in reviewing neuroimaging studies, maintain these suggest, for ADHD, the involvement of right frontal-striatal brain circuitry and that the cerebellum has a 'modulating influence'.

In 20–30 per cent of instances, particularly in severe cases of ADHD, such physiological features are caused by brain disease, brain injury or exposure to toxins such as alcohol or other drugs. To the extent that stimulant drugs such as methylphenidate are effective in reducing hyperactivity, this may indicate that hyperactivity results from an underarousal of the mid-brain, which leads to inefficient inhibition of movements and sensations. Stimulant drugs may stimulate the mid-brain sufficiently to suppress the overactivity.

One psychological theory is that there is a dysfunction of the psychological mechanism for self-regulation so that the child with ADHD has more difficulty than is typical in delaying a behavioural response. Another view is that characteristics of individuals with ADHD lead to difficulties with executive functions involving the mental filtering and checking processes that an individual uses to make decisions about how to behave. They involve: using inner speech (which may, for example, evaluate information held in the working memory); taking one's emotional state into account and recalling knowledge from situations similar to the one in which one finds oneself (Barkley, 1997).

Another theory questions the accuracy of the term ADHD. Evidence is cited suggesting there is in fact no deficit in attention in the sense that attention is in limited supply. Instead, there appears to be a deficit in the allocation of attentional resources as an aspect of executive function. The overarching executive function of self-control is thought to be a common feature explaining the apparent inattentiveness (an aspect of cognitive control) and the hyperactivity/impulsivity (an aspect of social-emotional control) associated with ADHD (Cutting and Denckla, 2003: 126).

Environmental factor, including family influences, may mediate other factors in influencing the probability of ADHD. One study found that a child with ADHD was more likely to have a mother with symptoms of anxiety or who had been recently seriously depressed than were other children. Where a child had ADHD and co-occurring conduct disorder and oppositional defiant disorder, the father tended to score higher on measures of neuroticism and lower on measures of agreeableness than fathers in a comparison group (Nigg and Hinshaw, 1998).

In a bio-psych-social model, a tentative picture of ADHD emerges from the factors that may be implicated. There may be differences in the brain morphology of individuals with ADHD and others, which may lead to cognitive differences in terms of how easily an individual can inhibit responses to stimuli. A particular child's circumstances, and his other skills and capacities, are likely to influence whether these cognitive factors lead to difficulties characterised as ADHD. (See also, Nigg, 2006.)

Identification and assessment

Criteria such as those already explained are used in identifying and assessing ADHD as part of wider assessment procedures. Ideally this involves bringing together information from different sources (child, parent, peers, teacher and other professionals) on how the child functions in different circumstances and settings.

Qualitative assessments include interviews, or using questionnaires for the child, members of the family, peers and teachers. Quantitative assessments may involve psychological, medical and educational information perhaps using standardised tests of cognitive performance; computerised tests of attention and vigilance and a medical examination including tests of hearing and vision (Cooper and O'Regan, 2001: 91).

Functional behavioural assessments for a child with ADHD can, in themselves, be informative and revealing and can have implications for provision. The teacher, parent, school psychologist and others may observe the child in different settings and develop hypotheses about why he is behaving the way that he is. For example, what function is served for the child by his being out of his seat often in class when he is meant to be working or at home when he is meant to be eating at table? What function is served by the child's work being untidy? (e.g. it is finished quickly.) Such observations and hypotheses can suggest ways of modifying the child's environment, such as the classroom setting to increase the behaviour that is required, for example producing written work of an acceptable level of neatness and legibility within the child's academic capability. It might suggest the need to teach new skills. The co-ordination of such approaches consistently across several setting can be beneficial.

Various commercially produced assessments and rating scales are available from test suppliers that seek to indicate ADHD. As with many difficulties and disorders, early identification and intervention tends to improve the outcome.

Provision

Curriculum and assessment

The condition or lack of provision for it may have led to lengthy periods out of school, when the child may have fallen behind in school subjects. Even when the child has attended school regularly, poor management of ADHD and associated lack of attention to lessons may lead to lowered attainment. In these instances the level of the curriculum may need to be lower than is age typical ensuring that the content of the curriculum is however at an appropriate interest level for the child's age. The curriculum may focus on literacy and numeracy skills, study skills training and computer skills to help the pupil gain fuller access to the curriculum and to build self-esteem in basic achievements. Practising motor skills has also been recommended for children with ADHD/DAMP (Gillberg, 1996).

Regarding the balance of other subjects, there is likely to be an emphasis on social skills training in discrete subject sessions such as 'personal and social development' and in aspects of other subjects such as drama (e.g. role play). There may be discrete sessions for behaviour management training. This has implications for curriculum flexibility and such sessions may need to be given priority before much progress in broader aspects of the curriculum is made.

Pedagogy

In general, classroom instructional approaches are very important in helping the pupil with ADHD. For example, providing good structure, short assignments with immediate feedback, clear directions and appropriate schedules of reinforcement are powerful techniques.

Concrete experience and active, experiential learning

To the degree that a pupil with ADHD favours concrete experience (over more abstract conceptualisation) and active, experiential learning (over reflective observation) (Wallace and Crawford, 1994) such experiences and approaches to learning can be optimised. This indicates that a pupil with ADHD is likely to learn best in participative drama, role-play and practical activities such as aspects of science and technology. Subjects normally involving abstract conceptualisation and reflective observation can be approached through concrete experience and active learning and supported by a continuation of these underpinnings. This recognises the requirement for activity in pupils with ADHD and helps attention and concentration because the physical and concrete constitute the medium of learning and at the same time act as multi-sensory prompts and aids.

More generally, the importance of remedial teaching is recognised focused on helping the child catch up on (or reduce attainment gaps in) areas of academic attainment in which he has fallen behind, such as reading, spelling and arithmetic.

Behaviour management training

It appears behavioural interventions are less effective on their own than stimulant medication but the use of behavioural methods can enable the dose of medication to be reduced while still achieving similar improvements. Behaviour management training was one of the interventions (the other being the psychostimulant methylphenidate) in a trial of the effects of single and combined treatments on the classroom performance of children with ADHD.

Performance was defined in terms of classroom behaviour, accuracy and academic productivity (Carlson, Pelham, Milich and Dixon, 1992). An 8-week programme involved 24 boys aged 6 to 12 years and two doses (0.3 mg and 0.6 mg) of methylphenidate (Ritalin) were crossed with two classroom settings:

- behaviour modification (token economy, time out and home report card);
- a classroom setting that did not use behaviour modification.

A combination of behaviour therapy and 0.3 mg of methylphenidate provided the maximal behaviour modification, nearly the same as 0.6 mg of methylphenidate alone.

A response cost approach (e.g. the loss of previously gained reward earning points) has been indicated to be effective with ADHD. This has been incorporated into an Attention Training System, a feedback module operated by battery that is placed on the child's desk and displays the running total of points a child has earned in a specified interval. For each minute the child is on task, a point is added, but each time the teacher sees the child off task, she presses a remote control button illuminating a red light on the module that tells the child a point has been deducted. At the end of the agreed period, the points are totalled and traded for a reward such as free time.

Behaviour management can also be linked to the implications of functional behavioural assessment mentioned earlier in the section, 'Identification and assessment'. For example, it may have been observed that the pupil produces sloppy work when academically capable of producing better. A functional behavioural analysis may lead to a hypothesis that the function of this for the child is to enable him to finish the work quicker so he can physically move to other activities. This might lead to the environment being modified to enable the work to be produced more neatly, for example by agreeing with the pupil that the work be done in two parts with a brief physical break in between. Such an approach would be monitored to ensure that the objective was reach and in this way the hypothesis would be confirmed or disconfirmed.

As with many behavioural approaches there is a concern that the required behaviours will not be generalised to other situations. Booster sessions and the reinforced opportunity to use the skills in the setting they are required may be used to encourage generalisation. Also the schedules of reinforcement can be gradually changed to move increasingly to the natural reinforcement more typically found in the classroom, for example from tokens/tangible rewards to teacher praise.

More broadly the teacher may use unobtrusive methods, aiming to encourage attention and concentration and discourage impulsivity and overactivity. For example, the pupil may be seated in a position enabling the teacher to see whether or not the pupil is giving attention, and the teacher can then encourage attention by using some previously agreed unobtrusive signal. Also, through discussion and sensitive 'feedback' about his behaviour, the pupil can be helped to recognise various feelings such as frustration, anger and disappointment, and develop a vocabulary enabling him to communicate these.

Cognitive behavioural approaches using behaviour management techniques combined with self-monitoring and problem-solving training appears to have no advantages over behaviour modification with regard to academic performance. Both behaviour modification alone and cognitive behavioural therapy alone are less effective than stimulant medication.

Biofeedback

Biofeedback involves the pupil monitoring the physiological manifestations of his own psychological processes. An instrument is used that responds to physiological changes and emits a signal such as a sound tone enabling the person to respond to the physiological changes and to try and control them. For example, in hyperactivity, the biofeedback signal is activated when muscle tension is high, enabling the child to become aware of this and use relaxation exercises to reduce the tension and relax. More generally, drawing on cognitive behavioural approaches, pupils may be taught to monitor their own behaviour and prompt themselves to keep track of how they are responding.

Social skills teaching and developing compensatory skills

For children with ADHD, social skills may be underdeveloped or lacking and the child may show aggression, further impairing popularity with peers and others. One way of seeking to improve social skills is through training to establish and reinforce them. The range of what can be taught includes conversational skills such as timing and showing interest in what others say. Methods used to develop these skills include: discussion, role-play and staff or other pupils modelling desired behaviours in both day-to-day contact and structured sessions (Hargie *et al.*, 1994).

Skills and behaviours are explicitly taught that concern the ability to concentrate, give attention, manage impulses and deal with social interactions (e.g. Kadesjö, 2001). Behavioural and cognitive behavioural methods, and parent training and social skills training for children, have been reviewed by Cousins and Weiss (1993). The acceptance of a child's peers after he has experienced social skills training is not automatic and there have been suggestions that involving peers of children with ADHD in social skills development might improve their acceptance of the child with ADHD.

Better pupil participation

Davis (2006) argues that approaches to ADHD, 'do not sufficiently engage with the sociological issues that influence children's and young people's lives' and consequently do not give enough consideration to how they can, 'take charge of resolving their own life issues' (ibid.: 45). Alternative social solutions might include 'restructuring the school system' (ibid.: 52). Also, children can be, 'encouraged to define their own life problems that have led to them being labelled ADHD and reflect on the solutions to their experiences' (ibid.: 56). Consulting children and including them as participants in the management of ADHD is suggested (ibid.: 57). The term 'agency' is sometimes used to convey this sense of developing autonomy.

Resources

No distinctive physical learning resources appear essential for pupils with ADHD beyond those required for biofeedback training, although physical aspects of classroom layout are relevant (please see following section).

Therapy/care

In the United States of America, around 90 per cent of pupils with ADHD receive medication of some kind (Greenhill, 1998). In the United Kingdom, about 10 per cent of pupils with ADHD are estimated to receive medication (Munden and Arcelus, 1999) with less than 6 per cent being administered the psychostimulant methylphenidate (Ritalin) (National Institute of Clinical Excellence, 2000). The effectiveness of psychostimulant drugs such as methylphenidate suggests, as indicated earlier, that hyperactivity results from underarousal of the mid-brain, which causes insufficient inhibition of movements and sensations and that stimulant drugs appear to stimulate the mid-brain sufficiently to suppress the overactivity. Stimulants can therefore act by improving the child's ability to concentrate when hyperactive behaviours are inhibited.

Electrophysiological investigations using neuroimaging have indicated that for children taking Ritalin stimulus recognition is improved in terms of better attention to auditory and visual stimuli (Seifert *et al.*, 2003). Methylphenidate is administered orally in tablet form usually in the mornings and afternoons and is not used with children under 4 years old. It is contraindicated where there is a high risk of cardiovascular disease, or tic disorders such as Tourette syndrome. Side effects that have been reported are insomnia and temporary loss of appetite.

Medication is used to try to improve the child's receptiveness, enabling him to learn more appropriate behaviours and skills such as better self-regulation and is used in combination with other approaches such as behavioural interventions. It is widely accepted that a thorough assessment is necessary before medication is used and that effects are continuously monitored, including monitoring by school and home.

Organisation

Breaks and structure

Arranging optimum breaks from class work tends to help reduce inattention and allow for the need for activity associated with impulsiveness. It appears there is a relationship between having insufficient time for breaks from class work and increases in pupils' disruption and inattention (Pellegrini and Horvat, 1995; Pellegrini *et al.*, 1996). This suggests that frequent short periods of physical activity interspersed with other work should improve attention.

Some research has indicated that pupils with ADHD can sustain effort and concentration in structured and controlled situations where the activity is stimulating, but find it particularly difficult to return to an activity once distracted (e.g. Borger and Van der Meer, 2000). This indicates that pupils with ADHD are likely to benefit from an environment which is structured and controlled, for example with predictable schedules; where the learning task is stimulating; and where distractions are minimised. In line with this, it has been recommended by a Swedish researcher that children considered to have ADHD/DAMP have breaks at regular intervals and short periods of concentrated work perhaps of only a few minutes for children in early school years (Gillberg, 1996).

Classroom layout

Being taught in small groups is a recommended strategy for children with ADHD/DAMP (Gillberg, 1996). Within such an arrangement, classroom layout and the general nature of the classroom environment require consideration so that the environment enables the child with ADHD to avoid distractions but is not bleak. A pupil with ADHD is likely to be able to concentrate better if seated away from windows, displays and other potential distractions. At times performance may be improved if the pupil works in an area facing a wall with partitions on either side in a position. The teacher should be able to see the pupil (from the back) and monitor whether he is carrying out the required activity (Cooper and O'Regan, 2001: 47).

Where discussion is part of a lesson, a pupil with ADHD may be less distracted working in a pair rather than in a larger group, although opportunities for the pupil to participate in larger groups of perhaps six pupils are also used.

Routines, sequences and duration

Providing clear routines that help him deal in a step-by-step way with the requirements of the school day can reduce a pupil's difficulty with attention and organising information. For pupils with ADHD, complicated timetabling arrangements are likely to require practical support. Among particularly confusing features might be rotating sessions each semester/term such as different aspects of a technology subject; or blocked subjects such as a 'French week'. Secure (but not over rigid) routines are intended to help a child with impulsive worries, and thoughts and feelings of insecurity so that the pupil knows what to expect. The intention is that over time, routines help the pupil internalise controls. Visual reminders of a task, perhaps in the form of a picture or a series of pictures, may be posted on the pupil's desk or on a nearby wall to help him remember the sequence of activities.

Because a pupil with ADHD tends to find sequences and sequencing difficult, the teacher will help if she gives clear guidance and instructions in manageable chunks reinforced as necessary by written and pictorial aids. She should ensure the pupil understands what is required through asking questions or encouraging him to indicate when requirements are unclear.

Helping the pupil develop an understanding of duration tends to reduce inattention and perhaps impulsivity. The teacher may set tasks with clear time limits that are conveyed to the pupil rather than having too many open-ended tasks. This can enable the pupil structure time better in aiming to complete the task. A clock or sand timer can help some pupils recognise the passage of time involved in an activity provided the time allocated for the task realistically matches the demands of the task and the pupil's capacity to concentrate for the required duration.

Criticisms of organisation involving separation and structure

A setting in Sweden of a classroom for six children aged 6 to 9 years with ADHD/DAMP is critically described by Hjörne (2006: 180) as being characterised by a high pupil/teacher ratio of six pupils and three teachers with two assistants; desks along the wall separated from one another; shields to separate the pupils and an extra classroom available if it is necessary to separate a pupil from the others. A concern was that the expectations of the children did not appear to be extended as they worked in the separate class, for example expecting them to work for longer periods or more independently. Also, tasks did not appear to always engage with the pupils' interests.

This suggests that the progress of pupils with ADHD be monitored in terms of the length of concentration and independent work and other areas of difficulty to ensure progress and to extend teachers' expectations.

Other provision

Parent training and support

Training programmes have been developed for parents of children with ADHD using a cognitive-behavioural approach. For example, one involves teaching parents special child management techniques and providing them with information about ADHD using cognitive therapy techniques to aid the parents' acceptance, management and understanding of ADHD (Anastopoulos and Farley, 2003: 187–203). Indications are that parent training combined with medication was superior to medication alone for some outcomes (e.g. family functioning) and for certain types of children (e.g. ones that are also anxious) and their families (ibid.: 202). Parent training appears to increase the child's compliance and shortens task completion time as well as tending to improve the parents' self-esteem as they learn to cope better and reduce parent stress.

Not all families are able to follow through the requirements of parent training and its persistent application. For these families as well as for others with children with ADHD, more general support is clearly important and may include respite care, extra assistance in the family home and practical help though family aides.

Diet

Although food allergy is popularly believed to be a common cause of hyper-activity, research studies indicate it is involved only rarely. Among exclusion-ary diets is the Feingold diet (Feingold, 1975) whose rationale is that some research has linked food additives to allergies and that hyperactivity may be a symptom of an allergic reaction. The diet seeks to eliminate the intake of salicylates found in certain fresh fruits and vegetables, food flavour-ings, food colourings and in some preservatives. Fonagy *et al.* (2005: 217) conclude that there is 'no good evidence' for rigorous exclusion diets despite one study (Feingold, 1975) suggesting around 5 per cent of hyperactive children show behavioural and cognitive benefits with an additive free diet. However, if parents observe adverse reactions to a certain food, it may be worth considering a trial period of excluding it.

Thinking points

Readers may wish to consider:

- how valid and reliable are the arrangements for identifying and assessing ADHD in the reader's setting (e.g. school, local authority);
- the extent to which a range of well thought out approaches for ADHD are in place and how these might be further developed.

Key texts

Barkley, R. A. (2006) (3rd edition) *Attention-Deficit Hyperactivity Disorder: A Handbook for Diagnosis and Treatment.* New York/London, Guilford Press.
This book is intended mainly for mental health professionals but there is also much to interest teachers and others. Parts cover the nature of ADHD; assess-ment and treatment. The treatment part includes chapters on 'Counselling and training parents'; 'Treatment of ADHD in school settings' and 'Student-mediated conflict resolution programmes'.

Barkley, R. A. (2006) *ADHD in the Classroom: Strategies for Teaching.* New York/ London, Guilford Press.
This source is in DVD and video format and, as the title suggests, shows teaching strategies for ADHD in the classroom.

Lloyd, G., Stead, J. and Cohen, D. (eds) (2006) *Critical New Perspectives on ADHD.* New York, Routledge.
This book presents criticisms of approaches to the identification and treat-ment of ADHD drawing on notions such as the construction of 'medical discourse', labelling and adult–child power relationships.

Nigg, J. T. (2006) *What Causes ADHD? Understanding What Goes Wrong and Why*. New York, The Guilford Press.
Draws on neuropsychological research to indicate the multiple genetic and environmental pathways by which ADHD develops.

Weyandt, L. L. (2007) (2nd edition) *An ADHD Primer*. New York, Taylor & Francis.
Summarises ADHD literature across the lifespan drawing out practical information and approaches for school and home.

Chapter 14

Communication disorders:
Speech

Introduction

The section that follows this introduction, 'Definitions, prevalence and causal factors', is a preamble not only to the present chapter, which looks at difficulties with speech, but also to the subsequent two chapters, which concern difficulties with respectively grammar and comprehension; and semantics (meaning) and pragmatics (use). (For an overview of child language disorders, see Schwartz, 2007.)

The chapter then looks at speech difficulties and their assessment; aspects of speech difficulties (phonetic, prosodic and phonological) and provision for phonological disorders in terms of curriculum and assessment, pedagogy (raising phonological awareness, encouraging phonological change and error analysis and articulation exercises), resources, organisation and therapy.

It is hoped this consideration of communication disorders in terms of speech, grammar, comprehension, semantics and pragmatics will allow teachers to contribute to improving a child's communication through familiar curriculum opportunities as well as in specific programmes. This educational typology reflects the training and expertise of teachers and others.

Naturally, the perspectives of a speech pathologist (the term used predominantly in the United States of America, Australia and Canada) or speech therapist (the expression often employed in the United Kingdom) is also informed by, among other factors, their particular training and expertise. Among the ways in which this may be reflected is in the frameworks for understanding that are used regarding speech and language development, pathology and remediation. For example, the speech pathologist may take a psycholinguistic perspective of communication. Such frameworks are in turn reflected in terminology which may often refer to clinical conditions such as dysarthria, verbal dyspraxia, dysphonia, dysphasia and so on, which are explained later.

Where educational and speech pathology perspectives do not overlap, the teacher and speech pathologist, school psychologist and others will need to work closely together to ensure that their aims coincide and that the educational and speech pathology terminology and perspectives are meshed together with regard to the interventions it is decided to follow.

Definitions, prevalence and causal factors

Delay and disorder

A distinction may be made between language delay and language disorder. Language delay is considered to be language similar to that expected of a younger child while language disorder is defined in terms of being different to what is expected both qualitatively and quantitatively. But the distinction is not as clear-cut as it might at first appear.

A child may use sounds, words and structures associated with a younger child but at this point it is not always possible without the power of looking into future paths of progress to determine whether the development is delayed or atypical. Later the child may develop language typical of his age when it would be possible looking back to say that the earlier language patterns were delayed. On the other hand, the child may not develop in this way and the problems may continue, in which case it would be justifiable looking back to say that the earlier language might have been disordered. In other words, the confirmation of delay or disorder may be a retrospective assessment.

The term 'specific language difficulties' might be used where the poor language development was discrepant with other more age typical levels of development. Related to this, a distinction may be made between language difficulties that appear to be related to other developmental difficulties, for example learning difficulties or hearing impairment and ones that are not. The term 'specific language impairment/difficulties' is used for the latter (e.g. Adams *et al.*, 1997).

Because of the retrospective nature of aspects of the assessment of delay or disorder, there is debate about the point at which, after initial observations, subsequent development can be taken to indicate one or the other. Also there is discussion about terms which might suggest that the difficulty is predominantly within the child or mainly environmental/contextual. The term 'impairment' is sometimes taken to imply a within child explanation and the expression language 'needs' may be preferred. However, the substitution of the word 'needs' raises difficulties of its own. While it might be taken to place greater emphasis on environmental factors, it does not make it clear how the supposed 'needs' arise nor who decides what the needs are. If the needs arise predominantly from within child factors, then the term is merely a euphemism for impairment (with the added implication that something should be done which is also superfluous given that this is what special education is about).

Diagnostic and Statistical Manual of Mental Disorders

This section outlines the framework for communication disorders used in the *Diagnostic and Statistical Manual of Mental Disorders Fourth Edition Text Revision* (*DSM-IV-TR*) (American Psychiatric Association, 2000: 58–69); describes the disorders of developmental verbal dyspraxia and dysarthria; and touches on other terms in common use.

The *DSM-IV-TR* (American Psychiatric Association, 2000: 58–69) delineation of communication disorders comprises:

- expressive language disorder;
- mixed expressive-receptive language disorder;
- phonological disorder;
- stuttering and
- communication disorder not otherwise specified.

(In the United Kingdom the term 'stammer' is often used instead of 'stutter'.)

Expressive language disorder is an impairment in expressive language development indicated by standardised assessment scores being substantially below standardised scores for non-verbal intellectual capacity and for receptive language. Where standardised tests are not used, functional assessments are made. Features vary but include a limited amount of speech and range of vocabulary; difficulty acquiring new words and word finding and limited types of grammatical structures. The most common associated feature of expressive language disorder is phonological disorder. Word finding difficulties just mentioned concern a child who is able to recognise a word and understand it, having difficulty in producing a needed word in conversation or when they are shown a picture. The difficulty appears to be in accessing retrieving the words (e.g. Dockrell *et al.*, 1998).

Mixed expressive-receptive language disorder is an impairment of both expressive and receptive language development. It is indicated by scores for these areas of development on standardised tests being substantially below those for intellectual capacity. Features are similar to those for expressive language disorder with the addition of a comprehension deficit. As with expressive language disorder, function assessments may be made in the absence of any standardised assessments. A child's receptive problems may be missed in the classroom because the child may copy others and therefore appear to manage adequately.

Phonological disorder involves failure to develop speech sounds appropriate for the child's age and dialect and may involve errors in 'sound production, use, representation, or organisation ...' (American Psychiatric Association, 2000; 65). These difficulties in speech sound production impede academic or occupational achievement or social communication, although of course some young adults with such difficulties are successful in finding suitable employment. Phonological disorder includes phonological production and cognitively based forms of phonological problems involving a 'deficit in linguistic categorisation of speech sounds' (ibid.: 65) and may involve errors in the selection and ordering of sounds within syllables and words. It is more common in boys than girls. Types of phonological disorder include developmental dyspraxia of speech/developmental verbal dyspraxia and dysarthria (see later). In some frameworks, the difficulties just outlined are considered motor/speech articulation problems rather than phonological disorders.

Stuttering/stammering involves a disturbance of 'normal fluency and time patterning of speech' inappropriate for the individual's age and typified by repetitions or prolongations of sounds or syllables. It interferes with academic or occupational achievement or social communication. For example, a child or young person who stammers may have particular difficulties communicating with peers. Prevalence is about 1 per cent in children and around 0.8 per cent in adolescents (American Psychiatric Association, 2000: 67) and the male:female ratio is around 3 to 1. In about 98 per cent of instances stuttering begins before the age of 10 years. There is strong evidence of a genetic factor (ibid.: 68). There is also evidence of multi-factorial causation. (See also www.nsastutter.org/index.php for the National Stuttering Association [United States of America] and www.stammering.org for the British Stammering Association). A therapy manual by Stewart and Turnbull (2007), *Working with Dysfluent Children*, concerns practical approaches for dysfluency.

Within the *DSM-IV-TR* (American Psychiatric Association, 2000) framework, communication disorder not otherwise specified includes voice disorder such as an abnormality of vocal pitch or loudness.

Developmental verbal dyspraxia and dysarthria

Two terms mentioned in the previous section in relation to phonological disorder were developmental verbal dyspraxia and dysarthria.

Developmental verbal dyspraxia (DVD) is also called 'apraxia of speech'. While it involves no obvious muscular abnormality, it is a difficulty 'in initiating, in directing and in controlling the speed and duration of movements of articulation' (Milloy and MorganBarry, 1990: 121). DVD, debatably thought to relate to immature neural development, affects the child's ability to co-ordinate the speech organs in order to produce sounds accurately. The child may avoid speaking because of difficulties with speech, particularly at speed and requires support, encouragement and practice before being able to 'incorporate new sounds into syllables at normal speed' (Kirby and Drew, 2003: 135). Speech may be '... slow or halting, and sometimes it appears to be a struggle to talk' (ibid.: 134–135). Often there are problems with vowels, which may ultimately be the main barrier to progress for speech intelligibility and literacy, especially spelling. There may be associated difficulties in language and literacy skills (Stackhouse and Wells, 1997).

Dysarthria is an 'impairment of movement and co-ordination of the muscles required for speech, due to abnormal muscle tone' (Milloy and MorganBarry, 1990: 109) and may be a feature of multiple sclerosis and cerebral palsy. Physical factors can affect speech at different levels. Neurological damage brought about by head injury or by brain damage before, during or soon after birth can sometimes lead to physical disabilities with associated speech difficulties. Neurological disease, for example meningitis or brain tumour, can be associated with speech difficulties, which may be progressive. For example, poor motor skills and poor co-ordination may lead to slurred articulation. Neurologically based speech difficulties may be so severe that they require the use of non-speech based communication.

Other terms

Further terminology includes:

* Aphasia – precisely used, the term refers to an absence of previously acquired language skills brought about by a brain disorder affecting the ability to speak and write and/or comprehend and read. The expression is sometimes used interchangeably with dysphasia. (Tesak and Code, 2007)
* Dysphasia – a broad expression for disturbance of language skills. Developmental dysphasia refers to such a language disturbance that does not appear to have a clear environmental cause. Acquired dysphasia refers to the loss of previously competent language skills through a trauma such as a road traffic accident.
* Anomia – word finding difficulties (in the United Kingdom, the word 'anomia' tends to be used with reference to adults and the phrase 'word finding difficulties' is commonly used with reference to children). (Laine and Martin, 2006)
* Dysphonia – defects of the sound system caused by disease of or damage to the larynx (voice box).

The broader term, 'specific language impairment' (SLI), describes children with a range of language profiles involving combinations of deficits in phonology, syntax, morphology, semantics and pragmatics. There are marked language difficulties but the cause is not evident and the child has normal cognitive abilities (Leonard, 1998, *passim*). This excludes children with autism (which is classified as a pervasive disorder not a specific one), general cognitive deficits and physical or neurological damage (e.g. head injury, cleft palate, cerebral palsy).

Having considered the framework for communication disorders in the *DSM-IV-TR* and briefly described developmental verbal dyspraxia and dysarthria and other terms, the remainder of this chapter looks at speech difficulties and their assessment; examines phonetic, prosodic and phonological difficulties and gives examples of interventions for speech difficulties.

Speech difficulties and their assessment

Given that language and speech are not synonymous terms, speech being only one (spoken) form of language, others being writing or signs, Thompson

(2003: 10) defines speech as 'the mechanical aspect of communication ... the ability to produce the sounds, words and phrases'.

Speech difficulties can be considered to occur when communication is impaired by the child's capacity for speech. Among reasons why speech may be unintelligible are:

- physical difficulties with articulation; and/or
- difficulties making sound contrasts that convey meaning; and/or
- problems in controlling pitch.

These three difficulties are aspects respectively of: phonetics, phonology, and prosody, each of which will be explained and considered later.

Turning to assessment, parents may notice their child's speech problems. The teacher may also have concerns. It is important to remember that speech and language are intertwined so that slow progress with language can have associated delayed speech. Therefore with a young child who appears to have speech problems and says very little, it may be better to focus on developing vocabulary and syntax. (Please see Chapter 19 in the present volume on 'Reading disorder', for example the section 'Phonological difficulties' for discussion of speech difficulties in relation to reading problems.)

The teacher may suspect difficulties when considering the pupil's attainments and progress in relation to usual developmental milestones or relatedly in terms of age typical curriculum achievements, for example in speaking and listening. Routine administration of screening procedures and other assessments such as checklists used by the school may suggest slow progress.

Such indications, informed by the teacher's experience and knowledge of typical child development may lead to her consulting a senior colleague. This might initially lead to an agreement to keep the child's progress under review, discussing the concerns with parents and gaining their perspective, and making further, perhaps more structured or standardised, assessments. Following this the advice of a speech pathologist/therapist may be sought who may observe the child and carry out specialist assessments and provide advice. The speech pathologist may look at sound production in single words and in continuous speech, establishing whether the child can make every individual sound in their spoken language then in single words and in continuous speech. Issues arise in connection with assessments of speech sounds in different language contexts: in isolation, in a syllable, in a word or in connected, perhaps conversational speech.

Assessments of individual speech sounds are sometimes carried out to measure the speed and accuracy of the child's articulation, which can indicate whether the child has difficulties with the co-ordination of speech muscles. A limitation is that some children may be able to make an individual speech sound (e.g. 'b') but be unable to make the sound in a word ('big', 'rib' and 'robber').

When assessing speech sounds in a syllable, single syllable words may be used in which the sound to be assessed is the initial or final sound and is minimally influenced by the other sounds of the syllable.

Assessing a speech sound in a word, perhaps by asking the child to name a picture, may be more natural than assessing the sound in isolation, but other speech sounds in the word may influence the target one. It is important therefore that the words and the position of the focus speech sound within it are chosen with care. For example, the sound of the 's' in the words 'saw' and 'straw' are influenced by the sound that follows the initial 's'.

If speech sounds are assessed as they occur in regular speech, this has the advantage of being more natural, but again the target sound may be influenced by the other sounds in the words used. This requires that conversational speech be analysed carefully perhaps by recoding it for later analysis. If this is done in different contexts such as school and home it gives the opportunity for the teacher, the parent and the speech pathologist to pool information and co-ordinate approaches. At the same time, it is pertinent to remember that the speech pathologist is the professional who is particularly trained to carry out a detailed analysis of the sound system.

It is important that speech difficulties are distinguished from problems with grammar. For example, a speech difficulty involving the sound 's' may make it hard for the child to indicate grammatical features such as plural endings (coat/coats) even if the child knows them. But other children may similarly tend not to indicate such endings even though they are able to make the necessary sound 's'. The difficulty then may be that they do not understand the grammatical convention. When interventions are made for phonological disorders, and speech improves because of successful interventions, this may reveal that the pupil has other difficulties, for example to do with grammar, that have previously been masked by the speech difficulties.

Behavioural and emotional difficulties may be associated with severe speech disorders. Children with speech disorders finding it difficult to communicate may become very frustrated. They may be reluctant to communicate or refuse to try. If required to communicate, they may show intense anxiety. The child may feel low self-esteem and may feel rejected by peers (and may indeed be rejected or even bullied by some). (See the Cleft Lip and Palate Association CLAPA at www.clapa.com and the American Cleft Palate Foundation at www.cleftline.org.) In this context, the child may develop emotional and behavioural problems. Recognising such pressures, the teacher, parents, speech pathologist and others will liaise closely to ensure the pupil is supported emotionally and socially.

Care needs to be taken that a pupil's speech difficulties are not incorrectly assumed to indicate a general difficulty with learning, risking having too low aspirations for the child's progress. If other pupils are allowed to make a similar assumption, their interactions with the pupil may similarly encourage low expectations, which can hinder progress and willingness to learn. Also, direct efforts to help the pupil communicate intelligibly are more likely to improve skills and self-esteem.

Children for whom English is an additional language who are experiencing speech difficulties may manifest difficulties in one language or both, making it necessary to assess in both languages before suitable strategies can be determined. Speech pathologists may be bilingual or work with co-workers who are bilingual or with interpreters.

Aspects of speech difficulties: Phonetic, prosodic and phonological

Phonetics (the study of articulation), prosody (an aspect of phonetics concerning such speech features as volume and pitch changes indicating e.g. surprise) and phonology (concerning differences in speech sounds that carry meaning) are inter-related aspects of speech although the causes of speech difficulties and intervention sometimes relate to one aspect more specifically than another.

Phonetics and phonetic difficulties

Phonetics is the study of articulation, a form of motor skill learning leading to the automatic moving of speech articulators in the mouth in 'rapid, precise and co-ordinated sequences' (Martin and Miller, 2003: 27). Phonetic aspects of speech include the speech sounds that can be segmented into the components of their articulation and into consonants and vowels.

In the case of articulation problems, speech difficulties are caused by motor skills being insufficient to produce the sounds for speech. Articulation difficulties may be caused by physical disability if learning of motor skills necessary for speech is affected. One physical cause is cleft lip and cleft palate, which can be brought about by drugs or viruses (e.g. rubella) in early pregnancy and can be treated surgically. Children with cleft lip/palate may also be at risk of having hearing problems and delayed language development. Speech skill deterioration may be linked with disability such as muscular dystrophy. Cerebral palsy may be associated with neurological effects on oral movements affecting articulation.

Also, hearing impairment may cause articulatory difficulties and children with intermittent hearing loss/glue ear can have speech problems. Among causes of dysphonia, a difficulty with voicing in which there is no voice at all or it is croaky, are a congenital malformation of the vocal chord; abnormalities in the structure of the larynx and paralysis of the vocal chords from accident or genetic factors related to certain syndromes. Voice problems can also be caused by the abuse or overuse of the voice, for example by excessive shouting. (See also Hunt and Slater, 2003 *passim*.)

Prosody and prosodic difficulties

Prosody is an aspect of phonetics concerning features of speech such as volume, patterns of intonation and changes in pitch that indicate, for example, questions, feeling and surprise. It also involves the rhythm and fluency of speech, which help convey meaning and therefore help the listener understand.

A phoneme is the smallest phonetic unit that can carry meaning. It distinguishes one word from another; for example in the words 'cat' and 'cap', the sounds for 't' and 'p' are phonemes. (In literacy phoneme-grapheme awareness is clearly important.) Onset and rime are units smaller than a syllable but larger than a phoneme. The 'onset' corresponds to the opening part of the syllable and the 'rime' contains the peak (or vowel nucleus) and the coda (the phonemes that come after it) (Howell and Dean, 1994: 94). When learning a new word, speakers attend especially to the onset and to the beat of the syllables, so, when teaching children new vocabulary, it is helpful to them to draw particular attention to these two features. Prosodic aspects of speech can affect the meaning of a complete utterance, as when the intonation is raised at the end of an utterance to indicate a question. Such instances have an effect at the phonological level of speech.

Prosodic difficulties have to do with such speech features as volume, patterns of intonation and changes in pitch, rhythm and fluency. A child with prosodic difficulties may also have problems with the use of language (pragmatics).

Stuttering, or stammering, is a difficulty with fluency that can make it more difficult for a listener to fully understand what is being said. It relates to prosody in that dysfluency disrupts the prosodic features of communication. A child who stammers is normally referred to a speech pathologist at an early age. Where stammering, unusually, occurs in adolescence social and emotional factors may be implicated and again referral to a speech pathologist is usual.

Phonology and phonological difficulties

Phonology has been said to refer to 'all the sound related aspects of language, knowledge and behaviour' (Watson, 1991: 26). It concerns the differences in speech sounds that carry meaning and has been described as 'the system with rules to organise speech sounds into sequences to make words' (Martin, 2000: 14).

Phonological knowledge enables the speaker to understand that, when a speech sound is changed in a word, meaning changes. Speakers come to learn distinctions such as 'dog'/'log' or 'pin'/'pig'. The speaker hears her own speech and modifies it as necessary to make the required word. The phonological system appears to lay down a sort of cognitive phonological representation of the speech-sound sequence, which is part of what enables the process to be automatic. Speakers can draw on this phonological representation when they are developing awareness of the different sounds in a word. (In reading in English, the 44 speech sounds are linked to written marks or graphemes so that the child develops a phoneme-grapheme correspondence.) Typically, the development of speech sounds is such that about 90 per cent of a child's speech is intelligible to a stranger by the time the child is 4 years old (Law *et al.*, 2000: 18).

With phonological problems, there is a difficulty in relating speech sounds to changes in meaning. There may be no obvious cause of the child's unintelligibility and a restricted speech sound system. Yet the child's development of the use of speech sounds to convey meaning has become individualistic rather than common with others. Those who know the child well may still be able to understand much of what the child wants to convey but others unfamiliar with the child will find it difficult to interpret what is intended. There is a distinction between phonological difficulties and dyspraxia here. Those familiar with a child with phonological problems understand their speech mainly because there is consistency in the sound patterns the child uses. However, with dyspraxia, there is a lack of consistency, making it difficult to understand the child. The child's speech profile may be specific or delayed or a mixture of the two. Specific and delayed profiles are managed differently. (See also, Lancaster and Pope, 1997 *passim*.)

Provision for phonological disorders

Curriculum and assessment

The curriculum for pupils with phonological disorders is likely to emphasise speaking and listening as an activity in English lessons and as an important aspect of all other lessons. Therefore, as well as structured sessions as necessarily focusing on improving phonological skills and knowledge, curriculum planning will ensure that in all aspects of the curriculum, phonological development is taken into account and supported. More time may be spent on developing phonology across the curriculum. Special programmes may be included in provision such as Metaphon, described later. Assessment of phonological development may be in small steps to provide the opportunity to recognised progress.

Pedagogy

Raising phonological awareness

Raising phonological awareness lends itself to whole class and small group teaching and can be interesting for all pupils including those with communication disorders of speech. It is also an important part of the overall curriculum and literacy development. Where new vocabulary is introduced, the teacher will encourage a keen interest in the word or phrase. She will explicitly teach (and check the pupils' understanding of) various aspects of the vocabulary including:

- Phonological – how do the sounds of the word break up and blend back together? Do the pupils know any similar sounding words? What are the syllables of the word? (Younger pupils may enjoy clapping them out.)
- Grammatical – how is the word used in sentences?
- Semantic – what does the word mean? Does it have interesting origins?

This can be routinely and briefly accomplished, for example if key words are introduced at the beginning of a lesson. In both elementary/primary schools and high/secondary schools, subject specialists other than English specialists can use the approach to reinforce new vocabulary. (These strategies are also important for children with word finding difficulties.)

Encouraging phonological change

Several programmes or resources aim to encourage phonological change. For example, the *Children's Phonology Sourcebook* (Flynn and Lancaster, 1997) intended for speech and language therapists/pathologists provides ideas and resources that can be copied for parents and teachers. Coverage includes auditory input, first words, speech perception and phonological representations and there is an emphasis on the auditory processing of speech. (See www.speechmark.net.)

'Metaphon' uses activities designed to bring about phonological change (Howell and Dean, 1994: vii). The *Metaphon Resource Pack* (MRP) (Dean et al., 1990), used mainly by speech and language therapists with children aged $3\frac{1}{2}$ to 7 years, provides phonological assessment. Therapeutic activities include practising and playing with language, for example rhyming activities, and spontaneous use of 'repairs' to communication.

Error analysis and articulation exercises

The view of speech development underpinning error analysis is that the child is thought to progressively develop sounds that become increasingly like those made by adults. Where there is a difficulty in speech this is regarded as the child having selected the wrong sound, hence the term 'error' analysis. The child is therefore taught the 'correct' sound. If the child tends to pronounce words like 'yes' and 'mess' as 'yeth' and 'meth' from no apparent phonological difficulty the approach would indicate enabling the child to recognise the sound that she is making and the distinction between it and the target sound. Articulation exercises would then be carried out to develop and encourage the correct sound. There may of course also be an articulation problem.

On the negative side, the approach seems to suggest that speech sounds are rather isolated from the meaning of language and that speech sounds develop individually rather than within a complex context of the child trying to convey meaning, and cultural and media influences. An alternative view is that the motivation for the child to be increasingly precise in making speech sounds is the desire to be understood. Encouraging that motivation is therefore important in the child developing increasingly precise speech sounds.

Where error analysis is used, the interventions may include exercises for breathing, swallowing and articulation. For example, activities may be designed to improve the child's awareness of speech mechanisms and gaining control over the lips, tongue, palate and breathing. Such activities are used when the problem is identified as an articulation/motor speech problem. They might include licking round the lips and modelling movements for the child to copy, the intention being to raise awareness and develop improvement in underlying muscular control. Specific sounds may be taught using a progressive approach from teaching and using the sound in isolation; in nonsense syllables; in initial and final positions in simple consonant-vowel-consonant words; in medial position and in consonant blends.

Cued articulation is also used as a teaching support for children with speech problems.

Alternative and augmentative communication

Where alternative and augmentative communication is used for children with speech problems the problems tend to be very severe. (For an overview see Cockerill and Carrollfew, 2007.)

Non-symbolic communication has been described as 'behaviours, gestures, expressions and/or object manipulations used to communicate with another person' (Bigge *et al.*, 2001: 230).

With symbolic communication, the focus of the present section, symbols are used, for example a word or a picture is used to stand for something. Communication may be non-aided or aided. 'Non-aided' communication involves the child making a movement or vocalisation that does not necessitate a physical aid or other device (Vanderheiden and Lloyd, 1986). Examples of such augmentative communication are oral language, manual sign languages or individualised communication (e.g. one blink for 'yes' and two for 'no'). A sign language is a system of communication using bodily signs: hand and finger movements, facial expressions and bodily movements. Among signing methods is the Paget-Gorman sign system, designed to closely parallel the grammar of spoken English. It is intended to complement speech and enhance the ability to write grammatically correctly. Signing may be used as means of communication other than speech or accompanying developing speech. Other examples of sign languages are deaf sign languages used in different countries.

'Aided' augmentative communication involves using a device or item other than one's own body, such as communication boards, eye gaze boards and electronic systems. Three categories may be identified (e.g. Bigge *et al.*, 2001: 237): non-electronic devices; dedicated communication devices and computer-based communication systems. These are considered below in the section on resources.

Resources

The following section refers mainly to children with very severe communication problems. Where a child has severe communication difficulties of which speech difficulties were one aspect, a communication board, a non-electronic device, might be used. Another non-electronic device is a communication notebook. Communication books can include photographs, symbols and words, enabling a pupil to find a symbol and show the particular page to someone who may not know the symbol so they can see the intended word.

Dedicated communication devices are electronic communication systems that speak programmed messages when the user activates locations marked by symbols. Computer-based communication systems may consist of a computer with input options, communication software and a speech synthesizer. Computer aided communication may involve the pupil having a voice production device with a computer-based bank of words and sentences that can be produced by pressing the keyboard keys.

Symbols may be part or whole objects used to represent an item or activity. Often what is meant when people refer to symbols is a system of graphical communication, with each symbol representing a concept such as an object, person, activity or attribute. Among the uses of graphic symbols is as communication tools for pupils with speech difficulties. Communication grids in which several symbols are set out in a specified order can enable a pupil to participate in a group sessions; for example, to support the retelling of a story. A sequence of symbols can be used to indicate a sequence of activities, including a school timetable for a pupil. Computer technology, using symbols, allows a large number of symbols to be used flexibly. There are symbol email programmes, and websites that use symbols. Among commercially available symbol sets are Rebus symbols and Blissymbols. The Picture Exchange Communication System (PECS) may also be used. Care is needed to ensure that the pupil makes the link between the real and intended object, activity or person and the symbol, as, although some symbols may seem obvious, they may not be so to a child.

An example of the flexible use of symbols to help convey meaning is 'talking mats'. These were developed by the research team at the Alternative and Augmentative Communication Research Unit at the University of Stirling, Scotland, and used to supplement AAC with children and adults. A textured mat is used to which symbols are attached as required covering issues, emotions and influences. The use of these symbols in sorted sets allows communication including choices and preferences (www.speechmag.com/archives/).

For children with motor difficulties, an important consideration is how the child will indicate a selection (pointing, using a head stick, eye pointing, light pointing); the vocabulary content available and the output method (Bigge *et al.*, 2001: 242–250). Among methods of teaching communication using AAC are environmental arrangement strategies, which involve rearranging the environment to increase the likelihood the pupil will communicate. For example, a desired object may be placed out of reach, the teacher may not give enough objects or pieces to complete a task, and the pupil may be offered a choice of items or activities (e.g. Kaiser, 2000).

Organisation

Where speech problems are very severe or where there are multiple communication problems, signing may be used. Classroom organisation may include where signing is used, that all pupils are able to see the communications as well as hear the accompanying words. Where a child's speech intelligibility is developing, in group and class settings it will be important that the acoustics are good so that the teacher and other children can hear what the child is saying.

It is also helpful to provide the correct model of the word rather than correcting a child. For example, a child who says 'gog' for 'dog' would be helped by hearing the teacher say, 'You've got a new dog', rather than the teacher saying, 'No, it's not "gog", its "dog"'.

Therapy

Speech and language therapy

The role and contribution of the speech pathologist/therapist is important for children with phonological difficulties, whether it involves the therapist working directly with the child or taking a more advisory or supervisory role. For example, individual task-based programmes may be developed jointly with the teacher and speech pathologist/therapist. Or the speech pathologist might work with a teaching assistant who continues the planned work when the therapist is not present.

The programmes may imply a psycholinguistic perspective focusing on cognitive and linguistic processing (e.g. Stackhouse and Wells, 1997).

The assessment of a child's difficulties is identified at different levels. For example, the pupil may have a difficulty at the level of receiving and recognising speech input because of a problem with auditory discrimination. Medical checks would ensure the child did not have a hearing impairment. (Hearing impairment affects the perception of some phonemes more than others.) An audiological assessment is carried out, among other things, to check whether a hearing loss is contributing to the speech difficulties, usually before a speech pathologist sees a child for therapy.

It may be judged that, once it is ensured that auditory discrimination is secure, the pupil would not be likely to have further difficulties with the processes of storing information or accessing and retrieving knowledge of phonological representations or transforming this knowledge into speech. The focus for intervention would therefore be on improving auditory discrimination.

But, because the levels are inter-related, work would continue at other levels too. The task-based programme in such an instance might include a series of activities in which the pupil listens to (perhaps recorded) sounds that are obviously different, then gradually become more similar, to encourage careful attention to sounds and help the child improve auditory discrimination.

The development of a psycholinguistic framework, to which the chapter has already referred, is an important aid to understanding and interpreting speech (and literacy) difficulties (Stackhouse and Wells, 1997, 2001; Pasco et al., 2006).

Other approaches may be used with a psycholinguistic perspective including phonological approaches and articulatory ones. For example, for children with persisting speech difficulties, such an eclectic approach may be effective (e.g. Pasco et al., 2006: 15–17).

Medical/surgical interventions

The school needs to be aware of any medical interventions that have occurred, or are ongoing or that are proposed, because of the impact that these can have on the pupil's progress. Surgery may be used, for example for cleft palate and cleft lip and for chronic middle ear infections. Many operations will be completed before the child starts school, but continuing hospital appointments and check-ups and the associated absences from school make it important that the child's learning is well supported. Medication such as antibiotics may be prescribed for persistent ear infections.

Thinking points

Readers may wish to consider:

- how best to ensure whole school structures that enable the teacher, speech pathologist/therapist and others to work together and liaise;
- how to prioritise the focus for liaison, for example in the development of individual education plans, joint assessment, planning and intervention.

Key texts

Cockerill, H. and Carrollfew, L. (2007) *Communicating without Speech: Practical Augmentative and Alternative Communication for Children*. New York, Blackwell Publishing.
Intended mainly for health professionals such as speech and language pathologists/therapists, this book is also relevant for other professionals including teachers. It concerns children who do not develop adequate speech because of

complex neurological conditions or learning disabilities and may require alternative and augmentative communication systems.

Kersner, M. and Wright, J. (eds) (2001) *Speech and Language Therapy: The Decision Making Process when Working with Children.* London, David Fulton Publishers.
This book, aimed mainly at speech and language therapists/pathologists but also written with educators in mind, includes chapters on working with children with unclear speech; cleft palate and velopharyngeal anomalies; children who stammer; and augmentative and alternative communication.

Kersner, M. and Wright, J. (2002) (eds) (3rd edition) *How to Manage Communication Problems in Young Children.* London, David Fulton Publishers.
Teachers may find the chapter by Rosemary MorganBarry and Jannet Wright on how to recognise speech and language problems particularly helpful.

Pasco, M., Stackhouse, J. and Wells, B. (2006) *Persisting Speech Difficulties in Children: Children's Speech and Literacy Difficulties, Book 3.* London, Wiley.
The title is self-explanatory and the previous two books in the series concerned respectively an introduction to a psycholinguistic framework, and a focus on identification and assessment.

Schneiderman, C. R. and Potter, R. E. (2002) *Speech-Language Pathology: A Simplified Guide to Structures, Functions and Clinical Implications.* San Diego, CA, Academic Press.
This clearly illustrated book introduces anatomy and physiology of speech, language and hearing mechanisms and the clinical implications of impairment to the structures involved. Chapters concern respiration, larynx and phonation, structures of resonation, skull and facial structures, the ear and hearing and the nervous system.

Taylor-Goh, S. (ed.) (2007) *RCSLT Clinical Guidelines.* Royal College of Speech and Language Therapists/Speechmark.
Intended for speech and language therapists/pathologists and others these guidelines concern specific disorders and conditions including those affecting pre-school children and school-aged children. Teachers and those working in the health and social services may also consult them.

Tesak, J. and Code, C. (2007) *Milestones in the History of Aphasia: Theories and Protagonists.* New York, Routledge.
A survey of the history of aphasia from ancient times to the present day aimed at a wide readership including teachers, psychologists and speech and language pathologists.

Chapter 15

Communication disorders: Grammar and comprehension

Introduction

This chapter considers grammar and its development; possible causes of problems with grammar; particular difficulties with syntax and morphology; the assessment of grammar and provision to help grammar development. It then similarly looks at comprehension; difficulties with comprehension; the assessment of comprehension and provision to improve it. When examining provision, for grammar and for comprehension, the focus is on pedagogy. The end of the chapter, to avoid repetition, briefly outlines features of the curriculum and assessment, resources, therapy and organisation with reference to both grammar and comprehension.

Grammar and its development

Grammar concerns the rules for putting words together to make sentences both in writing and in the sequences of words in spoken utterances. In sentences, some words that are closely grammatically related 'constituents' of the sentence (noun phrases, verb phrases, prepositional phrases, adverbial phrases, etc.) can often be replaced by a single alternative word. In the sentence, 'John Kelly had eaten the cakes', the noun phrase 'John Kelly' can be replaced by 'he'; the verb phrase 'had eaten' might remain; and the noun phrase 'the cakes' might be replaced by 'them' to make the sentence 'He had eaten them'.

There are rules for combining words at constituent, phrase and word levels. At the constituent level, making meaning in utterances is structured by the patterns in which combinations of words are placed such as noun phrase, verb phrase and word order. The phrase level involves function words such as 'the' and 'but' respectively in the sentences '*The* horse was galloping' and 'I tried to eat *but* I was not hungry'. At the word level, making meaning is structured by inflexions such as word endings and by function words like 'by', 'with' and 'of' which can be used to indicate a meaning relationship.

Grammar is also viewed in terms of syntax (the rules for making words into sentences) and morphology (grammatical changes to particular words). Morphemes may be 'free' or 'bound'. Free morphemes are single words ('dog', 'give') or function words ('the', 'under'); while bound morphemes are inflexions attached to words ('-ly' in happi*ly*, '-ing' in swimm*ing*).

To develop age appropriate grammar, a child needs a good vocabulary, so a child lacking this requires help developing it. It is also important to develop function words. In early language development, when children start making two word utterances, this is taken as an indication of the beginning of the child's awareness that putting words together has (grammatical) meaning.

Generally, until children are about 3 years old, development can be adequately described as moving from single word to four-word utterances but later they begin to use complex utterances with several clauses and phrases. Utterances begin to reflect the development of constituents, phrases, inflections and function words. Beyond the four-word stage, as utterances become increasingly complex, it becomes less and less satisfactory to describe or analyse utterances in terms of word count because this misses so much grammatical meaning. It is more productive to analyse the relationships of the grammatical constituents (noun phrases, verb phrases, adverbial phrases) and the development of phrase level structure.

Typically, children's grammar is seen to develop at constituent, phrase, inflection and function word levels. The utterances of children with grammatical difficulties may indicate development at the constituent level but less development at the phrase level (e.g. function word, adjective) and word level (inflections). Therefore, although the utterances tend to comprise the main information-carrying words, they sound stilted.

As children become able to grammatically connect two related ideas, compound utterances develop. Ideas might be related by:

*   similarity, ('We saw a dog *and* we saw a puppy');
*   difference ('I was warm *but* mummy said she was cold') or
*   sequence/causation ('Jenny knocked the glass over *and* the water went all over the table').

Other compound utterances involve embedding one sentence in another ('I like the coat *that* I bought last summer'). As constituent and phrase level grammar develops, so does morphemic level grammar affecting word level relationships in utterances (words, function words and inflections). Typically, many children have acquired many early emerging morphemes (including '-ing', '-ed', 'a' and 'the') by two and a half years old (Wells, 1985).

Causal factors and difficulties with syntax and morphology

Causal factors

For a small group of children, there may be a hereditary predisposition to language difficulties as suggested by prevalence among other members of the family, particularly males. Neurological weakness, for example through birth trauma, appears to be a factor in the language difficulties of some children. Physical damage to the brain through accident or viral infection may lead to severe language difficulties.

Where poverty or hearing impairment is associated with language difficulties, they are regarded as the primary difficulty while the language difficulty is considered a secondary concomitant of them. In a study of pre-school children from disadvantaged socio-economic backgrounds, over half were considered to have language delay and language skills were significantly below cognitive abilities (Locke *et al*, 2002). A child from a disadvantaged socio-economic background is also more likely to suffer illnesses leading to absences from school and have poorer nutrition than other children, both likely to hinder learning. A child with a hearing impairment may be taught a sign language which has grammatical implications. While 'national' Sign Language may have a grammatical structure at the constituent and word order levels, others (the Paget-Gorman system) reflect the phrase and word level grammatical structures of spoken language. Some children experience additional difficulties in developing grammatical structure.

Difficulties with syntax and morphology

A child may show indications of grammatical difficulties at about the age of 3 years. He may have difficulties with the order of words and with making sentences of four or more words. There may be a problem with function words, with the child using telegraphic utterances such as 'me tired' for 'I am tired' when it is no longer age appropriate. Key words are included but function words are often omitted.

A child while able to formulate simple sentences may have problems making compound ones perhaps because of difficulties with auditory sequential memory making him unable to handle long word sequences. The child may also have difficulties with the grammatical relationships implicated in connecting the ideas that are complicatedly hierarchical, dependent, embedded or causal (Martin and Miller, 2003: 73).

The child may lack the linguistic knowledge of the rules necessary to recognise the grammatical role of words, such as the difference between nouns and verbs. For similar reasons, he may not be able to recognise the appropriate structures for verbs (Van der Lely, 1994).

Short-term memory difficulties may cause problems formulating sentences; or the child may have difficulties with grammatical structures because these are embedded and hierarchical, leading also to problems formulating sentences. Pervasive memory and organisational problems may necessitate help and support with general organisation. Grammar difficulties may be a manifestation of processing difficulties relating to working memory, the child being unable to make sentence structures with familiar words or use a two-noun phrase with a verb because the demands of processing these requirements are too great.

From a broader cognitive perspective, the child may have problems with auditory memory, auditory sequencing, attention and reading and writing. To the extent that these contribute to grammatical development, remediating work may be undertaken. In parallel, the teacher can more directly help the pupil improve grammatical skills and understanding.

Morphology, for example prefixes (tidy/untidy), and suffixes (talk/talked; cat/cats), can add grammatical information and many children acquire a variety of these sorts of morphemes as early as two and a half years (Wells, 1985), if not expressively then receptively. Some children, however, will require specific teaching and practice in order to learn these. More complex aspects of morphology include changes to words that negate their meaning (stable/unstable) and suffixes changing the grammatical class to which the word belongs (adjective 'kind'/noun 'kindness').

Assessment

The subtlety and complexity of grammar suggests caution in applying a framework of typical development to inform assessment of grammar difficulties. A certain variation in development and the pace of development is considered statistically normal and occurs in children without necessarily indicating the existence of difficulties. However, timely intervention implies not treating possible early indications of difficulties too lightly. Tension between these two positions requires the teacher to make careful professional judgement supplemented with advice from colleagues and consultation with parents. A decision may be made to refer the child to a speech-language pathologist.

Assessments of the child's grammatical development are made in relation to curriculum expectations and by screening procedures and standardised assessments. An initial investigation might be made through checking the child's level of understanding of plurals, tenses, negatives, prepositions, pronouns and questions perhaps using assessment pictures or objects. For example, for prepositions the child can be asked to distinguish from two carefully designed pictures, which shows a ball 'in front of' and which 'behind' the box. Similar investigations can show whether the child understands plurals, negative and other features. If preliminary investigation suggests there might be difficulties, ongoing observation can be used to more closely monitor progress. Where a teacher has concerns, she is likely to observe the child over a period of time and gather information to check early impressions. If so, the views of a senior colleague may be sought and as necessary the advice of a speech pathologist/therapist. Even after a speech pathologist is involved the teacher's ongoing monitoring is still relevant.

Descriptive grammar may be used to inform assessment. It seeks to describe the rules that exist in a speaker's use of language and any variations from those rules but avoiding implications of correct or incorrect grammar from some imaginary point outside what real speakers say and how they say it. As such, it can indicate the development of a child's grammar at different points in time, including as it approaches the way adults usually use grammar. The descriptions can indicate the skills the child has acquired without necessarily overemphasising features not yet developed.

'Mean length of utterance' (MLU) is a popular index of grammatical complexity perhaps because it is easy to compute and because in normally developing children there is a fairly linear relationship between MLU and the child's chronological age (Bishop, 1997: 92). MLU involves analysing a sample of the child's spontaneous language and counting the number of morphemes in each of a number of utterances (e.g. 'I eat-ed a cake' = 5 morphemes). The number of morphemes in each utterance is averaged to give the MLU and typical MLUs for children of different ages are used for comparison (e.g. 2 morphemes at age 24 months; 4 morphemes at 40 months old) (e.g. Martin and Miller, 2003: 74–75).

More refined evaluations may bring greater precision to the assessment of specific language impairment. For example, attempts to find grammatical markers of specific language difficulty indicate that particular aspects of morphology (marking tense and subject-verb agreement) appear to better differentiate affected and unaffected children (Rice, 2000: 29).

Provision

Pedagogy

Sentence recasting

Sentence recasting involves an adult responding to a child's utterance by modifying it. The adult response maintains the meaning, context, referents and main lexical items of the child's utterance but modifies one or more of the sentence constituents (e.g. subject, verb) or changes the sentence modality (e.g. declarative to interrogative). The recasting often corrects errors in the child's utterance such as if the child says, 'He need it', the adults would recast as 'He needs it' (e.g. Fey and Proctor-Williams, 2001: 179). It is a conversational naturally occurring procedure that can be used in story reading or play, for example, and the adult does not attempt to get the child to correct his original utterance. Although recasting is a natural part of what parents, teachers and others do, it is suggested that children with language difficulties require more frequent recasting than other children in order to progress. Speech pathologists may teach parents and teachers the procedures which may be more successful if targeted on specific grammatical targets.

Elicited imitation

Elicited imitation typically involves:

- an adult showing the child a non-verbal stimulus such as a picture;
- the adult saying an utterance related to the picture and asking the child to repeat it;
- the child trying to repeat the utterance and
- the adult rewarding a correct response (or repeating the correct utterance if the child is wrong and asking the child to try again).

Gradually the adult utterance and the reward are phased out so the child responds correctly to the picture and question only. For example, the adult may be trying to encourage the imitation of the linking use of 'is' and might show a picture of a black dog with an exchange such as:

Adult: Look at this picture and say, 'The dog is black'.
Child: Dog black.
Adult: No. Try again. Say, 'The dog is black'.
Child: The dog is black
Adult: Well done. That's right.

A limitation of the procedure is considered to be that the adult controls the activity and the child may not be very motivated and also may not generalise the learned response to less structured utterances. However, the focused nature of the activity can ensure that targeted difficulties are tackled. Also, modifications have been made to the procedure to help ensure that utterances are meaningful even if the task is greatly broken down. For example, the adult would not begin with simply asking the child to say the word 'is' in response to a picture and build up to 'The dog is black' but to begin with 'dog' then 'the dog' then 'the dog black' then 'the dog is black' (e.g. Fey and Proctor-Williams, 2001: 180–183).

Modelling

Modelling is an aspect of social learning theory (Bandura, 1977, 1986) in which learning takes place as the learner observes and imitates another person more accomplished at the skill or task in question. In modelling as applied to developing grammar, typically the adult produces about 10 to 20 sentences expressing the target grammatical form, the sentences being, for example, descriptions of pictures or responses to questions. The child listens quietly to the whole sequence. The child is then asked to respond to the same or a different set of stimuli in the way the adult had demonstrated, for example trying to describe a picture. The purpose of requiring the child not to respond until the set is complete is to avoid any response interfering with the child's concentration on the forms being modelled.

Similar issues emerge in relation to modelling as arise with elicited imitation in balancing the didactic and the naturalistic. Using a varied selection of sentence recasting, elicited imitation and modelling around the same grammatical targets may optimise the strengths and mitigate against the weaknesses of the different methods.

Clear teacher communication

The teacher can adopt whole class or small group approaches that although they are not focused exclusively on children with grammatical difficulties, can help all the class. For example, clear teacher communication is aided by avoiding long rambling utterances and numerous simultaneous instructions, which, as any teacher knows, is easy in theory but difficult at the end of a fraught day. This does not necessitate the teacher becoming robotic in her language but simply being aware of clarity in expressions and requests. So, 'Just one more thing before you go out and I know I say this every lesson or at least I seem to, I know most of you listen but there are still one or two – anyway can you all – I mean all this time – put your books in your desks before you go out – and remember not to make a noise when you leave and don't all rush out at once like you did yesterday or someone is going to get hurt' might become, 'Listen. Please put your books in your desk now. That's it. Now this group go quietly to the door'.

Difficulties with comprehension

Comprehension may be seen as, 'a process whereby information is successfully transformed from one kind of *representation* to another' (Bishop, 1997: 2, italics added). A framework for analysing comprehension can be constructed involving a process ranging from sound to meaning.

When a sound is produced, as when a person speaks, sound waves of different frequencies are channelled through the hearer's ear canal to the middle ear reaching the tympanic membrane (eardrum) between the outer and middle ear and causing the membrane to vibrate at different speeds. Through mechanisms in the middle ear, vibrations are transmitted to the 'oval window' membrane and thence to the cochlea, a spiral shaped organ in the inner ear. There vibrations of the basilar membrane stimulate microscopic hair cells, which feed impulses into the auditory nerve, which, with sub-cortical systems, convey 'neurally encoded *representations*' (Bishop, 1997: 4, italics added) of the frequency and intensity qualities of the sound to the auditory cortex. In the auditory cortex, some brain cells fire selectively in response to sounds of certain frequencies while others respond to changes in frequency over a given range or direction. There appears to be an intermediate level of representation between the 'neural spectrogram' of responsiveness to certain frequencies, and word recognition, although ultimately the brain interprets the stream of sounds into the discrete units of individual words.

Early phonological development may involve progression from larger to smaller units of analysis. The child at first operates on words and perhaps short phrases encoding them in terms of salient aspects such as the presence of phonetic features and the number of syllables (e.g. Walley, 1993). By the age of 3 or 4 years, most children seem aware of the sub-syllabic units of onset and rime and later, perhaps having been exposed to print, recognise smaller phonetic elements. Some children aged 5 to 6 years seem unable to match or identify phonemes, so find difficulty learning letter-sound correspondences, but have no obvious difficulties in understanding or producing speech. This may relate to lack of one-to-one correspondence between segments of the acoustic signal and phonemes (Liberman *et al.*, 1989).

From the flow of speech, the child developing language identifies meaningful patterns, storing these in long-term memory so that when heard again, they are recognised as known words. Mental representations of words have information about both the word's phonological form and meaning. Acquiring vocabulary may be seen as storing representations of familiar speech sound sequences in a mental 'lexicon' and associating these with particular meanings. Items in the lexicon are matched with sequences of sounds in the incoming speech signal.

An incoming sentence must be parsed into phrases that correspond to units of meaning, and the relationships between these have to be decoded (Bishop, 1997: 11). Syntax and morphology describe this grammatical sequencing for meaning. Understanding sentences also requires the ability to use knowledge of grammar in 'real time' to interpret utterances. Drawing on general knowledge of the world to infer meaning from a given context makes the interpretation of an utterance at all levels clearer and the understanding of longer discourse also informs interpretations. To understand an utterance often necessitates interpreting the speaker's intentions as with pragmatic aspects of communication like sarcasm and metaphor.

Comprehension difficulties

Difficulties with comprehension may have various sources. A child may find it difficult to maintain *attention* because of visual or hearing impairment. For some children, maturation of the nervous system may be slower than typical leading to slower development of learning the skills of listening, looking and maintaining attention. Clearly, a child finding it difficult to control attention and attracted to/distracted by non-relevant sights and sounds will find it difficult to direct attention at the teacher's instructions, perhaps particularly in whole class sessions. If a child has difficulty *discriminating sounds*, he may not receive sufficient information necessary to comprehend an utterance in the first place. A child having difficulties *understanding adult like grammar* may be struggling with information storage and retrieval, particularly when the sequence of an utterance does not reflect the sequences of events they convey.

The hierarchical structure of some utterances tends to make processing more difficult. Sometimes a child may have poor short-term memory. Difficulties with *pragmatics* may extend to incorrectly interpreting others' non-verbal communication, and not understanding intention (e.g. humour) and other non-literal expressions. *Cognitive skills* may be implicated. If auditory processing is slower than typical, the child may be trying to understand one part of an utterance while the speaker is continuing with further information, which is therefore likely to be missed or only partially grasped.

Assessment

There is the potential for the teacher and others to misconstrue attention and comprehension difficulties as bad behaviour. If a child does not understand a request, his inability to comply might be misinterpreted as defiance or unco-operativeness. Should the pupil take longer than others to respond to a teacher's question because of information processing difficulties, the teacher might incorrectly assume he has not been listening. If on top of the child's difficulties, adults persistently misconstrue his behaviour as unco-operative, the pupil's difficulties are likely to be compounded and his frustrations increased. All this makes it important that comprehension difficulties are identified and suitable support provided.

Such assessment may be based on the child's progress compared with that which is age typical in terms of the curriculum, informed by the teacher's knowledge of child developmental variations. Where there are initial concerns, the teacher's classroom observation and recording of progress can be informed by consultation with a senior colleague and as necessary with a speech and language pathologist/therapist. Parents will be consulted to compare the child's comprehension at home.

Particular note is likely to be made of how the child responds to the language of the teacher, other adults and other children in relation to such features as the child's name being used, and requests made of him in different settings and with different people. It will be necessary to observe the child in different settings such as in class and small groups, and in various lessons of differing content, perhaps with sessions having different potential sources of interest (e.g. visual, auditory). Such observations should indicate areas of difficulty and strength. Videotaping a child in different environments, taking care to explain what is happening to the child and allaying any anxieties about the process, can provide useful analysable information.

More formal assessments include commercial tests that may be standardised for the country and the population concerned. For bilingual pupils, assessments may be developed in the pupil's first linguistic community language as well as in the national language. Assessments in both languages allow the strengths and weakness of the child's understanding (and expression) to be investigated, which should indicate whether the difficulties relate to one language or both.

Provision

Pedagogy

Teaching for (and reminders of) giving attention

Assessment information that has indicated various situations and stimuli differentially capture the pupil's attention, may inform interventions. For example where a pupil tends to pay better attention to visual stimuli, these may be linked to auditory ones to help attract and maintain attention. More generally, the teacher may provide visual clues such as a series of pictures to support sequences and instructions. The teacher can also name a child when giving instructions and can question the pupil to check attention, while remembering that the pupil may have been attending but may still not have comprehended.

Teaching listening behaviour

The pupil can be taught the prerequisites of listening such as: sitting still, looking at the speaker and watching gestures as well as listening to what is said. The teacher and teaching assistant/classroom aide can model good listening behaviour perhaps in role-play sessions. Humour can be introduced by having one of the adults model poor listening behaviour and asking pupils to comment on how good the listening was and how it could be improved. The adults then demonstrate good listening. Next each pupil with an adult or another child practises these skills, which are monitored and praised by the teacher. As pupils spontaneously demonstrate good listening skills in other settings, these are praised too.

Useful activities for introducing and practising listening include the following (Thompson, 2003: 30–33, 59–61). To help the pupil *identify sounds*, a recording might be used of various domestic, rural and urban sounds for the pupil to match sound to picture. Also the pupil can be asked to listen to various speech sounds and guess the speaker's gender, age and other features. Where the child has practised a sound (e.g. 's') and knows it, the teacher may *encourage comprehension of the sound*. Giving the child three pictures (e.g. indicating 'tea', 'sea' and 'pea'), the teacher asks the child to be ready to point to the one starting with a specific sound (e.g. 's') when the teacher says the word. The teacher then screens her mouth and says the three words clearly. The pupil is expected of course to indicate the picture of 'sea'. Using this structure allows practice in listening for the initial consonant of words. To help develop the *auditory discrimination* of two similar sounds (e.g. p/b, s/sk, t/d, k/g), the child is given pairs of picture cards (e.g. 'pear' and 'bear') and listens to the teacher saying one of the words before the child indicates the corresponding picture. To encourage *listening to initial sounds*, the teacher can give the child two letter cards with a related picture to provide a visual prompt. One card might show the letter/sound 'f' with a picture of a fish; the other the letter/sound 'th' with a picture of a thumb. The teacher says the word and the pupil says its initial sound.

Reducing processing demands

An example of a programme that seeks (among other things) to help language processing and comprehension is the Fast ForWord® training programme. This draws on evidence that language learning problems involve 'a basic processing constraint in the rate at which incoming sensory information is segmented and represented' and is affected by 'the frequency and obligatory nature of morphological structures in a target language' (Tallal, 2000: 143). Fast ForWord® is a hierarchy of computer-based training exercises that has two aims. It seeks to drive neural processing of rapidly successive acoustic stimuli to faster rates. It also aims to improve speech perception, phonological analysis and the awareness of language comprehension through training exercises within various linguistic contexts that use speech stimuli that have been acoustically modified 'to amplify and temporarily extend the brief, rapidly successive ... intrasyllabic cues' (ibid.: 143).

More generally, to help a child struggling to understand adult-like grammatical utterances, who appears to have difficulties storing and retrieving the necessary information, the teacher might use more single phrase utterances. Where longer utterances are used, the teacher can try to make sure the sequence supports understanding (e.g. requests correspond to the order in which they are to be followed). Accordingly, 'Please put on your aprons then come to the table' tends to be easier to understand than 'Before you come to the table, please put on your aprons'. A pupil having difficulties understanding the grammatical aspects of an utterance is likely to grasp key words conveying concrete meaning ('aprons', 'table'). If the context makes the meaning clear, the request is part of usual routine, and the pupil sees others complying, he is especially likely to understand. Teacher communication aids pupils' comprehension if it involves clear step-by-step explanations of what the pupil is expected to do and explanation of key words; and is optimal, being neither a constant stream of words nor oversparing. Similarly, the adult emphasising of salient features of an utterance can help the child by reducing processing demands.

Supporting pragmatic understanding

Because of the pervasiveness, subtlety and variety of pragmatic aspects of language improving understanding is likely to be a slow long-term process. Role-play sessions or video/DVD examples can illustrate the more usual exemplars of aspects of non-verbal communication, which can be discussed with a small group of pupils. Examples of intention can be provided and discussed so aspects of communication such as humour and sarcasm can begin to develop. More common non-literal expressions can be explained and discussed.

Allowing sufficient time to respond

In line with the limited processing capacity framework of language impairment, research has been conducted that varies different aspects of the 'input' of language to the child. Among these was an investigation of the 'wait time' in relation to discourse characteristics and verbal reasoning (Ellis Weismer and Schrader, 1993). This involved 8- to 9-year-old children with language learning difficulties and investigated wait time in interactions between the clinician and child using experiential (here and now) and narrative (decontextualised) tasks. Wait time was either the naturally occurring time of about a second or a manipulated wait time of at least three seconds for the child to respond. For the narrative task (the only one for which the effects of wait time was observed) longer wait time improved accuracy of responses to higher cognitive level questions for the children with language learning difficulties but had no significant effect on lower cognitive level questions.

The teacher may allow a pupil having difficulties with comprehension extra time to respond to a question. In whole class teaching this can be done at judicious moments so as not to slow the pace of the lesson for others. In small group work and individual work it is easier. Pre-lesson tutoring (including for curriculum subject specific vocabulary) may be used to prepare the pupil for what is to come, to further reduce processing demands.

Grammar and comprehension: Curriculum, resources, therapy and organisation

Curriculum and assessment

For difficulties with both grammar and comprehension, the curriculum may emphasise these aspects of communication both in terms of time spent on them and in relation to their being embedded in cross-curricular planning with subjects across the curriculum. Within subjects, there may be a particular emphasis and support for grammar and comprehension, for example in science, the curriculum planning may help ensure that the passive voice is explicitly taught and reinforced and that time is planned into lessons to ensure pupils have clearly understood the content. Assessment may adopt small steps with regard to the development of grammar and comprehension so that progress can be recognised and celebrated.

Resources

Comprehension can be helped if the teacher uses visual aids and encourages the pupil to use other sensory channels of communication to supplement the usual mode of auditory comprehension. Helping pupils to build a vocabulary for sensory modes can assist comprehension by further developing information about the pupil's experiences and the environment and relating it to language. For some pupils signing boards may be used to encourage kinaesthetic and visual memory to supplement comprehension. Communication boards and computer technology can assist comprehension as can reading and writing providing visual information to supplement the auditory.

Therapy

Therapy may involve the speech and language pathologist either working directly with pupils or working in a consultancy/monitoring role.

Organisation

No distinctive approaches to organisation appear essential for difficulties with grammar and comprehension.

Thinking points

Readers may wish to consider:
  For difficulties with grammar:

- the extent to which interventions successfully balance being relatively focused but isolated and being relatively general but contextual.

For difficulties with comprehension:

- school procedures for identifying difficulties early and ensuring they are not misconstrued as poor behaviour;
- the extent to which the teacher's communication might be improved to aid pupils' understanding and
- the effectiveness of the teacher's methods of checking the comprehension of all pupils.

Key texts

Bishop, D. V. M. and Leonard, L.B. (eds) (2000) *Speech and Language Impairments in Children: Causes, Characteristics, Intervention and Outcome.* Philadelphia, PA and Hove, UK, Psychology Press.
The book is based on plenary papers from the Third International Symposium on children's speech and language disorders held in York, England in 1999. Chapter 8 considers the research relating to the remediation strategy, FastForWord®. Chapter 10 concerns the grammar interventions of recasting, elicited imitation and modelling.

Bishop, D. V. M. (1997) *Uncommon Understanding: Development and Disorders of Language Comprehension*. Hove, Psychology Press.
This book vividly conveys some of the complexities involved in language comprehension.

Cain, K. and Oakhill, J. (eds) (2007) *Children's Comprehension Problems in Oral and Written Language: A Cognitive Perspective*. New York, Guilford Press.
Presents research to inform assessment strategies and interventions for children without an assessment of disability/disorder as well as children with specific language impairment and other conditions, including autism and attention deficit hyperactivity disorder.

Paul, R. (2007) *Language Disorders From a Developmental Perspective: Essays in Honor of Robin S. Chapman*. New York, Taylor & Francis.
The essays cover a much wider area than comprehension and grammar and concern psycholinguistic contributions to the understanding of child language disorders, their nature and remediation.

Chapter 16

Communication disorder: Semantics and pragmatics

Introduction

This chapter considers semantics and looks at labelling, packaging and network building difficulties; and difficulties with idiom; grammatical aspects of meaning and meaning relations. After touching on the assessment of semantic difficulties, the chapter sets out various aspects of provision. Next, it explains the nature of pragmatics; consider pragmatic difficulties; the assessment of such difficulties and provision. When looking at provision, for semantics and pragmatics, the focus is on pedagogy. The chapter, to avoid repetition, then briefly outlines features of the curriculum and assessment, resources, therapy and organisation with reference to both semantics and pragmatics.

Semantics

When examining meaning (semantics) in language, the unit of meaning or lexeme, can be conveyed in one word or several ('die', 'pass away', 'meet your maker'). For a lexeme to be meaningful the speaker requires some concept knowledge, for example having seen a dog and having some notion of the concept 'dog' before the word can be used meaningfully. Also, to grasp the meaning of lexemes implies that other cognitive factors support understanding of meaning. The child's memory needs to be able to link with the object and the word so when the object is next seen, the word will be available; or when the child next uses the word, it will be with some memory of the concept and object associated with the word.

The verbal context in which the word is used also indicates that the child has grasped its meaning. A child may use the word 'cat' in an utterance bearing no apparent relationship to the usual meaning of the word. If the context does not support the word, the child cannot normally be said to have understood the meaning. Aitchison (1987) suggests that in acquiring meaning, children have three basic, related tasks: labelling, packaging and network building.

Labelling difficulties

Labelling involves the child discovering that sound sequences can be used as names for things. While apparent early words may be better regarded as 'ritual accompaniments' to a whole situation (Aitchison, 1987: 88), as the child broadens the circumstances under which these are produced the word can be more accurately seen as labelling and symbolising. To understand the lexeme as a label is to regard it as a content word referring to an external phenomenon: object, person, action or attribute. From an early age the child interacts with parents who encourage linking sound with phenomena so the child comes to associate the two. Also, from about the age of 3 years, the child noticeably asks questions about objects and other features of the environment, a process apparently necessitating a certain level of maturation and skill development.

For example, labelling is facilitated if the child is able to: direct attention physically and cognitively to an object or event being named; has some notion of object permanence and recognises that objects and events can be symbolised by pictures or models. Being able to label also implies word finding: ability to access and retrieve words that connect with a stimulus such as a picture or item. As these skills and abilities are acquired in the course of development, the child gradually becomes more adept and comes to increasingly establish connections as in the adult system.

A child having difficulties with labelling may have problems with the above processes, for example making sense of and storing auditory information, beyond an age when it would be expected. A child may have word finding problems and may therefore make excessive use of expressions lacking meaning, sustaining the utterance ('uh', 'ehm'), stereotyped phrases ('sort of', 'kind of') and filler words ('pass me the *thingy*').

Packaging difficulties

In the packaging task, the child must discover which things can be packaged together under one label. A lexeme is also understood to include a package of conceptual and grammatical meaning. Conceptual meaning may be 'underextended' as when a child can label his own dog as 'dog' but not understand the word and its meaning in connection with other dogs. Concepts are 'overextended' if the word is used with too wide a reference (e.g. the word 'dog' refers to all small animals). This is thought to relate to lack of knowledge (the child knows and correctly uses the word 'duck' but also uses it for other birds, not knowing their correct names) or because the child works from certain prototypes but analyses them differently from adults (the word 'star' is used correctly but is also used for 'spoon' because it too is shiny). Grammatical meaning relates to the grammatical role of the word in a sentence that affects its meaning, for example, whether grammar conveys an active or passive role for the object 'milk' in 'The cat drank the *milk*' or 'The *milk* was drunk by the cat'.

Difficulties with packaging are indicated if a child continues beyond the typical age to show underextended or overextended conceptual meaning. Difficulties with the grammatical meaning aspect of packaging relate to problems understanding that the grammatical role of the word in a sentence affects the word's meaning.

Network-building difficulties

In the network-building task, children must show how words relate to each other. Networking concerns the lexeme gaining meaning from its relationship with other words because it is a synonym, antonym or is in the same category (as 'paper' and 'pencil' are both in the category 'stationery').

Children tend to learn words that happen to be subordinates ('blue', 'red') before superordinates ('colour'). Word relationships include those based on serial connection (e.g. months of the year); homonyms ('meet', 'meat') and homographs ('wind' the breeze/turning a mechanism). Some words are polysemic ('top' meaning a spinning toy, a summit, to better someone, to execute someone). The correct meaning is usually determined by the child using contextual cues as predictors so, in discussing mountaineering, 'top' is likely to convey summit. Similarly, different meanings are usually learned as the polysemic word appears and is taught in different contexts. Some polysemic words have a literal meaning and an abstract one, such as 'soft' meaning either not very resistant (material) or overcompliant (person). Grammatical context can change the meaning of polysemic words as in phrasal verbs such as 'put' functioning as a preposition ('put on', 'put across', 'put away') (Martin and Miller, 2003: 92).

Difficulties with networking relating to synonyms may occur because of the child's conceptual rigidity, the idea that one word can only mean one thing. Antonyms can be problematic for any child in that they can be relative with a mouse being 'small' compared with a 'big' elephant but 'big' beside a 'small' ant. Regarding subordinate and superordinate words, some children have difficulties keeping boundaries of different semantic fields and may include fruits in a list of vegetables and vice versa. Children may have difficulties with word relationships that concern serial connections (e.g. months of the year) but sequencing problems may go well beyond this. Difficulties with homonyms and homographs are likely to emerge in literacy work. With polysemic words, the child finds it hard to determine the correct meaning using contextual clues or recognising the abstract meaning. He may struggle to grasp that grammatical context can change the meaning of polysemic words.

Difficulties with idiom; grammatical aspects of meaning and meaning relations

An idiom is an expression meaning more than, or something different from, the sum of the individual words comprising it as with proverbs, sayings and sequences of words conveying an idea ('take away' for 'subtract'). Children learn them as chunks of meaning. Developmentally, children under 8 years old prefer to analyse each word or morphological unit in a series of words or utterances to help them with grammatical and lexical information. Older pupils and adults increasingly organise language into strings and formulaic sequences perhaps because this results in quicker processing (Nippold and Martin, 1989, cited in Wray, 2001). Idioms require a high degree of cognitive skill as well as experience to utilise the multiple referents that the expressions invoke. This sort of understanding therefore develops gradually. Difficulties might be suggested when children appear to be unable to learn idioms not as chunks of meaning but continue to regard them as literal sequences of individual words, rendering the holistic meaning inaccessible (Wray, 2001).

Regarding grammatical aspects of meaning, although words can be described according to the part of speech (word class) they occupy in an utterance (e.g. noun, adjective, pronoun) the same word can have different grammatical functions. In the sentences 'I bought a cat' and 'I closed the cat flap' the word 'cat' is used respectively as a noun and an adjective. As children develop language, it is as though they tend to assign to each word they use a single grammatical function with for example 'dog' invariably being a noun and 'red' always an adjective. Only gradually do they learn that the same word can have different grammatical roles and some children have difficulties with this beyond the usual age.

Turning to meaning relations, a sentence has a meaning structure that can remain the same even though the grammatical structure (e.g. active or passive voice) may change. Some children find it hard to retain meaning when changing from a sentence in the active voice ('The dog chased the rabbit') to the passive voice ('The rabbit was chased by the dog'). They might on hearing the two utterances think that the second meant the rabbit was chasing the dog. This is a complex process as moving between the active to the passive voice requires the child deviate from the 'order of mention' subject-verb-object strategy. It requires the ability to utilise linguistic traces and co-referencing to assign meaning of a grammatical structure to a thematic role. If a child has sequencing difficulties, for example related to developmental verbal dyspraxia, these are taken into account when assessing and remedying difficulties with meaning relations.

Assessment

Difficulties with meaning may be assessed according to progress made by a child in a curriculum that has developmental underpinnings, informed by the professional judgement of the teacher and others in terms of typically expected development. The teacher's ongoing observation in monitoring progress is supplemented as necessary by consultation with parents, senior staff and language specialists. Collecting and analysing examples of the child's spontaneous vocabulary can be useful if sampled from a variety of settings (home, several different subject lessons, group talk, whole-class sessions).

In some assessments the assessor points to a picture, object or activity and asks the child to name it necessitating the child being able to understand that, for example, a picture represents something and recognise what that 'something' is. Because the approach does not provide a context (or contextual clues) in which the word would normally be used it may not always reveal what the child knows. It is essential to know a child's understanding level before it is assumed there are difficulties with semantic knowledge, it not being uncommon to comprehend more than one can produce.

Where there are problems with the child's use and understanding of idiom, among assessments are word elicitation tasks showing the words a child retrieves in response to word stimuli. Younger children tend to choose words that co-occur with the stimulus word co-grammatically (e.g. anticipating 'play/toys' as chunks) while older learners tend to retrieve words from the same word class as the stimulus words, anticipating 'play/work' as chunks. Idioms are particularly difficult because they occur in a conversational context adding yet another level of cognitive challenge to the task of interpreting them. Formal assessments including standardised tests are available from test suppliers.

Provision

Labelling

Children having labelling difficulties may benefit from individual tutoring to help develop the skills and understanding necessary. This may include: making links between the spoken word and the object, action or other phenomena; developing more securely the child's concepts through experience (e.g. structured experience of chairs of different shapes and sizes); explicit teaching to direct attention to an object or event being labelled and explicit teaching and extensive structured experiences to encourage recognition of object permanence.

The child may need teaching that there are implied links between objects and events or pictures and other items (symbolisation) for example using pretend play (e.g. copying events such as washing) and using pictures representing objects and actions.

A child having difficulty storing the auditory information needed to make the links for labelling may benefit from the use of gesture or sign language. While this allows auditory information to be linked with the tactile, kinaesthetic and visual features and memory, sign systems still require a level of development commensurate with understanding their symbolic nature. Graphic symbols may be used to aid labelling, by providing visual clues and drawing on visual memory for a child with poor auditory memory.

A child may have a sense of symbolising through play and the use of pictures but still struggle to learn words because of problems making sense of and storing information. In such instances, picture matching, printed labels and sign language may be used (Martin and Reilly, 1995).

Packaging

An adult can help a child with underextended and overextended conceptual meaning by first analysing and understanding the way the child perceives the problematic concepts then correcting misconceptions. In one-to-one sessions focusing on underextended concepts the adult can show the pupil other examples. The child using 'dog' only for his own pet can be encouraged to talk about photographs, first of his own pet then of other dogs. Similar features can be pointed out extending the use of the word to other dogs perhaps beginning with dogs similar in appearance to the child's own (e.g. small, short hair, long tail) then gradually extending to less similar dogs to encouraging the child to generalise the concept. The approaches for teaching vocabulary will vary, depending on the child's age. For a younger child who is still extracting the rules and classifying, multiple experiential examples may be sufficient.

Conversely, a pupil having overextended conceptual meaning can be taught to particularise, making the necessary discriminations to distinguish small animals that are not dogs. Several photographs of dogs and of say rabbits might be used. The pupil is asked to look for ways in which the two creatures differ (tail, ears, what they are eating) initially using pictures where these are unambiguous. Other sets of photographs or video clips can be introduced once discriminations start to develop.

Difficulties with grammatical meaning in packaging may be helped by directly teaching from exemplars and by providing good models of the use of words in different grammatical roles. Another strategy is judiciously reshaping the child's utterances as appropriate, perhaps in time limited sessions.

Networking

Difficulties with networking relating to synonyms or antonyms can be helped by teaching them explicitly, often as they arise in curriculum subjects. Similarly, explicit teaching of and checking the understanding of subordinate and superordinate words and serial connections can be undertaken. Homonyms and homographs are likely to be taught in literacy work perhaps using approaches encouraging semantic links such as Mind Maps ™.

For difficulties with polysemy, the words can be taught and explained in their different subject contexts, perhaps using a few key words for each lesson.

The meaning would be explained with reference to synonyms; for example in science, 'class' could be explained as 'group of substances' and in general school usage as 'group of pupils'. In this way, meaning is related to distinctive contextual clues. Particular difficulties can arise with recognising the abstract meaning of a polysemic word, because physical exemplars are not possible and the analogous use of the word is very subtle. Such meanings can be discussed and directly taught, beginning with a concrete example of a word such as 'sharp' as in a blade and moving to 'sharp' as in taste (perhaps because the taste seems concentrated just as the blade edge is narrow).

If a child knows or remembers only one meaning of a word and becomes confused if the same word is used with a different meaning, he may be taught a synonym or antonym for the new meaning of the word. If a child knows 'bill' as a request for payment but is confused by its use for part of a bird, the new meaning can be taught by linking it to the synonym 'beak' or the word 'beak' may be substituted. Difficulties understanding that grammatical context can change the meaning of polysemic words can be helped by direct teaching using examples and discussing them with pupils. The specific approaches will vary depending on the child's age and explicit teaching will be different for a child aged 4 and a child aged 8 years.

Idiom; grammatical aspects of meaning and meaning relations

Analysing the child's processing, and examples and explanations, can help a child understand idiom. Where idiom involves using a word in a figurative sense the meanings need to be explicitly taught, explained and discussed. For example, the phrase, 'he was cold towards her' or 'she gave him the cold shoulder' will be related to the more literal meaning of cold temperature. Word elicitation tasks can provide useful information. These are used with learners experiencing difficulties with idiom and other multi-word strings. They help determine how the learner is storing and retrieving meaning through analytic and holistic processing. However, interventions need to take into account that idioms and figurative expressions are ultimately learned as holistic units.

Where there are difficulties with grammatical aspects of meaning, the teacher can explain the feature of language and give examples followed by practice and assessment as well as specific teaching and support to develop understanding of this feature. Approaches to teaching grammar vary according to the nature of the grammatical structure being taught, the child's cognitive level and the child's existing vocabulary level. Some children learn best in play or age appropriate experience. But the direct teaching of grammar requires an existing level of symbol-structure relationship, which if it is the basic problem, needs to be established first. Not all children will develop good metalinguistic skills.

Regarding understanding meaning relations, practice and exemplars can help with understanding of changing the grammatical structure while maintaining the meaning. Structured experience and overlearning can assist maintaining the meaning when hearing utterances in which grammatical structure is different from what was originally said or expected.

Pragmatics

Pragmatics, it has been said, 'covers all the ways in which grammar serves the needs of speakers as social human beings' (Foster, 1990: 6–7). When listening to another person, one has to interpret what is meant in excess of the structural properties of language, drawing on subtle skills and levels of understanding. Such skill and understanding is equally important for the speaker. Language is used for different purposes, each often requiring more than the literal content of the language used, as when being sarcastic, witty, ironic, polite or intimate.

Different contexts have been identified in which pragmatic skills are necessary (Anderson-Wood and Smith, 1997: 40–41). Depending on their culture and subculture, people may have different ideas of what constitutes politeness and rudeness. If a pupil is insufficiently aware of these, taking account of his age, his communicative partner is more likely to perceive him as impolite. A child may find it easier to communicate in certain situations (home, school, youth group) than others perhaps because he feels more at ease in some than others and because the topics and levels of shared understanding may be more accessible in some situations.

It tends to be easier to talk about current activities than past ones partly because in the former, unlike the latter, objects and circumstances are visible at the time of speaking providing a supportive context. Communication is likely to differ according to the role of the speaker, for example whether the speaker is communicating with an equal or someone in authority. Where a child with pragmatic difficulties does not grasp this, it is likely to affect the response of the person they are addressing. This in turn will affect the child.

One tends to communicate differently with people depending on the relationship (e.g. how well one knows them), because the history of the relationship provides reference points for communication not possible with comparative strangers. Communication is influenced by the current state of the relationship, for example whether one is on friendly terms with one's communication partner. The knowledge of the partner with whom one is communicating, such as their perceived emotional state and their knowledge, influences communication. The topic of a person's communication is influential, for example whether one is ignorant or knowledgeable about it.

The linguistic context refers to what has gone before in the communication and how we responded to it. This implies that for communication to go smoothly, what is said must fit a preceding pattern. Also implied is a sense of communicative direction – a predictable structure to longer stretches of communication. The inferential context refers to what one infers from what is said beyond the literal word meaning. It involves indicating that one has understood the communicative partner's apparent intention as well as the literal words spoken. This implies considering the significance of what has been said by both people.

Pragmatic difficulties

Pragmatic difficulties may affect both expressive and receptive pragmatic abilities. Children with pragmatic difficulties have primary difficulties with communication and conversation. But they do not necessarily have the behaviours associated with autism or difficulties with other aspects of language such as grammar. There is debate about the positioning of children as having predominantly features of autistic spectrum disorder, predominantly features of specific language disorder or being between the two classifications (e.g. Bishop, 2000: 99–113). Again, there is a developmental range. The boundaries of acceptability of the pragmatic behaviour of a 4 year old will be different to that of a 14 year old, especially in the social/linguistic sense.

Difficulties with basic skills and knowledge

Turn taking is a vital prerequisite pre-pragmatic skill. Early turn taking begins in infancy with parent–child games and simple parent–child bonding activities. A child may have difficulties with basic skills associated with pragmatics. These include the developing ability and motivation to interact (e.g. with another person initiating an interaction) or to take part in an activity (e.g. singing a song). Sharing attention is important.

Difficulties with grammatical sense in language use

Grammatical cohesion is achieved as utterances are: linked to one another to avoid unnecessary repetition, draw on shared assumptions and understanding, and keep the listener's interest. This is achieved through such means as reference, substitutions and conjunctions. In reference, grammatical short forms are used, for example to carry over meaning from earlier utterances (e.g. as when recurring words or phrases are replaced by a pronoun). In substitution, a synonymous word or phrase stands in place of an already used word as in the utterance, 'I bought a *calculator and compass* but I've lost the *equipment*'. Conjunctions join utterances to avoid repetition. So to avoid saying 'Robert went to the shops. Robert went to the post office. Robert went to the cinema', we say, 'Robert went to the shops, the post office and the cinema'. Difficulties are evident where a child is unable to use such devices. The marking of new information is relevant (e.g. 'I saw a car' and 'I saw the car'). Also relevant is providing references before using pronouns (e.g. the ambiguity of 'Jenny told her sister that *she* was going to be late').

Difficulties with social and linguistic sense

Several important features enable utterances to make social and linguistic sense. Speaker's intention relates to speaking for a purpose such as asking a question or making a criticism. Shared understanding of the context of an utterance concerns the speaker and listener understanding with whom they are communicating. Inference and implication involves the speakers and listeners understanding and being able to respond suitably to various conventions such as polite, indirect requests. To understand someone at a dining table asking, 'Is there any salt down there?' it is necessary to realise they are probably implying, 'Pass the salt please'. Where a pupil has difficulties in these areas, he may respond inappropriately to utterances and struggle to maintain meaningful exchanges.

Difficulties with conversational skills

Conversational skills involve being able to use suitable grammatical forms to convey information through such devices as reference, substitutions and conjunctions. Conversation involves various abilities, difficulties with which impair the activity.

Difficulties relating to topic in conversation may be indicated when a pupil tends to change topic excessively, or appears restless. Or the child might, in response to a topic being initiated by another person, respond tersely and be disinclined to extend the topic or introduce a new one. The pupil may not understand the signals conveying a topic is being introduced. A child having difficulties with turn taking in conversation may interrupt or fail to pick up signals that the other person wants a turn. Where a child has not learned to adapt forms of address to different situations and people, his speech can be condescending to adults or overformal towards other children.

A child may have difficulty recognising that a conversation is breaking down because of misunderstandings or interruptions and have difficulty in repairing the conversation. An important element here is the marking of new and old information and presupposition skills. Where the child contributes to the breakdown of the conversation, he may not realise. Difficulties may be experienced with conversations concerning matters that are not in the here and now, or reference to emotional states, hypothetical situations or causal links. In non-verbal communication there may be problems using suitable facial expressions, following expectations of bodily proximity, using gestures appropriately and matching body language and verbal language.

Semantic-pragmatic difficulties

For a lexeme to be meaningful, a speaker has to have a certain amount of knowledge of concepts. Also, to grasp the meaning of lexemes implies that other cognitive factors support the understanding of meaning. The context of word use is also an indication the child has grasped its meaning. Semantic-pragmatic issues therefore concern the interaction of pragmatic and semantic skills and knowledge.

'Semantic-pragmatic difficulties' concern both meaning and use of language and the term semantic-pragmatic disorder describes a developmental disorder of language meaning and function. It is debated whether 'semantic-pragmatic disorder' should be considered separately from autistic spectrum disorder (Gagnon et al., 1997). Children considered to experience 'semantic-pragmatic disorder' may be overliteral in their attempts to make inferences, have a primary difficulty with semantic knowledge and may have difficulties with grammar. They have problems with word finding, learning vocabulary and auditory comprehension. Also their poor socialising skills restrict socialising with peers.

Assessment

Possible causal factors of pragmatic difficulties include: semantic difficulties; impairment of cognition; impairment of imagination; institutionalisation; adverse environmental influences; lack of social experience influencing the development of appropriate styles of interaction and certain neurological conditions (Anderson-Wood and Smith, 1997: 32 paraphrased).

Assessment in difficulties can be informed by the child's progress in the curriculum with the teacher taking further advice as necessary. Where there are concerns, conversational skills may be assessed. A baseline assessment is made through observations and recording of conversational skills in different contexts. An audio or video recording may be made (the latter allowing the social setting to be seen and non-verbal communication to be assessed).

Assessment in different contexts is important because communication may vary in different settings (Stacey, 1994). Repeating the process at agreed intervals can enable progress to be monitored. Commercial tests, checklists and profiles are also available. In assessing pragmatic problems, it is also important to ensure that basic auditory comprehension skills are at age typical levels. A child with impaired comprehension may display inappropriate responses, which signify more a problem with reception than with social appropriateness.

Regarding bilingual children, a child brought up in a linguistic minority community may learn the home language first and English later, perhaps beginning at school. If so, the child will tend to develop the skills of communication associated with his first language. These may be interpreted as difficulties in the English-speaking context. For example, if it is acceptable that a child responds minimally in his first language community, this may be interpreted as a potential communication difficulty in school. This necessitates the teacher liaising with specialist teachers supporting the child's learning of English. If there do appear to be pragmatic difficulties the assessment of the child's communication in different contexts will include not only different situations but also different linguistic communities. There is debate about the balance between encouraging and respecting such cultural differences and teaching and encouraging the linguistic/pragmatic patterns of the predominant language of the country. Of course, speaking English as an additional language is a language difference not a language disorder, but the response still raises the question of what should and should not be 'corrected' to help ensure communication is understood.

Provision and pedagogy

Providing basic skills and knowledge

Among possible interventions for developing basic skills and knowledge are interactive activities such as peek-a-boo and rhymes and songs with repeated sounds and movements. Also used are communication facilitation techniques (CFT), which aim to be very responsive to the child's communicative attempts by encouraging the adult to attend less to the child's speech performance and more to the child's interests and preferred activities. CFTs can be used at a pre-linguistic level (e.g. attention sharing); the linguistic stage (e.g. repeating what the pupil says) and the complex language stage (e.g. making a statement that is likely to lead the child to say something). Furthermore, naturalistic interventions include the aspect of 'contingent responding' (e.g. Anderson-Wood and Smith, 1997: 85) which involves sensitively and alertly responding to what the child says or indicates.

Grammatical sense in language use

For difficulties involving grammatical sense in language use, the speech therapist, or the teacher working with the speech therapist, may provide models of grammatical cohesion devices and help the child practise them, perhaps using role-play.

Social and linguistic sense

Interventions to help with social and linguistic sense include being taught possible signals of the speaker's intentions and examples of implication and inference. Opportunities to use similar signals can be provided in role-play and encouraged when they appear in day-to-day communication. The assessment programme *Social Use of Language Programme* (Rinaldi, 2001) is also used as a teaching framework to develop language skills in real-life settings, teaching basic social communication skills and awareness of one's self and others.

Conversational skills

A child may have difficulty with conversational topic because he does not understand signals that the topic is being introduced. The child can be taught to recognise common opening gambits of an intention to start a new topic (e.g. the use of open-ended questions – 'What did you think of the movie last night?') and respond accordingly. This may involve asking a question ('You mean the horror movie?') or commenting from his experience ('It was good but not as good as *Dracula*'). If the child does not recognise when someone is trying to round off a conversation and has difficulty signalling that he wants to do so himself, he can be taught to listen to possible signals that someone would like to change topic ('I liked the school trip too, but I haven't told you about my friend's visit'). He can learn and practise more subtle ways of indicating a desire to change topic himself. A child having difficulties with turn taking can be taught the signals that the other person wants a turn (e.g. a pause or question) and to respond to them and also be taught to use such signals himself. Role-play and encouragement when such devices appear in everyday conversation can help. Where the child has not learned the correct forms of address for different situations and people, the teacher or other adult can point this out as it arises. Where it can be done in an encouraging way the adult can explain why the original form is not suitable while providing examples of more apt forms.

Should the child find it hard to recognise that conversation is breaking down and have difficulty repairing it, the signs of conversation breakdown can be taught. Also the skills for repairing it (e.g. asking clarifying questions) can be taught and practised. Where the child contributes to conversational breakdown without realising, the adult can signal the breakdown. For example, the adult can simply say she does not understand or can employ a clarifying question or other repair strategy.

Helping a pupil having difficulty with conversational abstractions has implications for all aspects of the curriculum. However, it may be more apparent in certain subjects (e.g. geography topics dealing with 'now' but not with 'here' and history topics concerning 'here' but not 'now'). Where the child has a difficulty with conversations involving abstractions, specific support may help for some subjects such as pre-teaching some concepts.

Help with non-verbal communication (NVC) will take account of its culturally variable nature. The teacher or others may model suitable NVC, helping the child practise it through role-play and encourage and praising suitable approximations as the child shows it in day-to-day communication.

Helping with semantic-pragmatic difficulties

It is important that pupils with semantic-pragmatic difficulties have help with communication interaction skills in the early years and at school. Support in the family is also important. Assessment could indicate that, centrally, semantic difficulties lead to and compound the pragmatic difficulties. In such a case, interventions may include those intended to improve semantic skills, for example developing phonological awareness skills through overlearning and practice.

Semantics and pragmatics: curriculum and assessment, resources, therapy and organisation

Curriculum and assessment

For difficulties with semantics and pragmatics, the curriculum may provide extra time for these aspects of communication. It can also ensure that work supporting semantic and pragmatic development is embedded in cross-curricular planning with subjects across the curriculum. Within subjects, there may be a particular emphasis and support for semantics and pragmatics. Assessment may adopt small steps with regard to the development of semantics and pragmatics so progress can be recognised.

Resources

There appear to be no distinctive resources essential for the development of semantics and pragmatics.

Therapy

The speech and language pathologist/therapist contribution may be through direct work with children or in a consultancy role.

Organisation

There appear to be no distinctive aspects of organisation essential for the development of semantics and pragmatics.

Thinking points

Readers may wish to consider:

- With semantics, how effective the balance is between providing individual teaching and support for persistent difficulties and providing teaching for small groups and classes that support the aims of more intensive sessions.
- With pragmatics, how the teacher and speech and language pathologist/therapist can determine the combinations of approaches

(direct teaching, modelling, role-play and encouragement of skills in day-to-day communication) that work best with particular children.
- How every social and educational task provides an environment where the child needs to utilise semantic, pragmatic and grammatical skills.

Key texts

Firth, C. and Venkatesh, K. (2001) *Semantic-Pragmatic Language Disorder.* Brackley, UK, Speechmark.
This resource pack provides a framework for identifying and making provision for semantic-pragmatic disorder in children. Intended mainly for speech and language pathologists/therapists, it includes materials aimed at encouraging close working with parents and teachers.

MacKay, G. and Anderson, C. (eds) (2000) *Teaching Children with Pragmatic Difficulties of Communication: Classroom Approaches.* London, David Fulton Publishers.
Chapters include, 'Action and interaction: the roots of pragmatic communication'; 'Pragmatic communication difficulties'; 'Primary age pupils with pragmatic difficulties'; and 'The school as an integrated support system for pupils with pragmatic difficulties'.

Chapter 17

Autism

Introduction

This chapter briefly mentions pervasive developmental disorders as a context for subsequently describing autistic disorder and Asperger's syndrome. It explains the prevalence of autism and its apparent causes before looking at the identification and assessment of autism and Asperger's syndrome. Turning to provision, the chapter considers curriculum and assessment; pedagogy (including the Lovaas programme [Applied Behaviour Analysis], discrete trial teaching and pivotal response training); resources; therapy; organisation (physical organisation of the classroom, working in pairs and groups, Learning Experiences – Alternative Programme for Pre-schoolers and Parents, managing transitions) and other aspects (managing challenging behaviour, family support and parent training). Readers wishing to access further information quickly may find the Autism Society of America (www.autism-society.org) a useful starting point for investigating other Internet sites.

Pervasive development disorders

Autism and Asperger's syndrome are classified in the *Diagnostic and Statistical Manual of Mental Disorders Fourth Edition Text Revision (DSM-IV-TR)* (American Psychiatric Association, 2000: 69–84) as pervasive developmental disorders. These disorders involve severe and pervasive impairment in several areas of development and involve significant problems with social skills and understanding, communication and behaviour. They comprise:

- autistic disorder;
- Asperger's syndrome;
- Rett's disorder (characterised by atypical social and language development and repetitive behaviour including stereotyped hand washing movements);
- childhood disintegrative disorder (which has features similar to autism but develops after a period of normal development of at least 2 years) and
- pervasive development order not otherwise specified.

The term 'autistic spectrum disorders' or 'autism spectrum disorders' is sometimes used as a synonym for pervasive developmental disorders.

Autistic disorder and Asperger's syndrome

In a paper published in the 1940s, Leo Kanner, a psychiatrist from the United States of America, described several children attending his psychiatric unit, noting their limited interest in other people, odd language, insistence on routines and repetitive behaviour (Kanner, 1943). In doing so, he used the Greek word 'autism' to convey the children's self-absorption, although the term 'Kanner syndrome' was used for some time afterwards and still persists, as does the term 'classical autism'.

Later definitions have centred around a 'triad' of impairments (Wing and Gould, 1979) which concern social isolation, communication difficulties and insistence on sameness. The *Diagnostic and Statistical Manual of Mental Disorders Fourth Edition Text Revision (DSM-IV-TR)* (American Psychiatric Association, 2000: 51–53) defines autism in relation to:

- social difficulties;
- communication impairment and
- restricted behaviours.

All three must be present, with the social deficit being particularly marked.

The diagnostic criteria concerning *social interaction*, of which at least two of the elements must be manifested, are: 'marked impairment in the use of multiple non-verbal behaviours ...; failure to develop peer relationships appropriate to developmental level; a lack of spontaneous seeking to share enjoyment, interests, or achievement with other people ...; lack of emotional reciprocity' (American Psychiatric Association, 2000: 75).

Regarding *communication and language*, impairments are manifested by at least one of the following (American Psychiatric Association, 2000: 75): 'delay in, or total lack of, the development of spoken language ...; in individuals with adequate speech, marked impairment in the ability to initiate or sustain a conversation with others; stereotyped and repetitive use of language or idiosyncratic language; lack of varied, spontaneous make-believe play or social imitative play appropriate to the developmental level'.

It has been estimated that between a third and a half of autistic children do not develop speech (Prizant and Wetherby, 1993) and may require teaching alternative ways of communicating such as using picture symbols, assistive technology devices, written words or signing. A central issue is that communication systems need to be universally understandable to others (Mezibov, 1988).

Turning to *thinking and behaving flexibly*, a child with autistic disorder shows 'restricted repetitive and stereotyped patterns of behaviour, interests and activities' (American Psychiatric Association, 2000: 75).

The disorder must manifest itself before the age of 3 years in relation at least one of the areas of social interaction, social language or symbolic or imaginative play.

With reference to sensory perception and responses, adults with 'autistic spectrum disorder' have reported being particularly sensitive to certain stimuli (e.g. Lawson, 1998) while some children seem undersensitive to some stimuli. It has been estimated that about a third of children with autism may have epilepsy (Volkmar and Nelson, 1990). The ratio of males to females with autism is around 4:1; or where there are learning difficulties 5:1 (Lord and Schopler, 1987).

Asperger's syndrome takes its name from Hans Asperger (1944), an Austrian paediatrician who described behaviours that have come to define the syndrome. Its identification and assessment, unlike autism, does not require that the child experience a communication deficit in the same way. Because many of the features of Asperger's syndrome may not be as marked as those of autistic disorder, they may not be noticed as early. There is debate about whether Asperger's syndrome is best considered as part of the same continuum as autistic disorder or as a separate entity. It is not possible to demonstrate on present evidence that children identified as having Asperger's syndrome differ in terms of clinical or neurological variables from children with an intelligence quotient within the normal range and diagnosed with autism (Mackintosh and Dissanayake, 2004).

The outcome for children with autism is poor with around 61 to 73 per cent unable to live independently and about 5 to 17 per cent developing to be able to live a normal social life and have a vocation (Gillberg and Coleman, 2000). If a child has a non-verbal IQ within the age typical range and has some functional language skills by the age of 5 years, the prognosis is better. In any event progress can be made with parents, teachers and others working closely together.

Prevalence of autism

In a review of literature, Gillberg et al., (1991) concluded that there was international agreement of a prevalence of autism of 7 to 17 per 10,000 children in both rural and urban settings. More recently, autism has been estimated to affect 10 to 30 children in every 10,000 although the rate for the population that includes older children and adults is thought to be even higher. Prevalence estimates for the broader category of autistic spectrum disorder is thought to be about 60 in every 10,000 children under the age of 8 years (Medical Research Council, 2001). Three or four times as many boys as girls are identified. This apparent increase in the prevalence of autism is open to different explanations including that there has been a real increase in the disorder, and that changes in clinical and administrative diagnostic practices have contributed.

Causes of autism

There is considered to be 'overwhelming evidence' that autism has a biological basis and a strong genetic component (Medical Research Council, 2001: 21). Autism is believed to have several causes, perhaps all affecting the same brain systems. Several genes may act with environmental factors to lead to autism (e.g. Rutter, 1996). The International Molecular Genetic Study of Autism Consortium (1998) first identified the location of a small number of susceptibility genes that might be involved in the causation of autism (Genes 2, 7, 16, 17 have been considered). Among other genetic research studies implicating susceptibility genes, the Autism Genome Project (www.naar.org) is including approximately 1,500 multiplex families (two children with autism and their parents).

Among possible environmental factors are: illness during pregnancy, childhood illness, food intolerance and reaction to pollutants. Regarding vaccines, the view of the United States of America Department of Health and Human Services, Centers for Disease and Control is that 'the weight of evidence indicates that vaccines are not associated with autism' (www.cdc.gov). It is apparent that children experience such environmental factors without developing autism, so it appears it is the interaction between such possible elements and proposed genetic and biological factors that is influential.

Among psychological theories seeking to explain characteristics of autism, is that people with autism do not have a sufficiently developed 'theory of mind' and experience particular difficulties recognising and interpreting the emotional and mental states of others, leading to social and communication difficulties (e.g. Baron-Cohen, 2000). Another theory is that there may be a joint attention deficit in children with autism (Mundy and Neale, 2001). This involves impairment in the capacity to attend to events jointly with others and impairment in the capacity to prefer social rather than inanimate events, both of which are considered to impair language, social communication and theory of mind. A further theory emphasises the importance of executive dysfunction (Ozonoff, 1997). Executive functions that are affected include the ability to plan actions, to disengage from the external context, to restrain unwanted responses, to maintain a cognitive focus and remain on task and to monitor one's performance.

Identification and assessment of autism and Asperger's syndrome

Early identification and assessment are essential. The identification of autism may be undertaken by a paediatrician, psychiatrist, school psychologist, clinical psychologist, speech and language pathologist or general medical practitioner. A multi-disciplinary assessment may be carried out drawing on the perspectives of parents, teachers and other professionals over an extended period of time. Some local authorities have designated particular profession-als with extensive experience of and knowledge of children with autism. Initial broad screening instruments are commercially available for autism and for Asperger's syndrome.

For a thorough diagnosis to be made, it is necessary to combine systematic observations of the child at home and/or in other settings, and an account of the child's history from birth to the time of the assessment. Diagnostic instruments have been developed using interviews, ratings and structured observations. For example, the *Autism Diagnostic Observation Scale – Generic (ADOS-G)* (Lord *et al.*, 2000) uses the observation of semi-structured activi-ties for individuals from pre-school to adulthood. 'The diagnostic interview for social and communication disorders' (DISCO) (Wing, 2002) employs a semi-structured interview with parents.

Further sources of information for diagnostic assessment include informa-tion from the child as appropriate, the child's parents and other members of the family, and discussions with professionals who know the child well. Discussions are required about how, when and by whom the diagnosis is con-veyed to the parents, the child and other family members so that this is done with both sensitivity and clarity.

Provision

Evidence-based practice research is beginning to point to approaches for which there is evidence of effectiveness, although careful judgements still have to be made about the potential suitability of an intervention for any par-ticular child. An example is research reported by Simpson (2005). This argues that approaches that can be considered as scientifically based practice are: applied behaviour analysis, discrete trial teaching, pivotal response training and Learning Experiences – Alternative Program for Preschoolers and Parents. Among approaches considered to represent promising practice are: the Picture Exchange Communication System, structured teaching, joint action routines, social stories and sensory integration.

Curriculum and assessment

It is important the curriculum is developmentally suitable and chronologi-cally appropriate. It is likely to emphasise communication, social skills and play as well as academic skills training. But it is key that methods of teach-ing and learning are used to enable these aspects of curriculum content to be made meaningful and tolerable to the child. It is important to incorporate the special interests of the child with autism to increase motivation, success and time spent on task.

Curriculum-based assessments are interpreted with care and draw on profes-sional knowledge and understanding of autism so that 'correct' responses are not always taken to reflect a pupil's understanding. For example, usual assessments of reading might appear to show a certain level of reading skill but facility in the mechanics of reading may conceal poor understanding of the content and its nuances to a greater degree than is expected with other children.

Pedagogy

In general, children with autism tend to respond to repeated brief structured sessions of teaching and learning drawing on behavioural and cognitive approaches. The focus is often on building skills including skills of social interaction with sensitivity. There also needs to be an attuned recognition that the process may be perceived to be confusing and threatening to the child at times. A range of approaches focus on communication and developing other social skills.

'Structured teaching'

Division TEACCH (Treatment and Education of Autistic and related Communication handicapped CHildren) (www.teacch.com) is a programme used in the state of North Carolina and elsewhere for people with autistic spectrum disorders and their families (Schopler, 1997). One element of the work has been the development of a structured teaching approach 'designed to address the major neurological differences in autism' (e.g. Mezibov and Howley, 2003: 8). ST involves organising the classroom to reduce visual and auditory distractions thus helping the child focus and ensuring that the teaching process and teaching styles are suitable for pupils with autistic spectrum disorder. Visual information is used to make things more meaningful and to encourage learning and independence. The main purpose of structured teaching is to 'increase independence and to manage behaviour by considering the cognitive skills, needs and interests of people with autistic spectrum disorder and adjusting the environment accordingly' (ibid.: 9). Four components of structured teaching are physical structures, daily schedules, work systems and visual structure and information.

Physical structure and organisation concerns arranging furniture, materials and general surroundings to add meaning and context to the environment. It may include such features as providing the child with a workstation, screening an area to reduce distractions and using different colours to designate a room or area for different activities.

Daily schedules involve such features as visual timetables and diaries, either written or using pictures and drawings or representative objects, to help the pupil organise moving from place to place or from activity to activity. A transition object can be presented to a child to indicate what he should do next (e.g. a picture of a coat to indicate going outside for break time). A simple sequence can be indicated by a tray labelled, 'first' and 'then', which contain items necessary for two different tasks. Alternatives offered in schedules can encourage pupils' choice and decision-making.

Work systems, presented visually, aim to aid the pupil in completing specific activities. The work system may be organised to go from left to right so that for example work concerning specific tasks and activities is placed on a tray on the pupil's left and, as work is completed, it is transferred to a 'finished' tray on the right. For higher attaining pupils, work systems can be written.

Visual structure and information concerning specific tasks and activities includes ensuring organisation and structures using the principles of visual clarity (e.g. colour coding), visual organisation (e.g. using organising containers) and visual instructions (e.g. written or pictorial cues).

Lovaas programme

The Lovaas programme, based on the principles of applied behavioural analysis, uses behavioural methods to teach skills and to reduce unwanted behaviour (Lovaas, 1987 and the Lovaas Institute for Early Intervention (www.lovaas.com). In the programme, some behaviours are considered to be in excess, such as obsessive behaviour, and some in deficit, such as communication and social skills. It follows that the aim is to decrease excess behaviour and develop and increase deficit behaviours.

Usually, the child is taught at home, one-to-one, by a therapist who is trained to use the programme, and by the child's parents and volunteers. It is recommended that, ideally, the programme should commence before the child is 42 months old. Teaching takes place in 10–15 minute sessions, followed by a period of play, followed by a further session of work. Normally, the child sits opposite the therapist at a table and instructions are given with physical prompts as necessary. Required responses are rewarded while unwanted responses are ignored or given time out.

Target behaviours are specified (e.g. repeating a word) and a sequence or 'drill' is presented to teach the target behaviour. The first three goals, 'come here', 'sit down' and 'look at me', are followed by work such as imitation, matching, labelling objects and pre-school academic skills.

Discrete trial teaching/training

Discrete trial training (DTT) (e.g. Committee on Educational Interventions for Children with Autism, 2001) is a method providing intervention. It is a structured and therapist-led intervention. DTT involves breaking behaviour into smaller parts, teaching one sub-skill before moving on to another, shaping required behaviours until they are securely learned and prompt fading. Reinforcement is directly related to the task. The approach can be described in terms of its components of presentation, response, consequence and pause:

- an adult *presentation* (providing a stimulus such as an environmental cue or an instruction that cues the child to carry out the required behaviour);

- the child's *response* (as a result of the cue);
- the *consequence* following the child's response (receiving the reward such as food, a toy or time to engage in a favourite activity for a correct response);
- a brief *pause* following the consequence and preceding the next instruction.

If the adult presentation does not have the desired effect, the adult may prompt the child, or model the action required. Teaching may use the basic presentation, response, consequence, pause structure informally and for many purposes. What makes DTT programmes more distinct is that they use this model predominantly. Also, they may involve intensive regular work sessions of one-to-one instruction several times per day building up from brief sessions to longer ones of perhaps several hours per day over many months. DTT programmes may differ in terms of the content they are used to teach. For example, DTT is used in the Lovaas programme beginning with early receptive language and leading to skill programmes in self-help, in the school and in the community. Other DTT programmes follow other curricula and other sequences of learning.

For example, a 'readiness' skill such as sitting on a chair may be taught. The adult would provide the stimulus to cue the required behaviour perhaps using a request or a signal. The correct response for the child would be to sit in the chair. The child would then receive a reward. There would then be a brief pause before the next instruction. The skill might be further broken down into steps such as approaching the chair, standing near the chair, facing the correct way and at the correct distance to sit in the chair and lowering oneself into the chair. Each of these steps would be taught using the same approach. If the child did not carry out the required behaviour when cued, the adult might guide the child to carry out the behaviour and reward him for doing so. In the next trial, the child might again need help but may be beginning to comply. In the next trial the child might make an effort to carry out the requested behaviour and would be rewarded again. In the subsequent trial the child might carry out the required behaviour unaided. The intensity of the DTT programmes and the time and effort they require indicates that care is taken to evaluate and monitor the effectiveness of the approach for particular children, and the effort required by the child's family and others and whether it is sustainable. Please also see the website of the Indiana Resource Centre for Autism (www.iidc.indiana.edu/irca/behavior/discretetrl.html).

Pivotal response training

Pivotal response training is intended to improve the social-emotional and communicative behaviour of young children (about 3 to 10 years old) with autistic spectrum disorders. It does not teach one behaviour at a time. On the contrary, it is a naturalistic intervention intended to target pivotal areas of a child's functioning that if developed would be likely to lead to broader changes in other behaviours not targeted in the intervention. Procedures are used to structure the environment to teach these pivotal skills so that broader areas of social and communicative functioning are improved (Koegel and Koegel, 1995). Two areas that are considered pivotal for children with autism are motivation and responsivity to multiple cues. An example of developing a pivotal area is increasing a child's motivation to learn new skills and to initiate social contacts and respond to others doing so. More generally motivation is increased through such approaches as turn taking, giving the child choices and reinforcing attempts (not just the successful completion of a task). In this way it is expected that the child will be enabled to respond to the opportunities to learn and interact that arise day-to-day.

Pivotal response training uses a model of Applied Behaviour Analysis involving positive child centred and family centred procedures. It may involve short sessions perhaps from 10 minutes to an hour several times a week (e.g. one study involved sessions several times a week until 16 hours had been spent on the intervention). It includes:

- using varied tasks that encompass mastered and novel activities;
- ensuring adequate modelling of the required behaviour such as turn taking;
- using naturally occurring reinforcers such as responding meaningfully to a child's requests (e.g. helping a child obtain a drink when a drink is requested);
- using activities the child prefers and allowing choices within these activities.

These and other procedures are incorporated into day-to-day teaching and learning opportunities in natural settings. Among other features, asking questions, giving instructions and giving the child opportunities to respond, should all be clear, uninterrupted and task appropriate.

A review of studies using this approach concludes that it is an effective intervention and that in educational settings, '... a child centred approach to intervention in natural environments can optimise communicative and social-emotional functioning' (Humphries, 2003: 5). (See also (www.research intopractice.info).

Sensory integration

The underpinning theory for sensory integration was developed by Jean Ayers, an occupational therapist. The implication as applied to autism is that an aspect of the condition is considered to be a difficulty, processing information received through the senses either relating to the speed of processing, how information is interpreted and how memory functions in relating current information to previous experiences. Sensory integration therefore aims to reduce sensory disturbances connected with touch, movement and sense of position and involves the tactile, proprioceptive and vestibular senses (Please see Chapter 18 on 'Developmental co-ordination disorder' for an explanation of these senses). It is thought that some behaviour that may be associated with autism, such as hand flapping and walking on the tips of one's toes, is related to dysfunctions of sensory integration.

Among examples of sensory integration techniques for problems with tactile sensitivity is using a soft surgical brush and brushing the arms, legs and back interspersed with compressing (the occupational therapist manually pushing together) the joints of the elbows, knees and arm and hip sockets. For proprioceptive problems, jumping on a small trampoline and the joint compression techniques mentioned already may be used. For vestibular problems, balancing exercises, activities involving the hand and arm crossing the body mid line and work with an occupational therapist to strengthen muscle tone may be employed. (See for example, Case-Smith and Bryant, 1999.)

Teaching language skills

Pupils with autistic spectrum disorder will have difficulties with both receptive and expressive communication, such as semantics (language meaning) and pragmatics (language use) and may, for example, try to understand idioms through understanding of the words not the possible intentions of the speaker. Teachers will need to explicitly teach aspects of conversational skills. Readers may wish to consult in the present text the chapter concerning 'Communication disorder: Semantics and pragmatics' (Chapter 16) as a reminder of some of the issues and strategies involved but bearing in mind the particular context of autism.

Work on improving communication skills is likely to include using intonation, non-verbal communication (including appropriate proximity to others when speaking with them, and orientating one's body towards the speaker or listener), reducing echolalia and correcting the common reversal of pronouns ('You want a drink' when the message is 'I want a drink'). These are often approaches using structured behavioural training but are likely to take a long time.

To increase spontaneous verbalisation for children with autism, case studies have suggested the effectiveness of using time delay (Ingenmey and Van Houten, 1991; Matson et al., 1993) or visual cue prompting such as coloured cards (Matson et al., 1993). Time delay procedure to develop spontaneous requests might involve presenting the child with a target stimulus to be requested such as a toy or food. The adult immediately models the response (in this case a request for the item). When the child imitates the response without error, the adult delays the prompting and at each trial the time delay is lengthened. A response, whether spontaneous or imitated, is reinforced by giving the child the item. As the stimulus/model interval increases, the child is expected to initiate the request independently before the prompt is given.

The Picture Exchange Communication System

The Picture Exchange Communication System (Bondy and Frost, 1994) aims to help children using pictures to request things from others and for other purposes (www.pecs.org.uk). The child 'exchanges' a picture or symbol representing, for example, an item or activity for the thing they would like. Single things are taught initially, such as 'drink'. Good practice in early stages involves not pre-empting the child's attempts to communicate by volunteering for him the communication that is anticipated, but waiting for the child to hand over the picture conveying the request. Later, to further develop communication, the child is taught to construct sentences and to use pictures to offer comments.

Manual signing systems

Manual signing systems using hand and arm positioning and movements to communicate include systems that adapt and simplify the nationally used sign language for the deaf. They may be used to encourage the development of verbal language skills. Signing systems might be expected to be effective as communication tools for children with autistic spectrum disorder partly because they are visual and the child's hand movements when he is signing can be modified and corrected by the adult. Yet many children with autistic spectrum disorder appear to have difficulties making signs and using them spontaneously (Attwood et al., 1988). It is considered more effective to use signs to help a child's understanding (e.g. used by the teacher to give an extra physical clue to what is being communicated) rather than to teach it to be used as a means of expression.

Intensive interaction

A principle of Intensive Interaction (e.g. Hewett and Nind, 1998) is that it is necessary to develop the child's ability to enjoy the company of others, and to develop his understanding of how to interact with others and how to communicate. It uses techniques relating to early parent–child interactions, in which the parent, through imitation and turn taking, invests the earliest possible random actions of the child with meaning. In Intensive Interaction, the adult acts as though the actions of the child were intended to communicate meaning, and follows what the child does. Short daily interactions in the classroom aim to develop communication and encourage learning, so that the developing relationship leads to others activities within a wider curriculum. Parents who have been trained can also use the approach at home. Using this approach, the progress of pupils with autism has been assessed and reported (Nind, 1999).

The Children's Talk project

The Children's Talk project is an evidence-based communication programme for children with autistic spectrum disorder developed in the United Kingdom. Parents receive consultation and training in particular parent–child communication skills (Aldred *et al.*, 2004). In order to help a child's capacity for social referencing, parents are shown how to improve parent–child joint attention. They are trained to provide a supportive commentary on their child's behaviour and how to show their child how language can be used to work for them by translating the child's non-verbal communication into simple words.

Parents also learn how to use language scripts in particular contexts to convey certain meanings and intentions so helping their child's understanding. In the programme parents and pre-school children attend monthly sessions for 6 months and for a further 6 months attend sessions less often. Having been coached in communication skills using video feedback, parents are asked to plan daily half-hour sessions to coach their child in the development of these skills.

Joint action routines

Joint action routines (e.g. Prizant *et al.*, 2000) involve using day-to-day routines that encourage communication. A routine might be preparing food such as making a sandwich. In this example the adult might set out the ingredients but require the child to request each one (bread, butter, ham). It should be clear who does what so that the child would request items and then spread the butter or he might spread the butter and place the slice of ham on the bread. In different activities the allocation of roles and who does what may be different. The activity will generally involve clear discrete parts and a clear sequence (first you get the bread, then you get the butter, then you get the knife, then you spread the butter on the bread and so on).

Initially it is important to establish the routine rather than request responses from the child. The adult may demonstrate what to do (modelling) and then convey the expectation that the child will do part of the routine, conveying the idea of turn taking.

To encourage communication the adult might pause in the routine activity and say what she wants the child to say (e.g. 'butter'). The child should say the word then the activity continues. If the child does not respond, the adult tries several more times and if there is still no response she will model the required response for the child and continue with the activity. The structure may be employed to encourage the use of the Picture Exchange Communication System or to encourage gestures or manual sign language. Once the routine is established and the child knows the previously modelled response the response might be elicited by offering the child a choice where one of the responses is the previously modelled one. The adult, holding up two items one which the child wants and one which the child does not require asks, 'What do you want, the butter or the sugar?' (Reversing the order from time to time so the child does not merely repeat the final word.)

Consistency is important until the response is securely learned and routines are followed carefully and the same words are used. Once the routine is very secure, learning opportunities for responses can be created by unexpectedly changing the routine so a response is necessary, for example giving the child the butter but no bread and allowing plenty of time for the child to respond.

Social stories

Social stories are intended to help pupils understand the social environment and how to behave suitably in it, focusing on a desired outcome. As originally conceived (Gray, 1994), social stories are written by someone who knows the child well and concern a social situation the child finds difficult. The format includes descriptive, perspective and directive sentences. Descriptive sentences concern what happens, where it happens, who participates, what they do and why. Perspective sentences describe the feelings and responses of others. Directive sentences provide guidance about what the pupil should try to do or say in the situation (I should try to ...). It is suggested that social stories should have proportionately more descriptive and perspective sentences than directive ones.

The pupil might write his own stories focused on matters and situations he finds difficult (e.g. Smith, 2003). The discussion centring on the developing story and the anticipation of the real-life situations it describes may be important components. As well as written stories a comic strip format can be used with characters having speech/thought bubbles to convey the information. Photographs and symbols can be employed. More evidence and information is required on what social stories are intended to achieve, whether they achieve it, which pupils tend to benefit and how long-lasting any effects are on the child's behaviour and well-being.

Resources

Resources associated with developing communication may be used, for example the Picture Exchange Communication System. Visual timetables and other resources aimed at helping structure the environment may also be used.

Therapy

Music therapy and art therapy are used with children with autism but it has been suggested (Simpson, 2005) that both are associated with only 'limited supporting information for practice'. Musical interaction therapy (e.g. Prevezer, 2000) seeks to develop the child's ability to enjoy the company of others and his understanding of how to interact and communicate. Wimpory and colleagues (1995) present a case study illustrating its use. Normal communication is seen as developing as the baby and familiar adult negotiate increasingly complex interactions in which the baby actively participates. The interaction takes place as the baby responds to the adult and invites a response so that a dialogue develops. Building on this apparent rationale, music interaction therapy involves the child's key worker or parent working with the child having autistic spectrum disorder, while a musician plays an instrument to support and encourage their interaction. The key worker might copy or join in with the child's actions as if they were intentional attempts to communicate.

Organisation

Physical organisation of the classroom

The physical organisation of the classroom is important in approaches such as structured teaching where physical structure adds meaning and context to the environment. For autistic children who are oversensitive to sensory stimulation in the environment, classroom areas that are quiet and have low visual stimulation may be used.

Working in pairs and groups

While social situations tend to be difficult for pupils with autistic spectrum disorder, much is learned in pairs or small groups in school, so strategies for encouraging group work reflect a tension between child resistance and educational facilitation requiring teacher sensitivity. Working on a principle related to desensitisation in behavioural approaches, the pupil with autistic spectrum disorder can be taught individually by the teacher or teaching aide but in successively closer proximity to a small group of pupils. The pupil with autistic spectrum disorder can then work with one other child on a familiar task so efforts at adapting are largely on the social aspects of the activity. These activities can be made more appealing to pupils with autism by incorporating their special interest in the task or activity. Both the task and the level of social interaction required can be gradually increased in complexity. Next, the pupil with autistic spectrum disorder can be encouraged to work in a group of three pupils where again the task and social requirements can be gradually increased. Larger group work would follow. Balanced against all this is the importance for the child of also having some time alone or pursuing a preferred activity.

Learning Experiences – An Alternative Program for Preschoolers and Parents

Learning Experiences – An Alternative Program for Preschoolers and Parents (LEAP) (e.g. Strain and Hoyson, 2000) is a programme originally started in the state of Colorado in the early 1980s involving pre-schooling classes in which children with autism learn with typically developing children. A programme teaches parents how to use behavioural skills with their child at home and in the community. Among the features of the approach are that typically developing peers are taught to help the social and language skills of children with autism; and data is collected each day on Individual Education Programme objectives to inform the next day's teaching plans.

Typically a LEAP classroom might have about four children with autism and perhaps ten who do not and a special education teacher helps the children with autism throughout the day. One of the principles is that the children with autism, being educated with typically developing peers, have the opportunity to see models of appropriate social skills and more opportunities to interact with their non-disabled peers.

Managing transitions

Because of the nature of autism, including resistance to change, major transitions, which can be difficult for any child, are often particularly demanding. These include starting school, moving to another school, moving home, moving from school to further or higher education require careful support (Jones, 2002: 104–114). Aids to successful transition include good local policies and procedures for transition, effective record keeping, good preparation for transfer and careful monitoring of the quality of procedures. On a smaller scale the care taken with visual timetables and communication helps indicate the child that a change is proposed from one activity to another, from one school area to another, from activity to leisure or from school to home.

Other aspects of provision

Managing challenging behaviour

Functional behavioural assessments contribute to the management of challenging behaviour in that they seek to understand the function the behaviour serves for the child or young person, its antecedents and consequences. Positive Behavioural Interventions and Supports (PBIS) may include examining what things should always be done to prevent problem behaviour from occurring, what short-term strategies are used, what replacement behaviours need to be taught that are as efficient and effective as the problem behaviour and how staff need to change their own behaviour when problem behaviour does occur. The United States Office of Special Education Programs (OSEP) has a website Technical Assistance Centre on Positive Behavioural Interventions and Supports (www.pbis.org).

Challenging behaviour in not a necessary concomitant of autism, but the context of autism can be influential in its prevention, and where it does occur, its management. Several issues arise relating to the context of approaches to challenging behaviour in children with autism. (These are summarised by Carr, 2006: 354.)

Among these issues are that children with autism perceive many situations (e.g. breaking into their routines or requiring that the child moves attention from one activity to another) as frightening or threatening that may not be interpreted in a similar way by other children. Also, because children with autism have difficulties with insight into how others think and how they might behave, they may find the behaviour of others confusing and potentially distressing. Oversensitivity to stimuli might lead a child with autism to react aggressively in a situation that for other children would only represent acceptable levels of stimulation. Where a child is unable to express wants and needs, this can further exacerbate difficult behaviour. Behaviour may become a default system of communication in the absence of a more reliable system.

Important considerations are the environment in which the challenging behaviour occurs, what seems to precipitate it, the challenging behaviour itself, and the response it elicits – all principles of evidence-based behavioural approaches. It is from these considerations that strategies are developed to prevent or manage challenging behaviour. The environment may be modified (as in structured teaching) or what is requested of the child may be refined (e.g. obsessional behaviour) is not prohibited but, provided it is harmless and required tasks are finished, is allowed in recreation periods. Also it is made clear to the child that certain behaviour is not tolerated, as in aspects of the Lovaas programme which seeks to reduce behaviour that is considered to be in excess. Learning the consequences of actions can be helped by the use of communication aids and alternatives, as in the use of the Picture Exchange Communication System. As a general thread running through the management of challenging behaviour, communication is important. The difficulties of lack of understanding of what is being communicated by others and not being able to communicate effectively one's requirements can exacerbate challenging behaviour if communication is not addressed. Replacement behaviours may be taught that serve the same function as the problem behaviour.

Drug treatments may be considered if behaviour therapies fail to reduce unwanted or harmful behaviour. The neuroleptic drug Haloperidol has been reported to produce significant decrease in unwanted behaviours such as aggression and stereotypies and is the only medication consistently reported to be effective, but it has major side effects such as tardive dyskinesia (a neurological syndrome associated with uncontrollable purposeless muscular movements such as grimacing and rapid eye blinking). See Campbell and colleagues (1996) for a review of the use of Haloperidol with autistic children and adolescents. Naltrexone is considered a safe drug that has been reported to reduce hyperactivity and disruptive behaviour.

Family support and parent training

Initially, important work will have hopefully been done by various professionals to explain to parents the diagnosis of autism and help parents begin to and continue to make sense of the disorder. This is unlikely to be achieved in a few meetings and parents may welcome ongoing opportunities to ask questions, seek clarification, gain support or make contact with other parents who have a child with autism.

As well as family support, including respite care and counselling, parents are helped by practical advice and training. Parent training appears to be an important part of many behavioural programmes. The importance of parents as co-therapists has been emphasised including helping parents to learn problem-solving skills so that as well as being able to deal better with current behaviour problems, they are more able to cope with future challenges. The school will seek to involve parents in setting clear educational goals for children and working with the school in a consistent way to reach these. Where these goals are expressed in unambiguous behavioural terms, it is easier to identify progress and to modify approaches where anticipated progress is not evident. In particular, families report wanting more information on why problem behaviour occur, how to help their child make choices, reducing family stress, sustaining energy levels and advocacy (Turnbull and Rueff, 1996).

Thinking points

Readers may wish to consider with reference to a particular school:

- the extent to which application of the broad approach of structuring the environment is successful;
- the relative effectiveness of the particular approaches used and the type and quality of evidence on which they are based;
- the effectiveness of working closely with the child's family in terms of support and training.

Key texts

Akshoomoff, N. (ed.) (2006) *Autism Spectrum Disorders*. New York, Guildford Press.
These *Child Neuropsychology* journal articles (October 2006) focus on characteristics of children later diagnosed as having autism spectrum disorders, neuropsychological testing and developmental data.

Gabriels, R. and Hill, D. E. (2007) *Growing Up with Autism: Working with School Age Children and Adolescents*. New York, Guilford Press.
Provides guidance for supporting positive behaviour, social skills and communication and dealing with issues of mental and physical health and sexuality.

Sewell, K. (2000) *Breakthroughs: How to Reach Students with Autism*. Verona, WI, Attainment Company.
Practical advice for educating students with autism.

Myles, B., Cook, K., Miller, N. *et al.* (2000) *Asperger's Syndrome and Sensory Issues: Practical Solutions for Making Sense of the World*. Shawnee Mission, KS, Autism Asperger's Publishing Company.

Wall, K. (2004) *Autism and Early Years Practice: A Guide for Early Years Professionals, Teachers and Parents*. London, Paul Chapman.
This contains a range of practical advice assuming largely a United Kingdom context.

Chapter 18

Developmental co-ordination disorder

Introduction

This chapter presents a definition of developmental co-ordination disorder (DCD); looks at estimates of its prevalence; considers possible causal factors; examines developmental processes considered to underpin DCD (gross and fine motor co-ordination, and perceptual-motor development) and looks at ways of assessing DCD. Turning to provision, the chapter outlines aspects of the curriculum; pedagogy; resources; therapy/care and organisation.

Definitions

Concerning DCD, not withstanding a consensus meeting held at the University of Western Ontario in 1994, at which participants agreed on the preferential designation DCD, to refer to children with developmental motor problems, a number of terms continue to be used in describing and diagnosing children with developmental motor difficulties. Neither has a universally agreed set of characteristics been identified for these children (Ahonen, et al., 2004: 269–270). This inconsistency in definition relates to the heterogeneous nature of the group of children considered to have DCD and its different manifestations.

There is debate about the definition of DCD and related matters including the extent to which there may be subtypes of the condition and the extent to which it is helpful to consider DCD in the context of a variety of learning problems such as reading disability, specific language disabilities and attention deficit hyperactivity disorder (e.g. Dewey, 2002: 40–53).

In a widely used definition, DCD is considered a 'marked impairment of motor co-ordination', which 'significantly interferes with academic achievement or activities of daily living' and is 'not due to a general medical condition' (American Psychiatric Association, 2000: 56–57). DCD is not associated with any medically evident neurological signs and this helps distinguish it from cerebral palsy and other conditions affecting motor co-ordination but in which there are overt neurological symptoms. (See also

Cermak *et al.*, 2002: 2–22.) The expression, 'clumsy child syndrome', that was more commonly used previously, conveys something of a common feature of DCD or at least a possible subtype (e.g. Cermak and Larkin, 2002).

Where the term 'dyspraxia' (from the Greek, 'difficulty in doing') continues to be used, definitions tend to focus on the organisation, planning and organisation of movement, and dyspraxia is sometimes seen as a subtype of DCD. For example, dyspraxia has been defined as a 'marked impairment in gross and fine motor *organisation* (which may or may not influence articulation and speech) which are influenced by poor perceptual regulation. These difficulties present as an inability to *plan and organise purposeful movement*' (Dixon and Addy, 2004: 9, italics in original). It appears the child knows how to carry out activities but has difficulty organising movements to accomplish them. Nevertheless dyspraxia still relates fundamentally to motor actions (see also Cermak and Larkin, 2002: 42–46). Developmental verbal dyspraxia is a speech difficulty considered briefly in Chapter 14, 'Communication disorders: Speech'.

Characteristics of the motor performance of children with DCD include: slower movement time; relying more on visual information than on than proprioceptive information and inconsistency in some aspects of motor performance in relation to other skilled movement. Related but more cognitive aspects include the child's failure to anticipate and use perceptual information and benefit from cues; and failure to use rehearsal strategies (Dewey and Wilson, 2001: 18 paraphrased). More generally, children tend to show difficulties with gross and fine motor skills in terms of both speed and accuracy owing to motor control and co-ordination problems as well as difficulties with sequencing movements. It is important for teachers and others to note the amount of effort and time it takes a child to perform a task as well as whether or not he can perform it (Cermak and Larkin, 2002).

Prevalence and co-occurrence

Estimates of prevalence of DCD vary widely from 6 per cent to 22 per cent, which is thought to be influenced by the assessment procedure and the background experience of the assessor (Kirby and Drew, 2003: 52). Related to difficulties estimating prevalence (and definition) is the complicating issue of the degree of co-occurrence of DCD with other conditions, the exact nature of which is debated (Martini *et al.*, 1999). For example, Gillberg (in Landgren *et al.*, 1998) identified 589 children aged 6–7 years in a Swedish community considered to have some form of neurological disorder, finding that of the children identified as having 'Deficit of Attention and Motor Perception' (DAMP), all had DCD and attention deficits and about half fulfilled the criteria for attention deficit hyperactivity disorder. Kaplan and colleagues (1998) noted an overlap between DCD, attention deficit hyperactivity disorder and dyslexia, finding 23 per cent of a diagnosed group having all three conditions.

Possible causal factors

The causes of DCD are not fully known although evidence points to the problems of children with DCD being multi-dimensional and no single factor has been identified as a direct cause. This has been taken to suggest the use of multi-causative models to understand the interconnections between genetic predisposition, brain structure, pre-natal influences and post-natal effects (Cermak *et al.*, 2002).

In the aetiology of DCD, there is debate about the relative importance of motor and of non-motor factors. 'Non-motor' refers to the processing of perceptual information in the service of action. 'Motor' concerns control processes responsible for selecting and programming an appropriate motor response taking account of environmental input (Wilson and McKenzie, 1998).

It has been proposed that influential non-motor factors, in relation to DCD, include:

- visuoperceptual deficits;
- visuospatial representation deficits;
- deficits in kinaesthetic function and
- deficits in visuomotor integration (Wilson, 2005: 292).

A meta-analysis of DCD literature (Wilson and McKenzie, 1998) suggested the main deficit associated with DCD was visuospatial processing irrespective of whether a motor response was required or not. Kinaesthetic perception, especially where active movement was involved, and cross-modal perception involving different modes such as visual and movement perception were also important factors. It has been argued that deficits in the visuospatial representation of *intended* movements may be an important part of the explanation of motor clumsiness in children (Wilson, 2005: 293).

An aspect of analysis of deficits in motor control involves studying how children make reaching movements to objects or targets in space. Children with DCD and other children without DCD are compared in relation to the temporal and spatial characteristics of their movements. Reaction time, movement time, movement accuracy and movement variability are studied to try to determine how children with DCD plan, organise and carry out motor responses. Studies of goal-directed arm movements have examined the ability of children with DCD to use visual and kinaesthetic feedback for movement control (e.g. Pryde, 2000). Such studies suggest that characterising the effects of DCD on manual aiming has to take account of the requirements of the aiming task such as whether the child is allowed to see his hand movements, the size of the target and the amplitude of movements. It has been argued (Roy *et al.*, 2004: 54–55) that overall, DCD does not affect the initial programming of movement but does affect the processing of feedback information and the integration of feedback from vision and proprioception.

Nevertheless, for some children, earlier programming stages do appear to be affected.

Developmental processes considered to underpin DCD

Fundamental to a child being able to plan and perform co-ordinated actions is that he correctly interprets incoming sensory information from the environment. Three key systems provide information to enable the development of co-ordinated and controlled movement: the sensory, proprioceptive and vestibular systems.

In the present context, the sensory system refers particularly to the senses of sight, hearing and touch and is sometimes taken to include the proprioceptive and vestibular systems too.

The proprioceptive system provides information concerning where the limbs are in relation to the rest of the person's body without him having to look (e.g. Estil and Whiting, 2002: 71). This involves receptors within the joints and muscles that monitor the stretch of muscles and indicate the position of each limb (e.g. Dixon and Addy, 2004: 15). Where for a child with DCD this information is not as acute as it is for other children, certain activities may be particularly difficult including dressing where many buttons are involved, and wiping the bottom after using the toilet. Gross motor movement is difficult and consequently the child may be heavy footed.

The vestibular system involves receptors in the inner ear sending impulses to the brain to assess the position and movement of the head relative to the rest of the body, which is important for balance and the sense of movement including velocity. Children for whom this system is dysfunctional tend to lack control of the speed of their movements. Also a child with DCD tends to have problems maintaining balance, that is, poor equilibrium, and may therefore be afraid of movement.

As well as affecting fine and gross motor movement, the sensory, proprioceptive and vestibular systems influence visual and auditory perception. Inter-related elements of perceptual-motor development affected include:

- visual-motor co-ordination;
- visual form constancy;
- spatial position and
- spatial relationships.

Where proprioception, vestibular feedback and sense of touch are not as acute as is typical, *visual-motor co-ordination* (eye-hand co-ordination) is affected. The proprioceptive system provides inaccurate and slowly processed information about where the arm and hand are positioned and about how much movement is required to reach an object. Visuospatial judgement is therefore affected, impairing fine motor control.

Visual form constancy involves being able to recognise that an object that may appear different, for example when it is in a different position from when first encountered, is still the same object. In the process of a child developing a mental map of an object and coming to recognise it as a 'category', touch is an important aid. A child with DCD getting incorrect information about an object because of a dampened sense of touch is unable to absorb important tactile cues about the object. A clear mental schema of the object is not developed and the child may have difficulty developing form constancy, having to rely excessively on the sense of vision to help.

Acquiring a notion of one's *spatial position* enables one to perceive depth in space; to perceive body position relative to surroundings (e.g. above or below); and develop a body schema and a realistic body image. Many learners with DCD have a poor sense of position in space. Consequently they have a poor understanding of self-image, a poor appreciation of body proportions and a lack of understanding of laterality. The latter can lead to difficulties locating left and right and, more, generally, poor orientation. The child may avoid crossing the body mid-line by turning the body so that the left hand can pick up an item on the child's right without the left arm crossing the body midline. The child's writing might be 'mirror' writing and letters in words might be reversed. Map reading will be very difficult.

Turning to *spatial relationships*, to understand these, the child has to be able to perceive the position of two or more objects in relation to one another and in relation to him. This in turn depends on developing adequate form constancy, position in space, and figure-ground discrimination. Because a child with DCD has problems assessing space and judging distance, he tends to have difficulties with activities such as negotiating his way to the front of the class, climbing stairs and with physical education activities like climbing wall bars, or vaulting. In writing, the size of letters may be variable and spacing between letters either excessive or insufficient. Columns for mathematical calculations may be inconsistent, causing errors. Activities such as crossing the road will be problematic and requiring adults to take great care when making judgements about a child's safety. Please see also the chapter 'Development of the Child' (Kirby and Drew, 2003; 27–50).

Identification and assessment

A multi-professional assessment of DCD will provide a range of useful information and may involve the physician (who may make the initial diagnosis), physical therapist/physiotherapist, occupational therapist, school psychologist, speech pathologist where there are language implications, and the teacher. When tests are compared that aim to assess DCD, they do not always consistently identify children as having or not having DCD (Crawford *et al.*,

2001) suggesting that information from standardised tests along with an assessment of functional performance may increase accuracy of identification. Observation and assessments based on professional judgement also contribute.

Assessment is also informed by the assessor being aware of possible characteristics. A child around 4 or 5 years old may find it more difficult than others of the same age to go up and down stairs; learns to use the toilet independently much later than peers, and may have difficulty handling toys and performing tasks requiring dexterity such as completing jigsaws.

A child around 5 to 11 years old might find it hard to generalise skills because they are not secure or automatic. So tasks such as adapting to catching various balls of different sizes which most pupils will perform with little difficulty may for the pupil with DCD be almost like learning a new skill each time. The child may also be accident prone, tending to knock things over or bump into objects. Older students may be disorganised, finding it difficult to move around a large high school/secondary school and get to lessons on time especially if there are stairs to negotiate or if the building is on a large site or several sites. For older and younger pupils, particular school subjects such as art, science and design and technology, pose their own challenges. In some subjects, safety implications loom large. For example, where hazardous substances are handled, the school will need to make pupil-specific risk assessments. DCD poses particular difficulties for handwriting, physical activities, and social and personal development (e.g. Cermak and Larkin, 2002, *passim*).

Provision

Curriculum and assessment

The overall levels of curriculum are likely to be broadly similar to that of children without disorders/disability but there will be particular care with areas where motor co-ordination is central. These include handwriting, physical education, art, geometry and aspects of social and personal skills development; subjects where it is necessary to use tools, such as craft or technology; and laboratory work, for example in biology, chemistry or physics. The balance of subjects is likely to reflect this with an emphasis on those areas where the child needs extra practice and support. Components within subjects that require co-ordination may also be emphasised, for example handwriting in English studies. Assessment may be finely grained in the areas of motor development to ensure progress is monitored.

Pedagogy

In general, pedagogy related to DCD includes identifying tasks that are difficult for the child and breaking them into smaller steps so that they may be easier to teach and to learn, so-called task analysis. These are taught in contexts where their usefulness is apparent. The activity may be adapted and/or equipment used to enable activities to be accomplished.

Handwriting

A difficulty with acquiring handwriting skills for a child with DCD is the difficulty with learning the motor plan or programme of the letters owing to problems in motor planning or spatial orientation. Additionally, the child may have problems with forming letters correctly and legibly because of motor control deficits.

A child with DCD may adopt a poor writing posture because of proprioceptive difficulties. The pupil is more likely to adopt a better posture if the chair and desk height produce a 90- degree angle between the line of the upper body and the line of the upper leg, and between the upper and lower leg and the knee. The position of the paper to be written on is important but the pupil with DCD may misjudge this because of spatial difficulties. A sheet of paper should be aligned with the child's arm and a marking on the child's desk or the use of a large card template will help ensure this is maintained (e.g. Benbow, 2002: 271).

For a pupil with DCD, developing a good pencil grip may prove difficult. Because of poor tactile sensation the child may grip tightly so as to feel the pencil better. Fluency may be further affected by poor proprioceptive sense in the joints of the fingers and hand. The muscles in the hand may be underdeveloped or muscle tone may be poor. This is likely to hinder the fluency and comfort of writing, impair legibility and cause fatigue. Pencil grip is improved by the pupil using the preferred hand and most children have a preferred hand by the age of 7 years (although for children with DCD it may be older). A three-cornered pencil grip or a pen with a rubber finger grip can help. Proprioceptive feedback may be improved by specific tasks aimed at enhancing dexterity.

The pressure of the pencil on paper may be too light or too heavy because of proprioceptive difficulties affecting co-ordination and exerting pressure. Physical tasks can be used to temporarily boost limb awareness, with the effects lasting typically for about 40 minutes before further exercises are necessary. One exercise is up to five repetitions of rotating horizontally held arms in small spirals gradually increased, then reversing the direction and reducing the spirals (Addy, 2004). A pen that illuminates when pressed for writing can help the pupil become more aware of pressure exerted when writing. A pupil tending to press too lightly will be encouraged to make the implement light up, while a child tending to press too heavily will be encouraged to avoid illuminating the pen.

Where a pupil has difficulty with eye-hand co-ordination he will find it hard to place the pencil on a particular point, an essential skill for writing.

This can be tackled by encouraging increasingly refined movements of the hand and fingers, then of placing a pencil point. The pupil can begin by placing a finger on a marked area of paper. Gradually the area is decreased so it is a spot. Next the pupil is asked to perform a similar series of tasks but using a pencil, eventually placing a pencil point on a specified dot (Dixon and Addy, 2004: 66–80).

Adequate form constancy is essential because a central part of handwriting involves: recognising, identifying and distinguishing shapes and different sizes of shapes; and reproducing shapes, correct in form and size. To help, multi-sensory approaches may be used to develop the child's experience and understanding of shapes and sizes. Soft clay material may be used to make different letter shapes. When a pencil is used, the child may make lines (horizontal, vertical, diagonal) and basic shapes (circle). A diagonal line is likely to be particularly difficult for a pupil having problems with laterality because it necessitates simultaneously crossing from left to right and from top to bottom.

The child can work on more recognisable pre-writing patterns to help develop the rhythm and fluency necessary for writing. When the child is taught to write letters of the alphabet, it can help to get the correct shapes if lined paper is used with a central line and a line above to indicate the height of the ascending letter and a line below to signify the depth of the descending letter. It helps if letters are taught with joins/integral exit strokes to aid learning of cursive script (Dixon and Addy, 2004: 66–80).

Turning to movement control, the child has to learn the forms of letters and how they join cursively. Because of processing difficulties the child may have difficulty stopping a letter and may run the line of a letter on so that, for example, a 'c' has a bottom tail that is far too long. The pupil will need to learn that the letters have a beginning and an end and this can be helped by providing some practice writing a series of letters in a specified short line in which the start and finish are marked by vertical lines. Because of difficulties with laterality and orientation, pupils with dyspraxia often reverse letters, for example 'b' for 'd' and 'p' for 'q' at an age when most pupils do not. This can be remedied by emphasising the writing of letters grouped according to whether they are formed by using a clockwise or an anticlockwise motion (Dixon and Addy, 2004: 76).

- Letters formed with a clockwise motion are 'b', 'h', 'j', 'm', 'n', 'p' and 'r'.
- Those shaped with an anticlockwise motion are 'a', 'c', 'd', 'e', 'f', 'o', 'q', 't', 'u', 'v' and 'w'.
- Ones requiring both motions are 'g', 's' and 'y'.

Kinaesthetic aids, such as the teacher having the pupil write letters in the air and guiding the movements as necessary, tend to help the pupil's visual orientation of the letter. Teaching cursive script from an early age tends to help with letter orientation. Pupils with DCD tend often to space letters and words poorly because of poor spatial organisation. To help, cursive writing can be introduced early and (when using pencil rather than pen which may smudge) the pupil can be encouraged to leave a finger space between words.

It has been suggested (Benbow, 2002: 269) that among reasons for favouring cursive writing are that the patterns of movement better enable more automatic motor learning; reversing and transposing letters is less likely; the connected line helps the learning of words as units; and writing is faster because the child does not have to start and stop as he does when printing letters.

Fluency in writing is difficult to attain for a child with DCD. Moving from pre-writing patterns to the formation of letters with joins/integral exit strokes to cursive writing can assist the pupil's fluency. The pupil is not taught to write 'separate' letters. A kinaesthetic approach, for example using a sand tray for writing letters, helps the child develop a mental image of the letter forms and how they link together. Commercial writing programmes may also be used. Other programmes include the cursive programme Loops and Other Groups (Benbow, 1990) and the pre-cursive programme by Clough (1999). Benbow (2002: 248–279) has also summarised aspects of hand skills and handwriting.

Physical education

It can raise self-esteem if the child finds some success in physical education. Bundy (2002) suggests a child may be seen to be participating in games and activities with other children but may not be getting as much enjoyment as others. Also, as children with DCD are likely to be less competent, they may be less accepted by peers, which can lead to feelings of isolation and low self-worth.

For a child with DCD, physical activities pose a challenge. Skipping with or without a rope may be difficult. Riding a bicycle is a complex task for anyone, involving balance, co-ordination and constantly processing and responding to visual information for steering. For a child with DCD, having difficulties with co-ordination, spatial difficulties and poor judgement of speed, it is hardly surprising the skill of learning to ride a bicycle is delayed.

In physical education lessons, spatial difficulties will make it hard for the child to move about among apparatus. Difficulties judging distance and velocity will make many ball games very challenging. With high school/secondary school students some co-ordination difficulties may be less noticeable, as many will be going through a clumsy period because of the adolescent growth spurt.

In the United States of America, 'adapted physical education' (APE) is an individualised programme provided by people who have studied the requirements of physical education instruction for children with disabilities.

The APE teacher concentrates on fundamental motor skills and physical performance of individual pupils and may work with pupils for a certain number of designated hours per week (Gabbard *et al.*, 1994). The classroom teacher and the APE teacher can work productively together to develop and teach programmes of physical education as well as leisure and recreation. This relates to pupils with DCD and to other pupils, for example those with health or orthopaedic impairments.

A pupil with DCD may see a physical therapist outside school time but there is scope for innovative work when the teacher of physical education and a physical therapist work together planning and implementing physical education lessons to include pupils with DCD.

Black and Haskins (1996) suggest ways activities can be structured to enable all pupils to participate in physical education lessons: parallel activity, inclusive adapted activity and discrete adapted activity. Using the example of ball skills, in a *parallel activity*, pupils play a game together but in their own way using different strategies to reach the same learning goal. To develop the skill to send and receive a ball, pairs of pupils having acquired this skill can pass the ball while moving and from several metres apart while others still developing the skill can pass while stationary and be closer to each other. An *inclusive adapted activity* involves games and activities are adapted so all pupils can participate. For older students, a game of volleyball can be adapted using a light sponge ball allowing more time for students lacking advanced skills in relation to the game to position themselves and reach the ball. Students adept at the game will tend to enjoy such variations occasionally because the changed timing of skills creates a different element of challenge. In a *discrete adapted activity*, pupils take part in pairs or practise individually. In developing skills for a game in which a bat is used to strike a ball (e.g. soft ball) a pupil with DCD may practise using a larger bat or a lighter ball.

A related approach to developing adaptations with reference to pupils with physical, health or multiple disabilities is to use adaptive words to act as a guide to help select and design suitable adapted physical activities. These include 'increase or decrease' which may involve increasing rest periods between sections of a game or decreasing the length of time for each segment of a game. 'Reduce or enlarge' suggests reducing the dimensions of a game such as having a smaller volleyball court or enlarging goals for a game of soccer. 'Raise and lower' might indicate raising the number of attempts allowed to successfully carry out an activity. For example, this might be raising the limit on three strikes and out in a kickball game or lowering the balance beam in gymnastics (Bigge *et al.*, 2001: 474–475).

Because a pupil with DCD may find physical education lessons daunting, having a space for each pupil to which they may return (for example in gymnastics) can help provide a sense of predictability and security that is reassuring. Floor markings to indicate the paths the pupils are expected to follow will help the child with DCD with orientation and direction. Changing for physical education and changing back into day clothes afterwards in the limited time usually allowed is difficult. Adapted clothing using false buttons and Velcro fasteners can help.

Personal and social development

Pupils with DCD can become frustrated and demoralised and come to have low self-worth because of the persistent difficulties they face that may not always be understood by others. Such feelings may emerge in the form of difficult behaviour. In these circumstances the teacher and others will try to establish the root cause of the behaviour. The more the teacher and others understand DCD and the greater their skills in supporting a pupil with DCD, the greater the likelihood that the pupil will be able to deal with the challenges of education and other day-to-day demands.

Several difficulties associated with DCD influence the development of social skills. Motor perceptual difficulties can make it difficult for the child or young person to realise they may be standing too close to a person with whom they are speaking. Because of spatial and orientation problems, the pupil may have a poor appreciation of his own body language and be insufficiently aware of the importance of and subtlety of gesture and body position. Gesture may be poorly co-ordinated with speech and the pupil may be unaware of other people's non-verbal signals, missing the clues that facilitate smooth communication.

Poor co-ordination may inhibit participation in social activities such as dancing, ice-skating and bowling. Using public transport and finding one's way after asking directions may be hindered by orientation difficulties. Handling small coins can be problematic, particularly if under time pressure as when at the front of a busy store queue.

At mealtimes, younger pupils with DCD may have difficulty co-ordaining a knife and fork, may spill liquids and may take a long time to finish eating a meal. Cutting food may be particularly difficult (Hoare, 1994). In preparing a meal, activities such as using a can opener and buttering bread may be tricky, so a wall can opener and cutlery with thick rubber handles are possible adaptations.

Moving about without bumping into people or knocking into or knocking over objects may be difficult in itself. Co-ordination difficulties hamper involvement in team games requiring high levels of motor co-ordination, such as football, some computer games and board games, limiting opportunities to socialise and participate.

Some social skills can be taught using established behavioural techniques such as positive reinforcement of behaviours approaching what is desired or using social learning methods such as modelling. One approach is having the adult model appropriate behaviour (such as standing an optimum distance from someone one does not know well when speaking) followed by the pupil engaging in role-play to practise the skill.

Both personal hygiene and personal appearance can influence peer acceptance. Children with DCD may have difficulty with areas such as washing hair, cleaning teeth and cutting fingernails (Gubbay, 1985). For younger pupils, using the toilet may be problematic because wiping the bottom involves spatial and proprioceptive skills as the part of the body concerned is out of view. Also, for girls, unless the technique of wiping the bottom with a movement towards the back is learned, there is a risk of urinary infection. False buttons above Velcro fasteners on clothing, and trousers with an elasticised waist can save time dressing and undressing for the toilet, an important factor if the child wishes to use the toilet in the allocated recess times without being late back for lessons. Wet wipes rather than dry toilet tissue can clean the bottom more thoroughly and easily. A small foot rest by the toilet can be useful for younger pupils so that the legs are not dangling down and the child does not have to hold on to the sides of the toilet to keep balance. A mirror behind the door of at least one toilet cubicle will allow the child with DCD to see himself when dressed to check he is tidy. In high school, hygiene may still be problematic. Girls may find changing sanitary products very difficult and may find it hard to apply make up sparingly requiring sensitive guidance from parents and the school. See also a chapter on daily living skills and DCD by May-Benson, *et al.*, (2002: 140–156).

Resources

Aids to more fluent writing include pencil grips and illuminating pens as described above. Special equipment for physical education may be used such as extra light balls and extra large bats. Adapted equipment may be used such as cutlery with thick rubber handles. False buttons above Velcro fasteners may be used on clothing, and trousers may have an elasticised waist.

Therapy/care

Since DCD affects activities of daily living, the occupational therapist can assist the child in their daily life activities such as organisational skills, dressing and school activities such as handwriting.

A pupil with DCD may see a physical therapist outside school time and, as mentioned earlier, there are good opportunities for innovative work with the teacher of physical education and a physical therapist or occupational therapist working together. The work of therapists indicates aspects of the debate about provision and its effectiveness centring around so-called 'bottom-up' and 'top-down' approaches.

Bottom-up approaches involve attempts to remediate supposed underlying motor deficits, which are expected to lead to improvements in motor performance.

Among bottom-up approaches are sensory integration (e.g. Ayres, 1989); process-orientated treatment (e.g. Laszlo and Bairstow 1985) and perceptual motor training (e.g. meta analysis by Kavale and Mattson 1983). In summarising evaluations of these approaches, it has been suggested (Mandich et al., 2001: 61) that no one approach or combination of approaches 'is superior to another in improving motor skill' and that none 'has been shown to be reliably better than no treatment at all'.

Top-down approaches include: task-specific intervention involving direct teaching of the task to be learned (e.g. Revie and Larkin, 1993) and cognitive approaches, which include 'cognitive orientation to daily occupational performance' (CO-OP) (e.g. Polatajko et al., 2001). Cognitive-behavioural techniques employ various methods enabling children to demonstrate suitable motor responses. The therapist's positive reinforcement of approximations to the desired responses and their successful performance helps the child subsequently initiate his own movements. It is considered rather early to make judgements about the efficacy of top-down approaches as they are relatively new, but early indications look promising.

For example, CO-OP developed for children with DCD (Polatajko et al., 2001) typically involves an occupational therapist working closely with parents and the child. It aims to help children discover the particular cognitive strategies that will improve their ability to carry out everyday tasks such as handwriting, riding a bicycle, using cutlery and catching a ball. CO-OP employs global and domain-specific strategies and guided discovery of strategies to enable the child to achieve goals he has selected. 'Dynamic performance analysis' is used to try to determine when a child has difficulties performing an activity so that the performance breakdown can be identified. The therapist teaches the child a global strategy called 'Goal-Plan-Do-Check' to act as a framework for solving motor-based performance problems. The therapist then guides the child to discover domain-specific strategies to enable the activity to be performed (Polatajko and Mandich, 2004). It has been suggested from a review of a series studies that CO-OP shows promise as an effective means of promoting skill acquisition and transfer in children with DCD aged 7 to 12 years (Polatajko et al., 2004: 461).

Organisation

The teacher's physical organisation of the classroom can help the child by ensuring relatively free movement around the room without unnecessary clutter. The child may sit close to the front of the class in a seat near to the entry door to avoid bumping into other children and objects.

It is likely to help if the classroom is large enough so that different furniture arrangements for different activities such as group work or whole class work can be laid out permanently. This allows the child with DCD to become accustomed to the layout rather than have to constantly adapt as furniture is moved into different arrangement for different activities. Where space is at a premium and stable layouts are not possible, the positions into which furniture is moved for different activities can be marked on the floor of the classroom so that the positions are predictable and consistent.

Thinking points

Readers may wish to consider:

- How effective approaches that will help pupils with DCD are across all areas of school life and in particular subject lessons.
- How teachers, teaching assistants and others can work more effectively with physical therapists and occupational therapists to enhance overall provision.

Key texts

Cermak, S. A. and Larkin, D. (2002) *Developmental Coordination Disorder*. Albany, New York, Delmar Thompson Learning.
Parts of the book successively concern subtypes and conditions that co-occur with DCD; assessment; mechanisms underlying the condition; functional implications and interventions.

Kirby, A. and Drew, S. (2003) *Guide to Dyspraxia and Developmental Coordination Disorders*. London, David Fulton Publishers.
A readable overview, this book includes separate chapters focusing on the younger child, the adolescent and the adult.

Missiuna, C. (ed.) (2001) *Children with Development Co-ordination Disorder – Strategies for Success*. New York, Haworth Press.
The chapters of this coherently presented book progress from seeking to define DCD, identifying the condition, considering evidence for various treatment approaches and looking in particular at cognitive orientation to daily occupational performance (CO-OP).

Sugden, D. and Chambers, M. (2005) *Children with Developmental Coordination Disorder* London, Wiley.
Intended for researchers and various professionals, this book links research findings and clinical work to inform practice.

Chapter 19

Reading disorder

Introduction

This chapter looks at definitions of reading disorder; its prevalence; some characteristics of reading difficulties; causal factors and identification and assessment. It considers possible associated difficulties, their assessment and related provision; and looks at provision for reading and for reading skills, reading fluency and reading comprehension. The chapter examines alternative and augmentative communication. The final section summarises provision in relation to curriculum and assessment; pedagogy; resources; therapy/care; and organisation.

Definitions

The *Diagnostic and Statistical Manual of Mental Disorders Fourth Edition Text Revision (DSM-IV-TR)* (American Psychiatric Association, 2000: 51–53) provides a definition of reading disorder. It is essentially identified by reading achievement being 'substantially below' what is expected given the child's age, measured intelligence and education. Reading achievement is assessed in terms of reading accuracy, speed or comprehension measured by individually administered standardised tests. Reading disorder 'significantly' hinders academic achievement of daily living activities requiring reading skills. Oral reading is characterised by 'distortions, substitutions or omissions' (ibid.: 52) and both oral and silent reading tend to be slow and involve comprehension errors. There is evidence that developmental delays in language may occur in association with reading disorder (and other learning disabilities).

The judgement that reading achievement is 'substantially below' expectations is often taken to mean two or more standard deviations below the expected level although one standard deviation may be considered sufficient in special circumstances, for example where the disorder has had a significant impact on performance in the test of general intelligence (e.g. Fonagy *et al.*, 2005: 360).

Contrary to the implications of the American Psychiatric Association (2000: 51–53) criteria, there is growing consensus that reading disorder has to be associated with reading achievement being below age expectations. Previously, some observers supported an achievement intelligence quotient (IQ) discrepancy view, defining reading impairment in terms of a discrepancy between a child's actual reading score and the reading score that would be predicted on the basis of chronological age or IQ (or both). Normally, discrepancy scores are defined as the difference between the score on a specified reading test and the score predicted from the regression of reading performance on a measure of IQ (that is the correlation between reading and IQ). A discrepancy of a specified value is taken as a measure of underachievement in reading. In the IQ-achievement discrepancy view, a child could be considered to have reading disorder if he performed at age average or better in reading achievement but had a high IQ suggesting he should be doing even better. This view seems evident in the rather odd assertion of Miles and Miles (1990: iv) that 'there is no contradiction in saying that a person is dyslexic while never the less being a competent reader'.

Typical of the modern view is that of Beitchman and Young (1997), who, reviewing studies over the previous 10 years, recommend that if a child is not functioning below the expected level for age or grade, he is unlikely to require special help and should not be considered to have a learning disorder even though there may be a substantial IQ-achievement discrepancy. Similarly, Dykman and Ackerman (1992) observe (the public school system in the United States of America parallels the maintained school system in the United Kingdom).

Regression formulas are well and good if the purpose is to identify all students who are underachievers. But it defies common sense to diagnose a child with an IQ of 130 and a reading standard score of 110 as having dyslexia. Certainly the public school system should not be expected to offer special services to such a child.

While the American Psychiatric Association criteria mention that reading disorder has also been called 'dyslexia' in fact there are differences between what is defined as reading disorder and some of the many definitions of dyslexia. Some definitions of dyslexia include disorder of written expression, whereas the American Psychiatric Association (2000) criteria separate reading disorder and disorder of written expression while acknowledging the two often occur together. Mathematics disorder is also commonly associated with reading disorder.

Where research refers to dyslexia, it sometimes defines this in terms of a discrepancy view. Readers when consulting research need to be careful to identify the position of the researchers on these questions of definition. Types of dyslexia have been suggested such as 'visual dyslexia' and 'verbal dyslexia'.

Prevalence

The prevalence of reading disorder is not easy to ascertain. Many studies fail to separate out disorders of reading, written expression and mathematics.

In different countries, prevalence rates vary according to the strictness of criteria. In the United States of America it is estimated that about 4 per cent of school-aged children experience reading disorder. Although more boys than girls are usually considered to have reading disorder, it appears that referral of boys may be increased because of associated behaviour difficulties and when careful diagnostic procedures are used (rather than school referral) a more equal gender balance is found (e.g. American Psychiatric Association, 2000: 52).

Causal factors

In exclusionary definitions, dyslexia is in part defined by excluding causation by general intellectual impairment, socio-cultural constraints or emotional factors. Among factors that are associated with reading disorder are: phonological difficulties, visual difficulties and visual processing difficulties; auditory perception and auditory processing difficulties; short-term verbal memory difficulties and sequencing difficulties (temporal order). Each of these is considered in the next section as possible associated difficulties and each in varying degrees can be seen as explaining something about literacy problems. If a child has phonological difficulties, for example, the relationship between the sound related aspects of language and the written text are likely to be problematic. At one level then such associated factors can be said to contribute to reading disorder although the relationship may be reciprocal. Another level of explanation implicates a consideration of how the 'associated difficulties' might have arisen. What led to the problems with information processing? Sometimes in connection with such issues, biological explanations are offered.

Studies considering heritable factors have implicated loci on chromosomes 2, 3, 6, 15 and 18 (Fisher and DeFries, 2002) for the transmission of phonological awareness deficits and subsequent difficulties with reading, although the detailed consequences of these findings are still to be developed. Research involving functional brain imaging with children and adults with dyslexia indicates a failure of left hemisphere posterior brain systems to function correctly during reading (e.g. Paulesu et al., 2001). Symmetry of the planum temporale owing to a larger right plana or a reversal of the normal pattern of left greater than right asymmetry has been found in individuals with developmental dyslexia (Hynd et al., 1990).

Identification and assessment

In general, the teacher or parent may have concerns about what is perceived to be slow progress or difficulties with reading. The teacher may gather evidence to consider further and will consult with others such as senior teaching colleagues or school psychologists. A speech pathologist may be consulted, for example, where there is concern that there may be phonological difficulties.

Certain characteristics are associated with reading difficulties. The child may when reading:

- hesitate over words;
- confuse letters with similar shapes such as 'u' and 'n', visually similar words like 'was' and 'saw' and small words such as 'it' and 'is';
- omit small words such as 'it' and 'is' other words, or word endings or
- make errors regarding semantically related words (reading 'cat' for 'dog'), polysyllabic words ('animal', 'corridor', 'family' and so on) or grammar (including inconsistent use of tense).

Therefore the identification and assessment of difficulties with reading is likely to include:

- a profile of the sorts of errors that the pupil makes (relating to the characteristics outlined above), for example using miscue analysis;
- an indication of how the pupil reads (e.g. whether he is hesitant over words);
- an indication of whether the pupil tends to prefer silent reading or reading aloud and whether one leads to better comprehension than the other.

Commercial assessments of 'dyslexia' are available in developed countries, standardised for the country concerned. They often sample what are considered to be component skills or necessary skills relating to reading such as rapid naming, phonemic segmentation, verbal fluency, backwards digit span, assessment of syllable and phoneme deletions (aimed at identifying phonological processing ability) and so on. There are also assessment implications of associated difficulties and these are touched on in the next section.

Possible associated difficulties, their assessment and related provision

It is important that various sub-skills relating to reading work together. If one or more sub-skills are dysfunctional, then the pupil may find it hard to improve the skill while at the same time maintaining the other component skills of reading. In reading, the pupil has to, among other requirements, visually focus on words effectively and track words across a written page; auditorily discriminate, sequence, blend and segment sounds in words; retain information in short-term memory while it is processed and organise information. Where these are underpinning or necessary skills, the pupil may find it difficult to improve them while sustaining other skills, so it is assumed that it is beneficial to approach some skills distinctively. A learner's other skills may also be used to compensate for weakness, for example when a pupil's difficulties with auditory processing and with blending and segmenting sounds in words is compensated for by multi-sensory methods, including teaching phonics linking visual and kinaesthetic modes with word sounds.

Phonological difficulties

Phonology difficulties involve relating speech sounds to changes in meaning. Phonological knowledge enables the speaker to understand that, when a speech sound is changed into a word, meaning changes. Speakers normally come to learn distinctions (e.g. 'dog'/'log' or 'pig'/'pin') and the speaker, hearing his own speech, modifies it as necessary to make the required word. The phonological system is considered to lay down a sort of phonological representation of the speech sound sequence at a cognitive level of language functioning, which helps the process to be automatic. Speakers draw on this phonological representation when they are developing awareness of the different sounds in a word. In reading English, the 44 speech sounds are linked to written marks or graphemes so that the child develops a phoneme-grapheme correspondence.

The phonological deficit theory maintains that in reading disorder, the main cognitive deficit is in a person's ability to represent or recall phonemes, that is, there is a problem with phonological representations. This phonological deficit leads to the poor mental mapping of letters of the alphabet to phonemes. Both the phonological deficit and the poor letter-phoneme mapping operate at the cognitive level but, behaviourally, both lead to difficulties with phonological tasks such as splitting words into their phonemes. Also, poor letter-phoneme mapping relates to reading difficulties.

Among extensive evidence in support of a phonological deficit theory is that people with reading disorder have difficulty retaining speech in short-term memory and consciously breaking it up into phonemes. For example, a person with reading disorder will tend to have difficulty deleting or substituting phonemes from words (Snowling, 2000). A phonological deficit in children at the age of 6 years was found in a Norwegian study to be a strong predictor of reading difficulties (Hagtvet, 1997). Speech rate has been identified as a predictor of dyslexic difficulties (e.g. Hulme and Snowling, 1997). A double deficit of phonological processing and naming speed has been suggested (e.g. Wolf and O'Brien, 2001)

Briefly, because in an alphabetical system the brain has to map the letters of the alphabet onto a mental representations of corresponding phonemes, problems representing and recalling phonemes is expected to lead to reading difficulties. However, the exact nature of the phonological deficit and its biological concomitants is not yet fully understood.

Identifying and assessing phonological difficulties is likely to include assessing whether expressive language includes errors, omissions or other difficulties in conversation or classroom interaction, suggesting there might be difficulties relating to the key meaningful elements of sound. It is likely also to assess whether the child has difficulty with the comprehension of speech, for example appearing not to understand instructions or questions, suggesting that the child may have difficulty with the elements of speech conveying meaning.

Information from assessment can suggest strategies to help the child's learning or identify strategies the child has already developed. For example, assessment could indicate mode of 'input' (verbal, written or visual) appears to aid comprehension. This could indicate a preference for visual input that might help comprehension where there are phonological difficulties. Or the child's expressive language can be observed in different contexts to see if communication is easier in some contexts than others.

Where there are serious phonological difficulties, a speech pathologist may work with the teacher to develop and oversee suitable programmes. More generally, a learner with phonological difficulties may be taught to become more aware of and to use in spoken language, sounds and sequences of sounds that convey meaning in speech. In his own speech, the pupil may practise sounds that he frequently misses, such as those at the beginnings and endings of words.

Similarly, speech comprehension practice is used to help the pupil notice key sounds that convey meaning and changes in meaning. For example, the learner can be taught to listen for and recognise the sound 's' at the end of a word when it signals a plural as in 'cat' and 'cats'. Speech comprehension can be aided by other sensory modes such as showing accompanying pictures or objects such as a picture of one 'cat' and several 'cats'. The teacher would be careful to establish that the difficulty is predominantly phonological rather than mainly grammatical.

To raise phonological awareness, where new vocabulary is introduced, the teacher can encourage pupils' interest in a word or phrase. She will explicitly teach and check the pupils' understanding of various aspects of the vocabulary: semantic and grammatical as well as phonological. Phonological aspects may include asking such questions as: How do the sounds of the word break up and blend back together? Do you know any similar sounding words? What are syllables of the word? (Younger children may enjoy clapping these out.) This can be routinely and briefly accomplished when key words are introduced at the beginning of a lesson, in both elementary/primary schools and high/secondary schools where subject specialists can use the method to reinforce new vocabulary.

An approach drawing on interest in speech sounds, used for example in England, is Metaphon, designed to bring about phonological change through enhancing knowledge of the phonological and communicative aspects of language (Howell and Dean, 1994: vii). The *Metaphon Resource Pack* (Dean *et al.*, 1990), used with children aged 3 years 6 months to 7 years, provides phonological assessment giving information about the child's pronunciation abilities. Please also see in the present volume Chapter 14 on 'Communication disorders: Speech'.

Visual processing difficulties

'Scotopic sensitivity' refers to a particular sensitivity to print on black paper. Irlen (1994) found that some students in high school and at university in the United States of America who were poor readers had a particular sensitivity to black print on white paper, especially where the print was faint, the paper was glossy and fluorescent lighting was used. Words appeared to move around the page and the glare from the page tended to cause eye irritation. For some pupils, spectacles with tinted lenses or coloured page overlays appear to reduce the glare and stabilise the image of words on the page.

Other visual factors concern convergence, accommodation and tracking. Convergence involves the eyes converging on letters of print or handwriting at a distance of about 30 centimetres to ensure that the brain receives a unified picture of the letters and words. It has been suggested that for some children with dyslexia, there may be visual convergence difficulties that may lead to binocular instability (Stein, 1995). Accommodation involves being able to quickly adjust eye focus to changing circumstances such as changing distances between page and eye as the eye moves down a page of writing, and difficulties with this clearly affect reading, writing and spelling. Tracking involves the skill of scanning a line of print from word to word and line to line while keeping one's place and difficulties with this lead to losing one's place in reading. However, as Beaton (2004: 219) points out, the general consensus in the literature is that 'abnormal eye movements are a consequence rather than a cause of reading disability'.

Some people with dyslexia appear to have difficulties with visual tasks such as those involving the perception of movement. One attempt to explain such findings, the magnocellular theory, is based on a distinction between two proposed neuronal pathways of the visual system: the magnocellular and parvocellular. It is hypothesised that the magnocellular system is abnormal in people with reading disorder causing difficulties in some aspects of visual perception and in binocular control that may lead to a reading difficulty. Impaired development of the magnocellular component of the visual system, which processes fast temporal information, may lead to visual confusions such as letters looking blurred or appearing to move round (e.g. Stein et al., 2001).

At the neurological level then there is considered to be a general magnocellular dysfunction. This leads to a visual magnocellular deficit and a temporal auditory deficit at the cognitive level (the temporal auditory deficit is believed to lead to the phonological deficit). Behaviourally, the visual magnocellular deficit is hypothesised to lead to difficulties with certain visual tasks, such as those requiring the perception of motion, and to reading difficulties. The temporal auditory deficit is thought to lead to, behaviourally, difficulties with certain auditory tasks requiring the perception of brief or rapid speech (or none speech) sounds.

The assessment of visual difficulties is likely to involve assessing that the pupil has age inappropriate difficulty discriminating between letters that appear the same ('m' and 'n'), or that are the same but in different forms ('M' and 'm'), or omits or transposes part of a word (which could indicate a difficulty with visual segmentation).

Turning to interventions, where visual discrimination is poor, the teacher may use one or more books or activities aimed at encouraging this skill. These may include several pictures of objects including one that is obviously different and progress to series where the difference is increasingly subtle. The teacher may use a series of letters with one letter that is obviously different, progressing to series where the difference is subtler. Practice in discriminating letters can involve overlearning one letter, for example, 'm' then introducing a letter with which the child often confuses it such as 'n'. Pupils may be directly taught the upper and lower case forms of the same letter. To aid segmentation, items may be used first. Using a row of coloured bricks, the teacher asks the pupil to space them into sets of one, or two, or three. Printed letters of the alphabet can later be used to form words and the pupil asked to make segments such as 'b' 'at' or 'su' 'n'. Practice in tracking can involve exercises requiring the pupil to give close attention to the text and track it from left to right (in English). For example, the learner can be encouraged to track along a sentence or sentences marking first the letter 'a' then the letter 'b' then 'c' and so on (e.g. The apple was big and cold and ...).

Auditory perception and auditory processing difficulties

Auditory perception and auditory processing difficulties are relevant because, given that some perceptual aspects of speech are relevant to developing phonemic awareness, reading ability may be related to speech perception. One aspect of auditory perception concerns phonetic categorisation. In making different speech sounds, there are deferent durations between the instant that air is released from the lips and the vocal chords vibrating (voice onset time) that is important as a cue in speech perception. Presenting sounds using a speech synthesiser, with a 0 millisecond (msec.) voice-onset time, produces a perception of a /ba/ sound. A 40 msec. voice onset time leads to a perception of a /pa/ sound. At voice onset times between 0 and 40 msec., people report hearing either a /ba/ or a /pa/ sound, not a sound somewhere between, a phenomenon called categorical perception. Some children with dyslexia have been found to be less consistent in their classification of stimuli and changed more gradually from one phonetic category to another than did a control group of children (Godfrey et al., 1981: 419–420). It was suggested that this inconsistency in phonetic categorisation might impair the ability to learn through forming 'inadequate long-term representations of

phonetic units'. This could adversely affect the reading process of transforming script into phonetic units of speech and ordering and combining those
units that constitute words.

The assessment of auditory processing difficulties is likely to involve identifying: difficulties with auditory discrimination; inability to perceive consonant sounds in different positions and difficulties with auditory sequencing,
blending and segmentation. Auditory discrimination may be practised
through the teacher encouraging the pupil to make progressively finer distinctions in set task and exercises such as recognising and discriminating
sounds, including letter sounds from an audio recording. Auditory segmenting and blending can be taught and practised, for example by playing an
audio recording and asking the pupil to listen for certain sounds (such as 'to').
The sounds would be obvious and the pace slow at first ('I am going out
tomorrow'). Auditory blending can be taught using phonics approaches such
as those in Phonographix™ (www.readamerica.net) which introduces letter
sounds and then their blends in teaching reading. The pupil can be taught to
listen to consonant sounds in different positions, for example by listening for
the final consonant in the words 'dog', 'log' and 'doll' or the initial consonant
in 'pit', 'pot' and 'dot' and identifying the odd one out. Multi-sensory teaching and learning may help auditory processing weakness because other preferred modes are likely to be presented that may reinforce learning in the
weaker (auditory) mode, for example supplementing the spoken word by
visual aids and gesture.

Short-term verbal memory difficulties

Studies of dyslexia have found problems with verbal memory and learning,
especially in tasks requiring phonological processes (Share, 1995), for example, children with dyslexia tending to have lower digit spans than control
readers (e.g. McDougal *et al.*, 1994). One possible explanation is that difficulties with verbal memory in some children with dyslexia relate to difficulties in phonological awareness because memory difficulties contribute to
problems with keeping in mind individual phonemes as part of a phonic
reading strategy (Beaton: 72). Other research suggests that good readers are
more likely to use verbal retrieval strategies or rehearsal strategies than poor
readers (e.g. Palmer, S., 2000). Memory span is longer for words than for
pseudo words of the same length, suggesting that when remembering lists of
items, it is easier to remember words from established representations in
long-term memory. It is suggested (Hulme *et al.*, 1997) that a partially
decayed memory trace may be reconstructed from stored knowledge about
the structure of words. If, for learners with dyslexia, this knowledge were
inefficiently represented, it would offer only limited help in supporting the
process of reconstruction, resulting in lower recall performance for learners
with dyslexia. Identifying and assessing memory difficulties is likely to

include a profile of the areas and circumstances in which these difficulties are apparent.

Short-term memory difficulties can be aided by encouraging the pupil to be aware of the settings and conditions he finds conducive to memorising well. These might include actively focusing on the task in hand and not trying to do something else at the same time and avoiding distractions by using a quiet place. Teachers' requests and instructions are more likely to be processed and remembered if given one at a time. Embedding in memory (using long-term memory) is facilitated if the pupil is interested and can relate the new information and ideas to what he already knows, suggesting teachers find out the pupil's interests and encourage the pupil to relate new information to these. Multi-sensory methods may be used and the material to be remembered should be well organised. Recall and recognition can be aided by drawing on different sensory modes and particular ways that are used in presenting, recording and studying the information, for example diagrams or mnemonics.

Sequencing difficulties (temporal order)

Several studies have found poor readers less able to remember the serial order of events than average or good readers. Where participants were required to reproduce a sequence of taps on a wooden block or to repeat a sequence of digits, a relationship was found between the accuracy of recall of sequence of events and reading attainment (Corkin, 1974). A temporal processing deficit has been proposed possibly involving a 'high degree of processing overlap associated with the parallel transmission of speech' (Share, 1995: 188), which could lead to poor phonological representations. Such a deficit could explain difficulties in the fast sequencing of speech motor acts needed for 'serial naming and verbal rehearsal'. Identifying sequencing difficulties is likely to involve identifying difficulties with the child sequencing information such as sequencing letters of the alphabet, words when reading.

Using various senses can assist learning sequences such as letters of the alphabet. The pupil places pieces of card, each bearing a letter, in front of him in an arc with the 'a' on the left and the 'z' on the right. Learning the letters in blocks reinforcing rhythm may help: 'a' through 'g'; 'h' through 'n'; 'o' through 'u' and 'v' through 'z'. Handling and laying out the cards uses kinaesthetic memory; speaking the letter sounds and hearing others saying them uses auditory memory, and seeing the letters employs visual memory, all helping to establish the sequence (Pollock et al., 2004: 118–119). Where a dictionary, encyclopaedia or other alphabetically organised reference book is used, the pages can be marked by tabs to separate the alphabetical sequence in the same way that the blocks of letters were learned, divided at 'g', 'n' and 'u' so the required word is easier to find.

Provision for reading skills

Early intervention: Direct code instruction

Foorman and colleagues (1998) assessed the reading development of 285 children in first and second grade in 66 classrooms in several Title 1 schools in Texas. The children had scored in the lowest 18 per cent on an early literacy assessment used by the school district. Three programmes were compared with the standard curriculum for the district. One programme provided direct instruction in letter-sound correspondences and practise decoding text (direct code); the second provided less direct instruction in letter-sound correspondences embedded in authentic literature samples (embedded code). The third offered implicit instruction in the alphabetic code while children read authentic text (implicit code). Children in the direct code approach, especially ones entering with the lowest levels of phonological awareness, showed better word identification skills and steeper learning curves in word reading than did children experiencing the implicit code instruction. Population based failure rates derived from this study suggested that 6 per cent of children would remain relatively weak in reading development (Torgesen, 2000), suggesting a remaining issue of how to improve the reading development of the most severe forms of reading disability.

Phonological training

Brooks (2002) reviewed and evaluated the effectiveness of various schemes in the report, *What Works for Reading Difficulties?* Among the interventions examined was Phonographix™. Taking as important the fact that English orthography is an alphabet for representing originally and in principle each distinctive speech sound with one symbol, Phonographix™ (www.readamerica.net) develops the notion that written English is a phonemic code with each sound in a spoken word being represented by some part of the written version. It teaches the phonological skills of blending, segmenting and phoneme manipulation required to use a phonemic code, explicitly teaching correspondences in sound-to-symbol relationships. The 'impact measures' of data on the approach included the largest ratio gain of all the studies reviewed in the Brooks report.

'Reading Intervention' was also reviewed and evaluated in the report, *What Works for Reading Difficulties?* (Brooks, 2002). It combines phonological training with reading, enabling pupils to isolate phonemes in words to come to recognise that sounds can be common between words and that specific sounds can be represented by certain letters. Several studies are reported. In one of these, poor readers aged 6 to 7 years were randomly assigned to one of four groups.

1   Received systematic training in phonological skills to promote phono-
    logical awareness and help in learning to read.
2   Received training in reading only.
3   Received training only in phonological skills.
4   Received normal teaching (controls).

Experimental groups 1, 2 and 3 received 40 by 30 minute sessions over a
period of 20 weeks. In group 1 the sessions were in three parts. The first part
involved the child reading a familiar book with the teacher making a written
record so the child could go over familiar words in different contexts. This
also involved phonological activities and letter identification using a multi-
sensory approach of feeling, writing and naming. The second part of the session involved writing a story and cutting it up. The third part introduced a
new book. The reading plus phonology group (group 1) made significantly
better progress than other groups (Hatcher, 2000). Brooks states the initia-
tive continues to be effective for poor readers, 'and even for children with
moderate learning difficulties or dyslexia' (Brooks, 2002: 39). Some studies
reported in support of this intervention take a discrepancy view of dyslexia
and readers may wish to consider the original reports carefully when judging
applicability.

Combination programmes

An intervention study by Olsen, Wise and colleagues (e.g. Wise *et al.*, 2000)
combined:

*   features of an oral-motor programme for training phonological aware-
    ness, reading and spelling skills (the Lindamood Auditory
    Discrimination in Depth programme);
*   the researchers' own computer-based reading training programme called
    Reading with Orthographic and Speech Support.

Two groups of children with reading disabilities from grades 2 through
5 received phonological decoding and digitised speech to help them read
unknown words in story reading on the computer. With this training one
group received further phonological awareness training using the Auditory
Discrimination in Depth programme oral-motor methods. The second
group received extra training in reading comprehension strategies. The first
group (receiving extra phonological awareness training) was better than the
second group at phonological awareness and phonological decoding skill
immediately after training and a year later. But they were not superior in
word recognition performance at 1- and 2-year follow up assessments, indicating a problem with generalising the improved phonological skills to
word recognition.

Assisting generalisation of phonological skills to reading

Research at the Hospital for Sick Children in Toronto, Canada, with children with severe reading disabilities has included reading interventions aimed at the problem of generalising instructional gains in word identification learning.

One approach, the Phonological Analysis and Blending/ Direct Instruction programme, comprises programmes training phonological analysis, phonological blending and letter-sound association skills in the context of intensive and systematic word recognition and decoding instruction.

Another approach, Word Identification Strategy Training, instructs the child through teacher-led dialogue, and teaches how to use and monitor the application of four metacognitive decoding strategies. Its word identification strategies include, for example, 'peeling off' suffixes and prefixes in a multisylabic word, and identifying parts of a word you already know. It includes a metacognitive 'game plan' to train flexibility in choice of strategy and the evaluation of their success.

Both of these approaches helped pupils generalise remedial gains. Positive effects were found even with children with the most severe reading disabilities (Lovett *et al.*, 2000).

In another study (Lovett *et al.*, 2000), 85 children aged 7–13 years and having severe reading disability were randomly assigned to 70 hours of remedial instruction in one of five conditions:

* Phonological Analysis and Blending/Direct Instruction programme followed by Word Identification Strategy Training.
* Word Identification Strategy Training followed by Phonological Analysis and Blending/ Direct Instruction programme.
* Phonological Analysis and Blending/Direct Instruction programme repeated.
* Word Identification Strategy Training repeated.
* Classroom Survival Skills (study skills) followed by mathematics.

Each child's skills were assessed before (once), during the programme (three times) and afterwards (once) using standard measures of word recognition, passage comprehension and non-word reading. The most superior outcomes and steepest learning curves were found for children in the group that had experienced Phonological Analysis and Blending/Direct Instruction programme followed by Word Identification Strategy Training. This condition was superior to each method alone on measures of phonological reading skill (non-word reading), tests of letter sound and key word knowledge, and three-word identification measures. Generalisation from non-word decoding to other reading measures it appears can be best achieved through a combination of remedial components. In line with this, is a review of intervention studies indicated that optimal approaches in instructing children with learning disabilities combine direct instruction and strategy instruction methods (Swanson and Hoskyn, 1998).

A programme, the PHAST Track Reading Programme (Phonological and Strategy Training) for 'struggling readers' seeks to integrate into the two approaches into a single programme (e.g. Lovett *et al.*, 2000) and has been extended to include reading comprehension, writing and spelling lessons. An adaptation PHAST PACES was developed for older (high school) readers and young adults.

Reading fluency

An experimental reading programme intended to aid the development of reading fluency RAVE-O (Retrieval, Automaticity, Vocabulary elaboration, Engagement with language, Orthography) has been devised (Wolf *et al.*, 2000). It is taught in combination with a systematic phonologically based programme teaching letter-sound knowledge, decoding and word identification skills while remediating speech based phonological processes. In combination with this, RAVE-O aims to:

* develop accuracy and automaticity in reading sub-skills and component processes;
* aid the development of fluency in word identification, word attack, and text reading, and comprehension processes;
* change the attitudes and feelings of pupils with reading disability in their approach to words and written language.

RAVE-O encourages children to learn to play with language through animated computer games, building imaginative word webs, instruction in word retrieval strategies that are playful but systematic, and reading one-minute mystery stories.

Provision for reading comprehension

Reading comprehension is essentially being able to get the gist or 'main idea' from a text. Once one has the main idea, one can draw inferences from the text. Difficulty with reading comprehension may be the result of lack of fluency in word recognition, but may also be related to cognitive processing problems such as limitations in working memory, lexical processing difficulties, poor inference making and poor monitoring of comprehension (Gersten *et al.*, 2001).

Work has been carried out on helping pupils grasp the main idea of texts. Normally achieving children in the fourth to sixth grades were asked to read a short paragraph and select an appropriate title from several choices and write a summary sentence for the paragraph. Performance was better when pupils had only to select the main idea from an array that when they had to formulate a summary sentence. This was replicated with children with LD (Taylor and Williams, 1983). However, pupils with LD differed from younger children without LD in their response to the inclusion of information that was unrelated to the main idea of the paragraph. Children with LD were able to identify the anomalous sentence the closer it was to the end of the paragraph, but children with LD were not. This suggested that pupils with LD were less able to gradually build up a representation as the information in each successive sentence was processed. From this work, an instructional sequence was developed using simple, highly structured paragraphs and emphasising a clear definition of what a 'main idea' is and a clear description of the task. In evaluating the model, 11-year-old children with LD were after 10 lessons found to be better able to identify anomalous sentences and write sentences on the materials (Williams *et al.* 1983).

In a similar way, research has been conducted into how pupils understand the theme of a story. An instructional model for pupils with LD was developed from this. The instruction involved teacher explanation and modelling, guided practice, and independent practice. (See summaries of this and related work in Williams, 2003: 293–305.)

Alternative and augmentative communication

Alternative and augmentative communication is considered in more detail in Chapter 14, 'Communication disorders: Speech', in the present book. This section looks more briefly at issues connected with reading and the use of symbols. Symbolic communication uses symbols, for example a word or a picture to stand for something. 'Non-aided' communication involves the child making a movement or vocalisation that does not necessitate a physical aid or other device (Vanderheiden and Lloyd, 1986). 'Aided' augmentative communication involves using a device or item such as a communication board, eye gaze board or electronic system.

Three categories have been suggested (Bigge *et al.*, 2001: 237). *Non-electronic devices* may include communication boards and communication notebooks. Communication books can include photographs, symbols and words, enabling a pupil to find a symbol and show the particular page to someone who may not know the symbol so they can see the intended word. *Dedicated communication devices* are electronic communication systems that speak programmed messages when the user activates locations marked by symbols. Computer-based communication systems may consist of a computer with input options, communication software and a speech synthesizer. *Computer-aided communication* may involve the pupil having a voice production device with a computer-based bank of words and sentences that can be produced by pressing the keyboard keys.

Symbols may be part or whole objects used to represent an item or activity. In a symbol system using graphical communication, each symbol represents a concept such as an object, person, activity or attribute. Communication grids in which several symbols are set out in a specified order can enable a pupil to participate in a group sessions; for example, to support the retelling of a story. A sequence of symbols can be used to indicate a sequence of activities, including a school timetable for a pupil. Computer technology, using symbols, allows a large number of symbols to be used flexibly. There are symbol email programmes, and websites that use symbols.

Curriculum and assessment; pedagogy; resources; therapy/care; and organisation

Curriculum

Given the centrality of reading to most subjects of the curriculum, the levels of curriculum for pupils with reading disorder are likely to be lower than those for other children and the curriculum will recognise this so that the pupil's progress can move from secure foundations. The balance of subjects may emphasise language and reading with necessary support, and within subjects the reading element will be an important focus of support. Small steps of assessment may be used with regard to language and reading to ensure progress is recognised. The curriculum may include programmes such as some of those described earlier that combine curriculum content, approaches to pedagogy and specific resources.

Pedagogy

Teaching and learning approaches may include support for any evident visual and visual processing difficulties, for example by ensuring materials avoid difficult tracking from one plane to another where possible. Pedagogy will also focus on phonological development; auditory perception training; support for difficulties with short-term memory and help with sequencing difficulties. Strategies are used to facilitate reading fluency and comprehension.

Resources

For a few pupils with visual processing difficulties, tinted lenses may be considered. Computer software that supports reading is also used. Materials such as printed lessons and computer activities associated with particular programmes may be used. Where symbols are used, the relevant resources are of course necessary.

Therapy/care

The speech and language pathologist may work directly or in a consultancy role to help with phonological difficulties.

Organisation

There do not appear to be any distinctive aspects of school and classroom organisation that are essential for reading disorder.

Thinking points

Readers may wish to consider:

- How convincing they find the view that, if reading disorder is associated with underlying difficulties, working directly on these will improve reading.
- The extent to which direct approaches to improving reading appear to tackle supposed related difficulties.

Key texts

Beaton, A. A. (2004) *Dyslexia, Reading and the Brain: A Sourcebook of Biological and Psychological Research*. London, Psychology Press.
A lucid and balanced presentation of a vast amount of research relating to reading and reading difficulties.

Klingner, J., Vaughn, S. and Boardman A. (2007) *Teaching Reading Comprehension to Students with Learning Difficulties*. New York, Guilford Press.
Research based recommendations for the classroom.

Rosen, G. D. (2006) *The Dyslexic Brain: New Pathways in Neuroscience Discovery*. New York, Taylor & Francis.
Examines neural components and functions involved in reading, possible sources of breakdown and interventions.

Swanson, H. L., Harris, K. R. and Graham, S. (eds) (2003) *Handbook of Learning Disabilities*. New York, The Guilford Press.
A well-structured overview of learning difficulties covering: foundations and current perspectives; causes and behavioural manifestations; effective instruction; formation of instructional models and methodology.

Chapter 20

Disorder of written expression

Introduction

This chapter looks at a definition of disorder of written expression, prevalence, causal factors, identification and assessment, and traditional and process-based approaches to teaching writing. In provision for writing and spelling, it examines: remediating sequencing, improving co-ordination skills for handwriting and teaching cursive script.

Turning to provision for writing composition, the chapter looks at frameworks for writing, reducing task demands, software for essay structure, note taking, writing for a purpose and developing self-regulation strategies. For spelling, it considers: multi-sensory aspects, Directed Spelling Thinking Activity and target words.

Although the chapter is concerned mainly with traditional orthography, it next considers the important matter of alternative and augmentative communication including the use of symbols. In the final section, it summarises provision in terms of curriculum and assessment; pedagogy; resources; therapy/care and organisation.

Definition

It is recognised that there are 'complex skills and sub-skills' involved in writing, for example organising ideas, forming letters, spelling and punctuation (e.g. Macintyre and Deponio, 2003: 67). The necessary abilities range from those associated with 'lower level transcription skills' to ones needed for 'higher level composing' (Gregg and Mather, 2002: 7). The inter-relationships of reading and writing are also recognised (e.g. Nelson and Calfee, 1998, *passim*).

The *Diagnostic and Statistical Manual of Mental Disorders Fourth Edition Text Revision (DSM-IV-TR)* (American Psychiatric Association, 2000: 54–56) outlines what it sees as the essential features of disorder of written expression. As measured by individually administered standardised tests of writing skills or functional assessment, these skills are substantially below age expectations, measured intelligence and 'age appropriate education'. Being substantially below age expectations is often taken to mean two standard deviations below average. The disturbance hinders academic achievement or daily living activities requiring the composition of written texts.

There is generally a combination of difficulties as indicated by errors in grammar and punctuation in written sentences, poor organisation of paragraphs, many spelling errors and very poor handwriting. Disorder in spelling and handwriting alone is not considered to meet the definition of disorder of written expression. If poor handwriting is the result of impaired motor co-ordination, it is suggested that a 'diagnosis' of developmental co-ordination disorder be considered (ibid.: 56).

Both disorder of written expression and mathematics disorder are commonly associated with reading disorder, it being comparatively rare for either to be found in the absence of reading disorder (ibid.: 52). Language deficits and perceptual motor deficits may accompany disorder of written expression (ibid.: 55).

Prevalence

Prevalence is difficult to establish because disorder of written expression is not often differentiated from reading disorder or mathematics disorder in research studies. However, developmental disorder of written expression appears to occur in about 4 per cent of children with boys being three times more likely to meet the criteria (Kavale and Forness, 1995).

Causal factors

The skills of spelling and handwriting influence the development of competency in written expression. Even leaving these aside there are still the components of executive functions (Wong, 1991) and semantic knowledge (Berninger, 1994) that are required. The complexity of the processes has perhaps been a factor in constraining research in this area. As Westwood (2003: 51) points out, 'Competence in writing relies heavily on competence in listening, speaking and reading, as well as on possession of necessary strategies for planning, encoding, reviewing and revising written language'. Pupils with learning difficulties tend to have great difficulties with writing, particularly with planning, sequencing ideas, editing and revising (Hess and Wheldall, 1999).

Sandler and colleagues (1992) suggested possible subtypes of 'written language disorder' drawing on cluster analysis of data. The first group, which was also the largest, had fine motor and linguistic deficits. The second had poor handwriting and visual spatial skills but good spelling and good ability to develop ideas. The third group had memory and attention problems. The fourth had difficulties with letter production, legibility and sequencing.

Many areas of the brain appear to be implicated in the complex activity of written expression. A central factor in disorder of written expression may be executive and working memory deficits as these have been associated with such aspects as poor sentence coherence and lexical cohesion (Wilson and Proctor, 2000).

Assessment

Although there are many standardised assessments of spelling ability, fewer such tests exist for writing. The teacher and others will need to compare several examples of the child's writing with that of other children developing age typically and consult others as necessary also taking into account the child's intellectual ability. Examples of the child's writing may be compared that involve copying, writing from dictation and writing spontaneously. It is not usually practicable to determine disorder of written expression very early because it is necessary for the child to have reached an age where it is expected that several types of writing will have been produced for comparison with that of others.

A child with disorder of written expression may be reluctant to write; have particular difficulty copying writing from the board, finding it easier to copy from material on his desk or table; and have an inconsistent handwriting style. Therefore the identification of such difficulties is likely to include: the pupil's approach to a writing task (e.g. reluctance); whether copying from the board appears particularly difficult; and the consistency of the child's handwriting style.

Regarding spelling, the pupil may have difficulties with: words ending in 'er', 'or' and 'ar', for example spelling 'paper' as 'papor' or 'papar'; commonly used words as well as less frequently used ones; and sounds such as 's' and 'z'. The child may tend to: spell phonetically (e.g. 'fotograf' for 'photograph'); omit the middle or end of a word; spell certain words inconsistently ('nesesery', 'nececary', 'nesacary' and so on for 'necessary') and write letters or syllables in the wrong sequence. Such difficulties are typical of pupils with dyslexia. It follows that the identification and assessment of a pupil's difficulty with spelling will include a profile of the sorts of errors made by the pupil in terms of the above characteristics.

Traditional and process approaches

It has been suggested that there are two broad approaches to teaching writing, the traditional and the process (e.g. writers' workshop) approaches (Pollington et al., 2001). The traditional approach tends to be skills based, involves sequential exercises and is teacher led. It may not be very motivating or interesting, the skills may not be generalised to the child's normal writing, and at its least productive does not involve the teacher in teaching anything, only assessing the child's efforts. However, it has the advantage that it can produce steady progress recognised by the child, is predictable and secure. Also, in the hands of an enthusiastic teacher, skills approaches can be made stimulating and enjoyable.

Process approaches tend to emphasise the processes of composing writing and editing it. Manifestations are 'writers' workshop' (e.g. Morrow, 2001) and 'guided writing' and an example of strategies for using process approaches in the classroom is *Writing Through Childhood* (Harwayne, 2001). Rather than be brought to believe that writing has to be exact as it is first produced the child is encouraged to see writing as often passing through several stages before it reaches what could be called a finished stage. This is not intended as an inevitable approach and indeed there are times when writing is well developed which requires the first attempt to be largely the final one as in examinations or in time-pressured work situations. Typical writers' workshop lessons are time-structured, involving teacher instruction, a section on an aspect of writing, then independent or group pupil work and finally sharing of the pupils' work in a plenary. Having seen and learned from the teacher modelling how to offer constructive criticisms of work, pupils then work together to comment on each other's writing and act as the audience for it. Where the groups involve pupils with disorder of written expression, the teacher may need to provide extra support to enable the structure to work and so that the pupil with difficulties does not feel demoralised. As well as being used in a class situation, guided writing may be used in one-to-one remedial work. It involves the teacher modelling a particular strategy followed by the pupil with guidance applying the strategy or principle.

While encouraging the independence and peer interaction associated with a process approach, the teacher of pupils with disorder of written expression will also need to provide the structure for small steps to success that is often associated with basic skills methods. The use of the methods and their relative application can be informed by how well the pupil progresses and enjoys the lessons.

A parallel dichotomy can be found in approaches to teaching spelling. These centre on teaching spelling skills explicitly, for example using groups of words with similar sounds and endings such as 'fish', 'dish' and 'wish' or on teaching the spelling of words in context as they are needed for writing. As with the teaching of aspects of composition, each approach has strengths and weaknesses, but is appears that it is particularly difficult for pupils with disorder of written expression to learn from only a contextual approach to teaching spellings as the intensive practice that is needed to embed the spelling is rarely possible. The aspect of spelling that is likely to need support is the move from basic phonologically recognisable spelling such as 'cort' or 'cot' for 'caught', to the use of visual checking (does the word look right?) and spelling words based on one's existing knowledge of how other words are spelt.

Provision for writing and spelling

Provision for handwriting

General

One principle of interventions for improving handwriting is that where there appear to be several aspects to the writing task, a focus on one of what appear to be underlying difficulties will enable progress to be made. For example, in copying a text, a pupil may find it difficult to co-ordinate movements in handwriting, while maintaining other aspects. These include retaining the visual memory of the words just read (in order to translate them into writing); and maintaining the sequence of different letters and words and translating these into written sequences.

If the combination of skills makes it difficult for the pupil to concentrate on and improve one aspect such as co-ordination, then the assumption is that the associated skills (that is, the difficulties associated with them) can be approached distinctively. Also, to the extent that writing difficulties relate to difficulties with reading, interventions appropriate for reading problems may be suitable for problems with writing too.

Remediating sequencing

Indirect approaches to remediating sequencing difficulties might include task such as laying out sequences of bricks from left to right on a table to introduce the pupil to positional words such as 'before', 'after', 'next to', 'first' and 'last' and encourage him to use them. This positional understanding and the language linked to it may help the pupil begin to recognise a sequence of letters in a word, be able to talk about their position and reproduce this in writing.

Improving co-ordination skills for handwriting

Teaching handwriting is also discussed in the chapter on developmental co-ordination disorder where the focus is on teaching handwriting to children with particular difficulties in motor co-ordination. If the co-ordination skills for writing are to be taught and improved the focus on reducing the demands of the other sub-skills of remembering and translating sequences of different letters from a page of print can achieve this. The task can involve, for example, the writing of one repeated letter shape related to handwriting such as the following:

ccccc

aaaaa

ggg

The early teaching of cursive script can help a pupil having difficulties with fine motor movements. This is because it is more flowing and controllable than forming separate letters and because it enables the pupil to learn handwriting as it were in one go rather than having to learn to write in separate letters then later change to cursive.

Where handwriting includes problems with letter orientation and the reversal of letters (a common feature of many pupils when they are learning to write), the correct formations may be taught directly. The pupil may begin with large letters, perhaps using a sand tray to aid orientation. The pupil can be encouraged to look at the letter and say the letter as well as tracing it. Later the pupil will write the letter in a series on paper.

Teaching cursive script

Where letter formation for handwriting is taught using a cursive script, the teacher may provide a chart to act as a reminder to the pupil of the shape of each letter. It is suggested (Pollock *et al.*, 2004) that a well-shaped letter 'c' is a good starting point. The individual letters should be written with an exit stroke so they can join other letters as follows, *cccc*.

This leads on to teaching the letters *aa,dd,gg* and *ee*. These units can then be the initial focus of practice in handwriting exercises even though other letters may be used in general writing. Other groups of letters can then be taught. The next group is the letters that determine the handwriting slant, such as *ll* and *jj*. Next are the letters that are a combination of curves and angles such as *bbb* and *fff*. Finally, the letters that can be formed in more than one way can be taught, for example *kkk* (ibid.: 109–111).

Compensatory tools for handwriting

Among computer-based strategies for bypassing handwriting problems are: using a keyboard, dictation using a voice recognition system and word prediction programmes, each of which has been shown to improve the writing accuracy of pupils with learning disabilities (Lewis *et al.*, 1998). As Berninger and Amtmann (2003: 351) point out, although these tools bypass handwriting difficulties, they each have their own demands which a particular pupil with learning disabilities may or may not find challenging.

Unless a pupil is able to automatise the letter finding and keyboard skills involved in word processing, it may not be fluent enough to be a viable alternative to handwriting. Although dictation using a voice recognition system can eventually lead to better and longer text than a pupil may produce by handwriting, it is not a panacea. It still involves the pupil learning the commands for monitoring and correcting errors and being able to dictate, self-monitor for errors and use the programme commands effectively, placing considerable demands on working memory (e.g. Berninger and Amtmann, 2003: 352). Word prediction software may also pose challenges for pupils having poor working memory or problems with attention or executive function because the pupil has to monitor the list of options that changes with each letter that is typed.

Provision for writing composition

Framework for writing

Supporting frameworks for writing can help the pupil with disorder of written expression in several ways. They can be used to get the pupil started, give a sense of direction to the task and build confidence.

For example, the teacher can develop with the pupil an understanding of the processes of developing ideas for writing, composing and editing. The teacher can model the processes and use sets of questions that the pupil can later use to structure his own attempts. In generating ideas, the questions might be for a fictional story, 'Who is in the story?' 'Where does it happen?' 'What is the main thing that happens?' 'What happens, first, next, finally?' The pupil gradually takes on more of the task of generating ideas.

Similarly, the steps in composing the piece of writing can be modelled and gradually taken over by the pupil. In a non-fiction piece of writing where the ideas have been generated, the teacher can model the task of setting out the ideas in some kind of understandable order. Questions might be, 'What are the main ideas? 'Which should come first?' 'What should come last?' Composition can then include taking each main idea in turn and expanding it into a sentence or two.

In editing, the teacher will show how she checks if the structure and shape of the piece of writing is good, whether paragraphs are used effectively, if grammar is clear, and if punctuation and spelling are correct.

Reducing task demands

To build confidence by providing initial success and to get a pupil started, reducing task demands can be useful. In story writing this can involve providing the beginnings of a series of sentences in a writing frame.

- When the light plane crashed, we found ourselves in the middle of the desert with no water and ...
- All we could do at first was ...
- Then we looked round the wreckage and noticed ...
- So we made a ....
- By nightfall it was ...

To aid fluency in writing longer pieces of work and to save the pupil time using a dictionary for many words, the teacher can provide key words that are likely to be used, or that the pupil indicates he wishes to use.

The underlying principle of reducing task demands is to enable the pupil to concentrate on smaller aspects of the overall task and improve on that by the teacher providing the structure for other aspects of the work so that a finished product is made. The initial focus might be on generating ideas, then composition, then editing and gradually the supports are faded out so that the pupil is able to carry out the whole process.

Software for essay structure

Software packages are available to help users develop and organise ideas, using diagrams to help. This allows ideas to be arranged, which can help with the structure of essays. Templates can be used for different subjects, including science and history. If a pupil is carrying out a piece of extended writing, such as an essay or research report, actively teaching the skills of how it should be presented is likely to be helpful (for all pupils).

More general software is also useful. Word processing packages such as Microsoft Word are useful at different stages of writing a piece of work: planning, composition, checking and correcting and publishing. Talking word processors allow users to hear, through synthetic speech, the sentences they are typing as they are being typed. This can help reassure the pupil that what they are writing makes sense, and, where it does not, allows the pupil to go back and check accuracy. Some programmes provide partial or complete sentences to support writing and allow the creation of personalised cloze procedure exercises.

Note taking

Note taking is a complex and difficult skill that is difficult for many pupils and where a pupil has difficulties with writing, demands are exacerbated. The pupil is likely to find it particularly difficult to concentrate on what is being said at the same time as keeping handwriting legible. The teacher can encourage the pupil to write down only the key words. Then at the end of the dictation, the teacher gives the pupil a copy of her notes and the pupil goes through them highlighting the key words he has identified. The key words act as a revision aid and an anchor for reading the notes.

Writing for a purpose

As a motivational aid and as an incentive to produce work of good quality, writing for a particular purpose is helpful. The pupil may write a letter of thanks to a speaker who has visited the school, contribute to a newsletter about school events, design and write a safety poster, write to a penfriend, send emails to pupils in other schools perhaps in different parts of the world, or write shopping lists for class projects that involve buying items such as creating a school garden or organising a school fair. He may write to the local newspaper, apply for a job, write a story book for younger children in the school, write letters on behalf of elderly and infirm people in a local old people's home, or prepare a cooking recipe. As well as being motivational such work of course provides invaluable opportunities for the pupil to consider the requirements of writing for different audiences.

Developing self-regulation strategies

Pupils with learning disabilities tend to do little planning before they write and their approach tends to involve little monitoring and evaluation (e.g. Graham, 1990). Their compositions are very short, with little detail or elaboration (Graham et al., 1991). One reason is their difficulty in sustaining the writing effort, for example in one study, fourth and sixth graders with LD were found to spend an average of only six minutes on writing an opinion essay. Yet with prompting, output could be considerably increased (Graham, 1990). Difficulties with the mechanics of writing such as spelling, punctuation and shaping letters also reduce content (Graham et al., 1991). When pupils with LD do attempt revisions of their work, these tend to focus on mechanical aspects and neatness rather than compositional aspects of writing.

When given procedural support to ensure elements of the revising process were co-ordinated and occurred in a regular way, the revising of pupils' with LD improved. For example, eighth grade students with LD were taught to make two passes through a composition. The first concentrated on global concerns such as there not being sufficient ideas, while the second pass focused more on sentence level concerns such as a sentence not sounding right or an idea being incomplete. This produced better and larger revisions (De La Paz et al., 1998).

One approach to directly teaching pupils with LD to use the same types of strategies as more competent writers is 'self-regulated strategy development' (e.g. see Graham and Harris, 2003: 328–331 for a summary), an example of a cognitive strategies instruction model. This approach is intended to enhance students':

- strategic behaviours;
- self-regulation skills;
- content knowledge and
- motivation.

For example, one writing study (Sexton et al., 1998) involved fifth and sixth grade students with LD who had a difficulty with writing, low motivation and unhelpful beliefs about the causes of writing success and failure. The students were taught a *strategy* for planning and writing an opinion essay, using steps to help them establish a goal for writing, creating an initial outline for their paper (using basic components of thesis, supporting reasons, and conclusion) and continuing the process of planning while writing. The necessary *content knowledge* of the structure of an opinion essay was taught by defining the above basic components, identifying them in essays by others, and generating ideas for each component. Students were helped to *regulate* their use of the strategy by the teacher modelling how to use it while thinking aloud, using self-statements such as 'What do I need to do?' and 'Did I say what I believe?' Teacher and students discussed these self-statements and students were praised when they later used them in learning the strategy. Motivation and unhelpful beliefs were also directly tackled.

Interventions for spelling

Multi-sensory aspects

There is a range of approaches using multi-sensory aids to teach spelling (e.g. Pollock *et al.*, 2004). For example, in teaching early letter sounds, the teacher can include the first letter of the child's name, say, 'p'. Other letters might be 'm' for 'mum'/'mom', 't' for 'tiger' and 'a' for 'apple'. Words are chosen that have a personal interest for the child and which can be illustrated and visualised. These are taught as the sound the letter makes rather than the pronunciation of the letter name (e.g. 'a' pronounced as in 'cat' not as in 'cape'). The teacher talks with the child about the letter sound and shape using cards on which the letters are written in front of them. This leads to basic word building with words like 'pat' and 'mat' depending on the first few letters that have been introduced. In the approach, 'simultaneous oral spelling', the pupil says the letters as he writes them, so linking kinaesthetic memory and auditory memory.

Visual recall can be aided by the teacher showing the pupils a written word and asking them to concentrate on the word and remember as much as possible about it. After removing the word from view, the teacher prompts with questions such as, 'How many letters in the word?' or 'Were any of the letters the same?' to encourage visual recall.

The auditory recall of words can be encouraged by games such as clapping out the syllables of the word or grouping words according to their sound, as with 'dog', 'bog', 'log' and so on. Rhymes, poems and songs of course help highlight the sounds of words. A child with auditory difficulties might not hear the similarities of words taught in clusters to aid spelling ('wish', 'dish') so the teacher will need to make sure that the common rhyme 'ish' is noticed.

Simply looking at words does not seem to be enough for most learners to be able to learn how to spell a word (Graham, 2000) and the contribution of kinaesthetic, speech motor and auditory senses are necessary. In the early stages of learning to spell (and in learning to read) phonemic awareness is important (Torgesen and Mathes, 2000) so that the different sound units of the word are linked to the graphic representation.

Multi-sensory work for writing and spelling draws on speech-motor, kinaesthetic, visual and auditory memory. Large letters may be drawn using the finger in a sand tray so that the shape and sequence of letters is emphasised. Smaller letters may then be traced, leading to the writing of letters on paper. Having the child say and sound out the word (for phonetically regular words) may further embed this. This brings in speech-motor memory as the child articulates and involves auditory memory as the child hears the sounds.

Often, a reading disorder appears to be related to a difficulty with phonological processing. In such instances, work on teaching and supporting better phonological awareness in conjunction with letter-sound instruction would be expected to contribute to improved spelling. The 'look-cover-write-check' approach is familiar to many, but by drawing on other senses too the strategy can be extended to 'look-say-finger-trace-cover-write-check'. This can include the strategy of looking at the word shape overall as well as looking at individual letters, given that the words where this approach is used are not normally phonetically regular words that can be guessed from knowing their sounds.

Directed Spelling Thinking Activity

In the Directed Spelling Thinking Activity (DSTA) (Graham *et al.*, 2000), a group of pupils study words, being helped to contrast, compare and categorise two or more words according to their finding similarities and difference in them. The aim is to raise awareness of spelling patterns and more complex grapho-phonological principles. For example, in examining words with a long /i/ sound as in 'thigh', 'by' and 'pie', they are encouraged to discover that the long /i/ can be made by the letters 'igh' as in not only 'thigh' but also in 'sigh'. It can be made with the letters 'y' in 'by' but also in 'try' and 'cry'. The long /i/ can be made by 'ie' as in 'pie' and in words such as 'lie' and 'die'. The pupils are encouraged to classify other similar words into groups or notice that they do not follow the common principle. Consolidating activities might be looking at a piece of writing in which examples of the words conforming to the rule appear (and which the teacher has previously checked to ensure this is the case). This approach has been suggested for use with pupils with 'learning disabilities' (ibid.). A similar approach, 'word sort', has been used with 'delayed readers' (Zutell, 1998).

Target words

Target words may reflect the recommendations for spelling programmes (Tiedt *et al.*, 2001) that is, they include high frequency core words, personal words and patterns of words illustrating some morphological or phonological principle. The personal words will include a list prepared with the pupil of the words used often in the week in various contexts and of course some of these may be high frequency core words also. Groups of words can be made in consultation with older students and subject specialist teachers of the words often needed in the subjects, for example in science or geography.

When the pupil works on words that have been misspelled in free writing sessions, the words to be worked on will reflect the school's spelling policy, and this is likely to be most helpful when it involves selecting only a few misspelled words from a piece of work, usually those which are very commonly used.

While repetition of spellings is a necessary aid, effort should be made to generate interest in the tasks involved. Short daily activities with weekly checks of progress are better than long drills. Games, puzzles and computer activities, as long as they focus on the important words, can be motivating and helpful. Software is available that allows the user to decide how words are grouped and to add words of the user's choice. Games and strategies to improve spelling may be included. Other software employs a 'look, cover, write and check' approach to learning spellings. The words are in 'families' or subject groups but personalised lists can also be made. Sometimes, remembering the spelling of target words can be made easier by using visual mnemonics and word associations (Mercer and Mercer, 1998) For example, a pupil who often misspells 'piece' as 'peice' might find the phrase 'a piece of pie' a useful reminder of the letter order.

Alternative and augmentative communication

Chapter 14 in this book on 'Communication disorders: speech' considers alternative and augmentative communication. This section briefly touches on its relevance to written communication through symbols and related matters. Symbolic communication involves the use of symbols, for example a word or a picture to stand for something. 'Non-aided' communication involves the child making a movement or vocalisation that does not necessitate a physical aid or other device (Vanderheiden and Lloyd, 1986), while 'aided' augmentative communication involves using a device or item such as a communication board, eye gaze board and electronic systems.

Three categories may be identified (e.g. Bigge et al., 2001: 237): non-electronic devices; dedicated communication devices and computer-based communication systems. *Non-electronic devices* may be communication boards and communication notebooks. Communication books can include photographs, symbols and words, enabling a pupil to find a symbol and show the particular page to someone who may not know the symbol so they can see the intended word. *Dedicated communication devices* are electronic communication systems that speak programmed messages when the user activates locations marked by symbols. *Computer-based communication systems* may consist of a computer with input options, communication software and a speech synthesizer.

Computer aided communication may involve the pupil having a voice production device with a computer-based bank of words and sentences that can be produced by pressing the keyboard keys.

Symbols may be part or whole objects used to represent an item or activity. Often what is meant when people refer to symbols is a system of graphical communication, with each symbol representing a concept such as an object, person, activity or attribute. Communication grids in which several symbols are set out in a specified order can enable a pupil to participate in a group sessions; for example, to support the retelling of a story. A sequence of symbols can be used to indicate a sequence of activities, including a school timetable for a pupil. Computer technology, using symbols, allows the pupil and the adult to use a large number of symbols flexibly. There are symbol email programmes, and websites that use symbols.

Curriculum and assessment; pedagogy; resources; therapy/care; and organisation

Curriculum and assessment

Given the centrality of writing to many school subjects, attainment in these may be lower than is age typical where written responses are required (although knowledge in the subjects may be the same as for other children). The balance of subjects may emphasise writing to encourage and support progress in this. Small steps of assessment may be used to recognise progress in written expression and spelling.

Pedagogy

Approaches for disorder of written expression include: remediating sequencing, improving co-ordination skills, teaching cursive script, frameworks for writing, reducing task demands, and support for note taking, and self-regulated strategy development. To improve spelling, interventions may involve multi-sensory approaches, Directed Spelling Thinking Activity and target words.

Resources

Among resources used for disorder of written expression is computer software to help with essay structure. Where graphical symbols are used the relevant resources are required.

Therapy/care

There appears to be no distinctive therapy necessary for disorder of written expression.

Organisation

There appears to be no distinctive organisation of the school or classroom necessary for disorder of written expression. However, as a supplementary approach to more direct interventions such as self-regulated strategy development, aspects of classroom environment have been identified. These involve developing an environment conducive to the development of self-regulation such as encouraging pupils to share their writing with others; securing classroom routines where planning and revising are expected and reinforced; and a classroom ethos that is supportive (e.g. Graham and Harris, 1997).

Thinking points

Readers may wish to consider:

- how the tensions between essential skills learning, which may lead to observable progress, and the use of learning in context, which may be more meaningful, are reconciled;
- how the effectiveness of the strategies mentioned above will be assessed for a particular pupil to help ensure they are helping progress;
- how links between the teaching of writing and the teaching of reading and speaking and listening will be inter-related so each enhances the others.

Key texts

Fletcher, J. M., Lyon, G. R., Fuchs, L. and Barnes, M. A. (2007) *Learning Disabilities: From Identification to Intervention*. New York, Guilford Press.
Drawing on genetic, neural, cognitive and contextual information, this book considers classification, definition, identification and assessment and intervention for disabilities in: reading (word recognition, fluency, comprehension), mathematics disabilities and written expression

Gunning, T. G. (2002) (2nd edition) *Assessing and Correcting Reading and Writing Difficulties*. Boston, MA, Allyn & Bacon.
The title is self-explanatory.

Chapter 21

Mathematics disorder

Introduction

This chapter considers definitions of mathematics disorder; its prevalence; causal factors and its identification and assessment. Provision is then described in terms of teaching prerequisite skills, general approaches, mathematics difficulties relating to developmental co-ordination disorder and mathematics difficulties relating to reading disorder. In the final section the chapter summarises provision in relation to curriculum and assessment; pedagogy; resources; therapy/care; and organisation. An example of an Internet site with a brief overview of mathematics disorder is (www.schwablearning.org/articles).

Definitions

Mathematics disorder, sometimes called dyscalculia, is considered to be a difficulty in understanding and learning mathematics that is not associated with general cognitive difficulties. In the *Diagnostic and Statistical Manual of Mental Disorders Fourth Edition Text Revision* (*DSM-IV-TR*) (American Psychiatric Association, 2000: 53) the essential feature of mathematics disorder is stated to be mathematical ability falling substantially below that expected for the child's chronological age, intelligence and age appropriate education. The disorder 'significantly interferes' with academic achievement of daily living that requires mathematical skills.

Dyscalculia' is defined in a document relating to a national numeracy strategy in England as:

> a condition that affects the ability to acquire mathematical skills. Dycalculic learners may have difficulty understanding simple number concepts, lack an intuitive grasp of numbers, and have problems with learning number facts and procedures. Even if they produce the correct answer or use the correct method, they may do so mechanically and without confidence.
>
> (Department for Education and Skills, 2001a).

A pupil with mathematics disorder may have difficulty performing simple calculations such as addition: have difficulty knowing how to respond to mathematical information; substitute one number for another; reverse numbers (e.g. 2 for 5); misalign symbols, for example when using a decimal point; and name, read and write mathematical symbols incorrectly. Attempts have been made to identify and delineate different 'types' of mathematics difficulty and these extend and supplement basic definitions.

- *Spatial dyscalculia* relates to difficulties in visuo-spatial assessment and organisation.
- *Anarithmetria* involves confusion with arithmetical procedures, for example, mixing written operations such as addition, subtraction and multiplication.
- *Lexical dyscalculia* (alexia) concerns confusion with the language of mathematics and its relationship with symbols (e.g. subtract, take away, deduct, minus and '-').
- *Graphic dyscalculia* refers to problems with being able to write the symbols and digits needed for calculations.
- *Practographic dyscalculia* is characterised by impairment in the ability to manipulate concrete objects or graphically illustrated objects. The child has difficulty in practically applying mathematical knowledge and procedures and may be unable to arrange objects in order of size, compare two items according to size or state when two items are identical in size and weight (Senzer, 2001).

Some of these purported types of mathematics disorder appear to be related conceptually to either dyspraxia or dyslexia. For example, spatial dyscalculia may relate to dyspraxic difficulties, while lexical and perhaps graphic dyscalculia may relate more to dyslexic difficulties (e.g. Jordan and Hanich, 2003; Jordan et al., 2003).

Prevalence

The prevalence of mathematics disorder is difficult to determine because it is not always regarded as a separate entity. Often it is associated with reading disorder or developmental co-ordination disorder and interventions are developed within that context. Also, the level at which difficulties with mathematics is sufficiently severe to constitute a disorder is not always agreed. It has, however, been estimated that about 6 per cent of students have significant difficulties learning basic mathematical concepts and skills (Fleischner and Manheimer, 1997). Regarding arithmetical disability, estimates taking into account studies in the United States of America, Europe and Israel suggest that 5 per cent to 7 per cent of school age children show some form of arithmetical disability (Geary, 2003: 200).

Causal factors

Foetal alcohol syndrome has been associated with babies being born with the parietal lobes being underdeveloped. These are considered important for numeracy, and underdevelopment is associated with the child later having difficulties with mathematical cognition and number processing (Kopera-Frye *et al.*, 1996).

Different neural systems contribute to mathematical cognition, one of which is a verbal system (Dehaene *et al.*, 1998). This appears to store, as well verbally rote learned information, number facts such as number bonds, and underpins counting and numerical rote learned knowledge like multiplication tables. If a child with mathematics disorder also has reading disorder, and if reading disorder has a phonological basis, then the neural system affected may be the verbal system underpinning counting and calculation (Goswami, 2004: 179). Another neural system concerned with the representation of number appears to underpin knowledge concerning numbers and their relations (e.g. one number being large or smaller than another) (Dahaene *et al.*, 1999). Located in the intraparietal areas of the brain, the system is activated by such tasks as number comparisons (whether using numerals, words or clusters of dots). Visuo-spatial regions may be involved with complex calculations (Zago *et al.*, 2001) where visual-mental imagery may be important. A particular parietal-premotor area is activated during finger counting and calculation (Goswami, 2004: 179).

Identification and assessment

In identifying mathematics disorder, the teacher will bear in mind the definition of mathematics disorder and its possible characteristic difficulties. The identification and assessment of mathematics disorder is also informed by other difficulties the pupil may have. For example, if the pupil is identified as having reading disorder or development co-ordination disorder, the mathematics disorder is assessed in those contexts. Among commercial assessments is the computer-based *Dyscalculia Screener* (Butterworth, 2004) for children aged 6 to 14 years, which measures pupils' response times and response accuracy. Typically, a score lower than the 20th or 25th percentile on a mathematics achievement test and a low average or higher IQ score are considered to indicate arithmetical disability (e.g. Geary *et al.*, 2000), although interpreting the detail of the tests and monitoring progress are important.

In curriculum terms, the pupil will be assessed to establish the gaps that exist in his mathematical knowledge and skills and this diagnostic approach will inform what is taught (e.g. Silver and Hagin, 2002). Good assessment will also influence the pace at which mathematics is taught, the contexts, the amount of support needed from concrete apparatus and other matters.

Provision

This section takes a pragmatic view looking at teaching prerequisite skills (relating to classification, number, length, area, volume, weight and position and movement); general interventions and approaches (reducing anxiety, using concrete experience and adapting and applying knowledge and mathematical problem solving); approaches relating to developmental co-ordination disorder; and approaches relating to reading disorder.

Teaching prerequisite skills

The development of subsequent skills and understanding necessary in mathematics are hindered if there is not a secure basis of certain prerequisite skills: classification, number, length, area, volume, weight, position and movement.

Classification begins with very simple distinctions such as 'same' and 'different' and extends to more sophisticated classifications such as grouping shapes with the same number of sides and angles. To help a pupil recognise patterns of relationships and recognise groups (e.g. groups of objects of the same colour) the teacher can provide practical experience of and practice in classifying, beginning with easy classifications and making them gradually more complex.

Number sense has been variously defined but may be taken to include: being able to subitise small quantities (that is rapidly, accurately and confidently judging number given a small number of items), recognise number patterns, compare numerical magnitudes, estimate quantities, count and carry out simple number transformations (e.g. Berch, 2005). If a pupil is having difficulty with number, it is helpful to check that precursors such as the following are in place and to teach them using practical examples and experience if they are not. The pupil may struggle with concepts relating to 'more' or 'less'. He may have difficulty learning that one number has a greater value than another (e.g. 5 and 3). There may be difficulty relating size and quantity, for example, knowing that five tiles laid out on a flat surface will take up a smaller space than ten tiles of the same size arranged similarly. The pupil may find it hard to estimate an answer before working a problem out. He may confuse the direction in which things get bigger and smaller. One source of this confusion may be that in a number line (1, 2, 3...), numbers to the left are progressively smaller while in value, while with digits, the value to the left is bigger in the sense that it represents tens, hundreds etc. (e.g. in '24' the '2' on the left represents '20') (Poustie, 2001b: 71). Difficulties with place value may relate to numbers being misread so that the correct information is not used; numbers being miswritten, in which case the pupil may know the correct answer to a calculation but miswrites it; and not understanding the concept, perhaps because of difficulties in understanding the language used. To rectify any mistakes relating to place value it is important the teacher asks the pupil to explain his working out so the correct remediating strategy can be determined.

A precursor to understanding *length* such as the length of a line is grasping that length is 'conserved' even when the line is bent or curved. A pupil having difficulty with this notion would be shown two straight pieces of wire and recognise they were the same length. If one of the pieces of wire were then bent (say into an 'S' shape) the pupil would not recognise or accept it was still the same length as its partner. He may assume length has to do with the length of the space the wire occupied (which is smaller when the wire is bent) rather than being a retained property of the wire. To rectify this, the teacher can provide plenty of experience that length stays the same by very gradually bending the wire and having the pupil agree it is the same length as before then progressively bending it a little more.

In order to understand *area*, it is necessary to be able to match circumscribed areas. For example the pupil should be able to match two squares of identical areas from several squares with different areas. This can be taught directly, giving the pupil plenty of experience of matching area visually. Initially, the pupil can be given a square and a choice of two other squares only one of which matches the pupil's square. Subsequently, the number of squares can be increased. Later still, the pupil can be asked to match two squares from several laid out on the table, so the pupil has to identify both squares.

To begin to understand *volume*, the pupil has to realise that volume is conserved even if the container of the substance is different in size and/or shape. The pupil should be given plenty of practical experience using liquids and containers of different sizes and shapes, care being taken not to spill the liquid so it can be demonstrated that the volume of liquid remains the same!

Among precursors of understanding *weight* is that the pupil grasps the conservation of weight, understanding that, if two malleable items weigh the same and one is then made into a different shape, it will still weigh the same as its partner. To teach this, the pupil might begin by reading his weight on scales when standing then checking the reading when crouching to show that weight is constant. This develops into weighing items and changing their shape and then weighing them again to confirm their weight is the same (Poustie, 2001b: 22–23).

For a pupil with difficulties regarding *position and movement* in mathematics, early work can involve the pupil developing an understanding of his own position in relation to other objects. He might be asked and if necessary guided to stand 'in front of' a box, 'beside' a box, 'behind' a box and so on. The pupil would later direct another person into similar positions to give the pupil practice in using the correct expressive vocabulary.

General approaches

Reducing anxiety

Some students become anxious when expected to demonstrate competence applying mathematical skills (Battista, 1999). Sometimes difficulties with attention are exacerbated by stress and anxiety about doing mathematics. Reassuring the pupil and trying to make mathematics enjoyable perhaps using games can help reduce anxiety and help the pupil relax and therefore concentrate and attend better. Where anxiety about mathematics is high, individual tuition can help ensure early success and reduce the anxiety of not getting the task right.

Concrete experience

Using concrete apparatus helps give the pupil experience and understanding of what is being done and a pupil with mathematics disorder may require consolidation using concrete items longer than most pupils. Even when more abstract methods are being used, concrete reminders can still be helpful for some tasks. Number lines or a box of physical shapes that are labelled are examples. Concrete material such as Dienes MAB blocks, Stern's equipment and Unifix blocks are useful in developing understanding of computation and other mathematical understanding. For example, Cuisenaire rods are useful physical aids using size and colour to help pupils' understanding of many aspects of mathematics (Poustie, 2001b: 61–63 gives many practical ideas).

Westwood (2000: 41) accepts that structural apparatus 'provides a bridge between the concrete experience and abstract reasoning by taking learners through experiences at intermediate levels of semi-concrete ... to the semi-abstract' but gives a timely reminder that such apparatus is by no means fool-proof in helping pupils acquire understanding. The pupil may not connect activities carried out using the apparatus with the mathematical concepts the teacher wants to convey, so the teacher still needs to discuss with the pupil the task and assess his understanding.

Adapting and applying knowledge and mathematical problem solving

The pupil may find it difficult to adapt existing knowledge, finding it hard to dispense with procedures unsuited to the task in hand. For example, phys-ically adding to 6 existing items different numbers of items, (e.g. 2, 3, 4) the pupil may count from 1 every time instead of adapting the counting approach and counting on from 6.

Regarding generalising mathematical skills, the pupil may learn an approach in one situation with one set of items but not apply it in another situation with other items when most other children would do so. Plenty of practice and application in other contexts can help embed mathematical con-cepts and terms.

To help a pupil apply and adapt mathematical learning such as being able to count money to practical situations like spending money in a shop, struc-tured practice of different teaching strategies and practice in using them can be used. Similarly, the pupil may be taught to apply approaches and skills to different situations. Applying knowledge can be helped if the teacher ensures the skills are very secure then gradually introduces the extra demands of applying the knowledge and skill in different circumstances. For example, using money for shopping can begin with buying a single item with a known price using the exact amount of money, allowing the pupil to cope better with the social demands of shopping. Later the task can be made increasingly complicated by requiring change and buying several items.

Related to the issue of generalisation arising in connection with adapting and applying knowledge, is the development of the ability to carry out mathematical problem solving. Fuchs and Fuchs (2003) research programme indicated that for pupils with mathematics disabilities (MD), a strong foundation in the rules of problem solving was necessary. Children had to master solution methods on problems with 'low transfer demands'. (These were problems that were worded the same as previous problems and in which only quantities and the cover stories were different.) After this foundation, it was possible to progress to problems with higher transfer demands. These require transfer to problems with certain differences making it more difficult to recognise the problem that is already known. Also explicit instruction on transfer was needed aimed at increasing the child's awareness of the connections between new and familiar problems. This is achieved by broadening the categories by which pupils group problems that require the same solution methods and by prompting pupils to search novel problems for these broad categories (increasing metacognition) (ibid.: 318).

Mathematics and DCD

Bearing in mind the underlying difficulties associated with developmental co-ordination disorder (DCD) and some of the approaches suggested in relation to handwriting in the chapter on DCD, it is possible to understand why certain difficulties arise in mathematics and how they might be tackled.

Number

Many students with learning disabilities have difficulty learning and recalling number facts and tables (Ostad, 1999). More specifically, because of such difficulties as those with fine motor co-ordination, eye-hand co-ordination and spatial relationships, the child with DCD may have difficulties writing numerals, for example getting the size correct. Squared paper with squares of a size allowing the child to write a number in each can be used to help with the size of numerals. It has also been suggested that numerals can be taught in groups that avoid the teaching very similar numerals that may be confused (3 and 5; 6 and 9). The groups would be introduced as 1, 2 and 3 with particular care that 3 was formed and practiced before 5 was introduced.

Next, 4, 5 and 6 would be taught with care that 6 is practised before 9 is taught. The next group would be 7, 8, 9 and 10 (El-Nagar, 1996).

If spacing between numerals is excessive or insufficient, or columns for calculations inconsistent so that errors are made, squared paper can help. Difficulties with orientation may make it hard for the pupil to follow and reproduce the sequence of a calculation from left to right or from top to bottom. This can be explicitly taught and the pupil reminded of the direction of the calculation by arrows of a different colour to that used for the child's calculations at the beginning of a horizontal sum and at the side of a top to bottom calculation as indicated below:

$$\rightarrow 6 + 7 = 11 \qquad \begin{array}{r} 6 + \\ 7 \ \downarrow \\ \hline \\ \hline \end{array}$$

Also, difficulties with motor co-ordination may lead to a symbol being incorrectly written or copied, for example 'x' for '+'. If therefore a pupil writes '5 + 2 = 10' this may reflect an incorrect calculation or indicate the pupil was trying to write '5 x 2 = 10'. It is important that place value is securely understood and where this is achieved, mistakes are reduced. More generally, it is essential to ask the pupil to explain the working out so such misunderstandings come to light.

Space, shape and measure

Because of such difficulties as orientation, the pupil with DCD may have problems understanding and using positional words and phrases such as 'up', 'down', 'behind' and 'in front' and linking them to different aspects of spatial relationships. These works need to be explicitly taught and linked with practical experience of the positions they convey. The teacher may begin by applying the words to the position of the pupil's body, for example teaching the pupil positions such as standing 'behind' a tree or 'in front' of a tree. Miniature models are then used (a figure representing the pupil and a model of the tree) with the pupil manipulating these to develop and confirm understanding. Next, two-dimensional representations are used such as immediately observed digital photographs (of the pupil standing behind/in front of the tree) and drawings.

Regarding shape, the pupil having difficulties with form constancy may not see shapes accurately and when required to reproduce them from memory will have difficulties replicating the correct form and size. This will be exacerbated if the pupil has difficulties with fine motor co-ordination that makes it hard for him to draw the shape even if he had visualised it accurately. Problems with laterality tend to make it hard for the pupil to draw shapes involving diagonals where the lines involve negotiating two sets of directions: left-right and up-down.

To help a child recognise shapes, a teacher can encourage him to handle and explore physical shapes such as a square or triangle. Multi-sensory approaches can help especially kinaesthetic and tactile methods to encourage the accurate reproduction of shapes, for example drawing shapes in a sand tray or making them from plasticine. The child may struggle to understand symmetry because of problems identifying left and right. This can be taught through games in which the child's body is the first indicator of what is left and right (not the teacher's left and right as she faces him). With his own left hand and right hand marked in an agreed way, the child is asked to go to his left or right. With a group, the game 'Simon Says' can be a vehicle for introducing and practising this. Later, looking at a shape that can be handled and which has a clear line of symmetry, the pupil is asked to show the left and right of the shape. Drawings of shapes can then be used to check the pupil's understanding of the concept and to teach and reinforce it further.

To help a pupil recognise three-dimensional shapes and drawings of such shapes and draw a three-dimensional shape, the teacher can provide plenty of guided opportunities for the pupil to handle and talk about three-dimensional shapes. A structured programme in which the child is introduced to two-dimensional representations of three-dimensional shapes while the latter are present can help the pupil begin to recognise and match the aspects of the three-dimensional shape and the representation.

Turning to weight, pupils with poor proprioception, whose muscle receptors are not as sensitised as most other children, have difficulty understanding weight. The pupil will benefit from being provided with structured experience of handling objects of different weights and terms such as 'heavy', 'light', 'heavier than' and 'lighter than' need to be learned and understood.

The pupil is introduced to measuring weight using a balance where respective relative weights are indicated by the position of the balance and the notions of 'heavier than' and 'lighter than' are refined. Spring scales can be introduced later. For linear measuring, where a pupil has difficulties with fine motor co-ordination, a ruler with a small handle can be used.

Mathematics and reading disorder

It appears that reading and language capabilities enable young children to compensate for deficits in certain areas of mathematics. For example, the reading and mathematics achievement and particular mathematical competencies of 74 children were tracked over second and third grade. Children were initially classified into one of four groups:

- moderate mathematics deficiencies but normal reading achievement;
- moderate mathematics deficiencies and moderate reading deficiencies;
- moderate reading deficiencies but normal mathematics;
- normal mathematics achievement and normal reading achievement.

Many of the children were not eligible for special educational services, their disabilities being relatively mild. The group with 'moderate mathematics deficiencies but normal reading achievement' and the group with 'moderate mathematics deficiencies and moderate reading deficiencies' both started out at the same level in mathematics, the former group passed the latter over time. Children with moderate mathematics deficiencies (whether or not they had reading deficiencies) tended to be weak in fact retrieval and estimation. The group with moderate mathematics deficiencies and normal reading performed better at problem solving than did the group that had deficiencies in both mathematics and reading (Jordan and Hanich, 2003).

Other relationships between reading disorder and mathematics disorder may be considered with regard to apparent underlying difficulties. Difficulties associated with reading disorder discussed in an earlier chapter included:

- phonological difficulties;
- auditory perception and auditory processing difficulties;
- short-term verbal memory difficulties and
- sequencing difficulties (temporal order).

Similar difficulties are considered below in relation to mathematics problems for the pupil with reading disorder.

Phonological difficulties and auditory perception and auditory processing difficulties

It has been suggested (Geary and Hoard, 2001) that there may be a relationship between deficits in processing sounds (a feature of reading disability) and accessing arithmetical facts from long-term memory. Certainly, learning number facts involves counting, which involves number words and the use of the phonetic system. But, as has been observed, (Jordan et al., 2003: 834) it is therefore unclear why children with mathematics disability only who presumably have intact phonetic abilities also demonstrate deficits in fact retrieval.

It is important that the teacher's use of language in explaining mathematical relationships corresponds to the student's comprehension level (Cawley et al., 2001). More specifically, difficulties with phonological representations and with auditory processing and auditory perception may make it hard for the pupil with reading disorder to develop a secure understanding of the language of mathematics. The pupil may have difficulty in acquiring and using mathematical language such as 'addition', 'place value', 'decimals' and 'fractions', perhaps having limited experience of mathematical vocabulary receptively and expressively. Using mathematical language correctly complements developing the understanding and skills with which the language is associated. The teacher can introduce and explain new words and display key words throughout the lesson, for example on a board. Wall displays with key words as their focus can be built up as new words are introduced.

Number stories aim to give the pupil a better understanding of word problems and how they are constructed (Poustie, 2001b: 33–34). The pupil might make up and tell a story about '3' and '7', perhaps that there were seven children in a camp in the forest and three of them went out to explore and three were left. The pupil would then be encouraged to write the different sums that could be made from the story such as '7 − 3 = 4'.

Potentially misleading language may require explanation and examples. The fact that the numbers in 'twenty three' are said with the 'tens' part of the number first but the 'fourteen' is said with the units part of the number first can confuse some children. A careful explanation with examples of the expression 'teen' meaning 'ten' and the rule that for numbers 13 to 19, the number is said in this way can help deal with this anomaly.

Difficulty with working memory

Difficulties with short-term verbal memory may be apparent in the pupil having difficulty with remembering: numbers, multiplication tables or the sequences of a mathematical operation. A pupil's difficulties remembering numbers can be helped by his using concrete items with if necessary one-to-one tuition to help the pupil retain the numbers mentally. Memorising multiplication tables can be helped by table grids using visual patterns such as having some of the numbers coloured, allowing the use of visual sense as the pupil scrutinises the grid and auditory sense as he or another person says the numbers.

To help the pupil remember instructions and sequences of numbers, multi-sensory approaches (including allowing the pupil to talk through a calculation) are useful along with regular practice and over-learning, though not to the point of boredom. Mnemonics can help, such as SOHCAHTOA to remember the relationships for sine (opposite over hypotenuse), cosine (adjacent over hypotenuse) and tangent (opposite over adjacent).

In mental mathematics, the pupil may have difficulty retaining the necessary information and simultaneously processing it to calculate the solution. The teacher might make only one part of the task mental allowing the pupil to write down the key number and the sign for the mathematical operation. For the problem 8x9, the pupil would write down 8x and remember the 9 mentally then work out the calculation mentally.

Physical aids to memory such as number lines and multiplication squares can assist calculations. Visualising may help the pupil deal with otherwise abstract problems. The calculation, '9 + 7 = 16' would be visualised as 'I have nine books and I get another seven books making sixteen'. Some symbols can be remembered better with a visual clue. If the easily confused signs < and >

are remembered as crocodile teeth with the mouth open more widely for the bigger number, it is easier to remember that '8 < a' means '8 is smaller than a'.

Sequencing difficulties

Effective planning often rests on the pupil knowing the sequence in which the tasks need to be done and where this poses difficulties, careful explanations and step by step guidance are important. Using Mind Maps™, which allow information including sequences to be presented visually, may help the pupil with planning and organisation.

Normally, calculations for x, – and + involve working from right to left as in the calculation below where one begins on the right adding the five units and the three units then moves to the left to add the 1 ten and the 8 tens.

$$15 + $$
$$83$$
$$\overline{}$$
$$98$$

But when dividing, one works from left to right as in the calculation below in which one first divides the 8 tens by 2 then moves to the right to divide the 4 units by 2.

$$84 \div 2$$

Sequences of numbers 1, 2, 3, 4 and so on may be taught in small steps so that the pupil will first learn the sequence 1, 2 securely then 1, 2, 3 and so on over several sessions as necessary. Time sequences, such as the days of the week and the months of the year, can similarly be explicitly taught and practised using multi-sensory aids such as pictures or photographs associated with different days. Again the sequence can be learned in small steps. An example of teaching the sequence of numbers on an analogue clock face (which also relates to constructional difficulties) was provided in Chapter 19 on 'Reading disorder'.

Curriculum and assessment; pedagogy; resources; therapy/care and organisation

Curriculum and assessment

Attainment in mathematics will be lower than age average and levels of the curriculum may be lower than age typical in areas where mathematics is a major component such as physics, chemistry, biology and geography.

The balance of subjects may emphasise mathematics so that progress can be encouraged and supported. Within subjects the mathematics elements will be highlighted for support. Small steps of assessment may be used to demonstrate progress in mathematics.

Pedagogy

Pedagogy includes: the explicit practically orientated teaching of prerequisite skills; general approaches (e.g. providing extensive concrete experience), approaches relating to developmental co-ordination disorder (e.g. help with the alignment of number calculations) and approaches relating to dyslexia (e.g. support for phonological difficulties and mathematics language).

Resources

There appear to be no distinctive resources essential for mathematics disorder beyond the use of concrete materials suitable for all children.

Therapy/care

There appears to be no distinctive therapy essential for mathematics disorder.

Organisation

There is converging evidence that explicit systematic instruction with numerous opportunities for students to respond and to talk through their thinking is helpful to students with mathematics disorder (e.g. Gersten *et al.*, under review). See also the Instructional Research Group, California (www.inresg.org). Therefore classroom and group organisation that facilitates this is likely to aid learning.

Thinking points

Readers may wish to consider with reference to a particular school:

- the extent to which there is effective provision for the prerequisites to mathematics;
- the effectiveness of general approaches used;
- the degree to which there is suitable provision for mathematics difficulties related to DCD and reading disorder;
- how these approaches are rationalised into a comprehensive and coherent set of interventions;
- how effectiveness of the overall provision is monitored and improved.

Key texts

Campbell, J. (ed.) (2005) *Handbook of Mathematical Cognition*. New York, Taylor &Francis.
A collection of chapters by researchers into the cognitive and neurological processes underlying mathematical and numerical abilities.

Chin, S. and Ashcroft, R. (2006) (3rd edition) *Mathematics for Dyslexics, Including Dyscalculia*. London, Wiley.
Written with a United Kingdom context in mind, this book provides information on dyscalculia, research evidence and resources.

Dowker, A. (2005) *Individual Differences in Arithmetic: Implications for Psychology, Neuroscience and Education*. New York, Taylor & Francis.
Reviews research into areas including arithmetical abilities, causes of arithmetical difficulties and interventions.

Westwood, P. (2000) *Numeracy and Learning Difficulties: Approaches to Teaching and Assessment*. Melbourne, Australian Council for Educational Research.
This book examines the various ways students acquire mathematical skills and suggests flexible methods of teaching to accommodate these. Problem solving strategies and skills to improve numerical literacy are discussed.

Chapter 22

Conclusion

This volume has looked at provision considered effective with special children. Provision was taken to concern curriculum and assessment; pedagogy; resources; therapy/care; and organisation. These were examined in relation to learners with disabilities and disorders who are considered to require special education in order to make optimum academic and personal/social progress.

The book attempted to identify various categories of disorder/disability and link group characteristics to provision, at the same time recognising that approaches common to all children and specific to the individual children were still possible; and that children other than those with disability/disorder might sometimes benefit from aspects of approaches used with pupils having a disability/disorder.

Either within a chapter or at the end of it, the provision was outlined in terms of the elements mentioned above. In this final chapter, therefore, it remains to set out in accordance with these elements, aspects of provision for different disorders/disabilities, not exhaustively but to illustrate the provision for each disorder/disability.

Curriculum and assessment

Provision for pupils with profound cognitive impairment includes a broad and rich curriculum informed by early infant development and integrating therapy and care; and very small steps of assessment reflecting the pupils' levels of attainment and responses that may not necessarily reflect 'vertical' progress but also experiences and reactions to these. Regarding pupils with moderate to severe cognitive impairment, provision increasingly concerns areas of the curriculum and activities with a more recognisable subject basis. Visual recognition is important in literacy where pupils have difficulties with phonological awareness and in mathematics where pupils may have poor auditory memory. There is direct teaching of aspects of personal and social skills that age typical pupils might pick up more casually. Cross-curricular links are used to reinforce and consolidate learning with a practical emphasis. Assessment reflects the levels at which pupils are working, involves small steps to demonstrate progress and takes account of the need to record skills and knowledge acquired across the curriculum and practised or consolidated in different contexts. The curriculum for pupils with mild cognitive impairment, while recognising pupils are significantly behind age typical peers, is securely subject based but content is broken down (without being made fragmentary) to ensure concepts are understood. More time than is typical is spent on communication, basic skills and social and personal development and these subjects are embedded in other subjects through cross-curricular planning. Assessment reflects the levels of attainment evident in curriculum content.

For children with hearing impairment, curriculum content and related assessment is influenced by whether oral, sign bilingual and total communication methods predominate. For children with visual impairment, the curriculum balance emphasises the development and use of tactile, mobility and orientation skills and knowledge. Regarding children who are deafblind, the curriculum highlights communication, and cross-curricular audits of skills and understanding may be used.

Curricular provision for disruptive behaviour disorders for *children* include social skills training and anger management coping skills training, problem-solving skills and classroom contingency management. For disruptive behaviour disorders in *adolescents* provision includes: combination packages of adolescent focused interventions; and school-based interventions appeared effective. For children with anxiety disorders, curriculum arrangements may emphasise opportunities to express concerns, develop confidence and be part of generally supportive ethos. With regard to depressive disorders, curriculum arrangements and time allocations allow close liaison between teachers and therapists. The balance of curriculum subjects encourages open communication. For children with attention deficit hyperactivity disorder, the content and balance of the curriculum emphasises active experiential areas.

Concerning children with communication disorders of speech, grammar, comprehension, semantics and pragmatics, the content and balance of the curriculum emphasises communication and its support with respect to the difficulty concerned. For children with autism, curriculum content and balance emphasises communication, interaction and social skills while building in opportunities for the pupil to follow other interests of his own.

Regarding children with developmental co-ordination disorder, curriculum content and balance emphasises the development of motor skills and co-ordination.

Concerning curriculum content and balance: for reading disorder, it emphasises the development of literacy and its apparent underlying skills; for disorder of written expression, it prioritises the development of writing and its component skills; and for mathematics disorder, it emphasises the development of mathematics and its apparent underlying skills and cross-curricular planning embeds this and ensures its application.

For children with *orthopaedic impairment*, the curriculum ensures the best involvement and support of the pupil in activities where special equipment may be necessary. Within safety requirements, many activities may still be available in physical education for pupils with an *orthopaedic impairment*. The teacher liaises with the physiotherapist and occupational therapist and where special programmes are necessary to develop skills or encourage movement, these are planned into the pupil's school day. For a child with *health impairments*, the school supports families wherever they can and collaborates with parents and others to help ensure that the child is not excluded unnecessarily from any part of the school curriculum. Curriculum flexibility is necessary. Participation in sports and other physical education may be restricted according to weather conditions and curriculum opportunities may be modified following risk assessments for some activities. For some pupils time may have to be allocated to physiotherapy. Turning to pupils with *TBI*, the curriculum may need to be modified by breaking down content into smaller steps while ensuring it is not fragmentary and smaller steps for assessment may be necessary to show progress. In physical activities non-contact sports are encouraged and safe rules followed.

In general, it will be seen that the broad curriculum may be modified in terms of level and content (as for pupils with cognitive impairment). Particular areas or subjects of the curriculum may be planned at a lower than age typical level where there are difficulties with certain areas such as mathematics. Within subjects and areas of the curriculum, certain threads may be taught at lower than age typical levels, for example writing. Curriculum subjects, or areas or threads within these, may be emphasised, such as communication, numeracy, mobility or social development, by increasing time allocated to these areas. Careful cross-curricular planning is used to ensure that for areas that require emphasis and development, other aspects of the curriculum are closely related to them so that they are regularly highlighted in different contexts. Assessment is made in small steps as necessary to recognise progress in areas of difficulty.

Pedagogy

Regarding profound cognitive impairment, the organisation of the learning environment and routines are finely tuned to encouraging and responding to the smallest signs of interest and responsiveness. Multi-sensory approaches are used to stimulate the sense and to form a range of experiences that over time may come to have more coherent meaning as a sequence or as part of a wider whole such as a story or a complete activity. Approaches to communication draw on research into and experience of early infant communication and involve the adult communication partner being sensitive to the slightest response that might through the adult's response come to be invested with communicative meaning. Task analysis approaches are used and community-based vocational training skills may be developed. For moderate to severe cognitive impairment, visual modes are capitalised on in such methods as the use of symbols and manual signing. Communication is aided by augmentative and alternative communication and approaches such as the behaviour chain interruption strategy. Autonomy and independence are increasingly encouraged through developing choices and decision making and using visual cues to aid self-monitoring of performance in tasks. Regarding mild cognitive impairment, literacy approaches tend to emphasise phonics while not ignoring the reading context. In mathematics, as well as in the curriculum more generally, concrete experiences are used to help concept development. Also important are making learning relevant to life-relevant situations to aid generalisation, and a slower pace for lessons while ensuring they are engaging.

For pupils with hearing impairment, approaches to communication reflect differing valuations of oral, sign bilingual and total communication methods. Literacy teaching similarly reflects adherence to oral or sign bilingual methods. In mathematics, presentational order, early emphasis on counting avoiding potential confusions, and capitalising where deaf children have spatial strengths contribute. For children with visual impairment, pedagogy involves: tactile representation and hands-on experience and teaching ways of gaining rapid access to information; teaching orientation and mobility; aids to self-help and independence skills; developing speaking and listening taking into account the lack of or very limited visual cues, reading using tactile methods such as Braille and writing using tactile code. Regarding deafblind children, specialist approaches to encourage and develop communication include co-creative communication, resonance work and co-active movement. Non-symbolic communication is developed using reflexive responses, signals and place or object cues, while symbolic communication may be developed through objects of reference, tactile symbols and Moon script, manual sign language and communication books. Also important are structured opportunities to interact with others, the environment, objects, places and activities.

Pedagogic provision for disruptive behaviour disorders for *children* comprised parent training, social skills training and anger management coping skills training, problem-solving skills and classroom contingency management. For disruptive behaviour disorders in *adolescents* effective approaches include those drawing several interventions together in a multiple level package. No specific pedagogic approaches appear essential with regard to anxiety disorders. For depression, teaching methods contribute to developing a calm ethos. For children with attention deficit hyperactivity disorder, optimum breaks and a supportive structure in the classroom; a layout of the classroom reducing distractions; clear routines, clear instructions and guidance; and active, experiential learning are helpful. Social skills teaching and the development of compensatory skills are used.

In pedagogical provision for phonological disorders, approaches to raise phonological awareness are used as well as specific programmes. Error analysis and articulation exercises; and individual task-based programmes are employed. For some pupils, communicating through methods other than speech (e.g. signing, symbols) is necessary.

Difficulties with syntax and morphology are provided for by sentence recasting; elicited imitation and modelling. Also helpful is ensuring teacher communication is direct and clear. Where the child has problems with auditory memory, auditory sequencing, attention and reading and writing, remediating work is undertaken. In parallel, the teacher can more directly help the pupil improve grammatical skills and understanding.

Difficulties with comprehension are helped by teaching in modes to hold the pupil's attention and providing reminders; teaching listening behaviour; reducing processing demands; supporting pragmatic understanding; sensory and other aids and allowing sufficient time to respond. Regarding semantic difficulties, children having labelling difficulties may benefit from individual tutoring to enable such features as making links between the spoken word and the object or other phenomena and developing more securely the child's concepts through experience. Regarding packaging, the adult addresses underextended and overextended conceptual meaning by analysing and understanding the way the child perceives problematic concepts then correcting misconceptions. Networking problems are addressed through careful identification and explicit teaching. Pragmatic difficulties are helped by such interventions as teaching and practising indications of speakers' intentions, and conversational skills building. Approaches used for pupils with autism (and as appropriate for Asperger's syndrome) include: 'Structured teaching'; the Lovaas programme; Intensive Interaction; Picture Exchange Communication system and manual signing; social stories and family support and parent training.

With regard to *developmental co-ordination disorder*, focuses for provision have been handwriting (help with posture, pencil grip/pressure, assisting eye-hand co-ordination for writing, multi-sensory approaches to improve form consistency and strategies for teaching the writing of letter shapes). In physical education, the teacher and physiotherapist liaise to develop suitable activities and lessons are planned to enable the participation of pupils with DCD. For personal and social skills, practical strategies and aids (e.g. adapted clothing) are developed to improve these.

For *reading disorder*, strategies used are those relating to possible associated difficulties: phonological difficulties, visual difficulties and visual processing difficulties, auditory perception and auditory processing difficulties, short-term verbal memory difficulties, sequencing difficulties – temporal order. Direct provision for reading tends to teach phonological skills necessary for using a phonemic code, and sound-symbol correspondences. Provision for *writing and spelling*, includes: remediating sequencing, improving co-ordination skills for handwriting and teaching cursive script. For writing composition, approaches may be frameworks for writing, reducing task demands, note taking and writing for a purpose. Spelling provision uses multi-sensory aspects, Directed Spelling Thinking Activity, repetition and target words. Provision for *mathematics disorder* focuses on prerequisite skills and how they may be taught. There are also general interventions. Other strategies draw on the influence of related conditions particularly developmental co-ordination disorder and reading disorder.

Pedagogy for pupils with *orthopaedic impairment* is not in itself distinctive from the pedagogy for children not having a disability/disorder. The issue is gaining access to the curriculum and to learning activities and in this, the use of specialist resources is important as the section below illustrates. The impact of other *health impairment* can vary from time to time because of variations in the condition but also because of different demands of the curriculum or the child's peer group. Therefore the child's educational provision needs to be responsive to changes in the child's physical and motor abilities and sensitive to the physical, psychological and any other effects of the medical condition. Particular requirements arise such as, for a child with epilepsy, having a structured framework and routine in which to locate information to help the student with information processing. For a child with *TBI*, pedagogy involves assisting attention (e.g. by routines, and clear instructions); aiding memory (e.g. presenting information repeatedly enabling extra rehearsal). Helping the child with visual functioning difficulties is likely to draw on assessments and advice of the ophthalmologist and occupational therapist. The child's positioning, for example at a desk, and the positioning of work surfaces, require care. The classroom environment is more comprehensible if it is orderly. Where the child experiences visual perception problems, materials such as texts used for teaching may be simplified. The amount of written work required might be reduced and extra time allowed to complete it. Impulse control may be helped (e.g. by teaching the child 'self-talk') and self-monitoring is encouraged. For younger children, social interactions might be more structured than usual. The teacher and others contribute to helping the children communicate, working closely with the speech and language pathologist/ therapist as necessary. Communications from the teacher need to be clear and understandable to the child and other systems of communication may be used temporarily. Among approaches to managing and behaviour and reducing problems are: behaviour management strategies, psychotherapy (individual and family) and environmental modifications and supports.

Resources

For pupils with profound cognitive impairment, technology is used to enable links to be made between the child's behaviour and what happens in the environment. With regard to moderate to severe cognitive impairment, technology is used to improve physical, supportive and cognitive access to the curriculum. For mild cognitive impairment, no distinctive resources appear essential other than a varied range of concrete apparatus and materials.

Concerning hearing impairment, the maintenance of hearing aids is encouraged. Regarding visual impairment, resources include: low vision devices and lighting; Braille or Moon materials and computer technology. For children who are deafblind, physical aids to mobility include tactile maps and clues in rooms and corridors.

For communication disorders relating to speech, as an alternative or augmentation to speech, computer aided communication may be necessary. For autism, resources include visual timetables and other materials emphasising visual clues.

For reading disorder, reading materials particularly supporting the development of phonics are used. Computer programmes are used to aid skills development. For disorder of written expression, computer software is used for essay structure and others support of writing. For mathematics disorder, there is an emphasis on concrete resources.

The choice of resources and their use for children with *orthopaedic impairment* will involve guidance from the physical therapist or the occupational therapist. Resources are used to ensure that children are correctly positioned and furniture takes account of pupil's stature and need for good posture and support. Hoists, assistive walking devices, or manual or powered wheelchairs may be used. Access to classrooms and other facilities is ensured. Also provided are separate rooms for personal care procedures. Toilets are adapted. Environmental modifications are made in terms of location of materials and equipment; work surface modifications and object modifications. Others issues are object stabilisation; boundaries and grasping aids and manipulation aids. Environmental control may involve the use of appliances such as communication devices. For a child with *health impairments*, resources may be required, depending on the condition and its severity, for example, the possible use of standing aids for a child with congenital heart defect where lessons require long periods of standing. Architectural/organisational implications include that, where the school building has stairs, the school may ensure that the classroom and other facilities are on the lower floor or minimise the necessity of stair climbing or a lift may be used (e.g. for a child with a heart condition). For children with *TBI*, resources may include adaptive equipment to help function, such as a wheelchair (which may be used temporarily or for some activities and not others), and environmental modifications. Technology may be used for example to help manual dexterity. Depending on the exact nature and consequences of the *TBI*, resources associated with *orthopaedic impairment* may be uses.

No specific resources appear essential for: disruptive behaviour disorders, anxiety disorders, depression or ADHD; developmental co-ordination disorder or for communication disorders concerning grammar, comprehension, semantics and pragmatics.

Therapy

For children with profound cognitive impairment, educational, therapeutic and care provision takes account of sensory impairment, physical disability and medical conditions. Regarding pupils with moderate to severe cognitive impairment, educational, therapeutic and care provision takes account of any sensory impairment, physical disability and medical conditions. For children with mild cognitive impairment, therapy and other support are provided for any 'additional' communication disorders and conduct disorder or anxiety or depressive disorder.

With reference to children with hearing impairment, or visual impairment, no specific therapy appears essential unless the child has other disabilities. Provision for children who are deafblind includes that the particularly wide range of professionals involved work together closely.

Provision for disruptive behaviour disorders for *children* comprised parent training. For disruptive behaviour disorders in *adolescents* provision includes family-based interventions, teaching family model in-group homes and fostering. For generalised anxiety disorder provision includes: cognitive-behavioural therapy, cognitive-behavioural therapy plus family management and focal psychodynamic psychotherapy. For obsessive-compulsive disorder provision includes medication, cognitive-behavioural therapy, combinations of medication and cognitive-behavioural therapy. Specific and social phobias respond to behavioural interventions and cognitive-behavioural therapy. For separation anxiety disorder, group cognitive behavioural therapy has been used. Regarding depressive disorders (major depressive disorder and dysthymic disorder), provision for adolescents includes: cognitive behaviour therapy with the concurrent treatment of any maternal depression, Interpersonal Therapy Adapted for Adolescents and the administration of serotonin reuptake inhibitors. Provision for attention deficit hyperactivity disorder includes medication, usually a psychostimulant drug such as methylphenidate; behaviour management training and a combination of the two. Parent training and support and biofeedback are also used.

With regard to children with communication disorders of speech, then speech and language therapy is provided. Surgical procedures may be used for conditions such as cleft palate. For a child with communication disorders of grammar, comprehension, semantics, or pragmatics, speech and language therapy is provided as necessary. For children with autism, musical interaction therapy may be used.

Concerning a child with developmental co-ordination disorder, physiotherapy is important, with the physiotherapist working closely with teachers and others of programmes and assessment. For a child with reading disorder, speech and language therapy may support the development of phonological skills.

For children with *orthopaedic impairments*, the support of services other than education is generally required. Medical practitioners, physiotherapists, occupational therapists, prosthetists and others contribute to the child's well being. Health care professionals provide training for school staff in intimate care procedures before these are carried out. Pastoral care will support the development of high self-esteem and counselling may be available to allow the pupil to talk through issues such restrictions on activities, developing relationships and so on. For a child with *health impairments*, medical intervention can include surgery to try to correct the abnormality or improve function, for example in the case of a congenital heart condition. Teachers and paraprofessionals carrying out specialised health care procedures, require sufficient training, help in developing policies and technical help. An important contribution is made by the individualised health care plan, developed under the guidance and leadership of a health care professional. School staff need to be aware of medical requirements and properly trained. The pastoral system may include opportunities for counselling. Staff are trained and supported to carry out any necessary procedures or to be aware of the implications of particular symptoms and how to act is important. The pastoral system may include opportunities for counselling and other provision to help raise self-esteem, help teenagers recognise and deal with the stress associated with delayed sexual maturity, support pupils with life limiting conditions or other matters. Regarding *TBI*, the speech and language therapist/pathologist has an important role in assessing the child with *TBI* drawing on standardised assessments of the child, interviews with parents and teacher, observing the child, making a curriculum-based language assessment and sampling narrative language. The SLP/SLT may work directly with him or in a consultancy role through others such as the parents and teacher who have regular contact with the child. Support for the child and the family may be provided by various professionals.

For disorder of written expression, and for mathematics disorder, no specific therapy/care appears essential.

Organisation

For a pupil with profound cognitive impairment, arrangements may include room management/responsive environment.

When a pupil has hearing impairment, the classroom is organised to optimise listening to and seeing others speakers. For a child with visual impairment, the classroom is organised to reduce background noise. For a child who is deafblind, the classroom is organised to optimise any hearing and visual sensitivity the child may have.

For autism, classroom physical structure adds meaning and context to environment (e.g. Structured Teaching) and is organised to reduce difficulties, e.g. daily schedule.

Turning to children with *orthopaedic impairments*, the school may adopt flexible arrival and departure times for lessons. If the pupil requires adult oversight of movement between lessons, and he leaves with other students, the adult can keep at a distance that does not inhibit the student's social contact with peers. Outside classroom, the level of supervision necessary for recess times will be determined to balance safety with encouraging socialisation and independence. Similarly in class where adult support is needed this should be given only as required encouraging the pupil to develop independence. Where trips and visits are planned, pre-visits can help check details of physical access. Flexible arrangements for pupil absences can include home tuition and emailed work to support home study. Where there are particular hazards, a risk assessment or similar procedure is carried out. Moving and handling some pupils with physical disability has potential hazards and risk assessments may be carried out on these procedures, supported by training for the adults involved. Fire procedures take into account any particular issues arising. Safety procedures are followed where adults help students in wheelchairs with steps using devices such as a 'stair climber'. Procedures and responsibilities for administering medication will be clear and supported by staff training as necessary. For a child with *health impairments*, school building design and use is important and care is taken in ensuring where necessary the child does not unduly exert himself because of carrying equipment round school. Risk assessments are made to avoid situations and activities that may affect the child adversely. Where necessary, flexible timescales for returning homework and possible home tuition are employed. Higher levels of supervision may be needed. Extra supervision may be necessary sometimes at specific times such as mealtimes or recess to ensure dietary or medication procedures are followed by pupils. The level of supervision for a child with *TBI* is an important consideration, ensuring it assists safety but does not damage social contact with peers. To encourage attention, the classroom layout (and physical aspects) should minimise distractions and the child may be taught, at least for a time, in small groups.

No distinctive organisation appears essential for: moderate to severe cognitive impairment, mild cognitive impairment; disruptive behaviour disorders (oppositional defiance disorder, conduct disorder), anxiety disorders, depression, attention deficit hyperactivity disorder; communication disorders whether of speech, grammar, comprehension, semantics or pragmatics; developmental co-ordination disorder, reading disorder, disorder of written expression or mathematics disorder.

Other aspects of provision

Other aspects of provision included for hearing impairment, visual impairment and deafblindness, specialist teachers. For disruptive behaviour disorder, parent training was suggested for children, family-based interventions and teaching family model in group homes/foresting for adolescents and for both, multi-agency working. For adolescents with mild depression, where cognitive behavioural therapy is indicated, concurrent treatment for any maternal depression was suggested. For children and young people with attention deficit hyperactivity disorder, and for autism, parent support and training is suggested.

Thinking points

Readers may wish to consider:

- The inter-relating contribution of elements of provision (curriculum and assessment, pedagogy, resources, therapy/care, and organisation) to different types of disability/disorder.
- The practical implications of educating pupils with predominantly different types of disorder/disability together for some or all of their education.
- The relative contributions of ordinary schools, units/resource rooms, special schools in provision for special children to ensure their optimum educational progress and personal and social development.

Bibliography

Abbeduto, L. and Hesketh, L. J. (1997) 'Pragmatic development in individuals with mental retardation: Learning to use language in social interactions', *Mental Retardation and Developmental Disabilities Research Reviews* 3: 323–33.

Achenbach, T. M. and Edelbrock, C. S. (1983) *Manual for the Child Behaviour Checklist and Revised Child Behaviour Profile*. Burlington, Department of Psychiatry, University of Vermont.

Adams, C., Byers Brown, B. and Edwards, M. (1997) (2nd edition) *Developmental Disorders of Language*. London, Whurr.

Addy, L. M. (2004) *Speed Up! A Kinaesthetic Approach to Handwriting*. Cambridge, LDA Ltd.

Ahonen, T., Kooistra, L., Viholainen, H. *et al*. (2004) 'Developmental motor learning disability: A neuropsychological approach', in Dewy, D. and Tupper, D. E. (eds) *Developmental Motor Disorders: A Neuropsychological Perspective*. New York, Guilford Press.

Aird, R. (2001) *The Education and Care of Children with Severe, Profound and Multiple Learning Difficulties*. London, David Fulton Publishers.

Aitchison, J. (1987) *Words in the Mind: An Introduction to the Mental Lexicon*. Oxford, Basil Blackwell.

Aitken, S. (2000) 'Understanding deafblindness', in Aitken, S., Buultjens, M. and Clark, C. *et al*. (eds) *Teaching Children who are Deafblind: Contact, Communication and Learning*. London, David Fulton Publishers.

Aitken, S., Buultjens, M. and Clark, C. *et al*. (eds) (2000) *Teaching Children who are Deafblind: Contact, Communication and Learning*. London, David Fulton Publishers.

Aldred, C., Green, J. and Adams, C. (2004) 'A new social communication intervention for children with autism: Pilot randomised controlled treatment study suggesting effectiveness', *Journal of Child Psychology and Psychiatry* 45: 1420–30.

Aldrich, F. K. and Parkin, A. J. (1989) 'Listening at speed', *British Journal of Visual Impairment* 7 (1): 16–18.

Alexander, J. F. and Parsons, B. V. (1982) *Functional Family Therapy*. Monterey, CA, Brooks/Cole.

Alexander, J. F., Waldron, H. B., Newberry, A. M. *et al*. (1988) 'Family approaches to treating delinquents', in Nunnally, E. W., Chilman, C. S. and Cox, F. M. (eds) *Mental Illness, Delinquency, Addictions and Neglect*. Newbury Park, CA, Sage, pp. 128–46.

Allen, J., Brown, S. and Riddell, S. (1998) 'Permission to speak? Theorising special education inside the classroom', in Clark, C., Dyson, A. and Millward, A. (eds) *Theorising Special Education*. London, Routledge.

Alton, S. (2001) 'Children with Down's syndrome and short term auditory memory', *Down's Syndrome Association Journal* 95 (Winter): 4–9.

American Psychiatric Association (2000) *Diagnostic and Statistical Manual of Mental Disorders*, Fourth Edition Text Revision. Washington, DC, APA.

Anastopoulos, A. D. and Farley, S. E. (2003) 'A cognitive-behavioural training program for parents of children with attention-deficit/hyperactivity disorder', in Kazdin, A. E. and Weisz, T. R. (eds) *Evidence Based Psychotherapies for Children and Adolescents*. New York, The Guilford Press. pp. 187–203.

Anderson-Wood, L. and Smith, B. R. (1997) *Working with Pragmatics: A Practical Guide to Promoting Communicative Competence*. Bicester, Winslow Press.

Antia, S. D. (1998) 'School and classroom characteristics that facilitate the social integration of deaf and hard of hearing children', in Weisel, A. (ed.) *Issues Unresolved: New Perspectives on Language and Deaf Education*. Washington, DC, Gallaudet University Press. pp. 148–60.

Antidote (2003) *The Emotional Literacy Handbook*. London, David Fulton Publishers.

Appleton, R. and Gibbs, J. (1998) *Epilepsy in Childhood and Adolescence*. London, Dunitz.

Armitage, I. M., Burke, J. P. and Buffin, J. T. (1995) 'Visual impairment in severe and profound sensorineural deafness', *Archives of Diseases in Childhood* 73: 53–6.

Armstrong, T. (2006) 'Canaries in the coal mine: The symptoms of children labelled "ADHD" as biocultural feedback', in Lloyd, G., Stead, J. and Cohen, D. (eds) *Critical New Perspectives on ADHD*. New York, Routledge.

Arvio, M. and Sillanpaa, M. (2003) 'Prevalence, aetiology and comorbidity of severe and profound intellectual disability in Finland', *Journal of Intellectual Disability Research* 47(2): 108–12.

Asperger, A. (1944) 'Autistischen Psychopathen in Kindesalter', *Archiv fur Psychiatrie und Nervenkrankheiten* 177: 76–136.

Atwood, A., Frith, U. and Hermelin, B., (1988) 'The understanding and use of interpersonal gestures by autistic and Down's syndrome children', *Journal of Autism and Developmental Disorders* 18: 241–57.

Avery, M. E. and First, L. R. (1994) *Paediatric Care*. Baltimore, Williams and Wilkins.

Ayres, A. J. (1989) *Sensory Integration and Praxis Tests*. Los Angeles, CA, Western Psychological Services.

Ayers, H. and Prytys, C. (2002) *An A to Z Practical Guide to Emotional and Behavioural Difficulties*. London, David Fulton Publishers.

Bailey, J. (1998) 'Medical and psychological models in special needs education', in Clark, C., Dyson, A. and Millward, A. (eds) *Theorising Special Education*. London, Routledge.

Baker, R. (1990) 'Developing literacy skills through dialogue journals', in *Bilingual Education for Deaf Children: From Policy to Practice*. Nottingham, Laser Conference Proceedings.

Bandura, A. (1977) *Social Learning Theory*. Englewood Cliffs, N J, Prentice-Hall.

Bandura, A. (1986) *Social Foundations of Thought and Action: A Social Cognitive Theory*. Englewood Cliffs, NJ, Prentice-Hall.

Bandura, A. and Walters, R. (1959) *Adolescent Aggression*. New York, Ronald Press.

Banks, J., Gray, P. and Fyfe, R. (1990) 'The written recall of printed stories by severely deaf children', *British Journal of Educational Psychology* 60: 192–206.

Barker, P. (1998) *Michel Foucault: An Introduction*. Edinburgh, Edinburgh University Press.

Barkley, R. (1997) *ADHD and the Nature of Self Control*. New York, Guilford.

Barkley, R. A., Shelton, T. L., Crosswait, C. C. *et al.* (2000) 'Multi-method psychoeducational intervention for preschool children with disruptive behaviour: Preliminary results at post treatment', *Journal of Child Psychology and Psychiatry* 41(3): 319–32.

Barnes, C. and Mercer, G. (1996) *Exploring the Divide: Illness and Disability*. Leeds, Leeds Disability Press.

Baroff, G. S. (1999) 'General Learning Disorder: A New Designation for Mental Retardation', *Mental Retardation* 37 (1): 68–70.

Baron-Cohen, S. (2000) *Understanding Others' Minds*. Oxford, Oxford University Press.

Barrett, P. M., Dadds, M. R. and Rapee, R. M. (1996) 'Family treatment for childhood anxiety: A controlled trial', *Journal of Consulting and Clinical Psychology* 64: 333–42.

Battista, M.T. (1999) 'The mathematical miseducation of America's youth: Ignoring research and scientific study in education', *Phi Delta Kappan* 80(6): 425–433.

Beaton, A. A. (2004) *Dyslexia, Reading and the Brain: A Sourcebook of Biological and Psychological Research*. London, Psychology Press.

Beirne-Smith, M. Ittenbach, R. F. and Patton, J. R. (2002) (6th edition) *Mental Retardation*. Upper Saddle River, NJ, Prentice-Hall.

Beitchman, J. H. and Young, A. R. (1997) 'Learning disorders with a special emphasis on reading disorders: A review of the past ten years', *Journal of the American Academy of Child and Adolescent Psychiatry* 40: 75–82.

Bellugi, U., O'Grady, L., Lillo-Martin, M. *et al.* (1994) 'Enhancement of spatial cognition in deaf children', in Volterra, V. and Erting, C. (eds) *From Gesture to Language in Hearing and Deaf Children*. Washington, DC, Galluadet University Press.

Benbow, M. (1990) *Loops and other Groups: A Kinaesthetic Writing System*. Tucson, AZ, Therapy Skill Builders.

Benbow, M. (2002) 'Hand skills and handwriting', in Cermak, S. A. and Larkin, D. (eds) *Developmental Coordination Disorder*. Albany, NY, Delmar Thompson Learning. pp. 248–79.

Berch, D. B. (2005) 'Making sense of number sense: Implications for children with mathematical disabilities', *Journal of Learning Disabilities* 38(4): 333–39.

Berninger, V. W. (1994) 'Future directions for research on writing disabilities: Integrating endogenous and exogenous variables', in Lyon, G. R. (ed.) *Frames of Reference for the Assessment of Learning Disabilities*. Baltimore, Brookes. pp. 419–40.

Berninger, V. W. and Amtmann, D. (2003) 'Preventing written expression disabilites through early and continuing assessment and intervetion for handwriting and/or spelling problems: Research into Practice' in Swanson, H., Harris, K. R. and Graham, S. (eds) *Handbook of Learning Disabilities*. New York. Guilford. pp. 345–63.

Bernstein, G. A. and Borchardt, C. M. (1991) 'Anxiety disorders of childhood and adolescence: A critical review', *Journal of the American Academy of Child and Adolescent Psychiatry* 30(4): 519–32.

Best, A. B. (1992) *Teaching Children with Visual Impairments*. Milton Keynes, Open University Press.

Best, S. J. and Bigge, J. L. (2001) 'Multiple disabilities', in Bigge, J. L., Best, S. J. and Heller, K. W. (eds) (4th edition) *Teaching Individuals with Physical, Health or Multiple Disabilities*. Upper Saddle River, NJ, Merrill-Prentice-Hall.

Biederman, J., Newcorn, J. and Sprich, S. (1991) 'Comorbidity of attention deficit hyperactivity disorder with conduct, depressive, anxiety and other disorders', *American Journal of Psychiatry* 148(5): 564–77.

Bigge, J. L., Stump, C. S., Spagna, M. E. *et al.* (1999) *Curriculum, Assessment, and Instruction for Students with Disabilities*. Belmont, CA, Wadsworth.

Bigge, J. L., Best, S. J. and Heller, K. W. (2001) (4th edition) *Teaching Individuals with Physical, Health or Multiple Disabilities*. Upper Saddle River, NJ, Merrill-Prentice-Hall.

Birmaher, B., Ryan, N. D., Williamson, D. E. *et al.*(1996) 'Childhood and adolescent depression: A review of the past ten years. Part 1, *Journal of the American Academy of Child and Adolescent Psychiatry* 35(11): 1427–39.

Bishop, D. V. M. (1997) *Uncommon Understanding: Development and Disorders of Understanding in Children*. Hove, Psychology Press.

Bishop, D. V. M. (2000) 'Pragmatic language impairment: A correlate of SLI, a distinct subgroup, or a part of the autistic continuum?', in Bishop, D. V. M. and Leonard, L. B. (eds) *Speech and Language Impairments in Children: Causes, Characteristics, Intervention and Outcome.* Philadelphia, PA and Hove UK, Psychology Press.

Black, K. and Haskins, D. (1996) 'Including all children in TOP PLAY and BT TOP SPORT', *British Journal of Physical Education*, Primary PE Focus, Winter edition 9(11).

Blagg, N. R. and Yule, W. (1984) 'The behavioural treatment of school refusal: A comparative study', *Behaviour Research and Therapy* 22(2): 119–27.

Blanchard, E. B. (1970) 'Relative contributions of modelling, informational influences, and physical contact in extinction of phobic behaviour', *Journal of Abnormal Psychology* 76: 55–61.

Blosser, J. L. and DePompei, R. (1994) 'Creating an effective classroom environment', in Savage, R. C. and Wolcott, G. F. (eds) *Educational Dimensions of Acquired Brain Injury.* Austin, TX, Pro-Ed. pp. 413–51.

Bonati, M. (2006) 'The Italian saga of ADHD and its treatment', in Lloyd, G., Stead, J. and Cohen, D. (eds) *Critical New Perspectives on ADHD.* New York, Routledge.

Bondy, A. S. and Frost, L. A. (1994) 'The picture communication system', *Focus on Autistic Behaviour* 9(3): 1–9.

Borduin, C. M. (1999) 'Multi-systemic treatment of criminality and violence in adolescents', *Journal of the American Academy for Child and Adolescent Psychiatry* 38(3): 242–9.

Borger, N. and Van der Meer, J. (2000) 'Visual behaviour of ADHD children during an attention test', *Journal of Child Psychology and Psychiatry* 4(4): 525–32.

Borkowski, J. G., Chan, L. K. S. and Muthukrishna, N. (2000) 'A process-oriented model of metacognition: Links between motivation and executive functioning', in Schraw, G. and Impara, J. C. (eds) *Issues in the Measurement of Metacognition.* Lincoln, NE, Buros Institute of Mental Measurements. pp. 1–41.

Borkowski, J. G., Carothers, S. S., Howard, K. *et al.*(2006) 'Intellectual assessment and intellectual disability', in Jacobson, J. W., Mulick, J. A. and Rojhan, J. (eds) *Handbook of Mental Retardation and Developmental Abilities.* New York, Springer.

Braden, J. P. (1994) *Deafness, Deprivation and IQ.* London, Plenum Press.

Brady, K. D. (2001) 'How TBI affects learning and thinking', in Schoenbrodt, L. (ed.) *Children with Traumatic Brain Injury: A Parent's Guide.* Bethesda, MD, Woodbine House.

Bransford, J. D., Delclos, V. R., Vye, N. J. *et al.* (1986) 'State of the art and future direction', in Lidz, C. S. (ed.) *Dynamic Assessment: An Interactional Approach to Evaluating Learning Potential.* New York: Guilford Press. pp. 479–96.

Brenner, C. (1973, revised edition) *An Elementary Textbook of Psychoanalysis.* New York, International Universities.

Brent, D. A., Kolko, D., Birmaher, B. *et al.* (1998) 'Predictors of treatment efficacy in a clinical trial of three psychosocial treatments for adolescent depression', *Journal of the American Academy for Child and Adolescent Psychiatry* 37(9): 906–14.

British Deaf Association (1996) *The Right to be Equal: British Deaf Association Policy.* London, BDA.

Brooks, G. (2002) *What Works for Reading Difficulties? The Effectiveness of Intervention Schemes.* London, Department of Education and Science.

Bundy, A. (2002) 'Play in children with DCD: What we know and what we suspect', 5th Biennial *Conference on Developmental Co-ordination Disorders.* Bannf, Alberta, Canada.

Butler, F. M., Miller, S. P., Lee, K. *et al.*(2001) 'Teaching mathematics to students with mild to moderate mental retardation: A review of the literature', *Mental Retardation* 39(1): 20–31.

Butterworth, B. (2004) *Dyscalculia Screener.* Swindon, NFER-Nelson.

Campbell, J. and Oliver, M. (1996) *Disability Politics: Understanding Our Past, Changing Our Future*. London, Routledge.

Campbell, M., Schopler, E. Cueva, J. E. *et al.* (1996) 'Treatment of autistic disorder', *Journal of the American Academy for Child and Adolescent Psychiatry* 35(2): 134–43.

Campbell, R. and Wright, H. (1990) 'Deafness and immediate memory for pictures: Dissociations between "inner speech" and the "Inner ear"', *Journal of Experimental Child Psychology* 50(2): 259–86.

Cantell, M., Kooistra, L. and Larkin, D. (2001) 'Approaches to intervention for children with developmental coordination disorder', *New Zealand Journal of Disability Studies* 9: 106–19.

Capute, A. J. and Accardo, P. J. (1996) 'Cerebral palsy: the spectrum of motor dysfunction', in Capute, A. J. and Accardo, P. J. (eds) *Developmental Disabilities in Infancy and Childhood, volume 2*. Baltimore, MD, Brookes.

Carey, W. B. (2002) 'Is ADHD a valid disorder?', in Jensen, P. S. and Cooper, J. R. (eds) *Attention Deficit Hyperactivity Disorder: State of the Science. Best Practices*. Kingston, NJ, Civic Research Institute.

Carlson, C. L., Pelham, W. E., Milich, R. *et al.* (1992) 'Single and combined effects of methylphenidate and behaviour therapy on the classroom performance of children with attention deficit hyperactivity disorder', *Journal of Abnormal Child Psychology* 20: 213–32.

Carpenter, B. (1994) 'Finding a home for the sensory curriculum', *PMLD Link* 19: 2–3.

Carr, A. (2000) *What Works with Children and Adolescents?* London, Routledge.

Carr, A. (2006) (2nd edition) *The Handbook of Child and Adolescent Clinical Psychology: A Contextual Approach*. London, Routledge.

Carter, M. and Grunsell, J. (2001) 'The behaviour chain interruption strategy: A review of research and discussion of future directions', *Journal for the Association of the Severely Handicapped* 26(1): 37–49.

Case-Smith, J. and Bryant, T. (1999) 'The effects of occupational therapy with sensory integration emphasis on preschool age children with autism', *American Journal of Occupational Therapy* 53(5): 489–97.

Cattanach, A. (2003) *Introduction to Play Therapy*. Hove, U.K., Brunner-Routledge.

Cawley, J., Parmar, R., Foley, T. *et al.* (2001) 'Arithmetic performance of students: Implications for standards and programming', *Exceptional Children* 67(3): 311–28.

Cermak, S. A. and Larkin, D. (2002) *Developmental Coordination Disorder*. Albany, NY, Delmar Thompson Learning.

Cermak, S. A. Gubbay, S. S. and Larkin, D. (2002) 'What is developmental co-ordination disorder?', in Cermak, S. A. and Larkin, D. (eds) *Developmental Co-ordination Disorder*. Albany, NY, Delmar.

Chamberlain, P. and Moore, K. J. (1998) 'A clinical model for parenting juvenile offenders: A comparison of group care versus family care', *Clinical Child Psychology and Psychiatry* 3: 375–86.

Christensen, J. R. (2001) 'What is Traumatic Brain Injury?', in Schoenbrodt, L. (ed.) *Children with Traumatic Brain Injury: A Parent's Guide*. Bethesda, MD, Woodbine House.

Clark, C. (2000) 'Personal and social development', in Aitken, S., Buultjens, M. and Clark, C. *et al.* (eds) *Teaching Children who are Deafblind: Contact, Communication and Learning*. London, David Fulton Publishers.

Clarke, G. N., Rohde, P., Lewinsohn, P. M. *et al.* (1999) 'Cognitive-behavioural treatment of adolescent depression: Efficacy of acute group treatment and booster sessions', *Journal of the American Academy for Child and Adolescent Psychiatry* 38: 272–9.

Clough, C. (1999) 'Teaching cursive writing', *OT Practice* 4(8): 41–2.

Cockerill, H. and Carrollfew, L. (2007) *Communicating without Speech: Practical Augmentative and Alternative Communication for Children*. New York, Blackwell Publishers.

Cohen, D. (2006) 'Critiques of the "ADHD" enterprise', in Lloyd, G., Stead, J. and Cohen, D. (eds) *Critical New Perspectives on ADHD*. New York, Routledge.

Committee on Educational Interventions for Children with Autism (2001) *Educating Children with Autism*. Washington, DC, National Academy Press.

Cooper, P. and O'Regan, F. J. (2001) *Educating Children with AD/HD*. London, Routledge-Falmer

Copeland, S. R. and Hughes, C. (2000) 'Acquisition of a picture prompt strategy to increase independent performance', *Education and Training in Mental Retardation and Developmental Disabilities* 35(3): 294–305.

Corkin, S. (1974) 'Serial order deficits in inferior readers', *Neuropsychologia* 12(3): 347–354.

Cornish, U. and Ross, F. (2003) *Social Skills Training for Adolescents with General Moderate Learning Difficulties*. London, Jessica Kingsley Publishers.

Cousins, L. S. and Weiss, G. (1993) 'Parent training and social skills training for children with attention deficit hyperactivity disorder: How can they be combined for greater effectiveness?', *Canadian Journal of Psychiatry* 38: 449–57.

Crawford, S. G., Wilson, B. N. and Dewey, D. (2001) 'Identifying developmental co-ordination disorder: Consistency between tests', in *Children with Developmental Co-ordination Disorder: Strategies for Success*. Binghamton, NY, Hawthorne Press.

Crocker, A. C. (1992) 'Human immunodeficiency virus', in Levine, M. D., Carey, W. B. and Crocker, A. C. (eds) *Developmental-behavioural Paediatrics*. Philadelphia, PA, W. B. Saunders. pp. 271–5.

Cutting, L. E. and Denckla, M. B. (2003) 'Attention: Relationships between Attention-Deficit Hyperactivity Disorder and Learning Disability', in Swanson, H. L., Harris, K. R. and Graham, S. (eds) *Handbook of Learning Disabilities*. New York, The Guilford Press.

DAHISS (1996) *English as a Foreign Language Curriculum*. Leeds, Leeds Deaf and Hearing Impaired Support Service.

Davis, J. (2006) 'Disability, childhood studies and the construction of medical discourses–Questioning attention deficit hyperactivity disorder: A theoretical perspective', in Lloyd, G., Stead, J. and Cohen, D. (eds) *Critical New Perspectives on ADHD*. New York, Routledge.

Day, J. (1995) (2nd edition) *Access Technology: Making the Right Choice*. Coventry, National Council for Educational Technology.

Deaf Education Through Listening and Talking (1997) *The Right to Hear and be Heard: Raising Standards in the Education of Deaf Children*. Haverhill, DELTA.

Dean, E., Howell, J. and Waters, D. (1990) *Metaphon Resource Pack*. Windsor, NFER-Nelson.

DeGrandepre, R. (1998) *Ritalin Nation: Rapid-fire Culture and the Transformation of Human Consciousness*. New York, W. W. Norton and Company.

Dehaene, S., Dehaene-Lambertz, G. and Cohen, L. (1998) 'Abstract representations of numbers in the animal and human brain', *Trend in Neuroscience* 21(8): 355–61.

De La Paz, S., Swanson, P. and Graham, S. (1998) 'The contribution of executive control to the revising of students with writing and learning difficulties', *Journal of Educational Psychology* 90(3): 448–60.

Denton, D. (1996) 'The philosophy of total communication', *Supplement to British Deaf News*. Carlisle, British Deaf Association.

Department for Education and Skills (2001a) *The National Numeracy Strategy Guidance to Support Pupils with Dyslexia and Dyscalculia*. London, DfES.

Department for Education and Skills (2001b) *Special Educational Needs Code of Practice.* London, DfES.

Department for Education and Skills (2005) (2nd edition) *Data Collection by Special Educational Need.* London, DfES.

De Silva, P., Rachman, S. and Rachman, J. (1998) *Obsessive-Compulsive Disorder: The Facts.* Oxford, Oxford University Press.

Detheridge, T. and Stevens, C. (2001) 'Information and communication technology', in Carpenter, B., Ashdown, R. and Bovair, K. (eds) *Enabling Access: Effective Teaching and earning for Pupils with Learning Difficulties.* London, David Fulton Publishers. pp. 156–69.

DeVeaugh-Geiss, J., Moroz, G., Beiderman, J. *et al.* (1992) 'Clomipramine in child and adolescent obsessive- compulsive disorder: A multicenter trail', *Journal of the American Academy of Child and Adolescent Psychiatry* 31(1): 45–9.

Dewey, D. (2002) 'Subtypes of developmental coordination disorder' in Cermak, S. A. and Larkin, D. (eds) *Developmental Coordination Disorder.* Albany, NY, Delmar Thompson Learning. pp. 40–53.

Dewey, D. and Wilson, B. N. (2001) 'Developmental coordination disorder: What is it?', in Missiuna, C. (ed.) *Children with Developmental Disorder: Strategies for Success.* New York, The Haworth Press. pp. 51–68.

Dewey, D. and Tupper, D. (eds) (2004) *Developmental Motor Disorders: A Neuropsychological Perspective.* New York, The Guilford Press.

DiScala, C., Osberg, J. and Savage, R. (1997) 'Children hospitalised for traumatic brain injury: Transition to post acute care', *Journal of Head Trauma Rehabilitation* 12(3): 1–19.

Dixon, G. and Addy, L. M. (2004) *Making Inclusion Work for Children with Dyspraxia: Practical Strategies for Teachers.* London, Routledge-Falmer.

Dockrell, J., Messer, D., George, R. *et al.* (1998) 'Children with word finding difficulties – prevalence, presentation and naming problems', *International Journal of Language and Communication Disorders* 33(4): 445–54.

Doll, R. C. (1996) (9th edition) *Curriculum Improvement: Decision Making and Process.* Needham Heights, MA, Allyn & Bacon.

Dowling, E. and Osborne, E. (1994) (2nd edition) *The Family and the School: A Joint Systems Approach to Problems with Children.* London, Routledge.

Drake, R. (1996) 'A critique of the role of traditional charities', in Barton, L. (ed.) *Disability and Society: Emerging Issues and Insights.* London, Longman.

Dykens, E. M., Hodapp, R. M. and Finucane, B. M. (2000) *Genetics and Mental Retardation Syndromes: A New Look at Behaviour and Interventions.* Baltimore, MD, Paul H. Brookes.

Dykman, R. A. and Ackerman, P. T. (1992) 'Diagnosing dyslexia: IQ regression plus cut points', *Journal of Learning Disabilities* 25(9): 574–6.

Ellis Weismer, S. and Schrader, T. (1993) 'Discourse characteristics of and verbal reasoning: Wait time effects on the performance of children with language learning disabilities', *Exceptionality Education Canada* 3: 71–92.

El-Nagar, O. (1996) *Specific Learning Difficulties in Mathematics: A Classroom Approach.* Tamworth, National Association of Special Educational Needs.

Emery, A. (1991) 'Population frequencies of inherited neuromuscular – A world survey', *Neuromuscular Diseases* 1: 19.

Emslie, G. H., Rush, A. J., Weinberg, W.A. *et al.* (1997) 'A double-blind randomised, placebo-controlled trial of fluoxetine in children and adolescents with depression', *Archives of General Psychiatry* 54(11): 1031–7.

Engel, J. (2001) 'ILAE Commission Report: A proposed diagnostic scheme for people with epileptic seizures and with epilepsy. Report of the ILAE task force on classification and terminology', *Epilepsia* 42(6): 1–8.

Esbensen, F. A. and Osgood, D. W. (1999) 'Gang resistance education and training (GREAT): Results from the national evaluation', *Journal of Research in Crime and Delinquency* 36(2): 194–225.

Estil, L. and Whiting, H. T. A. (2002) 'Motor/Language Impairment Syndromes – Direct or Indirect Foundations', in Cermak, S. A. and Larkin, D. (eds) *Developmental Coordination Disorder*. Albany, NY, Delmar Thompson Learning.

Evans, P. and Ware, J. (1987) *Special Care Provision*. Windsor, NFER-Nelson.

Eyberg, S. M., Boggs, S. R. and Algina, J. (1995) 'Parent-child interaction therapy: A psychosocial model for the treatment of young children with conduct problem behaviour and their families', *Psychopharmacology Bulletin* 31(1): 83–91.

Eyre, J. T. (2000) 'Holistic assessment', in Aitken, S., Buultjens, M. and Clark, C. *et al.* (eds) *Teaching Children who are Deafblind: Contact, Communication and Learning*. London, David Fulton Publishers.

Farrell, M. (2001) *Standards and Special Educational Needs*. London, Continuum.

Farrell, M. (2004a) *Special Educational Needs: A Resource for Practitioners*. London, Paul Chapman/Sage.

Farrell, M. (2004b) *Inclusion at the Crossroads: Special Education – Concepts and Values*. London, Paul Chapman/Sage.

Farrell, M. (2006a) *Celebrating the Special School*. London, David Fulton Publishers.

Farrell, M. (2006b) *The Effective Teacher's Guide to Behavioural, Emotional and Social Difficulties: Practical Strategies* (Part of the 'New Directions in Special Educational Needs' series). London, Routledge.

Farrell, M., Kerry, T. and Kerry, C. (1995) *The Blackwell Handbook of Education*. Cambridge, MA, Blackwell Publishers.

Feingold, B. F. (1975) 'Hyperkinesis and learning difficulties linked to artificial food colours and flavors', *American Journal of Nursing* 75: 797–803.

Fey, M. E. and Proctor-Williams, K. (2000) 'Recasting, elicited imitation and modeling in grammar intervention for children with specific language impairment', in Bishop, D. V. M. and Leonard, L. (eds) *Intervention and Outcome*. New York, Psychology Press.

Finnie, N. (1997) *Handling the Young Child with Cerebral Palsy at Home*. Oxford, Butterworth-Heinemann.

Fisher, S. E. and DeFries, J. C. (2002) 'Developmental dyslexia: Genetic dissection of a complex cognitive trait', *Nature Reviews, Neuroscience* 3(10): 767–80.

Fleischner, J. E. and Manheimer, M. A. (1997) 'Math intervention for students with learning disabilities: Myths and realities', *School Psychology Review* 26(3): 397–413.

Fletcher, J. M., Shaywitz, S. E. and Shaywitz, B. A. (1999) 'Comorbidity of learning and attention disorders: Separate but equal', *Paediatric Clinics of North America* 46(5): 885–97.

Fletcher, J. M., Morris, R. D. and Lyon, G. R. (2003) 'Classification and definition of Learning Disabilities: An Integrative Perspective', in Swanson, H. L., Harris, K. R. and Graham, S. (eds) *Handbook of Learning Disabilities*. New York, The Guilford Press.

Fletcher, J. M., Lyon, G. R., Barnes, M. *et al.* (2002) 'Classification of learning disabilties: An evidence based evaluation', in Bradley, R., Danielson, L. and Hallahan, D. P. (eds) *Identification of Learning Disabilities: Research to Policy*. Mahwah, NJ, Erlbaum. pp. 185–250.

Flynn, L. and Lancaster, G. (1997) *Children's Phonology Sourcebook*. Brackley, UK, Speechmark Publishing.

Fonagy, P., Target, M., Cottrell, D. *et al.* (2005) *What Works for Whom? A Critical Review of Treatments for Children and Adolescents*. New York, The Guilford Press.

Foorman, B. R., Francis, D. J., Fletcher, J. M. *et al.* (1998) 'The role of instruction in learning to read: Preventing reading failure in at risk children', *Journal of Educational Psychology* 90(1): 37–55.

Ford, D. (1999) *Theology: A Very Short Introduction.* Oxford, Oxford University Press.

Fortnum, H., Davies, A. and Butler, A. *et al.* (1996) *Health Service Implications of Changes in Aetiology and Referral Patterns of Hearing Impaired Children in Trent 1985–93 – Report to Trent Health.* Nottingham and Sheffield, Medical Research Council Institute of Hearing Research and Trent Health.

Foster, S. H. (1990) *The Communicative Competence of Young Children: A Modular Approach.* New York, Longman.

Foucault, M. (1965) *Madness and Civilisation: A History of Insanity Madness in the Age of Reason.* New York, Random House (translated from the 1961 French edition).

Foucault, M. (1977) 'Intellectuals and power: A conversation between Michel Foucault and Giles Deleuze', in Bouchard, D. (ed.) *Language, Counter-memory, Practice: Selected Essays and Interviews by Michel Foucault.* Oxford, Blackwell.

Foucault, M. (1982) 'The subject and power', in Dreyfus, H. and Rabinow, P. (eds) *Michel Foucault: Beyond Structuralism and Hermeneutics.* Brighton, Harvester.

Franklin, M. E., Kozak, M. J., Cashman, L. A. *et al.* (1998) 'Cognitive-behavioural treatment of paediatric obsessive-compulsive disorder: An open clinic trial', *Journal of the American Academy of Child and Adolescent Psychiatry* 37: 412–19.

Fuchs, L. S. and Fuchs, D. (2003) 'Enhancing the mathematical problem solving of students with mathematics disabilities', in Swanson, H. L., Harris, K. R. and Graham, S. (eds) *Handbook of Learning Disabilities.* New York, The Guilford Press.

Fujiki, M., Brinton, B. and Clarke, D. (2002) 'Emotion regulation in children with specific language impairment', *Language, Speech, and Hearing Services in Schools* 33(2): 102–11.

Fuller, C. (1999) 'Bag books and tactile stories', *The SLD Experience* 23: 20–1.

Funderburk, B. W., Eyburg, S. M., Newcomb, K. *et al.* (1998) 'Parent-child interaction therapy with behaviour problem children: Maintenance of treatment effects in the school setting', *Child and Family Behaviour Therapy* 20(2): 17–38.

Gabbard, C., LeBlanc, B. and Lowry, S. (1994) (2nd edition) *Physical Education for Children: Building the Foundation.* Upper Saddle River, NJ, Prentice-Hall.

Gagnon, L., Mottron, L. and Joanette, Y. (1997) 'Questioning the validity of the semantic pragmatic syndrome diagnosis' *Autism* 1 (1): 37–55.

Geary, D. C. (2003) 'Learning disabilities in arithmetic: Problem solving differences and Cognitive deficits', in Swanson, H. L., Harris, K. R. and Graham, S. (eds) *Handbook of Learning Disabilities.* New York, The Guilford Press. pp. 199–212.

Geary, D. C., Hamson, C. O. and Hoard, M. K. (2000) 'Numerical and arithmetical cognition: A longitudinal study of process and concept deficits in children with learning disability', *Journal of Experimental Child Psychology* 77(3): 236–63.

Geary, D. C. and Hoard, M. K. (2001) 'Numerical and arithmetical deficits in learning disabled children: Relation to dyscalculia and dyslexia', *Aphasiology* 15(7): 635–47.

Geldard, K. and Geldard, D. (2001) *Working with Children in Groups.* Basingstoke, Palgrave.

Geller, B., Reising, D., Leonard, H. L. *et al.* (1999) 'Critical review of tricyclic antidepressant use in children and adolescents', *Journal of the American Academy of Child and Adolescent Psychiatry* 38(5): 513–16.

Gersten, R., Fuchs, L. S., Williams, J. P. *et al.* (2001) 'Teaching reading comprehension strategies to students with learning disabilities: A review of research', *Review of Educational Research* 71(2): 279–320.

Gersten, R., Chard, D., Baker, S. *et al.* (under review) 'Experimental and quasi-experimental research on instructional approaches for teaching mathematics to students with learning disabilities. A research synthesis', *Review of Educational Research*.

Gibbs, J. C., Potter, G. B., Barriga, A. Q. *et al.* (1996) 'Developing the helping skills and prosocial motivation of aggressive adolescents in peer group programmes', *Aggression and Violent Behaviour* 1: 283–305.

Giedd, J. N., Blumenthal, J., Molloy, E. *et al.* (2001) 'Brain imaging of attention deficit/ hyperactivity disorder', in Wassertein, J., Wolf, L. E. and Lefever, F. F. (eds) *Adult Attention Deficit Disorder: Brain Mechanisms and Life Outcomes*. New York, New York Academy of Sciences.

Gillberg, C. and Coleman, M. (2000) (2nd edition) *The Biology of the Autistic Syndromes*. London, McKeith Press.

Gillberg, C. (1996) *Ett barn I varje klass. Om DAMP, MBD, ADHD*. Södertälje, Cura.

Gillberg, C. and Soderstrom, H. (2003) 'Learning disability', *The Lancet* 362: 811–21.

Gillberg, C., Steffenburg, S. and Schaumann, H. (1991) 'Is autism more common now than ten years ago?' *British Journal of Psychiatry* 30: 489–94.

Glang, A., Singer, G. H. Todis, B. (1997) *Students with Acquired Brain Injury: The School's Response*. Baltimore, MD, Brookes.

Godfrey J. J., Syrdal-Lasky, A. K., Millay, K. *et al.* (1981) 'Performance of dyslexic children on speech perception tests', *Journal of Experimental Child Psychology* 32: 401–24.

Goldstein, S. and Reynolds, C. R. (eds) (1999) *Handbook of Neurodevelopmental and Genetic Disorders in Children*. New York, The Guilford Press.

Goswami, U. (2004) 'Neuroscience, education and special education', *British Journal of Special Education* 31(4): 175–83.

Graham, S. (1990) 'The role of production factors in learning disabled students compositions', *Journal of Educational Psychology* 82(4): 781–91.

Graham, S. (2000) 'Should the natural learning approach replace spelling instruction?' *Journal of Educational Psychology* 92(2): 235–47.

Graham, S. and Harris, K. R. (1997) 'Self-regulation and writing: Where do we go from here?', *Contemporary Educational Psychology* 22(1): 102–14.

Graham, S. and Harris, K. R. (2003) 'Students with learning disabilities and the process of writing: A meta-analysis of SRDS studies', in Swanson, H. L., Harris, K. R. and Graham, S. (eds) *Handbook of Learning Disabilities*. New York, The Guilford Press. pp. 323–44.

Graham, S., Harris, K. and Loynachan, C. (2000) 'The directed spelling thinking activity: Application with high frequency words', *Learning Disabilities: Research and Practice* 11(1): 34–40.

Graham, S., Harris, K. R., McArthur, C. *et al.* (1991) 'Writing and writing instruction with students with learning disabilities: A review of a program of research', *Learning Disability Quarterly* 14: 89–114.

Gray, C. (1994) *The Social Stories Book*. Arlington TX, Future Horizons.

Greenhill, L. (1998) 'Childhood ADHD: Pharmacological treatments', in Nathan, P. and Gorman, M. (eds) *A Guide to Treatments that Work*. Oxford, Oxford University Press.

Greenspan, S. (2006) 'Functional concepts in mental retardation: Finding the natural essence of an artificial category', *Exceptionality* 14(4): 205–24.

Gregg, N. and Mather, N. (2002) 'School is fun at recess: Informal analyses of written language for students with learning disabilities', *Journal of Learning Disabilities* 35(1): 7–22.

Gregory, S. and Pickergill, M. (1997) 'Towards a model of bilingual education for deaf children', *Laserbeam* Spring, 28: 3–8.

Griebel, M. L. Oakes, W. J. and Worley, G. (1991) 'The Chiari malformation associated with myelomenigocele', in Rekate, H. L. (ed.) *Comprehensive Management of Spina Bifida*. Boca Raton, FL, CRC Press. pp. 67–92.

Gubbay, S. S. (1985) 'Clumsiness', in Vinken, P., Bruyn, G. and Klawans, H. (eds) *Handbook of Clinical Neurology Vol. 2 (46) Neurobehavioral Disorders*. New York, Elsevier Science. pp. 159–67.

Guess, D., Siegel-Causey, E., Roberts, S. *et al.* (1990) 'Assessment and analysis of behavioural state and related variables among students with profoundly handicapping conditions', *Journal of the Association for Persons with Severe Handicaps* 15: 211–30.

Hagtvet, B. E. (1997) 'Phonological and linguistic-cognitive precursors of reading abilities', *Dyslexia* 3(3).

Hale, J. B. and Fiorello, C. A. (2004) *School Neuropsychology: A Practitioner's Handbook*. New York, Guilford Press.

Hargie, O., Saunders, C. and Dickson, D. (1994) (3rd edition) *Social Skills in Interpersonal Communication*. London, Routledge.

Harwayne, S. (2001) *Writing Through Childhood*. Portsmouth, NH, Heinemann.

Hatcher, P. (2000) 'Sound links in reading and spelling with discrepancy defined dyslexics and children with moderate learning difficulties', *Reading and Writing: An Interdisciplinary Journal* 13: 257–72.

Heller, K. W., Alberto, P. A., Forney, P. E. *et al.* (1996) *Understanding Physical, Sensory and Health Impairments: Characteristics and Educational Implications*. Pacific Grove, CA, Brooks-Cole.

Heller, K. W., Fredrick, L. D., Best, S. J. *et al.* (2000) 'Providing specialised health procedures in the schools: Training and service delivery', *Exceptional Children* 66: 173–86.

Hemmens, A. (1999) 'Learning through the senses', *Primary Science Review* 59: 20–23.

Henry, L. C. and Maclean, M. (2002) 'Working memory performance in children with and without intellectual disabilities', *American Journal on Mental Retardation* 107(6): 421–32.

Hess, M. and Wheldall, K. (1999) 'Strategies for improving the written expression of primary children with poor writing skills', *Australian Journal of Learning Disabilities* 4(4): 14–20.

Hewett, D. and Nind, M. (1998) *Interaction in Action*. London, David Fulton Publishers.

Hjorne, E. (2006) 'Pedagogy in the ADHD Classroom: An exploratory study of "The Little Group"' in Lloyd, G., Stead, J. and Cohen, D. (eds) *Critical New Perspectives in ADHD*. New York, Routledge.

Hoare, D. (1994) 'Subtypes of developmental coordination disorder', *Adapted Physical Activity Quarterly* 11(2): 158–69.

Hodapp, R. M. and Dykens, E. M. (1994) 'Mental retardation's two cultures of behavioural research', *American Journal on Mental Retardation* 98(6): 675–87.

Hodges, L. (2000) 'Effective teaching and learning', in Aitken, S., Buultjens, M. and Clark, C. *et al.* (eds) *Teaching Children who are Deafblind: Contact, Communication and Learning*. London, David Fulton Publishers.

Hornby, G., Hall, C. and Hall, E. (2003) *Counselling Pupils in Schools: Skills and Strategies for Teachers*. London, RoutledgeFalmer.

Howell, J. and Dean, E. (1994) (2nd edition) *Treating Phonological Disorders in Children – Metaphon – Theory to Practice*. London, Whurr Publishers.

Hull Learning Services (2004) *Supporting Children with Medical Conditions*. London, David Fulton Publishers.

Hulme, C. and Snowling, M. (1997) *Dyslexia: Biology, Cognition and Intervention*. London, Whurr.

Hulme, C., Roodenreys, R., Schweikert, R. *et al.* (1997) 'Word frequency effects on short term memory tasks: Evidence for a reintegration process in immediate serial recall', *Journal of Experimental Psychology: Learning, Memory and Cognition* 23(5): 1217–32.

Humphries, T. L. (2003) 'Effectiveness of pivotal response training as a behavioural intervention for young children with autism spectrum disorders', *Bridges Practice Based Research Synthesis* 2(4): 1–10.

Hunt, J. and Slater, A. (2003) *Working with Children's Voice Disorders*. Brackley, UK, Speechmark.

Hunting, R. P. (1996) 'Does it matter if Mary can read but can't add up?', *Education Australia* 33: 16–19.

Hynd, G. W., Semrud-Clikeman, M., Lorys, A. *et al.* (1990) 'Brain morphology in developmental dyslexia and attention deficit hyperactivity disorder', *Archives of Neurology* 47: 919–26.

Ingenmey, R. and Van Houten, R. (1991) 'Using time delay to promote spontaneous speech in an autistic child', *Journal of Applied Behaviour Analysis* 24: 591–6.

Irlen, H. L. (1994) 'Scotopic sensitivity: Irlen syndrome hypothesis and explanation of the syndrome', *Journal of Behavioural Optometry* 5: 65–6.

International Molecular Study of Autism Consortium (1998) 'A full genome screen for autism with evidence for linkage to a region on chromosome 7q.', *Human Molecular Genetics* 7(3): 571–8.

Johnson, M. and Parkinson, G. (2002) *Epilepsy: A Practical Guide*. London, David Fulton Publishers.

Jones, G. (2002) *Educational Provision for Children with Autism and Asperger's Syndrome: Meeting Their Needs*. London, David Fulton Publishers.

Jordan, N. C. and Hanich, L. B. (2003) 'Characteristics of children with moderate mathematics deficiencies: A longitudinal perspective', *Learning Disabilities Research and Practice* 18(4) 213–21.

Jordan, N. C., Hanich, L. B. and Kaplan, D. (2003) 'A longitudinal study of mathematical competencies in children with specific mathematics difficulties versus children with comorbid mathematics and reading difficulties', *Child Development* 74(3): 834–50.

Kadesjö, B. (2001) *Barn med koncentrationssvårrigheter* (2nd edition) Stockholm, Liber.

Kaiser, A. P. (2000) 'Teaching functional communication skills', in Snell, M. E. and Brown, F. (eds) (5th edition) *Instruction of Students with Severe Disabilities*. Upper Saddle River, NJ, Merrill/ Prentice-Hall. pp. 453–92.

Kanner, L. (1943) 'Autistic disturbances of affective contact', *Nervous Child* 2: 217–50.

Kaplan, B. J., Wilson, B. N., Dewey, D. *et al.* (1998) 'DCD may not be a discrete disorder', *Journal of Human Movement Science* 17: 471–90.

Karchmer, M. A. and Mitchell, R. E. (2003) 'Demographic and achievement characteristics of deaf and hard of hearing students', in Marschark, M. and Spencer, P. E. (eds) *Oxford Handbook of Deaf Studies, Language and Education*. New York, Oxford University Press. pp. 21–7.

Kaufman, A. S. and Kaufman, N. L. (2004) *KABC-II Administration and Scoring Manual*. Circle Pines, MN, American Guidance Service.

Kavale, K. and Mattson, D. (1983) 'One jumped off the balance beam: A meta-analysis of perceptual-motor training', *Journal of Learning Disabilities* 16(3): 165–73.

Kavale, K. A. and Forness, S. R. (1995) *The Nature of Learning Disabilities: Critical Elements in Diagnosis and Classification*. Mahwah, NJ, Erlbaum.

Kazdin, A. (1995) (2nd edition) *Conduct Disorders in Childhood and Adolescence*. Thousand Oaks, CA, Sage.

Kazdin, A. E. (2003) 'Problem-solving skills training and parent management training for conduct disorder', in Kazdin, A. E. and Weisz, T. R. (eds) *Evidence Based Psychotherapies for Children and Adolescents*. New York, The Guilford Press. pp. 241–62.

Kazdin, A. E. and Wasser, G. (2000) 'Therapeutic changes in children, parents and families resulting from treatment of children with conduct problems', *Journal of the American Academy of Child and Adolescent Psychiatry* 39(4): 414–20.

Kazdin, A. E. and Weisz, T. R. (eds) (2003) *Evidence Based Psychotherapies for Children and Adolescents.* New York, The Guilford Press.

Keil, S. and Clunies-Ross, L. (2003) *Survey of the Educational Provision for Blind and Partially Sighted Provision in England,* Scotland and Wales in 2002. Peterborough, RNIB, Education and Employment Research Department.

Kelly, B. (1999) 'Circle Time – A systems approach to emotional and behavioural difficulties', *Educational Psychology in Practice* 15(1): 40–4.

Kendall, P. C., Aschenbrand, S. G. and Hudson, J. L. (2003) 'Child focused treatment of anxiety', in Kazdin, A. E. and Weisz, T. R. (eds) *Evidence Based Psychotherapies for Children and Adolescents.* New York, The Guilford Press. pp. 81–100.

Kenward, H. (1997) *Integrating Pupils with Disabilities in Mainstream Schools.* London, David Fulton Publishers.

Kersner, M. and Wright, J. (2002) (eds) (3rd edition) *How to ManageCommunication Problems in Young Children.* London, David Fulton Publishers.

King, N. J., Tonge, B. J., Heyne, D. *et al.* (1998) 'Cognitive-behavioural treatment of school refusing children: A controlled evaluation', *Journal of the American Academy of Child and Adolescent Psychiatry* 37: 395–403.

King, N. J., Tonge, B. J., Heyne, D. *et al.* (2001) 'Cognitive-behavioural treatment of school refusing children: Maintenance of improvement at 3 to 5 year follow up', *Scandinavian Journal of Behaviour Therapy* 30(2): 85–9.

King-de Baun, P. (1990) *Storytime: Stories, Symbols and Emergent Literacy Activities for Young Special Needs Children.* Park City, UT, Creative Communicating.

Kirby, A. and Drew, S. (2003) *Guide to Dyspraxia and Developmental Co-ordination Disorders.* London, David Fulton Publishers.

Kirchner, C. J. (2004) 'Co-enrolment: An effective answer to the mainstream debate', in Power, D. and Leigh, G. (eds) *Educating Deaf Students: Global Perspectives.* Washington, DC, Gallaudet University Press.

Kirigin, K. A. (1996) Teaching-family model of group home treatment of children with severe behaviour problems', in Roberts, M. C. (ed.) *Model Programs in Child and Family Mental Health.* Mahwah, NJ, Erlbaum. pp. 231–47.

Koegel, L. K. and Koegel, R. L. (1995) 'Motivating communication in children with autism', in Schopler, E. and Mezibov, G. (eds) *Learning and Cognition in Autism: Current Issues in Autism.* New York, Plenum Press. pp. 73–87.

Kopera-Frye, K., Dahaene, S. and Streissguth, A. P. (1996) 'Impairments of number processing induced by prenatal alcohol exposure', *Neuropsychologia* 34(12): 1187–96.

Kraemer, M. J. and Bierman, C. W. (1983) 'Asthma', in Umbriet, J. (ed.) *Physical Disabilities and Health Impairments: An Introduction.* Upper Saddle River, NJ, Merrill/Prentice-Hall. pp. 159–66.

Kraus, J. F., Rock, A. and Hemyari, P. (1990) 'Brain injuries among infants, children and adolescents, and young adults', *American Journal of Diseases in Children* 144(6): 684–91.

Kurtz, L. A. (1992) 'Cerebral palsy', in Batshaw, M. L. and Perret, Y. M. (eds) (3rd edition) *Children with Disabilities: A Medical Primer.* Baltimore, Brookes. pp. 441–69.

Kushlick, A. and Blunden, R. (1974) 'The epidemiology of mental subnormality', Clarke, A. M. and Clarke, A. D. B. (eds) *Mental Deficiency* (3rd edition). London, Methuen.

Lacey, P. (1991) 'Managing the classroom environment', in Tilstone, C. (ed.) *Teaching Pupils with Severe Learning Difficulties.* London, David Fulton Publishers.

Law, J., Lindsay, G., Peacey, N. *et al.* (2000) *Provision for Children with Speech and Language Needs in England and Wales: Facilitating Communication Between Education and Health Services.* London, Department for Education and Employment Research report RR239.

Laine, M. and Martin, N. (2006) *Anomia: Theoretical and Clinical Aspects*. New York, Routledge.

Lampert, M. (2001) *Teaching Problems and the Problems of Teaching*. New Haven, CT, Yale University Press.

Lancaster, G. and Pope, L. (1997) *Working with Children's Phonology*. Brackley, UK, Speechmark.

Lancioni, G. E., O'Reilly, M. F., Oliva, D. *et al.* (2002) 'Multiple microswitches for multiple responses with children with profound disabilities', *Cognitive Behaviour Therapy* 31(2): 81–7.

Landgren, M., Kjellman, B. and Gillberg, C. (1998) 'Attention deficit disorder with developmental coordination disorders', *Archives of Disease in Childhood* 79(3): 207–12.

Larkin, D. and Cermac, S. A. (2002) 'Issues in identification and assessment of developmental coordination disorder', in Cermak, S. A. and Larkin, D. (eds) *Developmental Coordination Disorder*. Albany, NY, Delmar Thompson Learning.

Laszlo, J. I. and Bairstow, P. J. (1985) *Perceptual-motor Behaviour: Developmental Assessment and Therapy*. New York, NY, Praeger.

Lawson, W. (1998) *Life Behind the Glass: A Personal Account of Autistic Spectrum Disorder*. Lismore, Southern Cross University Press.

Leeds Local Education Authority (1995) *Deaf and Hearing Impaired Support Services Policy Statement*. Leeds, Leeds LAE Publications.

Leonard, L. (1998) *Children with Specific Language Impairment*. Cambridge, MA, MIT Press.

Lewis, R., Graves, A., Ashton, T. *et al.* (1998) 'Word processing tools for students with learning disabilities: A comparison of strategies to increase text entry speed', *Learning Disabilities Research and Practice* 13(2): 95–108.

Lewis, A. and Norwich, B. (2001) 'A critical review of systematic evidence concerning distinctive pedagogies for pupils with difficulties in learning', *Journal of Research in Special Educational Needs* 1(1): 1–13.

Lewis, A. and Norwich, B. (eds) (2005) *Special Teaching for Special Children? Pedagogies for Inclusion*. Maidenhead, UK, Open University Press.

Lewis, S. (1998) 'Reading and writing within an oral/aural approach', in Gregory, S., Knight, P., McCracken, W. *et al.* (eds) *Issues in Deaf Education*. London, David Fulton Publishers.

Lewis, S. and Iselin, S. A. (2002) 'A comparison of the independent living skills of primary students with visual impairments and their sighted peers: A pilot study', *Journal of Visual Impairment and Blindness* 94: 335–44.

Lewinsohn, P. M. and Clarke, G. N. (1999) 'Psychosocial treatments for adolescent depression', *Clinical Psychology Review* 19(3): 329–42.

Liberman, I. Y., Shankweiler, D. and Liberman, A. M. (1989) 'The alphabetic principle in learning to read', in Shankweiler, D. and Liberman, I. Y. (eds) *Phonology and Reading Disability: Solving the Reading Puzzle*. Ann Arbour, MI, University of Michigan Press.

Lieberman, L. J. (2002) 'Fitness for individuals who are visually impaired or deafblind', *RE View (Rehabilitation and Education for Blindness and Visual Impairment)* 34(1): 13.

Lieberman, L. J. and McHugh, B. E. (2001) 'Health related fitness of children with visual impairments and blindness', *Journal of Visual Impairment and Blindness* 95(5): 272–86.

Light, J. (1989) 'Towards a definition of communicative competence for individuals using augmentative and alternative communication systems', *Augmentative and Alternative Communication* 5: 134–7.

Liptak, G. S. (1997) 'Neural tube defects' in Batshaw, M. L. (ed.) (4th edition) *Children with Disabilities*. Baltimore, Brookes. pp. 529–52.

Lloyd, G., Stead, J. and Cohen, D. (eds) (2006) *Critical New Perspectives on ADHD*. New York, Routledge.

Lochman, J. E. and Wells, K. C. (1996) 'A social-cognitive intervention with aggressive children: Prevention effects and contextual implementation issues', in Peters, R. E. and McMahon, R. J. (eds) *Preventing Childhood Disorders, Substance Abuse and Delinquency*. Thousand Oaks, CA, Sage. pp. 111–43.

Lochman, J. E., Barry, T. D. and Pardini, D. A. (2003) 'Anger control training for aggressive youth', in Kazdin, A. E. and Weisz, T. R. (eds) *Evidence Based Psychotherapies for Children and Adolescents*. New York, The Guilford Press. pp. 263–81.

Locke, A., Ginsborg, J. and Peers, I. (2002). Development and disadvantage: implications for the early years and beyond', *International Journal of Language and Communication Disorders* 37(1): 3–15.

Logan, K., Mayberry, M. and Fletcher, J. (1996) 'The short term memory of profoundly deaf people for words, signs and abstract spatial stimuli', *Applied Cognitive Psychology* 10: 105–19.

Lord, C. and Schopler, E. (1987) 'Neurobiological implications of sex differences in autism', in Schopler, E. and Mezibov, G. (eds) *Neurobiological Issues in Autism*. New York, Plenum.

Lord, C., Risi, S., Lambrecht, L. *et al*. (2000) 'The autism diagnostic observation schedule – generic: a standard measure of social and communication deficits associated with the spectrum of autism', *Journal of Autism and Developmental Disorders* 30(3): 205.

Lovaas, O. I. (1987) 'Behavioural treatment and normal intellectual and educational functioning in autistic children', *Journal of Consulting and Clinical Psychology* 55: 3–9.

Lovett, M. W., Lacerenza, L., Borden, S. L. (2000) 'Putting struggling readers on the PHAST track: A program to integrate phonological and strategy based remedial reading instruction and maximise outcomes', *Journal of Learning Disabilities* 33(5): 458–76.

Lovett, M. W., Lacerenza, L., Borden, S. L. *et al*. (2000) 'Components of effective remediation for developmental reading disabilities: Combining phonological and strategy-based instruction to improve outcomes', *Journal of Educational Psychology* 92(2): 263–83.

Lovett, M. W., Steinbach, K. A. and Frijters, J. C. (2000) 'Remediating the core deficits of developmental reading disability: A double deficit perspective', *Journal of Learning Disabilities* 33(4): 334–58.

Lyon, G. R., Fletcher, J. M., Shaywitz, S. E. *et al*. (2001) 'Rethinking learning disabilties', in Finn Jr., C. E., Rotherham, A. J. and Hokanson Jr., C. R. (eds) *Rethinking Special Education for a New Century*. Washington, DC, Thomas B. Fordham Foundation and Progressive Policy Institute. pp. 259–87.

McCracken, W. (1998a) 'Introduction' (to section 4, Audiology) in Gregory, S., Knight, P., McCracken, W. *et al*. (eds) *Issues in Deaf Education*. London, David Fulton Publishers.

McCracken, W. (1998b) 'Deaf children with disabilities', in Gregory, S., Knight, P., McCracken, W. *et al*. (eds) *Issues in Deaf Education*. London, David Fulton Publishers.

McDonnell, J., Hardman, M. L., Hightower, J. *et al*. (1993) 'Impact of community based instruction on the development of adaptive behaviour of secondary level students with mental retardation', *American Journal on Mental Retardation* 97(5): 575–84.

McDougal, S. J., Hulme, C., Ellis, A. *et al*., (1994) 'Learning to read: The role of short-term memory and phonological skills', *Journal of Experimental Child Psychology* 58: 112–33.

McInnes, J. M. and Treffry, J. A. (1982) *Deaf-blind Infants and Children: A Developmental Guide*. Toronto, University of Toronto Press.

MacKay, H. A., Soraci, S., Carlin, M. *et al*. (2002) 'Guiding visual attention during acquisition of matching to sample', *American Journal of Mental Retardation* 107(6): 445–54.

McSherry, J. (2001) *Challenging Behaviours in Mainstream Schools: Practical Strategies for Effective Intervention and Reintegration*. London, David Fulton Publishers.

Macintyre, C. and Deponio, P. (2003) *Identifying and Supporting Children with Specific Learning Difficulties: Looking Beyond the Label to Assess the Whole Child*. New York, RoutledgeFalmer.

Mackintosh, K. and Dissanayake, C. (2004) 'Annotation: The similarities and differences between autistic disorder and Asperger's disorder', *Journal of Child Psychology and Psychiatry* 45: 421–34.

Male, D. (1996) 'Who goes to special schools?' *British Journal of Special Education* 23(1): 35–41.

Mann, E. M., Ikeda, Y., Mueller, C. W. *et al.* (1992) 'Cross-cultural differences in rating hyperactive-disruptive behaviours in children', *American Journal of Psychiatry* 58: 336–44.

Mandich, A. D., Polatajko, H. J., Macnab, J. J. *et al.* (2001) 'Treatment of children with developmental coordination disorder: What is the evidence?', in Missiuna, C. (ed.) *Children with Developmental Disorder: Strategies for Success*. New York, The Haworth Press.

Mar, H. M. and Sall, N. (1999) 'Profiles of the expressive communication skills of children and adolescents with severe cognitive disabilities', *Education and Training in Mental Retardation and Developmental Disabilities* 34(1): 77–89.

March, J. S. (1999) 'Psychopharmacological management of paediatric obsessive-compulsive disorder (OCD)'. Paper presented at the 46th annual meeting of the American Academy of Child and Adolescent Psychiatry, Chicago.

Martin, D. (2000) *Teaching Children with Speech and Language Difficulties*. London, David Fulton Publishers.

Martin, D. and Miller, C. (2003) *Speech and Language Difficulties in the Classroom*. London, David Fulton Publishers.

Martin, D. and Reilly, O. (1995) 'Global language delay: analysis of a severe central auditory processing deficit', in Perkins, M. and Howard, S. (eds) *Case Studies in Clinical Linguistics*. London, Whurr.

Martini, R., Heath, N. and Missiuna, C. (1999) 'A North American analysis of the relationship between learning disabilities and developmental coordination disorder', *International Journal of Learning Disabilities* 14: 46–58.

Mason, H. and McCall, S. with Arter, C. *et al.* (1997) *Visual Impairment: Access to Education for Children and Young People*. London, David Fulton Publishers.

Mason, K. J. and Wright, S. (1994) 'Altered musculoskeletal function', in Betz, C. L., Hinsberger, M. M. and Wright, S. (eds) (2nd edition) *Family Centred Nursing Care for Children*. Philadelphia, Saunders. pp. 1825–73.

Matson, J. L., Sevin, J. A., Box, M. L. *et al.* (1993) 'An evaluation of two methods for increasing self-initiated verbalisations in autistic children', *Journal of Applied Behaviour Analysis* 26: 389–96.

Maxwell, M. (1992) 'Simultaneous communication: The state of the art and proposals for change', in Stokoe, W. (ed.) *Simultaneous Communication, ASL and Other Classroom Communication Modes*. Burtonsville, MD, Linstok Press.

May-Benson, T., Ingolia, P. and Koomar, J. (2002) 'Daily living skills and developmental coordination disorder', in Cermak, S. A. and Larkin, D. (eds) *Developmental Coordination Disorder*. Albany, NY, Delmar Thompson Learning.

Medical Research Council (2001) *Review of Autism Research: Epidemiology and Causes*. London, Medical Research Council (www.mrc.ac.uk)

Meese, R. L. (2001) (2nd edition) *Teaching Learners with Mild Disabilities: Integrating Research and Practice*. Belmont, CA, Wadsworth-Thompson.

Menzies, R. G. and Clarke, J. C. (1993) 'A comparison of in vivo and vicarious exposure in the treatment of childhood water phobia', *Behaviour Research and Therapy* 31: 9–15.

Mercer, C. D. and Mercer, A. R. (1998) *Teaching Students with Learning Problems*. New York, Merrill.

Mervis, C.A. and Boyle, C. A. (2002) 'Prevalence and selected characteristics of childhood vision impairment', *Developmental Medicine and Child Neurology* 44: 538–41.

Mescheryakov, A. (1974) *Awakening to Life*. Moscow, Progress Press.

Mesibov, G.B. (1988) 'Diagnosis and assessment of autistic adolescents and adults', in Schopler, E. and Mesibov, G.B. (eds) *Diagnosis and Assessment in Autism*. New York: Plenum Press. pp. 227–38.

Mezibov, G. and Howley, M. (2003) *Accessing the Curriculum for Pupils with Autistic Spectrum Disorders: Using the TEACCH Programme to Help Inclusion*. London, David Fulton Publishers.

Miles, T. R. and Miles, E. (1990) *Dyslexia: A Hundred Years On*. Buckingham, Open University Press.

Milloy, N. and MorganBarry, R. (1990) 'Developmental neurological disorders', in Grunwell, P. (ed.) *Developmental Speech Disorders*. London, Whurr Publishers.

Missiuna, C. (ed.) *Children with Developmental Disorder: Strategies for Success*. New York, The Haworth Press.

Mittler, P. (2001) 'Preparing for self advocacy', in Carpenter, B., Ashdown, R. and Bovair, K. (eds) *Enabling Access: Effective Teaching and Learning for Pupils with Learning Difficulties*. London, David Fulton Publishers.

Marcotte, A. C. and Morere, D. A. (1990) 'Speech lateralisation in deaf populations: evidence for a developmental critical period', *Journal of Brain and Language* 39: 134–52.

Moores, D. F. (2001) (5th edition) *Educating the Deaf: Psychology, Principles and Practices*. Boston, Houghton Mifflin.

Morrow, L. M. (2001) (4th edition) *Literacy Development in the Early Years: Helping Children Read and Write*. Boston, MA, Allyn & Bacon.

Mufson, L., Weisman, M. M., Moreau, D. *et al.* (1999) 'Efficacy of interpersonal psychotherapy for depressed adolescents', *Archives of General Psychiatry* 56(6): 573–9.

Munden, A. and Arcelus, J. (1999) *The AD/HD Handbook*. London, Jessica Kingsley.

Mundy, P. and Neale, A. (2001) 'Neural plasticity, joint attention and a transactional social-orienting of autism', in Glidden, L. (ed.) *International Review of Research in Mental Retardation. Autism*, vol 23, San Diego, CA, Academic Press. pp. 139–68.

Muratori, F., Picchi, L., Casella, C. *et al.* (2002) 'Efficacy of brief dynamic psychotherapy for children with emotional disorders', *Psychotherapy and Psychosomatics* 71(1): 28–38.

Nafstad, A. and Rodbrøe, I. (1999) *Co-creating Communication*. Oslo, Forlaget-Nord Press.

National Institute of Clinical Excellence (2000) *Guidance on the Use of Methylphenidate for ADHD*. London, NICE.

Nelson, N. and Calfee, R. C. (1998) *The Reading-Writing Connection*. Chicago, IL, National Society for the Study of Education.

Nelson, C., van Dijk, J., McDonnell, A. P. and Thompson, K. (2002) 'A framework for understanding young children with multiple disabilities: The van Dijk approach to assessment', *Research and Practice for Persons with Severe Disabilities* 27(2): 97–111.

Neville, H. J., Coffey, S. A., Lawson, D. S. *et al.* (1997) 'Neural systems mediating American Sign Language: effects of sensory experience and age of acquisition', *Brain and Language* 57(3): 285–308.

Nigg, J. (2006) *What Causes ADHD? Understanding What Goes Wrong and Why*. New York, Guilford Press.

Nigg, J. and Hinshaw, S. (1998) 'Parent personality traits and psychopathology associated with anti-social behaviours in childhood ADHD', *Journal of Child Psychology and Psychiatry* 39(2): 145–59.

Nind, M. (1999) 'Intensive interaction with autism: a useful approach?' *British Journal of Special Education* 26(2): 96–102.

Nind, M. and Hewett, D. (1994) *Access to Communication*. London, David Fulton Publishers.

Nind, M. and Hewett, D. (2001) *A Practical Guide to Intensive Interaction*. Kidderminster, British Institute of Learning Difficulties.

Nind, M. and Kellett, M. (2002) 'Responding to individuals with severe learning difficulties and stereotyped behaviour: challenges for an inclusive era', *European Journal of Special Needs Education* 17(3): 265–82.

Norwich, B. and Kelly, N. (2004) *Moderate Learning Difficulties and the Future of Inclusion*. London, RoutledgeFalmer.

Nunes, T. and Moreno, C. (1997a) 'Is hearing impairment a cause of difficulty in learning mathematics?' Report to the Nuffield Foundation.

Nunes, T. and Moreno, C. (1997b) 'Solving problems with different ways of presenting the task: How do deaf children perform?' *Equals* 3(2): 15–17.

Nunes, T. (2005) *Teaching Mathematics to Deaf Children*. London, Wiley.

Ollendick, T. H. and King, N. J. (1998) 'Empirically supported treatments for children with phobic and anxiety disorders', *Journal of Clinical Child Psychology* 27(2): 156–67.

Organisation for Economic Co-operation and Development (2000) *Special Needs Education: Statistics and Indicators*. Paris, OECD.

Orlove, F. P. and Sobsey, D. (1991) *Educating Children with Multiple Disabilities: A Transdisciplinary Approach*. Baltimore, Paul H. Brookes.

Ostad, S. A. (1999) 'Developmental progression of subtraction strategies: a comparison of mathematically normal and mathematically disabled children', *European Journal of Special Needs Education* 14(1): 21–36.

Ouvry, C. and Saunders, S. (2001) 'Pupils with profound and multiple learning difficulties', in Carpenter, B., Ashdown, R. and Bovair, K. (eds) *Enabling Access: Effective Teaching and Learning for Pupils with Learning Difficulties*. London, David Fulton Publishers. pp. 240–56.

Ozonoff, S. (1997) 'Components of executive function in autism and other disorders', in Russell, J. *Autism as an Executive Disorder*. Oxford, Oxford University Press.

Pagliano, P. (2002) 'Using all the senses', in Ashman, A. and Elkins, J. (eds) *Educating Children with Diverse Abilities*. Sydney, Prentice-Hall-Pearson Educational.

Palmer, R. (2000) 'Feeling the music philosophy' (www.kolumbus.fi./ritta/lahtinen).

Palmer, S. (2000) 'Phonological recoding deficit in working memory of dyslexic teenager', *Journal of Research in Reading* 23: 28–40.

Panter, S. (2001) 'Mathematics', in Carpenter, B., Ashdown, R. and Bovair, K. (eds) (2nd edition) *Enabling Access: Effective Teaching and Learning for Pupils with Learning Difficulties*. London, David Fulton Publishers. pp. 36–51.

Partridge, S. (1996) 'Video stories for 7 to 11s', in Galloway, C. (ed.) *Using Videos with Deaf Children*. Manchester Centre for Audiology, Education of the Deaf and Speech Pathology, University of Manchester.

Pasco, M., Stackhouse, J. and Wells, B. (2006) *Persisting Speech Difficulties in Children: Children's Speech and Literacy Difficulties, Book 3*. London, Wiley.

Pastor, P. N. and Reuben, C. A. (2002) 'Attention deficit hyperactivity disorder and learning disability: United States, 1997–98', *National Center for Health Statistics. Vital Health Statistics* 10: 208.

Patterson, G. R. and Chamberlain, P. (1988) 'Treatment process: A problem at three levels', in Wynne, L. C. (ed.) *The State of the Art in Family Therapy Research: Controversies and Recommendations*. New York, Family Process Press. pp. 189–223.

Patterson, G. R. and Forgatch, M. S. (1995) 'Predicting future clinical adjustment from treatment outcome and process variables', *Psychological Assessment* 7(3): 275–85.

Pau, C. S. (1995) 'The deaf child and solving the problems of arithmetic', *American Annals of the Deaf* 140(3): 287–90.

Paulesu, E., Demonet, J. F., Fazio, F. *et al.* (2001) 'Dyslexia – Cultural diversity and biological unity', *Science* 291(5511): 2165–7.

Pease, L. (2000) 'Creating a communicating environment', in Aitken, S., Buultjens, M. and Clark, C. *et al.* (eds) *Teaching Children who are Deafblind: Contact, Communication and Learning.* London, David Fulton Publishers.

Pellegrini, A. and Horvat, M. (1995) 'A developmental and contextualised critique of AD/HD', *Educational Researcher* 249(10): 13–20.

Pellegrini, A. Hubertey, P. and Jones, I. (1996) 'The effects of recess timing on children's playground and classroom behaviours', *American Educational Research Journal* 32(4): 854–864.

Pellegrino, L. (1997) 'Cerebral palsy', in Batshaw, M. L. (ed.) (4th edition) *Children with Disabilities.* Baltimore, Brookes. pp. 499–528.

Phoenix, S. (1988) *An Interim Report on a Pilot Survey of Deaf Adults in Northern Ireland.* Belfast, Northern Ireland Workshop for the Deaf.

Piaget, J. (1970) 'Piaget's theory', in Mussen, P. H. (ed.) *Manual of Child Psychology.* London, Wiley.

Piaget, J. and Inhelder, B. (1966/1969) *The Psychology of the Child.* London, Routledge & Keegan Paul (translated from the French by Helen Weaver).

Pickersgill, M. (1998) 'Bilingualism – current policy and practice', in Gregory, S., Knight, P., McCracken, W. *et al.* (eds) *Issues in Deaf Education.* London, David Fulton Publishers.

Pickersgill, M. and Gregory, M. S. (1998) *Sign Bilingualism: A Model.* London, Adept Press.

Pintrich, P. R. (2000) 'The role of goal orientation in self-regulated learning', in Boekaerts, M., Pintrich, P. R. and Zeider, M. (eds) *Handbook of Self-regulation.* New York: Academic. pp. 452–502.

Poizner, H. and Tallal, P. (1987) 'Temporal processing in deaf signers', *Brain and Language* 30(1): 52–62.

Polatajko, H. J., Mandich, A. D, Miller, L. T. *et al.* (2001) 'Cognitive orientation to daily occupational performance (CO-OP): Part II – The evidence', *Physical and Occupational Therapy in Paediatrics* 20(2/3): 83–106.

Polatajko, H., Mandich, A., Missuina, C. *et al.,* (2001) 'Cognitive orientation to daily occupational performance (CO-OP): Part III – The protocol in brief', *Physical and Occupational Therapy in Paediatrics* 20(2–3): 107–23.

Polatajko, H. and Mandich, A. (2004) *Enabling Occupation in Children: The Cognitive Orientation to Daily Occupational Performance (CO-OP) Approach.* Ottawa, CAOT Publications.

Polatajko, H. J., Rodger, S., Dhillon, A. *et al.* (2004) 'Approaches to the management of children with motor problems', in Dewey, D. and Tupper, D. (eds) *Developmental Motor Disorders: A Neuropsychological Perspective.* New York, The Guilford Press.

Pollington, M. F., Wilcox, B. and Morrison, T. G. (2001) 'Self-perception in writing: The effects of writing workshop and traditional instruction on intermediate grade students', *Reading Psychology* 22: 249–65.

Pollock, J., Waller, E. and Pollitt, R. (2004) (2nd edition) *Day-to-Day Dyslexia in the Classroom.* London, RoutledgeFalmer.

Porter, J., Miller, O. and Pease, L. (1997) *Curriculum Access for Deafblind Children: Research Report No. 1.* London, Department for Education and Employment/Sense.

Prevezer, W. (2000) 'Musical interaction and children with autism', in Powell, S. (ed.) *Helping Children with Autism to Learn.* London, David Fulton Publishers.

Prizant, B. M. and Wetherby, A. M. (1993) 'Communication in pre-school autistic children', in Schopler, E., Van Bourgondien, M. E. and Bristol, M. M. (eds) *Preschool Issues in Autism*. New York, Plenum.

Prizant, B. M., Wetherby, A. M. and Rydell, P. J. (2000) 'Communication intervention issues for children with autism spectrum disorders', in Prizant, B. M., Wetherby, A. M. (eds) *Autism Spectrum Disorders: A Transactional Developmental Perspective*. Baltimore, Brookes. pp. 193–224.

Poustie, J. (2001a) *Mathematics Solutions: An Introduction to Dyscalculia Part A – How to Identify, Assess and Manage Specific Learning Difficulties in Mathematics*. Taunton, Next Generation.

Poustie, J. (2001b) *Mathematics Solutions: An Introduction to Dyscalculia Part B – How to Teach Children and Adults who have Specific Learning Difficulties in Mathematics*. Taunton, Next Generation.

Power, D. (1998) (3rd edition) 'Deaf and hard of hearing students', in Ashman, A. and Elkins, J. (eds) *Educating Children with Special Needs*. Sydney, Prentice-Hall.

Power, D. and Leigh, G. (eds) (2004) *Educating Deaf Students: Global Perspectives*. Washington, DC, Gallaudet University Press.

Pryde, K. M. (2000) *Sensorimotor functioning in developmental coordination disorder: A kinematic and psychometric analysis*. Unpublished doctoral dissertation, University of Waterloo, Waterloo, Ontario, Canada.

Qualifications and Curriculum Authority (1999) *Shared World – Different Experiences: Designing the Curriculum for Pupils who are Deafblind*. London, QCA.

Qualifications and Curriculum Authority (2001a) *Planning, Teaching and Assessing the Curriculum for Pupils with Learning Difficulties: English*. London, QCA.

Qualifications and Curriculum Authority (2001b) *Planning, Teaching and Assessing the Curriculum for Pupils with Learning Difficulties: Mathematics*. London, QCA.

Qualifications and Curriculum Authority (2001c) *Planning, Teaching and Assessing the Curriculum for Pupils with Learning Difficulties: Personal, Social and Health Education and Citizenship*. London, QCA.

Quinn, M. M., Kavale, K. A., Mathur, S. R. *et al.* (1999) 'A meta-analysis of social skill interventions for students with emotional or behavioural disorders', *Journal of Emotional and Behavioural Disorders* 7: 54–64.

Rachman, S. (2004, 2nd edition) *Anxiety*. London and New York, Taylor & Francis.

Raine, A. (2002) 'The role of prefrontal deficits, low autonomic arousal, and early health factors in the development of antisocial and aggressive behaviour', *Journal of Child Psychology and Psychiatry* 43: 417–34.

Reddy, G. L., Ramar, R. and Kasuma, A. (2000) *Education of Children with Special Needs*. New Delhi, Discovery Publishing House.

Revie, G. and Larkin, D. (1993) 'Task-specific intervention with children reduces movement problems', *Adapt. Phys. Activ. Quarterly* 10: 29–41.

Richardson, A. J. and Ross, M. A. (2000) 'Fatty acid metabolism in neurodevelopmental disorder: A new perspective on associations between attention deficit/hyperactivity disorder dyslexia, dyspraxia and the autistic spectrum', *Prostaglandins, Leukotrienes and Essential Fatty Acids* 63(1/2): 1–9.

Rice, M. L. (2000) 'Grammatical symptoms of specific language impairments', in Bishop, D. V. M. and Leonard, L. B. (2000) *Speech and Language Impairments in Children: Causes, Characteristics, Intervention and Outcome*. Philadelphia, PA and Hove UK, Psychology Press.

Riddle, M. A., Reeve, A. E., Yaryura-Tobias, J. A. *et al.* (2001) 'Fluvoxamine for children and adolescents with obsessive-compulsive disorder: A randomised, controlled, multicenter trail', *Journal of the American Academy of Child and Adolescent Psychiatry* 40(2): 222–29.

Ridgeway, S. (1998) 'A deaf personality', in Gregory, S., Knight, P., McCracken, W. *et al.* (eds) *Issues in Deaf Education*. London, David Fulton Publishers.

Rinaldi, W. (2001) *Social Use of Language Programme*. Windsor, NFER-Nelson.

Rose, R. (1991) 'A jigsaw approach to group work', *British Journal of Special Education* 18(2): 54–8.

Roth, A. and Fonagy, P. (2005) (2nd edition) *What Works for Whom? A Critical Review of Psychotherapy Research*. New York, The Guilford Press.

Roy, E. A., Bottos, S., Pryde, K. *et al.* (2004) 'Approaches to understanding the neurobehavioral mechanisms associated with motor impairment in children', in Dewey, D. and Tupper, D. E. (eds) *Developmental Disorders: A Neurological Perspective*. New York, The Guilford Press.

Royal College of Surgeons of England (1999) *Report of the Working Party in the Management of Patients with Head Injuries*. London, The Royal College of Surgeons of England.

Rumeau-Rouquette, C., du Mazaubrun, C., Cans, C. et al. (1998) 'Definition and prevalence of school-age multi-handicaps', *Archives of Paediatric and Asolescent Medicine* 5 (7): 739–44.

Rutter, M. (1996) 'Autism research: Prospects and priorities', *Journal of Autism and Developmental Disorders* 26(2): 257–75.

Sage, R. and Sluckin, A. (2004) *Silent Children: Approaches to Selective Mutism*. Leicester, University of Leicester.

Sandler, A. D., Watson, T. E., Footo, M. et al. (1992) 'Neurodevelopmental study of writing disorders in middle childhood', *Journal of Developmental and Behavioural Paediatrics* 13(1): 17–23.

Savage, R. C. and Wolcott, G. (eds) (1995) *An Educator's Manual: What Educators Need to Know About Students with Traumatic Brain Injury*. Washington, DC, Brain Injury Association.

Schoenbrodt, L. (2001) 'How TBI affects speech and language', in Schoenbrodt, L. (ed.) *Children with Traumatic Brain Injury: A Parent's Guide*. Bethesda, MD, Woodbine House.

Schopler, E. (1997) 'Implementation of TEACCH philosophy', in Cohen, D. and Volkmar, F. (eds) (2nd edition) *Handbook of Autism and Pervasive Developmental Disorders*. New York, Wiley pp. 767–95.

Schwartz, R. G. (2007) *The Handbook of Child Language Disorders*. New York, Routledge.

Schweigert, P. and Rowland, C. (1992) 'Early communication and micro technology: Instructional sequence and case studies of children with severe multiple disabilities', *Augmentative and Alternative Communication* 8: 273–84.

Scott, C. I. (1989) 'Genetic and familial aspects of limb defects with emphasis on the lower extremity', in Kalamachi, A. (ed.) *Congenital Lower Limb Deficiencies*. New York, Springer-Verlag. pp. 46–57.

Seifert, J., Scheuerpflug, P., Zillerssen, K. E. *et al.* (2003) 'Electrophysiological investigations of the effectiveness of methylphenidate in children with and without ADHD', *Journal of Neural Transmission* 110(7): 821–8.

Sense (2004) *Reaching Out: A Toolkit for Deafblind Children's Services*. London, Sense.

Senzer, B. (2001) *Dyscalculia: A Brief Overview* (www.rivermall.com/math/dyscalcr.htm)

Sexton, R. J., Harris, K. R. and Graham, S. (1998) 'The effects of self regulated strategy development on essay writing and attributions of students with learning disabilities in a process writing setting', *Exceptional Children* 64: 295–311.

Shapiro, D. R., Lieberman, L. J. and Moffett, A. (2003) 'Strategies to improve perceived competence in children with visual impairments', *RE View (Rehabilitation and Education for Blindness and Visual Impairment)* 35(2): 69–80.

Share, D. L. (1995) 'Phonological recoding and self teaching: *sine qua non* of reading acquisition', *Cognition* 55(2): 151–218.

Silver, A. A. and Hagin, R. A. (2002) (2nd edition) *Disorders of Learning in Childhood*. New York, Wiley.

Simonoff, E. (2001) 'Genetic influences on conduct disorders', in Hill, J. and Maughan, B. (eds) *Conduct Disorder in Childhood and Adolescence*. Cambridge, Cambridge University Press. pp. 202–34.

Simpson, R. L. (2005) 'Evidence based practices and students with ASD', *Focus on Autism and Other Developmental Disabilities* 20(3): 140–9.

Smith, C. (2003) *Writing and Developing Social Stories: Practical Interventions in Autism*. Oxford, Harcourt Assessment.

Snell, M. and Brown, F. (2000) (5th edition) *Instruction of Students with Severe Disabilities*. Upper Saddle River, NJ, Merrill.

Snowling, M. J. (2000) *Dyslexia*. Oxford, Blackwell.

Sparrow, S. S., Chicchetti, D. V. and Balla, D. A. (2006) (2nd edition) *Vineland Adaptive Behaviour Scales* (Vineland II). Pearson Assessments.

Spivak, G. and Sure, M. B. (1978) *Problem Solving Techniques in Child Rearing*. San Francisco, Jossey-Bass.

Spivak, G. and Sure, M. B. (1982) 'The cognition of social adjustment: Interpersonal cognitive problem solving thinking', in Lahey, B. and Kazdin, A. (eds) (Vol. 5) *Advances in Clinical Child Psychology*. New York, Plenum. pp. 323–72.

Stacey, K. (1994) 'Contextual assessment of young children: moving from the strange to the familiar and from theory to praxis', *Child Language Teaching and Therapy* 10 (2): 179–98.

Stackhouse, J. and Wells, B. (1997) *Children's Speech and Literacy Difficulties Book 1: A Psycholinguistic Framework*. London, Whurr Publishing.

Stackhouse, J. and Wells, B. (2001) *Children's Speech and Literacy Difficulties Book 2: Identification and Intervention*. London, Whurr Publishing.

Strain, P. and Hoyson, M. (2000) 'The need for longitudinal, intensive social skill intervention: LEAP follow-up outcomes for children with autism', *Topics in Early Childhood Special Education* 20(2): 116–22.

Stieler, S. (1998) (3rd edition) 'Students with physical disabilities', in Ashman, A. and Elkins, J. (eds) *Educating Children with Special Needs*. Sydney, Prentice-Hall.

Stein, J. F. (1995) 'A visual deficit in dyslexia?', in Nicholson, R. I. and Fawcett, A. J. (eds) *Dyslexia in Children: Multi Disciplinary Perspectives*. Hemel Hempstead, Harvester Wheatsheaf.

Stein, J. F., Talcott, J. and Witton, C. (2001) 'Dyslexia: The role of the magnocellular system'. Paper presented at the 5th British Dyslexia Association Conference.

Steinberg, A. G. and Knightly, C. A. (1997) 'Hearing: Sounds and silences', in Batshaw, M. L. (ed.) *Children with Disabilities*. Sydney, Maclennan and Petty.

Stewart, E. and Ritter, K. (2001) 'Ethics of assessment', in Beattie, R. G. (ed.) *Ethics of Deaf Education*. San Diego, CA, Academic Press.

Stewart, T. and Turnbull, J. (2007) *Working with Dysfluent Children*. Brackley, UK, Speechmark.

Stillman, R. (1978) *Callier Azusa Scale*. Austin, TX, University of Texas.

Strauss, C. C. and Last, C. G. (1993) 'Social and simple phobias in children', *Journal of Anxiety Disorders* 7: 141–52.

Stright, A. D. and Supplee, L. H. (2002) 'Children's self-regulatory behaviours during teacher-directed, seat-work, and small-group instructional contexts', *Journal of Education Research* 95: 235–45.

Swanson, H. L. and Hoskyn, M. (1998) 'Experimental intervention research on students with learning disabilities: A meta-analysis of treatment outcomes', *Review of Educational Research* 68(3): 277–321.

Swanson, H. L., Harris, K. R. and Graham, S. (eds) (2003) *Handbook of Learning Disabilities*. New York, The Guilford Press.

Swanwick, R. (1993) 'The use of DARTs to develop deaf children's literacy skills within a bilingual context', *Deafness and Development* 3(2): 4–9.

Swanwick, R. (1998) 'The teaching and learning of literacy within a sign bilingual approach', in Gregory, S., Knight, P., McCracken, W. *et al.* (eds) *Issues in Deaf Education*. London, David Fulton Publishers.

Swanwick, R. (2003) 'Sign bilingual deaf children's writing strategies: Responses to different sources for writing', in Galloway, C. and Young, A. (eds) *Deafness and Education in the UK – Research Perspectives*. London, Whurr Publishers.

Tallal, P. (2000) 'Experimental studies of language learning impairments: From research to remediation', in Bishop, D. V. M. and Leonard, L. B. (eds) *Speech and Language Impairments in Children: Causes, Characteristics, Intervention and Outcome*. Philadelphia, PA and Hove UK, Psychology Press.

Tannock, R. (1998) 'ADHD: Advances in cognitive, neurobiological and genetic research', *Journal of Child Psychology and Psychiatry* 39(1): 65–99.

Target, M. and Fonagy, P. (1994) 'The efficacy of psychoanalysis for children with emotional disorders', *Journal of the American Academy for Child and Adolescent Psychiatry* 33: 361–71.

Taylor, M. B. and Williams, J. P. (1983) 'Comprehension of LD readers: Task and text variations', *Journal of Educational Psychology* 75: 743–51.

Teacher Training Agency (1999) *National Special Educational Needs Specialist Standards*. London, TTA.

Teasedale, G. and Jennet, B. (1974) 'Assessment of coma and impaired consciousness: A practical scale', *Lancet* 2: 81–4.

Thompson, G. (2003) *Supporting Children with Communication Disorders: A Handbook for Teachers and Teaching Assistants*. London, David Fulton Publishers.

Tiedt, P. L., Tiedt, I. M. and Tiedt, S. W. (2001) (3rd edition) *Language Arts Activities for the Classroom*. Boston, MA, Allyn & Bacon.

Toren, P., Wolmer, L., Rosental, B. *et al.* (2000) 'Case series: Brief parent-child group therapy for childhood anxiety disorders using a manual based cognitive-behavioural technique', *Journal of the American Academy for Child and Adolescent Psychiatry* 39(10): 1309–12.

Torgesen, J. K. (2000) 'Individual differences in response to early interventions in reading: The lingering problem of treatment registers', *Learning Disabilities Research and Practice* 15(1): 55–64.

Torgesen, J. K. and Mathes, P. G. (2000) *A Basic Guide to Understanding, Assessing and Teaching Phonological Awareness*. Austin, TX, ProEd.

Tucker, C. L. (2001) 'How TBI affects behaviour', in Schoenbrodt, L. (ed.) *Children with Traumatic Brain Injury: A Parent's Guide*. Bethesda, MD, Woodbine House.

Turnbull A. and Ruef, M. (1996). 'Family perspectives on problem behaviour', *Mental Retardation* 34(5): 280–93.

Turnbull, R., Turnbull, A., Shank, M. *et al.* (2002) (3rd edition) *Exceptional Lives: Special Education in Today's Schools*. Upper Saddle River, NJ, Merrill-Prentice-Hall.

Turner, J. C. (1995) 'The influence of classroom contexts on young children's motivation for literacy', *Reading Research Quarterly* 30(3): 410–41.

United States Department of Education (2002) *Twenty fourth annual report to Congress on the Implementation of the Individuals with Disabilities Education Act*. Washington, D.C., United States Department of Education.

Vanderheiden, G. C. and Lloyd, L. L. (1986) 'Communication systems and their components', in Blackstone, S. W. and Bruskin, D. M. (eds) *Augmentative Communication: An Introduction*. Rockville, MD, American Speech-Language-Haring Association. pp. 29–162.

Van der Lely, H. (1994) 'Canonical linking rules: Forward versus reverse thinking in normally developing and language impaired children', *Cognition* 51(1): 29–72.

van Dijk, J. (1989) 'The Sint Michilsgestel approach to diagnosis and education of multi sensory impaired persons', in Best, A. B. (ed.) *Sensory Impairment with Multi Handicap: Current Philosophies and New Approaches*. A European Conference, Warwick University, 6–11 August 1989: Papers on the Education of the Deafblind, International Association for the Education of the Deafblind.

van Dijk, J. (2004) 'Educating deaf students with multiple disabilities', in Power, D. and Leigh, G. (eds) *Educating Deaf Students: Global Perspectives*. Washington, DC, Gallaudet University Press.

Vellutino, F. R., Scanlon, D. M. and Fletcher, J. M. (2002) *Research in the study of reading disability (dyslexia): What have we learned in the past four decades?* Unpublished manuscript (cited in Fletcher, J. M., Morris, R. D. and Lyon, G. R. (2003) 'Classification and definition of learning disabilities: An integrative perspective', in Swanson, H. L., Harris, K. R. and Graham, S. (eds) *Handbook of Learning Disabilities*. New York, The Guilford Press, p. 31.

Volkmar, F. R. and Nelson, D. (1990) 'Seizure disorders in autism', *Journal of the American Academy for Child and Adolescent Psychiatry* 29(1): 127–29.

Walker, S. and Wicks, B. (2005) *Educating Children with Acquired Brain Injury*. London, David Fulton Publishers.

Wallace, B. and Crawford, S. (1994) 'Instructional paradigms and the ADHD child', in Weaver, C. (ed.) *Success at Last: Helping Students with AD (H)D Achieve Their Potential*. Portsmouth, NH, Heinemann.

Walley, A. C. (1993) The role of vocabulary development in children's spoken word recognition and segmentation ability', *Developmental Review* 13(3): 286–350.

Ware, J. (2003) *Creating a Responsive Environment for People with Profound and Multiple Learning Difficulties*. London, David Fulton Publishers.

Ware, J. (2005) 'Profound and multiple learning difficulties', in Lewis, A. and Norwich, B. (eds) *Special Teaching for Special Children? Pedagogies for Inclusion*. Maidenhead, Open University Press.

Watson, I. (1991) 'Phonological processing in two languages', in Bailystok, E. (ed.) *Language Processing in Bilingual Children*. Cambridge, Cambridge University Press.

Watson, J. and Fisher, A. (1997) 'Evaluating the effectiveness of intensive interactive teaching with pupils with profound and complex learning difficulties', *British Journal of Special Education* 24(2): 80–7.

Weaver, C. (ed.) *Success at Last: Helping Students with AD (H) D Achieve Their Potential*. Portsmouth, NH, Heinemann.

Webster-Stratton, C. and Reid, M. J. (2003) 'The incredible years parents, teachers and children training series', in Kazdin, A. E. and Weisz, J. R. (eds) *Evidence Based Psychotherapies for Children and Adolescents*. New York, Guilford Press. pp. 224–40.

Wechsler, D. (1991) *Wechsler Intelligence Scale for Children – Third Edition*. San Antonio, TX, Psychological Corporation.

Wechsler, D. (2003) *Wechsler Intelligence Scale for Children – Fourth Edition*. San Antonio, TX, Psychological Corporation.

Wehmeyer, M. L., Sands, D. J., Knowlton, E. *et al.* (2002) *Teaching Students with Mental Retardation: Providing Access to the General Curriculum*. Baltimore, MD, Paul H. Brookes Publishing.

Weinberger, S. E. (1993) 'Recent advances in pulmonary medicine', *The New England Journal of Medicine* 328(19): 1389–97.

Weiner, J. M. and Dulcan, M.K. (3rd edition) *The American Psychiatric Publishing Textbook of Child and Adolescent Psychiatry*. APA.

Weisz, J. R., Weisz, B., Han, S. S. *et al.* (1995) 'Effects of psychotherapy with children and adolescents revisited: A meta-analysis of treatment outcome studies', *Psychological Bulletin* 117: 450–468.

Weisz, J. R., Southam-Gerow, M. A., Gordis, E. B. *et al.* (2003) 'Primary and secondary control enhancement training for youth depression: Applying the deployment-focused model of treatment development and testing', in Kazdin, A. E. and Weisz, T. R. (eds) *Evidence Based Psychotherapies for Children and Adolescents*. New York, The Guilford Press. pp. 165–83.

Wells, G. (1985) *Language Development in the Preschool Years*. Cambridge, Cambridge University Press.

Wellesley, D., Hockey, K., Montgomery, P. *et al.* (1992) 'Prevalence of intellectual handicap in Western Australia: A community study', *Medical Journal of Australia* 156(2): 94–6, 100, 102.

Westwood, P. (2000) *Numeracy and Learning Difficulties: Approaches to Teaching and Assessment*. London, David Fulton Publishers.

Westwood, P. (2003) (4th edition) *Commonsense Methods for Children with Special Educational Needs: Strategies for the Regular Classroom*. London, RoutledgeFalmer.

Williams, J. P. (2003) 'Teaching text structure to improve reading comprehension', in Swanson, H. L., Harris, K. R. and Graham, S. (eds) *Handbook of Learning Disabilities*. New York, The Guilford Press. pp. 293–305.

Williams, J. P., Taylor, M. B., Jarin, D. C. *et al.* (1983) *Determining the main idea of expository paragraphs: An instructional program for the learning disabled and its evaluation* (Technical Report #25). Research Institute for the Study of Learning Disabilities Teachers College, Columbia University.

Wilson, J. and Frederickson, N. (1995) Phonological awareness training: An evaluation', *Educational and Child Psychology* 12(1): 68–79.

Wilson, B. M. and Proctor, A. (2000) 'Oral and written discourse in adolescents with closed head injury', *Brain and Cognition* 43: 425–429.

Wilson, P. (2005) 'Visuospatial, kinesthetic, visuomotor integration, and visuoconstructional disorders: Implications for motor development', in Dewey, D. and Tupper, D. E. (eds) *Developmental Disorders: A Neurological Perspective*. New York, The Guilford Press.

Wilson, P. H. and McKenzie, B. E. (1998) 'Information processing deficits associated with Developmental Coordination Disorder: A meta-analysis of research findings', *Journal of Child Psychology and Allied Disciplines* 39(6): 829–40.

Wimpory, D., Chadwick, P. and Nash, S. (1995) 'Musical interaction therapy for children with autism: An illustrative case study with a two year follow up' *Journal of Autism and Developmental Disorders* 25(5): 541–452.

Wing, L. and Gould, J. (1979) 'Severe impairments of social interaction and assorted abnormalities in children: Epidemiology and classification', *Journal of Autism and Childhood Schizophrenia* 9: 11–29.

Wing, L., Leekam, S. R., Libby, S. J. *et al.* (2002) 'The diagnostic interview for social and communication disorders: background, inter-rater reliability and clinical use', *Journal of Child Psychology and Psychiatry* 43(3): 307–25.

Wise, B. W., Ring, J. and Olsen, R. K. (2000) 'Individual differences in gains from computer assisted remedial reading', *Journal of Experimental Psychology* 77(3): 197–235.

Wolf, M., Miller, L. and Donnelly, K. (2000) 'Retrieval, automaticity, vocabulary elaboration, orthography (RAVE-O): A comprehensive, fluency-based reading intervention program', *Journal of Learning Disabilities* 33(4): 375–86.

Wolf, M. and O'Brien, B. (2001) 'On issues of time, fluency and intervention', in Fawcett, A. (ed.) *Dyslexia: Theory and Good Practice*. London, Whurr.

Wolfenden, S. R., Williams, K., and Peat, J. K. (2003) 'Family and parenting interventions in children and adolescents with conduct disorder and delinquency aged 10–17', (Cochrane review) in *The Cochrane Library* Issue 4. Chichester, UK, Wiley.

Wong, B. Y. L. (1991) 'On cognitive process-based instruction: An introduction', *Journal of Learning Disabilities* 25(3): 150–2, 172.

World Health Organisation (2001) *International Classification of Functioning, Disability and Health*. Geneva, WHO.

Wray, A. (2001) 'Formulaic sequences in second language teaching: Principle and practice', *Applied Linguistics*. 21(4): 463–89.

Ylvisaker, M. (1998) (2nd edition) (ed.) *Traumatic Brain Injury Rehabilitation – Children and Adolescents*. Boston, MA, Butterworth-Heinemann.

Zago, L., Presenti, M., Mellet, E. *et al*. (2001) 'Neural correlates of simple and complex mental calculation', *Neuroimage* 13(2): 314–27.

Zutell, J. (1998) 'Word sorting: a developmental approach to word study for delayed readers', *Reading and Writing Quarterly* 14(2): 219–38.

Index

eBooks

eBooks – at www.eBookstore.tandf.co.uk

A library at your fingertips!

eBooks are electronic versions of printed books. You can store them on your PC/laptop or browse them online.

They have advantages for anyone needing rapid access to a wide variety of published, copyright information.

eBooks can help your research by enabling you to bookmark chapters, annotate text and use instant searches to find specific words or phrases. Several eBook files would fit on even a small laptop or PDA.

NEW: Save money by eSubscribing: cheap, online access to any eBook for as long as you need it.

Annual subscription packages

We now offer special low-cost bulk subscriptions to packages of eBooks in certain subject areas. These are available to libraries or to individuals.

For more information please contact webmaster.ebooks@tandf.co.uk

We're continually developing the eBook concept, so keep up to date by visiting the website.

www.eBookstore.tandf.co.uk